OUR FINEST HOUR

DAVID J. BERCUSON

HarperCollins*PublishersLtd*

DEDICATION

At 2134 on the evening of August 16, 1944, Halifax MZ-899 "O", coded BM-D, of the RCAF's No. 433 Squadron, lifted off the runway at Skipton-on-Swale, Yorkshire, climbed low over the hills separating the Vale of York from the North Sea, and headed for the coast of Denmark. The Main Force of Bomber Command, including 171 aircraft of No. 6 Group (RCAF), was due to bomb Kiel and Stettin that night, but Halifax MZ-899 "O" and eighteen other RCAF aircraft were assigned to "gardening" or minelaying missions, instead. Halifax MZ-899 "O" was never seen again; all seven crew members perished.

This book is dedicated to the crew of MZ-899 "O": Pilot Officer J.G.M. Savard from Montreal, Quebec (pilot); Pilot Officer M.E. Fairall from Toronto, Ontario (air gunner); Pilot Officer B. Bercuson from Regina, Saskatchewan (wireless operator/air gunner); Flying Officer H. Grimble from Sturgeon Creek, Manitoba (navigator); Flying Officer J.L. Baillargeon from Windsor, Ontario (bomb aimer); Pilot Officer A.W.J. Drennan from Windsor, Ontario (bomb aimer); Sergeant R.I. Atkinson of the Royal Air Force (flight engineer)—and to the 42,029 other Canadians and the hundreds of thousands of other Allied soldiers, sailors, and airmen who died in the cause of freedom in the greatest war in history.

Our Finest Hour
Copyright © 2015 by David J. Bercuson.
All rights reserved.

Published by HarperCollins Publishers Ltd

First Canadian edition

Page 487 constitutes a continuation of this copyright page.

Maps by Dawn Huck

HarperCollins books may be purchased for educational, business,
or sales promotional use through our Special Markets Department.

HarperCollins Publishers Ltd
2 Bloor Street East, 20th Floor
Toronto, Ontario, Canada
M4W 1A8

www.harpercollins.ca

Library and Archives Canada Cataloguing in Publication
information is available upon request

ISBN 978-1-44341-873-7

Printed and bound in the United States of America
RRD 9 8 7 6 5 4 3 2 1

CONTENTS

PREFACE

The Second World War shaped the modern world, this nation, the people who fought in it or lived through it, and me. I was born two days before the formal Japanese surrender was signed on the USS *Missouri* in Tokyo Bay on September 2, 1945. When I was a small boy, the recently completed war seemed to have an impact on many important aspects of my life. I vividly remember my mother's European relatives—refugees from the Holocaust—bunking in our small apartment on Maplewood Avenue in Montreal just after they arrived from the displaced persons camps of Europe. I thought them strange and somewhat repulsive. They ate herring, had gold teeth, spoke a language I did not understand, and pinched my cheeks a lot. My sister was born at the end of 1949 with a congenital hip problem. It was attended to by Dr. Breckenridge, who had achieved fame as an army doctor in the war and was still in the army reserves. I remember the photo in his office of him in his army uniform. My uncle, who had been a wireless air gunner with the RCAF's No. 6 Group, Bomber Command, had been badly injured in the crash of his bomber. I remember him telling me about the war and showing me his flying helmet.

The war was all around me as I grew up. At our family table, we talked about Douglas MacArthur, Dwight D. Eisenhower, Harry Truman. My parents took me to Hyde Park, New York, to see where Franklin D. Roosevelt was buried. My father told me about his cousin from Calgary who had been killed in action in 1944; he had flown away from England one night and had not come back. Most of my friends had dads or uncles who had served in the armed forces. My father had been in the reserves, then worked for RCA Victor building tank radios. My mother had photos of her two brothers in the living room; both had served in the US armed forces, one just after the war in occupied Germany. I still have a cigarette case he gave me with a map of the US zone of occupation on it. My mother's uncle had been a US Army doctor in Normandy, her cousin a Boeing B-29 pilot based on Saipan.

At home we avidly watched *Victory at Sea* on television. My father brought home documentary films about the war to show on his new sound projector. Our class collected money for infirm veterans at Christmas. My male high-school teachers were all veterans. One had suffered from battle fatigue (we called it shell-shock) and sometimes grew erratic in front of our class. We feared him when that happened. In class we debated whether it was important to buy poppies on Remembrance Day, whether the war should be remembered year after year. When the Israelis captured Adolf Eichmann in Argentina in 1959 and spirited him to Israel to face trial for war crimes, we debated whether they should hang him or let him go, to show the world how truly "Christian" and forgiving they were (I attended a Protestant school). I was glad when he was hanged.

We were war babies, not baby boomers. My generation was born during or immediately after the war, when the veterans came home to start families. The streets were filled with mothers wheeling baby carriages. The nursery schools and kindergartens were jammed. War books, war comics, and war movies were the fare of every boy. We refought the war with our toy guns, trying to emulate the scruffy infantrymen we saw shuffling in the newsreels. We were acutely conscious that there had been a war, that it had been very important, and that most of our fathers, uncles, teachers, and friends' fathers had been in it.

Those days are gone. Ask a Canadian high school graduate today about Dieppe or Juno Beach or the Canadian liberation of Holland, and you will usually get only a blank stare. To them veterans are old men with blazers, berets, and chests full of medals seen on TV every now and then, marching to mark some occasion no one else seems to remember or care about. Our governments had better things to do after the war than make sure the memory of it stayed alive. In the 1960s, curriculum experts in provincial ministries of education from coast to coast decided that "social studies" were more important than history, and we stopped teaching history—of Canada or anything else—to the next generation. Students learned little about Canada's unique history and heritage, and virtually nothing of its contribution to the defeat of Nazism in the Second World War. That contribution was important both to Canada and to the Allies; Canadian soldiers, sailors, and airmen fought in virtually all the major theatres of war. They were infantrymen, bomber pilots, merchant seamen, corvette captains, tankers, reconnaissance pilots, submarine hunters, and more.

Our Finest Hour is a complete revision of *Maple Leaf Against the Axis*, a book I wrote in the early 1990s to commemorate the fiftieth anniversary of the Allied victory in the Second World War, published in 1995. In that book, I drew on the latest research in Canadian military history to tell that story, with all its sweep and grandeur, in one volume. I decided to ignore the home front, and there was nothing in that book about the impact of the war on Canadian society, nothing of the rise of trade unionism, the start of the welfare state in Canada, the evacuation of Japanese Canadians, and the role of women on the home front. Two major homefront events—the story of the British Commonwealth Air Training

Plan and the two conscription crises of 1942 and 1944—were mentioned briefly, but only as they had a direct impact on the fighting forces.

In 2012 I decided it was time to completely revise that book and this time to include new chapters on the home front and on Canadian war strategy. The most important job in completely revising *Maple Leaf* was to review more than twenty years of new books, articles, theses, papers, and even television documentary programs to discover what additional information historians had learned about Canada's role in the Second World War and to review my own attitudes and interpretations about the people and the events that had shaped Canada's role in that war. *Our Finest Hour*—a title proudly borrowed from the second volume of Winston Churchill's history of the Second World War—is the result.

I wrote this book to refresh our memories of those now mostly gone Canadians in the armed forces of Canada and its allies who served their country and the cause of human decency in the years between 1939 and 1945, when the fate of the world hung in the balance. It does not matter to me why each one went—for adventure, out of boredom, for three square meals a day, to save democracy, to stop Hitler. What matters is that they did go and that, when they got to where the shooting was, they gave everything they had to give. What also matters is that many never came back to their wives, sweethearts, parents, children, friends, and siblings. I believe it is essential for the integrity and honour of this country that they all be remembered for the part they played in shaping modern Canada and the world. This book is my thanks to them all.

ACKNOWLEDGEMENTS

I had a great deal of help in the writing and preparation of this book. My agent, Linda McKnight, encouraged me in my belief that it was a good idea to revise *Maple Leaf Against the Axis* and came up with the new title. Jim Gifford, Editorial Director, Non-fiction, at HarperCollins, took another chance on me. The original manuscript of this book was read by Jack Granatstein, Syd Wise, Marc Milner, Norman Hillmer, and Jack English. Jack Granatstein, Terry Copp, Sebastien Cox, and Randall Wakelam read all or part of *Maple Leaf* to tell me what I must do to improve the book, update it, and revise it to reflect what we know today about Canada in the Second World War. I benefited greatly from their comments, suggestions, and criticisms. Peter Archambault helped with the research for *Maple Leaf.* Brock Reumkens collected and organized the photos for the new version. David Moule, Christine Leppard, and Laurel Halladay researched the material for the revision. As always my wife, Barrie, encouraged me throughout this project. Ultimately, however, I take full responsibility for any errors or omissions.

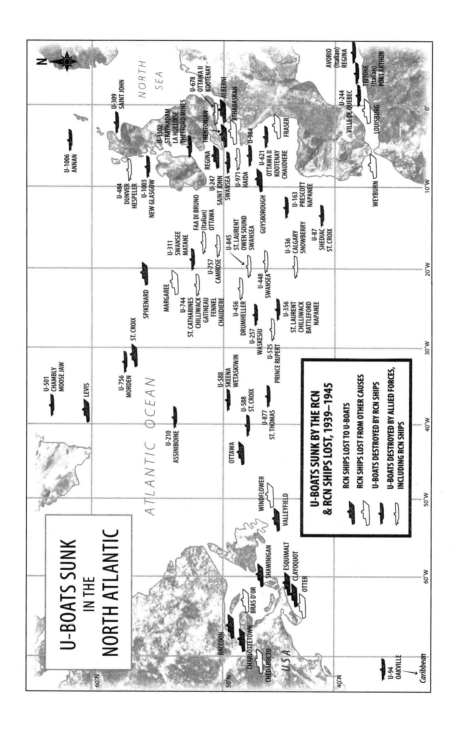

U-BOATS SUNK
IN THE
NORTH ATLANTIC

U-BOATS SUNK BY THE RCN
& RCN SHIPS LOST, 1939–1945

RCN SHIPS LOST TO U-BOATS
RCN SHIPS LOST FROM OTHER CAUSES
U-BOATS DESTROYED BY RCN SHIPS
U-BOATS DESTROYED BY ALLIED FORCES,
INCLUDING RCN SHIPS

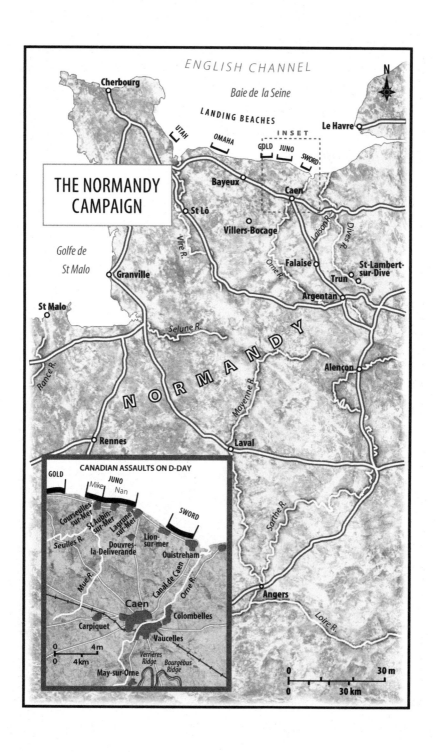

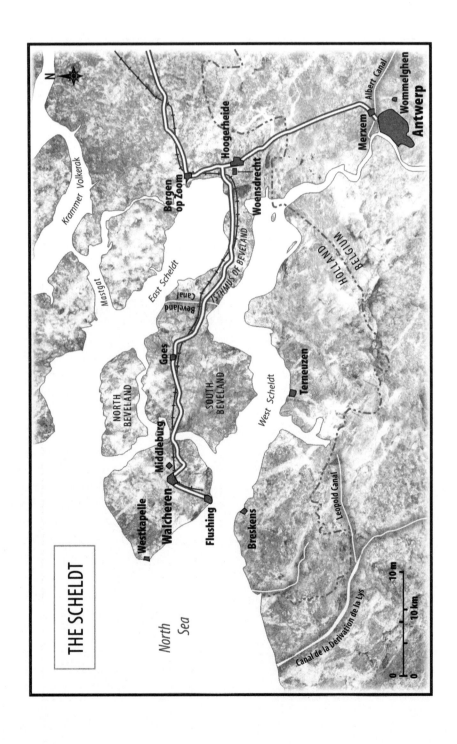

THE SCHELDT

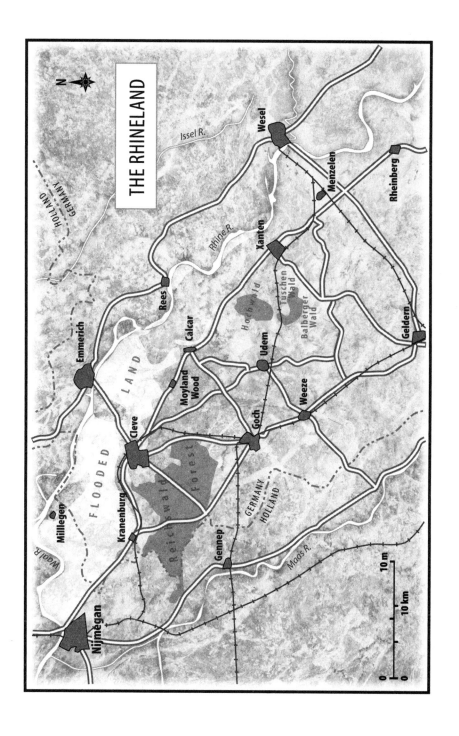

THE RHINELAND

NO. 6 GROUP
BOMBING TARGETS
1943–1945

ENGLAND

6 GROUP

4 GROUP

1 GROUP

5 GROUP

100 GROUP

8 GROUP

3 GROUP

London

ENGLISH CHANNEL

BAY OF
BISCAY

FRANCE

NETHE

**V-1 sites
Pas-de-Calais
2152/8014/5**

Brussels/Melsbruck
98/478

The
Hag

Domburg
33/160

Calais
659/3176/1

Cap Griz Nez
162/815

Le Clipon
42/151

St-Omer
12/30

Ghent
220/999

Bourg-L

BELGIUM

Louvain

149

**V-1 sites
Somme
972/3726/1**

Neufchatel
69/275

Boulongne
514/2336/3

Courtrai
45/258

Lille
106/528/2

43/2

M

Lens
153/782/1

53/329

St. Valery en Caux
105/479

St. Pol
95/348

Arras
86/300/6

Haine St. P
72/325/6

Aulnoy
160/77

Au Févre
118/444

Caen
515/2243/4

Le Havre
226/1074

Amiens
98/505

Cambrai
181/658/11

Somain
112/507/1

Valenci
8/2

Longues
24/77

Nucourt
64/300

Thiverny
89/437

Laon
89/411/1

St-Leu d'Esserent
240/1193/1

Chantilly
190/706/1

Brest
35/171

Coutances
125/463

Merville
136/528

Meulen
60/280

Paris

Valres
74/310/1

Connantre
99/351

Ile de Cezembre
187/909/1

Houlgate
103/395/1

Achères
94/345/5

Condé-sur-Noireau
112/385

Falaise
258/1165

Trouville
54/180

Trappes
117/565

Noisy le Sec
137/646/4

Lorient
441/993/9

Dongas
99/396

Mayenne
80/282/1

Le Mans
391/1614/2

Versailles
114/418/4

Villeneuve St. Georges
243/1022

St. Nazaire
213/475/3

Forêt de Montrichard
99/343

Le Creusot
39/98/1

Montluçon
63/117/2

RUHR

Gladbeck
95/340

Scholven-Buer
4/225/2

Castrop-Rauxel
398/14334/4

Bottrop/Whehim
172/735

Wanne-Eickel
397/1344/5

Kamen
109/364/1

Sterkrade
334/1149/13

Bochum
587/2050/26

Dortmund
900/3141/16

Oberhausen
244/995/6

Gelsenkirchen
256/1114/9

Witten
83/253/3

Duisburg
1312/4903/25

Mülheim
41/102/6

Essen
1117/3595/22

Hagen
333/1369/6

Krefeld
58/145/8

Neuss
220/948

Düsseldorf
719/2739/35

Wuppertal
111/349/6

Mönchen-
Gladbach
83/207/3

Remscheid
32/80/2

Grevenbroich
134/355

Opladen
146/613/2

Leverkusen
121/303/4

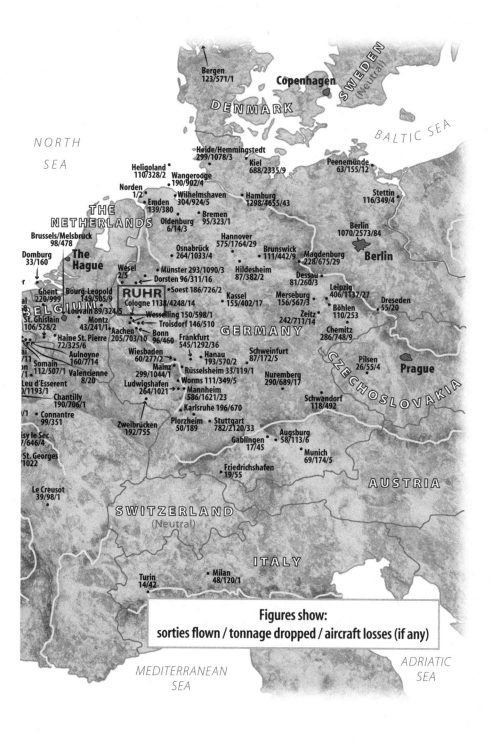

Bergen
123/571/1

Copenhagen

SWEDEN (Neutral)

DENMARK

NORTH SEA

BALTIC SEA

Heide/Hemmingstedt
299/1078/3

Heligoland
110/328/2
Wangerooge
190/902/4

Kiel
688/2335/9

Peenemünde
63/155/12

Norden
1/2

Wilhelmshaven
304/924/5

Hamburg
1298/4655/43

Stettin
116/349/4

Emden
139/380

Bremen
95/323/1

Oldenburg
6/14/3

THE NETHERLANDS

Brussels/Melsbruck
98/478

Hannover
575/1764/29

Berlin
1070/2573/84

The Hague

Domburg
33/160

Osnabrück
264/1033/4

Brunswick
111/442/9

Magdenburg
228/675/29

Berlin

Wesel
2/5

Münster 293/1090/3

Hildesheim
87/382/2

Dessau
81/260/3

Leipzig
406/1137/27

Ghent
220/999

Bourg-Leopold
149/505/9

Dorsten 96/311/16

RUHR

Soest 186/726/2

Merseburg
156/567/3

Dreseden
55/20

BELGIUM

Louvain 89/324/5

Cologne 1138/4248/14

Kassel
155/402/17

Böhlen
110/253

St. Ghislain
106/528/2

Wesseling 150/598/1

Zeitz
242/711/14

Montz
43/241/1

Troisdorf 146/510

GERMANY

Chemitz
286/748/9

Haine St. Pierre
72/325/6

Aachen
205/703/10

Bonn
96/460

Frankfurt
545/1292/36

Aulnoyne
160/7/14

Wiesbaden
60/277/2

Hanau
193/570/2

Schweinfurt
87/172/5

Somain
112/507/1

Valencienne
8/20

Mainz
299/1044/1

Rüsselsheim 33/119/1

Pilsen
26/55/4

Prague

Leu d'Esserent
/1193/1

Ludwigshafen
264/1021

Worms 111/349/5

Nuremberg
290/689/17

CZECHOSLOVAKIA

Chantilly
190/706/1

Mannheim
586/1621/23

Connantre
99/351

Karlsruhe 196/670

Schwandorf
118/492

sy le Sec
/646/4

Plorzheim
50/189

Stuttgart
782/2120/33

Augsburg
58/113/6

St. Georges
/1022

Zweibrücken
192/755

Gablingen
17/45

Munich
69/174/5

AUSTRIA

Le Creusot
39/98/1

Friedrichshafen
19/55

SWITZERLAND
(Neutral)

ITALY

Turin
14/42

Milan
48/120/1

MEDITERRANEAN SEA

ADRIATIC SEA

Figures show:
sorties flown / tonnage dropped / aircraft losses (if any)

INTRODUCTION

The beachside towns on the east coast of the Normandy peninsula are tourist meccas each summer. The narrow coastal highway links them together like pearls on a string. Visitors arrive on ferries from the United Kingdom or by car from Paris and other parts of France. Holiday traffic moves slowly on the narrow blacktop roads that parallel the beaches; cars filled with families pull trailers, young men and women on motorcycles or motor scooters thread their way around the slow-moving vehicles from towns such as St-Aubin-sur-Mer, Bernières-sur-Mer, and Courseulles-sur-Mer. On warm summer days it is impossible to get a parking spot near the beach; parked cars line both sides of the road and the small municipal parking areas are jammed to overflowing. It would be easy to mistake these small beach resorts on the coast of the English Channel as nothing more than vacation destinations for sun-seeking tourists, but these little towns have a deep and significant meaning for Canadians, even if most Canadians are unaware of that connection. Nowhere is that connection best symbolized than on a narrow, triangular stretch of land between the Quai des Frères Labreques, the Voie des Français Libres, and the English Channel in Courseulles-sur-Mer. There, just a few hundred metres south of the beach is the Juno Beach Centre, Canada's only Second World War memorial and education centre in Europe. Opened in 2003, the centre tells the story of Canada's role in the defeat of Nazi Germany from the latter days of the Great

Depression through Canada's mobilization for war in 1939, and the story of the more than one million Canadian veterans who fought in the Second World War—those who survived the war and those who did not.

Courseulles-sur-Mer lies roughly near the centre of what is known to history as Juno Beach. At approximately 0745 on the morning of June 6, 1944, Canadian infantrymen of the 7th Canadian Infantry Brigade, supported by the 6th Canadian Armoured Regiment, attacked the German defences in and around the town from the sea as part of the greatest assault landing in history. To the left and right flanks of the Canadians, the British landed at Sword and Gold Beaches; away to the west the Americans came ashore at Omaha and Utah Beaches. By the end of the day, the Allies were firmly lodged on the Normandy coast, but the British had failed to penetrate inland to the key city of Caen. The long and brutal Battle of Normandy was about to begin.

The Juno Beach Centre is the most visible sign of Canada's contribution to the eventual Allied victory in the battle for Normandy that began on June 6, 1944, and ended only in late August. But in many other places in Normandy, there are signs of the passing of the Canadian Army in that hot summer of 1944. In the small beach towns and inland, along the long and tortuous road from the beaches to the ancient Norman capital of Falaise, to the crossing of the Seine near Rouen, there are markers, memorials, and plaques attesting to the sacrifice of this or that regiment. There are also the remains of the formidable German defences that were overcome with bombs and shellfire and rockets and, in the end, the sheer determination of mortal men who pitted flesh against steel and concrete, and finally prevailed.

Not far from Juno Beach is the Canadian War Cemetery at Bény-sur-Mer where those Canadians killed in action on D-Day and in the fight for Caen lie buried. It is only one of many Canadian war cemeteries around the globe from Hong Kong to Holland. Each cemetery, each gravestone, is tangible proof that when called upon to do its part in the terrible struggle to defeat the most powerful evil the world has yet known, Canada did its duty. Each cemetery, each gravestone, marks Canada's final induction into the family of free and independent nations.

In the close to six years during which the Second World War ravaged much of the world, some 1,100,000 Canadians served in the three armed forces of their country. In places as far afield as Ceylon, the Aleutian Islands, the North African desert, the ocean run to Murmansk, Hong Kong, Italy, and northwest Europe, Canadian soldiers, sailors, and airmen played a full role in the Allied war effort. Canadians guarded convoys across the North Atlantic, took part in the bomber offensive against Germany, and contributed close to six full divisions to the Allied armies in the campaign to liberate Europe.

The Canadian contribution to victory pales beside that of the British, the Americans, or the Soviet Union, of course. The Allies would have prevailed without Canada. But Canada helped immensely, and at certain times and in particular circumstances, Canadians played a decisive role in building the Allied momentum to victory. The Canadian war effort was one that a small nation, barely three-quarters of a century old, could be proud of—one that Canadians today ought to recognize with pride. And yet it started from virtually nothing.

* * * *

The Canada of 1939 was a very different place than the Canada of today. There were a little over eleven million Canadians, almost half of whom lived on farms or in small towns or villages. Some 5.7 million Canadians considered themselves to be of British origin, 3.5 million thought of themselves as French. The other 20 percent or so were heavily European. Hardly anyone was black. There were few Asians in Canada except in British Columbia, where a large Japanese and Chinese community lived. Most Canadians had been born in Canada—about 9.4 million.

As a country largely dependent upon the extraction and sale of natural resources, Canada had suffered greatly in the Great Depression. The products of farm, mine, and forest are usually hardest hit in economic downturns, because raw materials are the first thing that factories cut back on when orders dry up and the last thing to be reordered when factories reopen or resume full production. There are no truly accurate figures as to the number of unemployed Canadians in the worst years of the Great Depression, but conservative estimates put the number at some 25 percent of the employable work force. Whole areas of Saskatchewan were virtually depopulated; armies of single unemployed men roamed the country in boxcars. Farmers in Ontario, Quebec, and Atlantic Canada were reduced to subsistence levels; formerly middle-class families became mired in poverty and were forced to live on handouts, welfare, or the meagre money from make-work projects. The social safety net that Canadians take for granted today did not exist.

By the late 1930s, a long, slow climb from the depths of the Depression in 1933 had produced a modicum of recovery, but the nation still had far to go before employment and income levels came close to what they had been in 1929. As late as 1938 there were still mobs of unemployed men rioting in the streets of Vancouver. It was small wonder that the great majority of Canadians paid little attention to events taking place in far-off corners of the world, as funny-looking men strutting about in comical uniforms made speeches about recovering lost honour, or the need for greater cooperation among Asian peoples, or the need to rid the world of Jews, Communists, or other undesirables. There was no instant Internet or satellite news then—and besides, what did any of that have to do with putting food on the table in Canada? Those who had experienced the war of 1914 to 1918 first-hand, or those who listened to idealists and isolationists spin yarns about how the conspiracies of arms merchants (the merchants of death) had dragged Canada and other nations to war in 1914 wanted nothing to do with Europe anyway. As one Canadian diplomat had declared in 1924, Canadians lived in "a fire-proof house, far from inflammable materials."

No one appeared to be a greater advocate of isolationism than the man who was prime minister for most of the interwar period, William Lyon Mackenzie King. King first came to power in 1921 at a time when Canadians were bitterly divided over issues that had been raised during the war, or because of it. In the months following the end of the war, labour fought capital, often in the streets; farmers battled the cities; and western Canadians struggled against eastern Canadians. But none of these schisms was as serious as the deep chasm that had opened between French- and English-speaking Canadians as a result of the introduction of conscription in 1917. King saw himself as a man with a sacred mission to reunite Canadians and to do all in his power to ensure that the fissures that had opened up in the First World War would never open again. This was the reason for his refusal to allow Canada's young and idealistic diplomats to be any more active than necessary on the world stage. If Canada led a diplomatic crusade against fascism, he reasoned, it might be called upon to participate in a military crusade as well. And when that happened, the danger of conscription and national division would rise once again. Thus it was King's policy to say and do as little as possible that might give Quebec, or Canada's isolationists, the notion that the government was preparing for another foreign war.

But King actually played a double game in the late 1930s, as crisis followed crisis in Europe. Until the Munich crisis in the fall of 1938, he studiously avoided any public act, no matter how symbolic, that might be read as preparation for war or support for other nations (especially Britain or France) that were preparing for war. He declared time after time that "Parliament would decide" Canada's course if and when the time came to determine Canadian participation in another conflict. There would be no joint planning with Britain or the United States for a possible war, no mobilization of Canadian resources for the military, no Canadian resources made available for others to build weapons, no commitments. King played down the importance, or the danger, of Hitler and was a strong supporter of the British and French policy of appeasing the dictators.

Behind the scenes, however, it was another matter. King was enough of a realist to know that English-speaking Canadians, with the strong emotional ties of loyalty to Britain that they then possessed, would never allow their government to remain neutral in a conflict that pitted Britain against Germany. They had fought beside Britain in the last war, most were the sons and daughters of British immigrants, and many had strong family ties to the United Kingdom. And virtually all of them believed that Britain and the British Empire embodied the ideals of Christian civilization, freedom, liberty, and decency that they themselves professed to believe in. As King told Hitler in a private conversation he had with the dictator when visiting him in 1937, Canada would never stand idly by while German bombs rained on London. In fact, at the height of the Munich crisis, the Cabinet secretly decided that it had no option but to declare war on Germany if Britain did. In 1914, Canada was only a self-governing colony with virtually no control over its foreign affairs; legally Canada had gone to war when Britain had. Now, in the late 1930s, Canada was a fully self-governing nation with the right to total control over its foreign policy and even over the decision to declare war. Canada's strong ties to Britain made it plain to King that the decision to follow Britain into a war with Germany would be virtually automatic, even though Parliament would vote on the declaration of war—something it had had no right to do in 1914. But he rarely spoke of this reality prior to the Munich crisis, almost as if he might wish away the signs of impending war.

The Munich crisis changed all that. Suddenly King realized that war between Germany and the United Kingdom was not only possible, it was looming ever larger. King's official biographer, H. Blair Neatby, described Munich as a "personal crisis" for King, who now concluded— and made clear to his ministers—that he would insist that Canada do all it could "to destroy all those Powers which are basing their actions on might and not right and that I would not consider being neutral for a moment." Thus he was also distancing himself from the strongly held views of his deputy minister for foreign affairs, Dr. Oscar Douglas Skelton, who was pushing for Canadian neutrality in the event of another European war. King instead became convinced that Canada's "real self-interest [lay] in the strength of the British Empire as a whole . . . not to recognize this would be to ultimately destroy the only great factor for world peace, to lose the association between the United States and the British Empire and all that it would mean for world peace." He was even prepared to face down Quebec if it came to that.[1] Thus he supported increases in the defence budget from $33 million in 1937–38 to $65 million for 1939–40.

King's double game was thus a game with a purpose: to forestall preparations for war that might divide the nation in peacetime in order to make sure that if Canada did go to war, it would do so as a united country. That plan worked well when the time came. Germany's invasion of Poland on September 1, 1939, set the machinery in motion for Canada's participation in the greatest war of modern times. When Hitler ignored a British and French ultimatum to withdraw from Poland, those two countries declared war on Germany on September 3. Canada's tiny armed forces had already been put on alert, as had the Royal Canadian Mounted Police, and the first stages of the mobilization of the 1st and 2nd Canadian Divisions had already been launched as Parliament gathered in Ottawa on September 7 to debate Canada's declaration of war. That declaration was made on September 10, 1939, and for the second time in the twentieth century, tens of thousands of Canadians were called upon to make the ultimate sacrifice. From a political perspective, King's plan was a great success. But the nation entered war virtually unprepared, despite the increases in the defence budget just prior to the outbreak of war.

* * * *

At the close of the First World War in November 1918, Canada had possessed a large army with four heavy divisions in the field, a tiny navy, and a rudimentary air force, even though large numbers of Canadians had distinguished themselves in the Royal Flying Corps and the Royal Naval Air Service. Canada's major contribution to the victory of 1918 had come in the form of its four-division Canadian Corps, commanded by Lieutenant-General Sir Arthur Currie, a Canadian who had gained a reputation as being one of the best tacticians on the Western Front. Through trial and error, the Canadian Corps had learned how to fight; a militia-based army officered and manned by weekend warriors had become a tough, battle-hardened force. The Canadians had paid a high price for that transition: some 65,000 Canadians were killed in action and 172,000 were wounded, out of a total of 620,000 who served. But at least they had learned through their errors and by the end of the war, the Canadian Corps had taught itself or adopted advanced techniques of assault and defence that rivalled those of any other army on the Western Front.

When the war ended, neither Canadians nor their government showed any inclination to maintain the magnificent instrument they had created. The nation was war weary and no one wanted to risk tearing the national fabric by bringing up the disturbing prospect of war planning.

The army's Defence Scheme No. 3, first circulated in 1931 and revised twice before war broke out, at least raised the possibility that Canada would send an army overseas in the event of a war; but it effectively hid that possibility behind the notion that what the army really needed was a cohesive plan for the defence of Canada at a time when international tensions were clearly on the rise in both Asia and Europe.[2] The adoption of Defence Scheme No. 3 produced two important results. The first was that planning for possible war revolved around the idea that Canada could field an army of five to six divisions for service outside of Canada organized into two corps with an army headquarters. The second was a major reorganization of militia regiments across Canada, with many being abolished and others consolidated into larger units in order to have a realistic mobilization plan ready to execute in the event of war.[3]

The Canadian Army had no control over the purse strings of government, no real say as to its size or the state of its equipment, but it did control the doctrine and training that its officers were taught at the Royal Military College in Kingston or at militia staff courses. It decided who was worthy for promotion and who was to be sent to British Army Staff Colleges at Quetta (in what is now Pakistan) or Camberley in the

United Kingdom. In the interwar years, and especially in the 1930s, the process by which new officers were selected and trained was dominated by Lieutenant-General Andy McNaughton, who had been a militiaman prior to the First World War. He was a professional engineer with a master's degree who had joined the militia in peacetime. In the war he had learned to be a very good artillery officer, specializing in finding and destroying enemy artillery—counter-battery fire. He joined the Permanent Force (PF) after the war (many veterans did not) and rose to become Chief of the General Staff (Canada's highest-ranking officer) in 1929, a post he occupied to 1935.

McNaughton believed that the proper basis for educating Canadian officers was to teach them how to think scientifically in Canada and then send them to a British staff college. One Canadian military historian has concluded that McNaughton's army paid "scant attention . . . to developing higher commanders capable of managing a battle."[4] McNaughton seemed to believe that military knowledge or experience was something that a good officer just picked up if he was properly educated as a civilian. This was the antithesis of the belief that had been developing in most modern militaries since the mid-nineteenth century: the idea that modern warfare (beginning in the Napoleonic wars at least) had become so complex and technological that its soldiers needed to become "professional" at what they did, and that modern armies had to conform to the standards of a profession of arms. Another Canadian military historian has observed, "General McNaughton's views on what constituted a sound officer development system were to be proved wrong. It took more than a keen mind, a scientific education, and attendance at British army staff courses."[5]

This is all very ironic because McNaughton, who came back to the military in 1939 to command the 1st Canadian Infantry Division, and who was later named General Officer Commanding-in-Chief (GOC-in-C) of the First Canadian Army, was the one man Canadian soldiers seemed to worship most at the start of the war. And yet his ideas on officer training ensured that when Canadians first went into battle, they would initially be led, for the most part, by men who had no business on a battlefield.

Between the wars, the Permanent Force was never larger than 4,125 soldiers; the officer corps contained fewer than 450 men. Inevitably many of these 450 were incapable of command in modern battle. Some were too old (including dozens of First World War veterans) who no longer had the strength, stamina, or vigour that would be required. Others lacked imagination, education, charisma, or technical skills. They were willing, but not able. Yet there was a youngish core of men, some with First World War experience in junior ranks, others entering the PF in the 1920s or early 1930s, who recognized how much the tank, the airplane, and modern communications and logistics were already changing war. Some of these few wrote for *Canadian Defence Quarterly*, founded in 1923 not as an official professional journal of the PF, but as a privately published magazine in which soldiers (and others) might write on important military topics of the day. Although it was subsidized by the Department of National Defence, many of the views expressed in its pages ran counter to official policy or doctrine. The magazine eventually developed a circulation of some 2,000—far more copies than the number of Canadian officers—and published some of the leading military thinkers of the day. Many of the men who emerged to command the Canadian Army after 1939 published in its pages, as did such foreign, soon-to-be military luminaries as George Patton and Bernard Law Montgomery. Much of the attention of its writers in the 1930s focused on mechanized warfare with its use of tanks, trucks, and personnel carriers to enhance manoeuvres on the battlefield. Its pages certainly cannot be said to represent an ebullient and intellectual PF officer corps, but they do demonstrate that a few dozen, perhaps, of Canada's younger officers were well aware of the challenges that a mechanized war would pose for Canada's army.[6]

Though severely restricted by a lack of government funding during the Depression years, things did change slowly within the army after 1935. Officers returned from British Army Staff Colleges having been introduced to the controversies and reforms aimed at making tanks and armoured warfare central to the land power role. Canadians such as E.L.M. Burns, Guy Simonds, Ken Stuart, and others pressed for change, which was slow to come because of government penury. Nonetheless, by the late 1930s Canada's artillery and logistics units were no longer horse-drawn, the army had acquired a small number of tracked and wheeled armoured vehicles, and it even owned two small Vickers tanks, built in the United Kingdom.

Appropriations for the army were about doubled between 1935 and the outbreak of war, and the size of both the Permanent Force and the militia was expanded; when war was declared, there were 4,268 men in the former, 86,308 in the latter. In the spring of 1937 the government reluctantly accepted the idea that Canada would likely have to dispatch an expeditionary force overseas in the event of war, but although the army was planning on an overall force of one cavalry and six infantry divisions, no final decision was made on the size or composition of the overseas contingent until after war was actually declared.

In the late 1930s, with growing international tensions in Europe and Asia, Mackenzie King remained suspicious of the military and was reluctant to expand it. When McNaughton retired in 1935, he prepared a survey of Canada's defences, which Mackenzie King did not read until 1936. When he did, he was shocked at the state of the nation's defences. There soon began the first of a number of modest increases in the defence budget and, with the establishment of the Cabinet Defence Committee, an effort at some coordinated military planning at the Cabinet level. Mackenzie King, however, directed that most of the new money would go to the navy and the air force; these two services might be built up for the defence of Canada itself without stimulating much public debate about whether they were being prepared for an overseas war. That would not have been true if King had promoted the expansion of the army and allowed open planning for overseas army operations.

Thus the Royal Canadian Navy fared somewhat better than did the army in the post-1935 expansion of the defence program. The backbone of the Canadian fleet in 1935 were the two new British-built destroyers acquired by Canada in 1931. HMCS *Saguenay* and HMCS *Skeena* were named after Canadian rivers and thus designated River Class destroyers. They were modern warships in every sense of the word, displacing 1,360 tonnes, with a top speed of 31 knots, a main armament of four 4.7-inch guns, and a normal complement of 181 officers and men. But then, there were only two of them and they were not equipped with sonar or asdic, as the British and Canadians referred to it throughout the Second World War (short for Allied Submarine Detection Investigation Committee), which had been developed at the end of the First World War. Asdic consisted of a device, fitted to the bottom of a warship, which transmitted sound pulses through the water and then received them. If a sound pulse struck an underwater object such as a submarine, it was reflected back to the transmitting vessel. The time lapse between the emission of the pulse and its receipt was supposed to tell the operator of the asdic how far and what depth the submerged object was. When echoes were successive, the asdic operator was also supposed to be able to discern where (i.e., in what direction) the object was. In theory, this was supposed to give the captain of the escort vessel all the information he needed before beginning a depth charge attack.

Like the army, the Royal Canadian Navy consisted of a professional corps of "regulars" and two militia-like auxiliary forces named the Royal Canadian Naval Reserve (RCNR) and the Royal Canadian Naval Volunteer Reserve (RCNVR). The latter was often referred to as the "wavy-navy" because of the wavy gold stripes on the cuffs of its officers' uniforms. The RCNR had been set up in 1923 with an authorized establishment of 500 men in nine ports. In fact, it was usually only half that size through most of the interwar period. RCNR members were required to have a maritime occupation in civilian life and to possess a professional knowledge of ships and the sea. They received four weeks of training each year aboard RCN vessels. Members of the RCNVR came from virtually all walks of life. During the week they were lawyers or accountants or salesmen; they qualified for membership by having an interest in the sea—by owning a yacht, for example—and being willing to devote some time to rudimentary training. They were treated to thirty evenings of training during the winter and two weeks at sea in the summer. There were never more than 1,500 members of the wavy-navy between the wars. The professional core of the RCN, the "regulars" numbered about 3,500 at the outbreak of the Second World War. These men were careerists, but the training they received, like that of their counterparts in the army, was well short of what would be required when war broke out.

It was taken as a given that when the Royal Canadian Navy next went to war, it would do so as a part of a larger Royal Navy war effort, and that RCN ships would serve alongside RN vessels and under the overall command of RN officers. Thus RCN training, tactics, and equipment in the interwar period followed that of the RN. In fact, most of the RCN's warfare training was carried out during participation in annual winter exercises with the RN's Atlantic and West Indies squadrons. The RN devoted scant attention to anti-submarine warfare in the interwar period even though it had virtually pioneered it. RN strategists (and, of course, the RCN officers who trained with them) assumed that asdic gave defenders such a powerful tool for the detection of enemy submarines that there would be no repeat of the U-boat scourge that had virtually brought Britain to its knees in the First World War. RN destroyers were not considered primarily as anti-submarine vessels but as fleet destroyers to protect the main fleet from enemy aircraft and to harass the main enemy fleet through daring torpedo and gunnery attacks. Thus RCN officers and crew members received virtually no training in modern anti-submarine warfare in the interwar period.

The prewar Royal Canadian Navy was deficient in one other area: an appreciation of the need for modern technological advances such as radar and for Canadian sources of supply. As historian David Zimmerman has observed, "Of the three [Canadian] services, the RCN was least committed to a program of scientific research conducted by the National Research Council."[7] The RCN saw no practical need to install radar on its vessels in the late prewar period, for example. In addition, the RCN, in Zimmerman's words "was content to be totally reliant on the RN for all its technical and scientific needs." The result of this was that when war broke out, the RCN was often a generation behind the Royal Navy in utilizing the latest in radar, asdic, and anti-submarine weaponry. The U-boat war turned out to be a highly technical war and the RCN was far from prepared to fight it in 1939, even though convoy escort and anti-submarine warfare eventually constituted the greatest part of the RCN's responsibilities.

In the late 1930s, Ottawa perceived a growing threat from Japan to the Canadian West Coast and was anxious not to leave the protection of the coast in the hands of the United States Navy. Thus Commodore Percy Walker Nelles, appointed Chief of the Naval Staff in 1934, pushed hard to expand the fleet. Four former RN Crescent Class destroyers, similar to the River Class vessels but somewhat larger, were purchased from the United Kingdom as additions to the River Class fleet. These were recommissioned as HMC ships *Fraser*, *St. Laurent*, *Restigouche*, and *Ottawa*. HMS *Kempenfelt*, a larger destroyer than the preceding six, was purchased after the outbreak of war as a flotilla leader and recommissioned as HMCS *Assiniboine*. Though these seven destroyers were not identical, they were all designated as River Class destroyers. Anticipating that the greatest direct threat to Canada was from Japan, the bulk of these ships, and Canada's small fleet of home-built mine sweepers, were stationed at Esquimalt, on the West Coast, in the summer of 1939.[8]

The state of the Royal Canadian Air Force in the interwar years was, for the most part, worse than the Royal Canadian Navy or the army. Established as a separate branch of the Canadian armed forces in 1924, the RCAF remained under the overall command of the Chief of the General Staff (i.e., army) until December 1938. After that the RCAF was headed by a Chief of the Air Staff (CAS). The first CAS was George M. Croil, a First World War infantryman who had joined the Royal Flying Corps in 1916. Most of the duties performed by the fledgling RCAF in the 1920s and early 1930s were actually civilian in nature because the force functioned as the air transport arm of the federal government; the RCAF was, in effect, the government's mapping, surveying, and bush-flying arm. That ended in 1936 when the Department of Transport was created to fill the government's civil needs, leaving the RCAF to concentrate on military duties. The change was connected to a rethinking of the air force's future role in the defence of Canada. The air staff identified two priorities that had always existed for the RCAF, but which had been almost completely ignored. One was participation in an overseas war, particularly what was then called army coopera-tion, and the other was the direct defence of Canada in the event of war, most likely with Japan. This meant coastal defence and the need to acquire amphibious bombing or torpedo-carrying aircraft to patrol the Pacific approaches to Canada.

The new emphasis on Canada's air defence needs did not bring a sudden splurge of spending on new aircraft and bases, but it did put an end to the use of the Royal Canadian Air Force as a government-owned freight and passenger airline for the North and direct it toward military objectives. A small number of Canadian flyers were sent to the United Kingdom in the interwar years to attend RAF staff school and became familiarized with the new theories of how air forces might be used to win future wars with the bombing of enemy civilian centres of produc-tion and even attacks on civilian populations to undermine morale, but the prewar RCAF had no resources to focus on building a strategic bombing force even if some Canadian airmen had the desire.

As late as the Munich crisis of September 1938, the RCAF was totally unprepared for war. With a permanent establishment of less than 1,000 and only obsolete and obsolescent aircraft, it was little more than a flying joke. When No. 1 Fighter Squadron was formed on March 1, 1937, for example, it was equipped with Armstrong Whitworth Siskin fighters, purchased from the Royal Air Force in the late 1920s and early 1930s. The Siskin was a biplane with an open cockpit and a fixed undercar-riage. It had a top speed of 190 kilometres per hour. At a time when the Luftwaffe was already flying all-metal, enclosed-cockpit Messerschmitt Bf-109s (Me-109s) with retractable landing gear and top speeds of more than 500 kilometres per hour in the Spanish Civil War, sending a pilot to war in a Siskin would have been as useful as shooting him in the head.

The government began to get serious about the air force after Munich. King's prime motivation for bolstering Canada's air defences was to both supplement and complement the navy's task of defending Canada. In fact, the air force was to be the nation's first line of defence because aircraft could range farther from shore in shorter periods of time to detect and deter potential enemy vessels. In the 1937–38 fiscal year, the budgets of the air force began to expand. It shortly acquired twenty Hawker Hurricane Mark I fighters from Britain, one of which was the pattern aircraft for the production of more Hurricanes at the Canadian Car and Foundry plant in Fort William, Ontario; the remaining planes went to replace the Siskins of No. 1 Fighter Squadron. The Hurricane was a closed-cockpit monoplane with retractable landing gear, a service ceiling of about 11,000 metres, and a top speed of 530 kilometres per hour. It was not a match for the Me-109 in a number of performance areas, but in the hands of a skilled pilot it could emerge victorious in a dogfight. It was more than a match for the Luftwaffe's bombers and the twin-engine Me-110 fighter. The problem was, there were so few of them in Canada.[9]

This, then, was the state of Canada's army, navy, and air force on the eve of war. Years of neglect and budget cutting had left all three services in a bad state. There was a dearth of equipment, and much of the equipment on hand was out of date. There was only a small core of professionals, and the training and skills levels for most of the militia and auxiliaries were patchy and inadequate. Neither the army nor the navy were being prepared to fight the type of war they would soon face, and the air force had no specific pre-assigned overseas mission at all. The government feared the consequences of war with Japan much more than the possibility of war with Germany, and much of the navy and air force were assigned to the West Coast. The King government, in power since 1935, had moved very cautiously to improve matters, but it continued to fear that any outright effort to ready the armed forces for war would produce a political crisis at home. The armed forces of Canada, and the soldiers, sailors, and airmen who served in them, would eventually pay a high price so that Mackenzie King could lead a united nation into war.

CHAPTER 1

RUDE AWAKENING

The train ride east from Brest, France, was slow, halting, and hot. Inside the crowded railway cars, men of the 1st Canadian Infantry Brigade talked, smoked, gawked at the countryside, and drank the cheap wine they bought at every stop. Lieutenant Farley Mowat was one of these men, a platoon commander with the Hastings and Prince Edward Regiment, the Hasty P's. He later wrote, "The train crawled on and at the first light of dawn it came into the town of Laval, almost 200 miles inland, where it was halted by a frenzied station master. He was beside himself. 'Are you Canadians insane?' he cried. Do you not know that Paris has fallen and that all resistance is at an end? Do you not know that *les boches* are only forty miles away?"[1] It was June 15, 1940—just thirty-six days after Hitler had unleashed his panzer (armoured) forces in the west. France was in chaos, and a handful of green Canadian troops were on the verge of stumbling into the spearheads of Field Marshal Fedor von Bock's Army Group B.

On May 10, 1940, the German army, backed by the Luftwaffe, had sliced through Belgium and Holland. Then, in a brilliant execution of tactical surprise, the Germans infiltrated through the Ardennes Forest, outflanked France's Maginot Line, split the Allied forces, and caused the virtual collapse of the French armies. The British Expeditionary Force (BEF), accompanied by a number of French troops, began to fall back on the English Channel port of Dunkirk. Between May 26 and June 4 about 300,000 men, mostly British but including about 70,000 French soldiers, were evacuated to the United Kingdom. The remnants of the French army took their stand along the Seine River to make a last-ditch effort to halt von Bock and Field Marshal Gerd von Rundstedt's Army Group A. The demoralized French were no match for the Wehrmacht; they were swept aside and Paris surrendered on June 14. It was no place for the Canadians to be.

* * * *

If William Lyon Mackenzie King had had his way, no Canadians would have been there at all. Just as he had been adamant about delaying a buildup of the Canadian armed forces as late as he could in the troubled years after 1935, he also wanted a Canadian war effort with a minimum number of casualties once Canada had declared war. In effect, he wanted Canada to fight a "limited liability" war by concentrating on providing raw materials, munitions, and war *materiél* to the Allies rather than sheer manpower. He would have been completely satisfied if the air force had virtually restricted itself to the defence of Canada's coasts, the navy to guarding the sea lanes on the approach to East Coast ports, and the army to sending as few combat units as possible to European battlefields. This would keep casualties low and make the possibility of conscription remote.

King was not alone in his hesitant approach to war; Britain and France were almost as hesitant as he was in the first eight to nine months of war. Certainly both Britain and France began to mobilize after they declared war on Germany, but neither country was willing to wage all-out war, and both countries seemed to want to wait until the Germans acted before doing anything substantial. Poland was quickly overrun; neither the British nor the French made any effort at all to help the Poles resist the Germans, not even to demonstrate across the German frontier, let alone make an attempt to penetrate it. Once Poland had been swallowed by the Germans—with the Soviet Union taking its share of the spoils in accordance with the Nazi–Soviet Pact signed in late August 1939—neither Britain nor France were eager to begin offensive operations against the Nazis. The French packed their troops into the Maginot Line, the British sent a small British Expeditionary Force to France to shore up French defences north of the Maginot Line, and both countries waited for Belgium to decide whether or not to renounce neutrality so that the Belgian army, and Belgian defences, could be integrated into the Allied war effort. The Royal Air Force spent the first months of this Phoney War (*Sitzkrieg,* or "sitting war") dropping leaflets on Germany. War had been declared, but neither France nor Britain showed any enthusiasm for fighting it.

In Ottawa, there were at least two continuing themes in the government's approach to the Canadian war effort. First, Ottawa insisted that Canada's war effort be paid for by Canada and that it be as self-contained as was practical. That meant that although Canadians would fight under the overall command of British (and later also American) commanders, Canadian units would maintain their integrity as Canadian units and would almost always be commanded by Canadians. Second, the government aimed to make the Canadian war effort highly visible to Canadians and to Canada's allies.

There was a reason for this approach: the government believed that

Our Finest Hour

Canadian unity could be guaranteed for the duration only if the war effort was seen by the people of Canada to be Canadian. In effect, that Canada was fighting as an ally, to achieve its own war aims, and not as a lesser party in a large coalition. Fielding an identifiable Canadian army or air force might do that. It would also make it more difficult for the major Allies to downplay the Canadian contribution to the war. The lesson Ottawa had learned from the First World War was that when it came to making the peace, or playing a role in designing the post-war world, one of the qualifications for inclusion in the process was the importance of a nation's war effort.

Although Canada did not declare war until September 10, 1939, the armed forces began to gear up for the coming conflict in late August. The government's Defence Scheme No. 3 called for the formation of a mobile force to defend Canada, and on August 25 a number of militia units were activated to assist in the protection of federal property, guard essential communications, and man coastal defence installations. On September 1—the day Germany invaded Poland—an order was issued establishing the Canadian Active Service Force (CASF) to consist of two infantry divisions and ancillary troops. Canada's three Permanent Force infantry regiments—the Princess Patricia's Canadian Light Infantry (PPCLI), the Royal 22e Regiment (R22eR), and the Royal Canadian Regiment (RCR)—were mobilized with one battalion in each brigade of the 1st Canadian Infantry Division to give that division a professional core. Fourteen militia regiments from across Canada were also mobilized to form the balance of the 1st and all of the 2nd Canadian Infantry Division. On September 19 King announced that the 1st Division would be available for overseas service if required (i.e., if requested by the British) and that the 2nd Division would be kept under arms in Canada for the time being.

Across Canada, militia regiments opened the doors of their armouries, set up a rudimentary selection procedure, dug musty uniforms out of storage, and went looking through armoury basements and storage lockers for First World War–era Lee-Enfield .303 rifles, Lewis guns, mortars, any military arm they could find. There were only twenty-three Bren light machine guns in the entire army. There was virtually nothing else besides rifles. There were no modern uniforms, no combat boots, no field equipment, no overcoats, no pre-packaged rations, almost no up-to-date crew-served weapons such as artillery, and fewer than a dozen tanks. In the militia units being mobilized—at that early stage of the war, most were not mobilized—new recruits wore crazy combinations of civilian clothes and bits of First World War uniforms. The absence of appropriate army boots posed a particular challenge because much of the so-called training the men would receive in the coming months was in the form of long route marches. Neither the lack of equipment nor the poor state of readiness seemed to bother the potential volunteers; throughout September and into October they lined up at recruitment centres and waited patiently to be processed. There were more volunteers than the army needed for its two divisions and many were turned away.

Why did they join? There is no doubt that many of them sought relief from unemployment or from dreary, low-paying jobs. Others thought the army and the war would be a chance to get away from home, see some of the world, and take part in a great adventure. Still others joined out of genuine patriotism, or from a belief that Hitler was wrong and had to be stopped. There was no great outpouring of the sort of naive, wide-eyed patriotism that had marked the first year or so of the First World War. There were few crowds cheering marching soldiers, no jingoistic music hall songs, little boisterousness in the whole business of recruiting and training. The prevailing feeling throughout the country was one of resignation and grim determination.

Lack of equipment, lack of space for training, and a poorly designed divisional structure were not the only difficulties hampering the Canadian Army in 1939; leadership was a major problem, especially in the early stages of the war when most of the officers in charge of army units were incapable of leading men into battle. Since most of the army units being prepared for war in the fall of 1940 were militia units, most of the officers were militia officers. Few of them lasted even until their units entered battle; many of those who succeeded them in command proved inadequate. Many were veterans of the First World War and too old or too set in their ways to fight a new kind of war. For one thing, they did not have the sheer physical stamina that younger men possessed. When British General Bernard L. Montgomery inspected Canadian units and their commanders in the spring of 1942, he concluded that most of the battalion commanders were totally unsuited to the job of training their men or leading them in combat. As a result, there was a wholesale housecleaning of officers right up to the divisional level. But in an army as wedded to the regimental system as the Canadian Army was, some of the newly appointed battalion commanders were little better than the men they replaced. Still, there were some militia officers who were excellent and by the time the war moved into its final year, they had, for the most part, come to the fore from the battalion level right up to divisional commands. Two of Canada's best field generals—Bert Hoffmeister, who eventually commanded the 5th Canadian Armoured Division, and A.B. Matthews of the 2nd Canadian Infantry Division, were both militiamen.

It was clear from the start of this war that Permanent Force officers would fill virtually all the staff, planning, and support positions. In the spring of 1939, the PF officer corps numbered just 446 men. In the words of Chris Vokes, who later commanded the 1st Canadian Infantry and 4th Canadian Armoured Divisions, "Over 50% of the then serving officers in the PF were useless for active service, either from old age, ill health or inefficiency."[11] The vast majority of Canadian army officers were graduates of the Royal Military College, located in Kingston, Ontario, and founded in 1876. An excellent academic institution, RMC did not do enough in the interwar years to prepare PF officers for the most important job a military officer can have: command in battle. In large measure, that reflected the approach of A.G.L. McNaughton, whose philosophy regarding arms and war dominated the army's thinking in this era.

When the government decided that it was going to send a Canadian division overseas in the first weeks of the war, there was little doubt that McNaughton was going to be its General Officer Commanding (GOC). From that position McNaughton was eventually elevated to GOC First Canadian Corps and then GOC-in-C First Canadian Army. An intelligent and innovative engineer, McNaughton had distinguished himself in the artillery in the First World War, but he did not apparently believe that a field officer required special knowledge about tactics, uses of weaponry, leadership techniques, etc. Thus the Royal Military College gave Canadian officers a good education and taught them leadership, but most received little realistic training about leading soldiers in war.

McNaughton was a strong Canadian nationalist and believed that Canada's army in the Second World War should fight together as the Canadian Corps had in the First World War. He bitterly resisted any attempt by the British, no matter how trivial, to interfere in the daily administration of the Canadian Army. But the legal and command position that McNaughton was in was full of contradictions. In matters considered operational, Canadian units in the field were under the overall command of the British. In other words, McNaughton always had a British superior officer above him in the chain of command. Nevertheless, McNaughton was also the ranking Canadian officer in the United Kingdom and was, thus, charged by the Canadian government with overall responsibility for the Canadian Army there. He could, for example, refuse an assignment his British superiors wished the Canadian troops to carry out. In administrative matters, he was the ranking Canadian officer in charge of Canadian Military Headquarters (CMHQ), established in London in November 1939 and responsible only to the Chief of the General Staff in Ottawa and, through him, to the minister of national defence. Later in the war, when the First Canadian Army was fighting on the Continent, a de facto division of function evolved between CMHQ, increasingly seen as the forward echelon of National Defence Headquarters, and Headquarters, First Canadian Army.

On December 10, 1939, convoy TC 1 sailed from Halifax with 7,400 men of the 1st Division; it reached the United Kingdom seventeen days later. The rest of the division arrived in subsequent convoys with the last men arriving on February 7, 1940. The division was settled in Aldershot, near Salisbury Plain, a familiar base to any Canadian who had gone overseas with the army in the First World War. The winter was cold and wet, the housing conditions poor, and the English food bad and difficult to get used to. The Canadians had been sent to England so soon in the mistaken belief that opportunities for training would be much better there than in the harsh Canadian winter. But it was difficult to train in the cold and wet, and the Canadians were little better trained for war by the early spring of 1940 than they had been when they left Canada. That was not much of a problem at that point, however, because the German invasion of Poland had long since ended, and an eerie quiet had settled over the European battlefields. Over the winter of 1939–40, Hitler's generals prepared for an all-out offensive in the west while Hitler held out the hope that Britain and France would now reverse the decision they had made on September 3, especially since Poland could no longer be saved. It was the time of the Phoney War, or *Sitzkrieg*, and the Canadians could sit as well as the best of them.

* * * *

Like the army, the Royal Canadian Navy was alerted to prepare for hostilities even before Canada declared war. By the end of August 1939, the RCN consisted of six River Class destroyers and a handful of small minesweepers and other auxiliary vessels, eleven ships in all. This fleet was certainly not the navy that Vice-Admiral Percy Nelles had dreamed of; in May 1939, the government had announced plans to build or acquire eighteen Tribal Class destroyers—powerful, fast, and very well-armed warships that were considered by some to be the equivalent of small cruisers—eight dedicated anti-submarine vessels, sixteen minesweepers, and eight fast motor torpedo boats to be divided between Halifax and Esquimalt. The Tribal Class destroyer had become the mainstay of British fleet destroyers in the late 1930s. Much larger than previous British destroyers, the Tribal had an average displacement of 2,000 tonnes, carried six 4.7-inch guns in three double turrets as main armament, and was equipped with a wide array of anti-aircraft and heavy machine guns as well as torpedoes. It also had a top speed of 36 knots. But Canadian shipyards were incapable of building these vessels; Canadian industry could not even supply suitable steel for warships. Thus the question remained unanswered at the outbreak of the war as to how Percy W. Nelles, Chief of the Naval Staff (CNS) since 1934, would be able to obtain these destroyers.

Nelles had had a career rather typical of Royal Canadian Navy officers; he had served aboard British cruisers in the First World War and risen to command of a British destroyer in the Atlantic and West Indies squadrons in 1929. He was the first captain of the destroyer HMCS *Saguenay* and spent a year at the Imperial Defence College in the United Kingdom before returning to Ottawa to become Chief of the Naval Staff in 1934. He was a strong traditionalist but equally a strong believer that Canada's eventual major contribution to the war at sea was not being recognized by its British and (eventually) American allies—and he fought hard to change that fact, eventually succeeding by the fourth year of the war. Nelles and the rest of the RCN's high command would pursue the desire to build a "big ship" navy throughout the war and would, in part, succeed. But the reality of the war at sea that began to unfold in the late summer of 1940 presented the navy with a very different set of circumstances; the hard facts that then emerged ensured that these aims would be undermined by the need to put Canadian escort ships—whatever was available—into action as quickly as possible.

On August 26, the Royal Canadian Navy issued orders that no merchant vessel could take to sea from a Canadian port without RCN authority; a similar order had already come from London regarding British merchant ships and the Royal Navy. Thus began the regime known as Naval Control of Shipping by which the two navies assumed full authority to control all merchant and passenger traffic across the North Atlantic for purposes on instituting a convoy system at the very beginning of the war. Then, five days later, *Fraser* and *St. Laurent* sailed for the East Coast from Esquimalt; they arrived at Halifax on September 15 and were sent to sea as escort vessels for convoy HX 1 one day later.

Both Nelles and the Royal Navy expected the Royal Canadian Navy to be put under command of the RN upon the outbreak of war and the small Canadian fleet to be deployed as the British required. King strongly resisted. As far as he was concerned, the RCN had been built up for the defence of Canada. In practical terms, this meant escorting convoys from the East Coast and preparing to defend Canadian waters from whatever might threaten them. Not until the German attack westward in the spring of 1940 did King relent and allow Canadian warships to be deployed across the Atlantic in aid of the British fleet.

The North Atlantic was one of the most important theatres of the Second World War and the RCN was in the battle from the very beginning. If anyone needed proof of how desperate the coming war at sea would be, that proof was provided within hours of the British declaration of war on Germany when the German submarine U-30 sank the British passenger ship *Athenia*, bound for Montreal from the United Kingdom, some 400 kilometres west of Ireland. The attack came without warning, in contravention of rules governing submarine warfare laid down in the 1930 London Naval Treaty and signed by Germany in 1936; 118 lives were lost. And although the sinking of the *Athenia* was clearly the act of one submarine commander and not, at that time, a reflection of a general German policy of embarking on unrestricted submarine warfare, it was only a matter of time before that happened. As an anti-commerce weapon, the submarine was most effective when it struck without warning, wreaked as much damage as it could as quickly as possible, and then escaped as fast as it could without stopping to ensure the safety of any survivors.

The outcome of the war in the North Atlantic helped determine the course of the entire conflict. As one of Canada's foremost naval historians, Marc Milner, has pointed out, "without secure use of the sea Anglo-American land and air campaigns could not have been mounted and sustained."[12] In fact, one study conducted in 1937 estimated that

Britain in wartime would need at least forty-seven million tons of imports of all kinds every year. From pork to petroleum products, the British depended on overseas suppliers to sustain themselves. Thus the war in the North Atlantic ultimately boiled down to this: to win the war in Europe against Germany, the Allies would eventually have to mount a major land operation supported by air power. To do that, they needed to have a Britain peopled by a reasonably well-fed and well-provisioned population as a base of operations. And, since British industry could never supply all the tanks, artillery, aircraft, etc., that would be necessary to beat the Germans, much (and eventually most) of the war *materiél*—as well as most of the soldiers—would have to come from the United States by sea. None of that was possible unless the sea lanes were secure. The German objective was to stop that from happening; the Allied objective was to make sure that the Germans did not succeed. One lesson that the British Admiralty had learned the hard way during the First World War was that merchant ships travelling in convoys protected by escort vessels were much more likely to reach their destinations than single ships sailing alone. That did not mean that convoys did not create difficulties for the Allies. For example, convoyed vessels had to waste time gathering in ports of departure while the arrival of a convoy at a port of destination taxed the unloading facilities. But on balance, there seemed little doubt that convoys offered significant protection, especially to slower vessels.

The war at sea was a war of attrition in which Vice-Admiral Karl Dönitz's men attempted to sink Allied merchant vessels (and neutral ships chartered by the Allies) at a much faster clip than they themselves were being sunk. Dönitz called this war of attrition *Tonnagekrieg,* reasoning that every successful attack by a submarine, no matter where or what kind of ship was attacked, would inevitably undermine, and perhaps even destroy, merchant traffic to the United Kingdom.

Dönitz's U-boats were not true submersibles. Both main types of U-boats utilized by the Germans, the long-range Type IX and the shorter-range Type VIIc, were diesel vessels that ran on battery power when submerged. Their maximum underwater endurance was about one day. Neither type could make more than 7 knots under water; the VIIc could do 17 knots on the surface and the Type IX 19 knots. Therefore, their underwater range and endurance were strictly limited. For the most part, therefore, these boats were really torpedo boats best used on the surface but with an ability to submerge when necessary to avoid detection. It was not until the Germans began to organize "wolf packs" of U-boats attacking on the surface at night, starting in August and September 1940, that they began to do serious damage to the North Atlantic commerce lifeline.

The Type VIIc was the mainstay of the U-boat fleet in the early stages of the Battle of the Atlantic; it had the rather limited range of about 10,400 kilometres and at the start of the war had to travel north of Scotland from Germany's Baltic Sea ports to reach the Atlantic. In the first year of the war, the limited range of these U-boats led the British Admiralty to believe that they posed a serious threat to commerce only in the eastern Atlantic and on the approaches to UK ports, and that the major threat to transatlantic shipping came from German surface raiders: battleships and pocket battleships, cruisers, etc. Therefore, convoy escort from Halifax to UK waters consisted of capital ships from the Royal Navy's Atlantic and West Indies squadrons. This left the Royal Canadian Navy to escort convoys from Halifax and other East Coast ports to the point in the western ocean where the Royal Navy's capital ships took over. That point was dubbed the Western Ocean Meeting Point or WESTOMP, though it was moved around at different stages of the war.

The best way to make sure that merchant ships would get through was to avoid submarines. To have U-boats constantly roaming the sea lanes looking for victims would have been a tremendous waste of submarines. Thus Dönitz introduced what was termed *Rudeltaktik*—wolf-pack tactics—whereby groups of U-boats were assigned particular patrol areas and did not move out of those areas unless told to do so by the BdU (*Befehlshaber der Unterseeboote*), or U-boat central command; the challenge to the Allies was to figure out where those patrol areas were. Therefore, much of the Battle of the Atlantic involved the rather undramatic job of trying to figure out where the U-boats were and routing convoys around them. The chief means of doing that over the course of the war was through signals intelligence—the breaking of the German naval codes—and radio direction finding, which pinpointed the location of German submarines from their radio transmissions. The Germans were able to counter Allied efforts to divert convoys because of a signals intelligence triumph of their own; they broke the key Royal Navy code even before the start of the war and were able to decipher radio traffic from the Allied command to the convoy escorts and thus to reposition their submarines to counter Allied moves to avoid them.

The Royal Canadian Navy was not ready to fight an anti-submarine war; two of its destroyers had to be fitted with asdic, and neither officers nor ratings (the navy's word for "other ranks") knew how to protect a convoy or kill a U-boat. It was fortunate that there was virtually no submarine action in the western Atlantic in the first six months of the war. During this early period, U-boats generally sailed alone and attacked individual merchantmen one by one; of the 164 ships sunk, only seven were part of an escorted convoy.

The Royal Canadian Navy continued to dream of eventually putting a small but powerful force of fleet destroyers to sea to help the Royal

Navy perform a variety of tasks. That, after all, was what the navy had trained for. If Canada wanted Tribals at that stage of the war, it would have to buy them from Britain, or barter for them. The ship that Canada proposed to swap for the Tribals was the corvette. A British-designed utility vessel patterned after a whale catcher, the corvette was originally ordered by the RCN as an all-purpose auxiliary ship to operate in Canadian coastal waters. Corvettes would sweep mines, patrol harbour entrances, and do escort duty for coastal convoys. They would definitely not be used in mid-ocean. In February 1940, Ottawa ordered sixty-four Flower Class corvettes to be built by Canadian shipyards in expectation that ten of these would be swapped for four British-built Tribals. The government also decided to build twenty-four Bangor Class minesweepers, smallish vessels built to commercial standards that could also perform coastal escort duties or sweep mines from harbour entrances. The original swap agreement fell through, although the British eventually agreed to build four Tribals for the RCN and the RCN eventually turned ten Canadian-built corvettes over to the Royal Navy. The RCN also requisitioned three Canadian Pacific Steamship Lines passenger vessels—*Prince Henry, Prince Robert,* and *Prince David*—and converted them to armed merchant cruisers, and a number of large yachts, most acquired in the United States and converted to small patrol vessels. But the RCN's mainstay for most of the war remained the corvette; by the end of the war, 122 had been turned out by Canadian shipbuilders.

The Flower Class corvette displaced only 935 tonnes, carried one 4-inch gun as its main armament, and had a top speed of only 16 knots. (British Flower Class corvettes were named after flowers; Canadian corvettes were named after Canadian towns and cities.) It was a miserable ship to sail on and to fight in. In British and Canadian warships of that day, the men slept and ate where they fought and worked (i.e., the mess deck), the food being brought to them from the galley. The early versions of the corvette had no covered passageway between the galley, which was aft, and the forward mess deck. Meals brought forward in inclement weather were invariably cold and wet. The corvette was very seaworthy but pitched and bucked in a heavy sea like a fiend possessed. Sea water sloshed into galleys, mess decks, officers' cabins, wardrooms, everywhere. The vessel was normally not fast enough to catch a U-boat on the surface and was originally equipped with obsolete asdic and a magnetic compass totally unsuitable for convoy escort work. When U-boats started to carry 5-inch deck guns, the corvette did not even have heavy enough armament to duke it out with them on the surface. It often seemed that the best a corvette could do was to ram a submarine, at great risk to itself. When the Royal Canadian Navy finally got around to equipping its escort vessels with radar, it put the obsolete Canadian-built SW1C on board because the much better British-built 271 radar was not available. The SW1C was virtually useless in detecting a surfaced U-boat. The only thing a corvette could do better than just about any other escort vessel was turn on a dime.

The burgeoning Royal Canadian Navy suffered tremendous teething problems. As the U-boat war widened after May 1940, there was virtually no time to either train men at specific tasks or even get them used to working with one another and under their assigned officers. The unreliability of the corvette and other RCN ships made it almost impossible for the RCN to set up permanent escort groups (a specific group of corvettes working with one or two destroyers) to work and train together. These problems stemmed from the navy's unpreparedness for war—despite its limited prewar expansion and Mackenzie King's desire, arrived at only late in the decade, to build a navy for home defence. Nonetheless, by July 1940 King recognized that the rapid growth of the navy necessitated the appointment of a minister of national defence for the naval services as, in effect, an adjunct to Minister of National Defence J.L. Ralston. On July 12 Angus L. Macdonald, former premier of Nova Scotia, was selected for the job and retained it until the last few months of the war. A new minister of national defence for air, Charles Gavin "Chubby" Power, was added to the Cabinet at the same time.

* * * *

Like the army and the navy, the Royal Canadian Air Force also hurried to ready itself for war. Before Parliament declared war, the RCAF's eight permanent and eleven auxiliary squadrons were placed on active service even though only two flew modern aircraft. Official historian W.A.B. Douglas summed up the state of the RCAF at the outbreak of war: "Of the fifty-three aircraft 'able to take their place on active service,' including eight on the west coast and thirty-six in the east, many were civil types converted with floats for patrol work and most of the others were obsolescent."[13] Of the fifteen squadrons that the RCAF was capable of putting into the air, twelve were allocated to home defence and three were selected to be sent overseas: a fighter squadron equipped with the first version of the single-engine Hurricane fighter and two army cooperation squadrons flying Lysanders.

On December 17, 1939, Canada, Britain, Australia, and New Zealand reached agreement on the establishment of the British Commonwealth Air Training Plan (BCATP), with costs to be shared by all four countries. Canada was to pay the largest portion as part of its contribution to the war effort. The BCATP would largely use Canadian bases and training facilities to train Commonwealth aircrew, who would then enter overseas service with the Royal Air Force. The RCAF was to operate the BCATP in Canada, which began to graduate aircrew in late 1940. By 1942, the BCATP operated 107 schools across Canada; by the end of the war, more than 131,000 flight crew had been turned out, of whom approximately 73,000 were Canadians.

Canada was chosen as the venue for the great bulk of BCATP training because of its distance from the European war zone, but also the relative ease that its graduates had getting to the United Kingdom. The Canadian West, especially, was perceived to enjoy clear blue skies for much of the year and vast distances between cities and town that would afford clear flying over unpopulated areas. But although the RCAF was supposed to oversee and administer the scheme, very few Canadian military pilots had enough flying experience to qualify as instructors; many civilians, including bush pilots, were hired. Their knowledge of military flying was minimal. In the early years of the course, not enough instruction was given (twelve weeks of training, as opposed to twenty weeks in 1943), and severe flight disciplinary problems, including "beating up" airfields at low levels, produced large numbers of casualties. As late as 1941, 40 of the 170 fatalities among BCATP trainees were caused by low flying. Accident reports recorded these small individual tragedies: "A Sergeant instructor with a student flying a Stearman aircraft engaged in unauthorized low flying. Through an error of judgment the aircraft struck the water of the Bow River and both occupants were killed . . . A Pilot Officer with a student in a Crane aircraft engaged in unauthorized low flying collided with a straw stack and crashed. Both instructor and student were killed." Problems also arose for BCAPT graduates due to the lack of training in instrument flying, needed in bad weather. Canadian skies, particularly over the Prairies, could be inordinately clear; European skies, by contrast, were generally overcast, requiring that pilots be skilled in instrument flying. Although good pilots generally learned how to cope despite the lack of instrument flying training in Canada, those with only marginal skills "wiped themselves out very early" according to one Canadian commander who had himself instructed in the BCATP.[14]

Canada insisted on two provisions of the BCATP that directly affected the development of the RCAF. Article 14 of the agreement guaranteed Canada a supply of aircrew for what the RCAF termed its Home War Establishment—the squadrons to be used for the defence of Canada, including for anti-submarine defence. Article 15 provided that twenty-eight RCAF squadrons would be formed overseas using Canadian BCATP graduates. These "Article 15 squadrons" would fly under the command of the Royal Air Force and be paid for by it. Ottawa's aim was not to create a separate RCAF presence in the United Kingdom, with its own training, administrative, and flying operations establishments, but simply to have squadrons of Canadians flying together in squadrons designated as RCAF. In fact there were many more Canadian graduates of the BCATP than these Article 15 squadrons could hold; most joined Royal Air Force squadrons that had large contingents of Canadians while still others were actually placed in the RAF.

A number of RCAF personnel were already in the United Kingdom serving with the RAF when war began, but the first all-RCAF squadron to go overseas, No. 110 "City of Toronto" Squadron, left Canada for the United Kingdom in February 1940. An "army cooperation" squadron (i.e., reconnaissance), it was equipped with single-engine Westland Lysander aircraft. Since there was little for the squadron to do in the United Kingdom, it continued to train for its army cooperation role after it arrived. It was redesignated No. 400 Squadron on March 1, 1941. No. 110 Squadron was followed in June 1940 by No. 112 Squadron, also an army cooperation squadron, and by No. 1 Fighter Squadron equipped with its Hurricane I fighters.

On April 9, 1940, Germany invaded Norway and occupied Denmark; within days the British began to mount a counter-invasion aimed at Narvik and other sites. They planned a second strike on Trondheim and approached Canadian Military Headquarters (CMHQ) in the United Kingdom with a request that infantrymen from the 1st Canadian Infantry Division be made available for this attack. They initially asked for eight parties of about 100 men each to help seize a number of German-held forts at the head of Trondheim fjord in a frontal assault. McNaughton agreed, but the Canadians never left for Norway. The British Chiefs of Staff changed their minds about the operation, always considered risky, primarily because of the danger that the Luftwaffe posed to the invasion fleet. Since British troops to the north and south of Trondheim seemed to be doing well, there was thought to be no need for the operation. The Canadians remained in Scotland for several days as Canadian Military Headquarters (CMHQ) in London and the British tried to decide how they were to be used, if at all. By April 26 they were back in their barracks at Aldershot. The British and French troops in Norway fought on against growing odds but finally began to pull out at the start of May. The last Allied soldier departed on June 8, and Norway was occupied by the Germans until the end of the war.

Although strategically important, Norway was just the opening round in Hitler's assault on western Europe. The main feature began May 10 with the German invasion of the Low Countries and France. Much has been written about the brilliance and daring of the German attack, the failures of Allied strategy and tactics, the collapse of morale in the French army, and the Dunkirk evacuation. It was only after most of the damage had been done and the Dunkirk evacuations completed

(June 3) that the British decided to try a second time to save France—or, at least, a piece of it—by scraping together enough units to form a second British Expeditionary Force (BEF). The 1st Canadian Infantry Division was to be part of that new BEF.

McNaughton thought that his troops would land at Brest, then concentrate in an assembly area to the northeast of that port, but he was wrong. When the lead elements of the 1st Brigade, the artillery, and a Royal Canadian Army Service Corps (RCASC) supply column landed at Brest on June 12 and 13, the British put them aboard trucks and railcars bound for an assembly area near Laval and Le Mans, more than 100 kilometres from the line that the Canadians thought they were going to help hold across the base of the Brittany peninsula in the vicinity of Rennes. The British and the French were weighing a scheme to hold Brittany both as a redoubt and as a launch point for future efforts to retake the rest of France, but the situation in France had deteriorated to such an extent that this was quite impossible. Churchill changed his mind and ordered all British and Canadian troops not already under command of the French army to be evacuated.

On the ground, confusion reigned. With the German spearheads drawing dangerously close to the Canadian concentration area near Rennes, the lead troops of the 1st Brigade, the artillery, and the RCASC began to move back the way they had come. Farley Mowat, then a young lieutenant in the Hastings and Prince Edward Regiment—the Hasty P's—recorded the retreat in his history of the regiment: "The holiday mood was certainly at an end. As the train retreated coastward, the face of the country underwent a terrifying change. Every little station was jammed with refugees fleeing westward." It seemed impossible that the train would reach Brest without suffering German air attack, but reach Brest they did without incident.

There, all was chaos. Refugees crowded the port to escape the German juggernaut; everyone who could beg, borrow, or steal a ferry ticket to Britain jammed the quays. Those Canadians who had not left their ships simply sailed back to the United Kingdom, but those who crowded in by rail and by road seemed at first to have no means of escape—there were no ships to take them to England. It was not until a whole day had been lost that three ships arrived and the men began to embark. Their vehicles were left outside town and destroyed, while guns and ammunition trailers were taken to the east quay. They, too, were supposed to be destroyed, but the local British garrison commander, a Royal Military College graduate, was persuaded to at least let the Canadians try to load them. He told them to get as much as they could aboard ship by 1600; that was less than two hours away. Working at a feverish pace, they managed to put aboard all twenty-four field guns and much other equipment; that which remained was rendered inoperable. The ships sailed at 0515 on June 17 and arrived back in the United Kingdom the next day; six men had gone missing but the formation had survived, something that most certainly would not have happened if it had pressed on to meet the Germans. The Royal Canadian Horse Artillery war diary called it "a rout."

The fall of France put a whole different complexion on the war; Britain now had no major partners, and Canada was its largest ally. Mackenzie King's limited-liability war effort was dead. Henceforth Canada would have to do all that it could on land, sea, and air to aid the cause. Back home, Parliament passed the National Resources Mobilization Act on June 21, providing for universal conscription for the defence of Canada. NRMA conscripts would not be sent overseas but could volunteer to "go active" (i.e., switch to the Canadian Active Service Force) if they desired. Then, on August 18, 1940, King and US President Franklin

D. Roosevelt concluded the Ogdensburg Agreement to establish the Permanent Joint Board on Defence (PJBD) to be in charge of joint Canada-US defence planning. To shore up British defences and strengthen the Canadian overseas contingent, Ottawa announced on May 20 that the 2nd Canadian Infantry Division would be sent to the United Kingdom as soon as possible, that the two divisions would form a Canadian Corps, and that a third infantry division would also be raised for overseas service. Eventually, a fourth and fifth division were formed and sent to the United Kingdom, a 2nd Canadian Corps was set up, and First Canadian Army was authorized.

The brigades of the 2nd Division had been concentrating at training areas in Canada since the spring; in June, seventy-six officers and 2,577 of these men were sent from Canada to Iceland as Z Force, to help the British guard the vital island from a possible German takeover. The Royal Regiment of Canada and Les Fusiliers Mont-Royal stayed in Iceland until October, then rejoined their division in the United Kingdom; the Cameron Highlanders stayed the winter and arrived in the United Kingdom in the spring of 1941. The rest of the 2nd Division landed in Britain between August 1 and December 25, 1940.

★ ★ ★ ★

The fall of France drastically changed the nature of the U-boat war. Suddenly, Dönitz had French ports available from which his submarines could be sent directly to the mid- and western Atlantic and thus forego a long, hazardous, and fuel-consuming route north of Scotland. Once through the Bay of Biscay, the U-boats could reach their patrol areas within days. The reduced transit time meant that more boats could be sent to sea at one time than before. That fact, and the lengthening nights of the late summer and early fall of 1940 made it an ideal time to introduce wolf-pack tactics.

Vice-Admiral Karl Dönitz had served aboard German submarines in the First World War and had seen the rapid change in the balance of the first Battle of the Atlantic when the Allies switched from individual sailings of merchant vessels to convoys. That switch and the improvement of devices to detect and attack U-boats eventually swung the war in the Allies' favour. But now Dönitz commanded better submarines equipped with advanced coding machines and powerful radio transmitters. He also had at his disposal information gleaned from the Admiralty due to the successful breaking of Royal Naval codes by the German intelligence service in the late 1930s. He used these assets to devise his wolf-pack tactics. The wolf pack was a temporary group of submarines deployed in long patrol lines across the likely routes of either westbound or eastbound convoys. Since the U-boats did not have radar, the patrol lines were organized in such a way that the field of visual detection of the lookouts on the U-boat conning towers would overlap each other. Depending on weather and sea conditions, the boats might be as far as fifteen to twenty nautical miles from each other and, depending on the number of boats available, a patrol line might stretch for hundreds of nautical miles. If a submarine spotted a convoy, it shadowed it, radioed news of its find to U-boat headquarters, and began to broadcast a homing beacon around which the other submarines in the patrol line could gather. The submarine that first contacted the convoy was forbidden to attack until other submarines reported that they too were in contact. The wolf pack then waited for dark, slipped through the escort screen and attacked on the surface. The almost total lack of Allied air cover over vast stretches of the Atlantic allowed them to stay on the surface when shadowing their prey by day; the longer nights of August and

September 1940 gave them plenty of darkness to cover their approach. The result was a slaughter on the high seas—the U-boat commanders called it the "happy time"—when the submarines sank hundreds of thousands of tons of Allied shipping with few losses to themselves.

The Royal Navy was virtually alone in trying to cope with the U-boat packs in the waters off the French and British coasts in the summer of 1940. On May 24 King finally relented and allowed his small navy to sail to European waters. *Skeena, Restigouche,* and *St. Laurent* were the first to go, departing from Halifax. *Fraser* left from Bermuda. The other three destroyers would make their way across when they could. The Royal Canadian Navy's first wartime task was to help with the evacuation of British troops and civilians from French ports. While performing this duty, *Fraser* was sliced in two by the British cruiser HMS *Calcutta* in the Gironde estuary on June 25, 1940. She sank with the loss of forty-seven of her crew, the first Canadian naval vessel to be sunk in the Second World War. After the fall of France, *St. Laurent, Restigouche, Ottawa, Skeena,* and *Margaree* (which the Royal Canadian Navy had acquired from the Royal Navy to replace *Fraser*) were sent to join the Clyde Escort Force, taking convoys from UK ports to about 15 degrees west and then meeting inbound convoys. On one of these escort missions, *Ottawa* joined with HMS *Harvester* on November 6 to sink the Italian submarine *Faà Di Bruno*—Canada's first submarine kill. On December 1 *Saguenay* was torpedoed by another Italian submarine while escorting a convoy from Gibraltar. It did not sink, but twenty-one crew members were killed.

The Royal Canadian Navy's escort force was augmented in the third week of September 1940, when six US-built, First World War–vintage destroyers arrived in Halifax to be commissioned into the RCN. These vessels were the RCN's allotment of fifty old destroyers obtained by Britain from the United States in exchange for ninety-nine-year leases on a number of British bases stretching from Newfoundland to the Caribbean. Known as Town Class destroyers (because the Royal Navy named them after British and American towns with the same name), the RCN named most of them for rivers that flowed along the Canada-US boundary. The Towns were flush-deck, four-stack destroyers with a top speed of 36 knots but they had serious drawbacks; they were top-heavy, they were narrow of beam, and their steering gear was obsolete and prone to break down in winter conditions. Eventually, to reduce top weight, the RCN cut several metres off the top of the three aft stacks, removed the four outboard multiple torpedo launchers and replaced them with a single multiple launcher amidships, and removed as much extraneous equipment as possible. Still, the ships rolled badly and were almost impossible to handle in a beam or a heavy following sea.

One of these Town Class destroyers was HMCS *St. Croix*, originally commissioned into the United States Navy on April 30, 1919. *St. Croix* arrived in Halifax on September 20, 1940, and sailed for the United Kingdom on November 31 with *Niagara* and *St. Clair*. The latter two arrived safely, but *St. Croix* was pounded mercilessly by a North Atlantic storm and suffered extensive superstructure damage. Unable to steer easterly, and suffering from frequent failure of its steering equipment, it was forced to "heave to" to ride out the storm and was roughly handled by a following sea. For two days the ship struggled against the storm until, on December 10, it turned south in search of calmer seas. It then struggled back to Halifax via St. John's, Newfoundland. It arrived back on the 13th and then, four days later, went out again to escort the battleship HMS *Revenge*. *St. Croix* was destined to become a mainstay of the RCN's anti-submarine war.

As the U-boat war intensified, the Germans completed their occupation of northern France (the Vichy regime controlled southern France) and prepared for the next stage of the war. Plans were laid for an invasion of the United Kingdom—Operation Sea Lion—but before the assault could be launched, the RAF had to be vanquished. The Battle of Britain, the epic struggle for control of the skies over the United Kingdom, began in mid-July with Luftwaffe attacks on British coastal shipping; in mid-August the Luftwaffe began to concentrate on British ports, airfields, aircraft factories, and radar sites. At the end of August the first deliberate bombings of British cities began; on September 7 the Luftwaffe turned its attention to London, first in daylight raids, then in night attacks that lasted into the spring of 1941.

The Royal Canadian Air Force's No. 1 Fighter Squadron arrived at Royal Air Force station Middle Wallop on June 21, 1940. It brought its Canadian-built Hurricane fighters with it, but they were outdated and were replaced with newer models by the RAF by the end of the month. On August 17 the squadron went operational at Northolt; on August 24 it went into action for the first time and promptly shot down two RAF Blenheim patrol bombers, which its pilots mistook for German JU-88 bombers. That disastrous introduction to battle was kept secret for years; RCAF headquarters in London did not inform Ottawa about it until 1947. The squadron's next engagement two days later was a very different affair. Taking off in the mid-afternoon, the Canadians were vectored to a formation of about thirty Dornier-215s flying at about 4,600 metres. The German Me-109s were drawn off by RAF Spitfires, and the RCAF Hurricanes dove into the formation. German gunners poured fire into the attacking fighters, which shot three bombers down and severely damaged three others. But the Canadians paid a heavy price—three fighters were shot down and one pilot killed.

The Battle of Britain dragged on, day by day, and the lone RCAF squadron did its part. So did other Canadians flying with the RAF; one of the more famous groups of Canadians formed part of No. 242 Fighter Squadron. Canadian Johnny Kent helped No. 303 Polish Squadron to become operational and then was given command of the RAF's No. 92 Squadron. Recent estimates indicate that some ninety Canadian pilots flew with the RAF during the Battle and that twenty of these were killed in action. But the largest concentration of Canadians was in the RCAF's No. 1 Fighter Squadron, which flew out day after day to do battle and which suffered heavy casualties in dead and wounded and destroyed aircraft, as did the rest of Britain's aerial defenders. Possibly the best day the squadron had was on September 27, when it is estimated to have shot down seven German aircraft even though it could put up barely half a dozen fighters. On that day the unit war diary, usually sparse and laconic, recorded, "By the end of the day the Squadron was a very tired, unshaven group of warriors. They are so tired that they immediately drop asleep, not hearing or caring about the funny noises that go on in the neighbourhood."[15]

No. 1 Squadron would continue to lose planes and men at a rapid pace until the German daylight raids petered out and the night blitz of London intensified toward the end of September. Hitler postponed Operation Sea Lion indefinitely on September 17; his Luftwaffe had badly hurt the RAF, but it had not won air superiority over the United Kingdom. As the winter nights grew long, the Luftwaffe pounded London and other British cities night after night, killing tens of thousands of civilians, but with little impact on the overall British war effort. The RCAF recovered much of its strength as more and more Article 15 squadrons were established.

In those same months, Hitler turned away from the west, temporarily gave up his dream of conquering Britain, and began to plan the invasion of the USSR. The war was just a little more than a year old, but already Canadians were in it up to their necks. For much of the next year, the Royal Canadian Navy would bear the brunt of Canada's war.

CHAPTER 2

THE RCN ENTERS THE BATTLE OF THE ATLANTIC

Four hours before midnight on July 11, 1941, convoy HX 138 slowed as it entered foggy waters west of the Strait of Belle Isle. HMCS *St. Croix* moved to the flank of this motley collection of plodding merchantmen to give the ships as wide a berth as possible. More than ten hours earlier, *St. Croix* had slipped its moorings at HMC Dockyard, Halifax, and, in company with *Annapolis*, another Town Class destroyer, had headed for a rendezvous with HX 138, already escorted by HMS *Aurania*. *St. Croix*, *Annapolis*, and the other escorts were slated to accompany HX 138 eastward until they met Royal Navy escorts that would take the convoy the rest of the way to the United Kingdom.

HX 138 was a "fast" convoy, which had gathered in Bedford Basin, part of Halifax harbour, before heading to sea. The designation "HX" was given to convoys departing from Halifax that would maintain a steady speed of from 9 to 13 knots on their way across the North Atlantic. The very first of these, HX 1, had departed Halifax on September 16, 1939, escorted by the Canadian destroyers *Saguenay* and *St. Laurent*. On August 15, 1940, a second series of convoys began to sail from Sydney, Nova Scotia. These were the SC or "slow" convoys made up of ships that could steam no faster than 8 knots. In both cases, however, the speed of the slowest ship in the convoy was the speed of the convoy. Ships that could steam at 15 knots or better were allowed by naval authorities to make their way across the Atlantic alone because it was believed that they were fast enough to avoid submarine attack.

As *St. Croix* steamed to the rendezvous point, her crew completed calibration of the recently installed direction-finding (D/F) gear designed to pick up U-boat radio signals and give the vessel some idea of just where the German submarines were lying in wait.

St. Croix's career as an RCN destroyer had had an inauspicious start; severely damaged in its first attempt at passage to the United Kingdom in December 1940, the ship had been laid up for repairs until mid-March. On 14 March, 1941, *St. Croix* had taken to sea again but had been relegated to escort duties in Canadian coastal waters and checking on fishing boats from St-Pierre and Miquelon. Since those two islands now came under the jurisdiction of Vichy France, the RCN feared that their fishing boats might radio reports of convoy movements to the Germans.

St. Croix and the other ships of HX 138 cleared the fog bank in the pre-dawn hours of July 12 but slowed again just after noon when the fog closed in once more. At 2035, still enshrouded in fog, the convoy began a pre-planned change of course. Suddenly, from out of the gloom came the unmistakable sound of steel grinding against steel; in two separate collisions four ships, including that of the commodore, were badly damaged.

The damaged ships left the convoy and, unescorted, proceeded slowly back to Halifax. The rest of the convoy sailed on to meet another section of HX 138. The two groups of ships joined up on the morning of July 14 and moved slowly to the narrow strait that separates Newfoundland from Labrador. About 355 kilometres west of the entrance to the strait, the convoy ran into a large field of icebergs and reduced speed to

6 knots. After dark fog rolled in again, increasing the danger from the icefield. *St. Croix* illuminated the largest of the icebergs with its powerful searchlight, thus avoiding further collisions. But *St. Croix* lost much of its power the next morning when a main steam pipe collapsed on its starboard engine; it then returned slowly to Halifax, arriving three days later.

There was little dramatic about the passage of HX 138 through Canadian waters: no deadly encounter with German surface raiders, no running battles over many nights with U-boat wolf packs. But the story of this convoy's departure does reveal the constant frustration of doing convoy escort with outmoded equipment, the dangers of weather, and the problems posed by the almost constant presence of ice in northern waters. It was routine in one way, but not routine in another; a head-on collision with any of the 60-metre-high icebergs that drifted near the entrance to the strait would have been the end of *St. Croix*, and in these northern latitudes, men in the water would quickly die from hypothermia.

* * * *

At the outbreak of the war, the Admiralty had feared that German surface raiders would pose the major threat to transatlantic shipping. There had been some dramatic encounters between German ships and Allied merchantmen and naval vessels in both the North and South Atlantic. The epic fight of the British armed merchant cruiser *Rawalpindi* against the German cruiser *Scharnhorst* in November 1939 and the Battle of the River Plate off the coast of Uruguay one month later seemed to bear out British fears. For the most part, however, the small German surface fleet was successfully bottled up by the Royal Navy in Germany's Baltic seaports. When the powerful battleship *Bismarck* broke out into the North

Atlantic in May 1941, it managed to sink HMS *Hood*—long thought of as the pride of the Royal Navy—but was then destroyed by a large British fleet. In the end, the German surface raider threat turned out to be mostly illusory.

That was not true of the U-boats. In the spring of 1941, the new, longer-range Type IXs, based at French ports, pushed farther west, beyond the range of the Royal Navy's escort vessels based in the United Kingdom. The Royal Navy still did not have enough escorts to accompany convoys all the way across the Atlantic, but Dönitz now had close to 100 submarines under his command, enough to put at least thirty boats to sea at any one time and three times more than he had had a year earlier. Sinkings increased dramatically. In March Winston Churchill declared that Britain was now fully engaged in the Battle of the Atlantic and charged the RN with closing the escort gap between Canadian waters and Ireland. Britain then occupied Iceland and the Royal Navy set up a supply base in Hvalfjordhur in April to replenish and resupply RN escorts in the mid-ocean. Dönitz countered by deploying his wolf packs even farther to the west, in the waters between Newfoundland and Iceland. In May one unprotected convoy lost five merchantmen before it dispersed in panic; U-boats then picked off some of the lone ships as they scurried away.

After the end of the Second World War, an argument was put forward by some historians that Britain had so large a merchant fleet at its disposal in 1940 and 1941, and so much food and productive capacity of its own, that it would have been well-nigh impossible for the German submarine campaign to strangle the United Kingdom at that point in the war. One historian wrote, "The German campaign against trade in the winter of 1940–41 could only have been successful had a total blockade of Britain been established, and that was an extremely difficult thing to do." However, the British themselves estimated in a study done in 1937 that Britain would need to import at least forty-seven million tons of goods per year to maintain normal life and production. When war broke out, severe rationing certainly lowered the minimum annual tonnage of food, fuel, and other key imports that Britain would require to approximately twenty-seven million tons. In January 1943 British import tonnage had been reduced to about half of what it had been twenty-four months earlier, and nearly half of British consumption of raw materials came from stocks.

U-boats were sinking about 250,000 tons a month over the winter of 1940–41, but even if that rate of sinking would not have been enough to knock Britain out of the war, it had a devastating impact on Britain's ability to build its war machine. Britain's ultimate war aim was not simply to survive, but to win. To do that, it needed to expand its military capability with raw materials and weaponry from North America. That meant that it had to preserve, and even increase, its carrying capacity. Besides, these huge losses came at a time when British leaders were already contemplating a further stretching of their own naval resources in possible theatres of war, from the waters of Southeast Asia to the coast of North Africa, while Dönitz's deadly fleet continued to expand. The balance sheet at that point was unmistakable: three merchant ships were going down for every new one built, and eight new U-boats were being launched for every one destroyed. In order to help the Royal Navy fight the growing menace, Canada's River Class destroyers were sent to shore up the Clyde Escort Force in British home waters. On October 22 HMCS *Margaree*, the very destroyer that had been acquired from the Royal Navy to replace HMCS *Fraser*, was sunk in a collision with a merchantman. Of the ship's company of 181 men, 142 were killed, including many *Fraser* veterans who had been reassigned to the *Margaree*. This devastating loss was only partially offset by the sinking, some two weeks later, of an Italian submarine by *Ottawa* and the Royal Navy destroyer *Harvester.*

Thus on May 20, 1941, the Royal Navy requested that the Royal Canadian Navy help close the escort gap by sending its growing corvette fleet (along with its small destroyer force) to St. John's, Newfoundland, from where it could begin to assume mid-ocean escort duties. The RCN and RN escorts based at St. John's were shortly thereafter designated as the Newfoundland Escort Force (NEF) under the command of RCN Commodore Leonard Murray. It consisted of thirteen destroyers (six Canadian, seven British) and twenty-one corvettes (seventeen Canadian, four British). Henceforth, convoys sailing from Sydney or Halifax were escorted by the RCN's smaller and more outmoded ships (the Local Escort Force) to a point off Newfoundland. Those escorts would then put into St. John's, replenish, refuel, and then return to Nova Scotia. The Newfoundland Escort Force would pick up the convoy from the Western Ocean Meeting Point and accompany it to waters south of Iceland, where they would hand it over to Royal Naval escorts, which would accompany the convoy into British home waters. The NEF ships would then proceed north to Hvalfjordhur, resupply, replenish, and refuel, and then sail south to pick up westbound ON (fast) or ONS (slow) convoys returning to North America.

The Royal Navy's Western Approaches Command, in overall charge of convoy escort, decided in the winter of 1940–41 that the prime duty of escort ships was the "safe and timely arrival of the convoy." That meant no wild goose chases after submarines; the escorts were to stay with the convoy no matter what. Thus an escort might drop one or two depth-charge patterns on a contact, but then it would have to return to the convoy regardless of the result of its attack. It was a doctrine that the professional RCN, with its interwar offensive training, had trouble swallowing. This was a frequent cause of British complaints about the way the RCN was carrying out its duties.

The RCN also gave the RN other cause for complaint. Canadian escort ships either had no radar or mounted a Canadian-built radar that was almost completely ineffective. They had obsolete asdic. They still used wireless for ship-to-ship communication rather than radio-telephone (R/T). The gun armament on the early Canadian corvettes was obsolete (First World War Lewis guns) or too light to be effective against U-boats. Instead of gyrocompasses, Canadian corvettes used magnetic compasses, which were both unreliable and useless in mounting a depth-charge attack. At a time when the U-boat war was becoming highly technical, the RCN failed to measure up. With a lack of ships and a dearth of trained manpower, the RCN was clearly at a severe disadvantage in doing escort work. The case of the corvette HMCS *Amherst* was all too typical. The keel for *Amherst* was laid at Saint John, New Brunswick on May 25, 1940. Launched on December 4, *Amherst* was completed in the early summer of 1941, underwent sea trials in July and was commissioned on August 5. The ship left Saint John on August 21 and arrived in Halifax the next day. Then, between August 27 and September 6, *Amherst* engaged in a grand total of five days of training alongside a number of other corvettes and destroyers before putting to sea on September 18 for her first escort assignment. British training was far more extensive and utilized RN submarines to teach asdic and radar operators what a U-boat sounded like and looked like on their asdic and radar screens.

The Royal Canadian Navy had one other serious disadvantage: the greatest (and a growing) part of its escort fleet was made up of Flower Class corvettes that had never been designed for mid-ocean escort duty and were, to all intents and purposes, unfit for the job. The Royal Navy began to make major modifications to its corvettes early in the conflict—changes designed to make them more seaworthy, more stable, and more comfortable for the crews. But although the RCN eventually moved in that direction, they steadfastly continued to order original-pattern corvettes from Canadian shipyards, even though these early ships had more than demonstrated their many failings. Turning out the same old, early version of the corvette added to the problem of modernizing the existing ships when the RCN eventually got around to it. This was a major RCN failure that haunted ships and crews throughout the early part of the war. Thus RCN crews lived for days at a time in cold, wet, cramped quarters in ships that tossed and twisted at the first sign of a heavy sea. James Lamb chronicled what life aboard a corvette was sometimes like: "A wall of water, tons of it, sweeps across our fo'c'sle to hurl itself against our bridge structure with a resounding thump. Water sweeps everywhere; even in the shelter of the dodger we are drenched, and from below comes a series of bangs and crashes, from mess decks and galley and upper deck, where a hundred items, big and small, have bumped and smashed and clanged and rattled under the impact of the heavy sea." With galley fires constantly doused, a hot meal was a rarity. If it left the galley hot, food was usually cold and wet when it arrived at the mess deck. RCN sailors began to suffer respiratory illness from mould and dampness. This life was debilitating, it drained the men of their energy, and it ground them into a numbing tiredness. Even when ships blew up around them on a dark night, the adrenalin rush was barely able to outstrip their fatigue.

In the last half of 1941, two breakthroughs, one technological, the other in the realm of intelligence, began to hold promise of effective defence against U-boats. The first was Ultra, the code name given by British intelligence to information gained from cracking the most secret German ciphers. Using a mechanical encoding device known as an Enigma machine, which was built around three complex rotors, top secret German diplomatic, governmental, and military information was broadcast hourly to and from German land, air, and naval forces and diplomatic posts around the world. Tipped off to Enigma even before the war began, the British were able to build a decryption machine; they were eventually able to crack the German codes, and the naval code was first deciphered in the summer of 1941 after code books and two complete machines were captured from German weather ships and U-110, forced to the surface and boarded before it actually sank. This allowed the RN to read some of Dönitz's radio traffic to his submarines and to determine his plans. At this stage of the war, however, deciphering was slow and could be done only on a selective basis. At the beginning of February 1942, the Germans introduced a new Enigma machine with four rotors, which once again stymied all efforts to read the German codes. This signals intelligence blackout lasted for a little more than a year before the British were able to break this more complex code. The Germans enjoyed a major code-breaking achievement of their own: even prior to the outbreak of war, they broke Royal Navy ciphers and were able to read Western Approaches instructions to escort group commanders. Thus they had advance warning of many convoy sailings and of Western Approaches' instructions to convoys to change directions and outflank wolf packs.

The other development was the establishment of a chain of shore-based high-frequency direction-finding (HF/DF) stations capable of detecting U-boat radio messages and pinpointing the locations from which the submarines were transmitting. Whenever a U-boat transmitted, the emissions could be picked up by these stations, the direction of the transmission determined, and the position fixed by cross-referencing. That allowed the Admiralty to try to route convoys around the known location of enemy submarines. By the end of 1941, many British escort vessels also had the equipment installed, and at least one ship in every escort group was able to pick up U-boat transmissions. This sometimes gave the escort groups warning that enemy submarines were close. Canadian ships, too, had HF/DF installed, but at a much slower pace than their British and US counterparts.

There was one bright spot emerging in the Royal Canadian Navy's escort picture in mid-1941: Commander J.D. "Chummy" Prentice, one of Canada's little-known war heroes, was beginning to leave his mark on the state of preparedness of RCN escorts. Born in Victoria, British Columbia, in 1899, Prentice had served twenty-two years in the Royal Navy before retiring to the business world in his home province in 1937. When war broke out, he volunteered for RN service but was offered a commission in the RCN instead and was eventually posted to Murray's staff in Halifax (prior to the formation of the NEF). With a rimless monocle ever present in his right eye, a British accent, and a cigarette almost always in his right hand, Prentice quickly became a legend throughout the fleet. But Prentice's real contribution to the RCN was not as some flamboyant imitation of a Royal Navy gentleman; he strongly believed that thorough training was necessary not only to familiarize men with their vessel and teach them the demanding skills of anti-submarine warfare (ASW), but also to work with other ships to provide effective escort. The hallmark of Prentice's service in the RCN, aside from his command of an escort group at sea, was his constant push to train escorts in groups and to do it as soon as newly commissioned vessels arrived in St. John's. In the last half of 1941, that was to prove well-nigh impossible, due to the shortage of Canadian escort ships; later in the war, Prentice's efforts would pay large dividends.

The NEF was scarcely a month old when it fought its first full-scale convoy battle. On June 21 convoy HX 133, with fifty-eight ships, sailed from Halifax; near St. John's, the local escort handed HX 133 off to a group of four corvettes (three Canadian and one British) led by *Ottawa*, a River Class destroyer. The convoy was spotted by U-203 south of Greenland on June 23; the submarine then radioed its position and sought permission to attack. Interception and decryption of the traffic between U-boat headquarters and U-203 indicated that Dönitz was trying to organize a wolf pack of at least ten submarines to attack the convoy. To counter the threat, the Commander-in-Chief (C-in-C) Western Approaches directed two escorts from a second escort group, led by the corvette *Wetaskiwin*, then sailing south from Iceland to meet westbound convoy OB 336, to go to the aid of HX 133.

U-203 waited for nightfall, then moved in on the surface, penetrated the escort screen, and torpedoed one ship. On board *Ottawa*, Captain E.R. Mainguy tried to coordinate the defence of HX 133, but the Canadian corvettes did not have R/T and their wireless sets were not working properly. The submarine escaped unscathed. At about 2300 the following night, another ship was torpedoed and a U-boat surfaced astern of the convoy. *Ottawa* and a corvette chased it briefly but turned back at the sound of still another torpedo explosion. Mainguy again tried to mount a coordinated hunt, but inadequate equipment and poor seamanship foiled the effort. When C-in-C Western Approaches received Mainguy's report of these latest sinkings, he ordered *Wetaskiwin* and its two consorts to go to the aid of HX 133. *Wetaskiwin*, at that point, was preparing to comply when it intercepted an urgent radio message that the unescorted OB 336 was also under attack. The escort commander decided to take matters into his own hands, ignore the order to join HX 133, and proceed as fast as possible to the vulnerable convoy. *Ottawa's* escort group handed HX 133 over to a powerful RN force shortly afterwards; eventually, the British ships went on to sink two U-boats. The convoy itself lost a total of six ships (OB 336 lost another two), not a heavy loss by any means, but the performance of *Ottawa*'s escort group was cause for serious concern and an indicator of just how many obstacles the RCN still had to overcome.

* * * *

For the remainder of the summer of 1941, the Admiralty maintained an edge over the U-boats by using Ultra information to route convoys past danger. But that edge seemed to have disappeared entirely after nightfall on September 9 when torpedoes slammed home against SS *Muneric*, a ship in convoy SC 42 in the waters south of Greenland. With its bottom blasted out, *Muneric* sank quickly and the epic battle of SC 42 was on. It would demonstrate all too clearly just how poorly equipped the RCN was to guard convoys even two years after the outbreak of the war.

Sailing from Sydney on August 30, SC 42 was a slow convoy consisting of sixty-four merchant ships guarded by a Canadian escort group from the NEF, which initially consisted of the destroyer *Skeena* and three corvettes. The convoy was making for the Strait of Belle Isle when, on September 1, Ultra intercepts carried warnings of a major U-boat concentration in the northwestern Atlantic. In St. John's, Chummy Prentice in *Chambly* obtained permission to sail to the area of danger accompanied by *Moose Jaw*: both of these ships were supposed to be part of a training group of five vessels that he was trying to put together. As Prentice proceeded eastward, he received garbled instructions to go to the aid of convoy SC 43, but he chose instead to sail to a position about 500 kilometres east of Cape Farewell (the southern tip of Greenland)

and bide his time until it became clear which convoy, SC 42 or SC 43, was in greatest danger.

In the meantime, convoy SC 42, then to the south-southeast of Cape Farewell, altered course and sailed due north, toward the Greenland coast, in an attempt to pass around the concentration of U-boats. The sea was rough and the convoy could make only 5 knots. Darkness began to envelope the ships, spread out over the seascape, as they turned northeastward toward Iceland. Inside the ships, the men prepared for the long night with a sense of foreboding; if nothing else, the course change told them that somewhere far to the east, their fate was being decided on the chartboards of the Admiralty and U-boat headquarters. Those not on watch turned in fully dressed, the better to abandon ship if a torpedo struck home. As the darkness deepened, the moon rose, silhouetting the ships to any submarine stalking them. That was when the first torpedoes struck; SC 42 had run into a full-blown wolf pack of eight to twelve U-boats.

In the chaos of the next few hours, *Skeena* and her consorts raced about, asdic pinging, lookouts straining in the explosion-lit dark to spot the surfaced U-boats. They were easy enough to see; every few minutes it seemed as if another surfaced submarine was reported by another merchantman. Tracer whipped across the seascape as the gunners aboard the freighters tried to hit back at their attackers. Explosion after explosion gave notice of yet another German triumph as the tell-tale sounds of the submarines were lost to the asdic operators in the swirling waters stirred up by the screws of the advancing merchantmen. The escorts sometimes gave chase, sometimes turned back to protect their charges, and sometimes stopped to rescue men still in the water.

Just after midnight, as the beleaguered convoy was making ready for a course change, a U-boat was spotted on the surface inside the convoy, running up between two columns of freighters. *Skeena* turned into the convoy and raced after it. The U-boat cut across a column of ships, reversed course, then speeded back in the opposite direction. The destroyer and the U-boat raced past each other, each in a separate lane; the two vessels closed in too quickly for *Skeena* to bring its guns to bear, especially since a line of merchantmen lay in between. The U-boat then began a crash-dive as the convoy began to execute its turn. For one panic-stricken moment, the slender *Skeena* lay directly in the path of a lumbering freighter; *Skeena*'s captain, Commander J.C. Hibbard, ordered all astern, and *Skeena* backed away just in time to avoid being cut in two.

As the submarines attacked again and again, Prentice was ordered to come to SC 42's aid. He was not certain of the exact position of the convoy, and his 15-knot maximum speed put him the better part of a day's sailing away. In the meantime, the U-boat attacks continued through the night and into the early dawn of September 10. With the exception of Hibbard aboard *Skeena*, the escort captains seemed confused about both what was happening and what their responsibility was. They wasted valuable time pulling men from the water when they ought to have been keeping to their stations and deterring further attacks.

Daylight brought no immediate respite; the U-boats dove and continued their onslaught against the slow convoy, which tried to twist and turn out of danger as it proceeded inexorably up the east coast of Greenland. Each turn seemed to bring it into torpedo range of yet another submarine. As darkness fell once again, the U-boats came to the surface and the attacks were stepped up. Once again the night was illuminated by star shells, tracer, and exploding ships; but this time they helped guide Prentice and his small flotilla of reinforcements to the stricken convoy. *Chambly* and *Moose Jaw* had actually sailed past the convoy, but when they spotted the pyrotechnics they turned toward it. Prentice reasoned that the enemy submarines would be on the surface on the dark side of the convoy and that he might catch them illuminated to the south, as they had caught their victims. His asdic operator obtained a firm contact close inboard some twenty-six minutes after midnight, and *Chambly* moved in quickly to drop a pattern of depth charges. Prentice then brought *Chambly* around in a tight turn to try to regain contact. As he did, U-501 popped to the surface about 350 metres from *Moose Jaw*. Hal Lawrence was aboard the second corvette: "Water streaming from her sides, U-501 set off in the general direction of Germany. We gave chase, the captain maneuvering to ram. With our primitive weapons, this was the surest way for a kill; a corvette in exchange for a U-boat was a bargain." *Moose Jaw* rammed the U-boat and raked its deck with gunfire to keep the Germans from their deck guns. Then Prentice pulled alongside and put a boarding party onto the German submarine to see what might be salvaged. But it was quickly obvious that the Germans had opened the seacocks and that the submarine was going down; the Canadians retreated from their victim, and U-501 sank with one Canadian seaman still inside. *Chambly* and *Moose Jaw* then joined the convoy escort screen.

The following day, nine Royal Navy escorts, including five destroyers, came to the aid of *Skeena* and her consorts, and the Battle of SC 42 effectively ended. One submarine had been sunk, but sixteen merchantmen had been lost. It was more than obvious that the Canadian escorts had been unable to mount an effective and coordinated defence of their charges. The four escorts had been not only outnumbered but, with the exception of Hibbard's, also outmanoeuvred and out-thought. This would happen time and time again until the Royal Canadian Navy could bring better vessels, more trained men, and more advanced weapons and detection gear into the fight. In mid-September SC 44 lost four ships and the corvette *Lévis* in one night. One month later, SC 48 suffered a terrific mauling despite a much heavier escort. At the beginning of November, SC 52 was actually driven back to port by U-boats, the only convoy to take such action in the entire war.

There was no let-up as the winter gales began to lash the North Atlantic. In fact, the load on the RCN increased as the RN pulled escort groups out of the North Atlantic and redeployed them to the South Atlantic. RCN ships and men were pushed to the limit. Ships like *Chambly* spent virtually every day at sea. The strain on the men and the equipment took its toll. What was worse, there was no time for men to learn better ways, for crews to jell, for ships to be refitted with better equipment. Each time a new corvette was commissioned, existing crews were stripped of their most experienced men, who were then ordered aboard the new vessels. The Admiralty asked the RCN to strengthen its escort groups by adding one corvette and one destroyer to each, but there were nowhere near enough destroyers to go around.

The slaughter at sea that occurred with SC 42 might have been avoided had the British and Canadians been able to mount effective air cover over the convoys. For the wolf-pack tactic to work, for example, the U-boat that initially spotted a convoy had to stay on the surface, shadowing its prey, broadcasting its position with a homing beacon, until the other submarines arrived and a night attack could be coordinated. Aircraft circling over the sea on the fringes, or in the path, of a convoy forced shadowing submarines down. Once under, U-boats were usually too slow to track the convoy. Thus constant air patrol over SC 42 and the other convoys might have helped the escort overcome the long odds against it, but this was simply not possible in the fall of 1941.

The Royal Air Force's Coastal Command had consisted of nineteen squadrons at the start of the war, but most of the aircraft available to it were both obsolete and short-range. The RCAF's Eastern Air Command (EAC) suffered from the same disadvantage but was in worse shape because it was even smaller. It counted only a single bomber reconnaissance squadron (No. 10) in its order of battle when war broke out, although a second squadron (No. 11) was formed shortly after. The BCATP (British Commonwealth Air Training Plan) added to the problem of building up these and other anti-submarine reconnaissance squadrons because it limited the number of aircrew that the RCAF could divert to EAC from overseas operations.

The greatest part of the North Atlantic crossing was beyond the range of shore-based aircraft for all of 1941, but even when British or Canadian aircraft caught a U-boat on the surface, poor training or inadequate weapons and equipment generally stymied a successful attack. Like the Royal Canadian Navy, the Royal Canadian Air Force lagged behind its British counterpart in acquiring the latest radar and anti-submarine weapons. Its ability to cooperate with the surface forces was also handicapped by poor organization and communications. Whereas Coastal Command and the Royal Navy had been cooperating since the late 1930s (and Coastal Command came under the operational control of the RN in April 1941), the RCAF jealously guarded its independence until much later in the war. This hampered cooperation between the two services and undermined their ability to kill submarines together.

* * * *

One reason why the buildup of Eastern Air Command units was so slow in 1941 was that it was generally assumed by the Canadians, the British, and the Americans that the United States, not Canada, would be primarily responsible for hemispheric defence, even though the United States was not then a participant in the war. According to war plans drawn up by the British and the Americans in early 1941, Canada would take responsibility only for its own airspace and coastal waters; the Newfoundland Escort Force was to be only a stopgap measure until the United States Navy could more fully deploy its strength in the North Atlantic theatre of operations.

As long as the United States was not officially at war, US President Franklin D. Roosevelt had to be careful regarding the use of US naval vessels in convoy escort, lest the neutralists in the United States accuse him of provoking Germany. Nonetheless, US naval units began to involve themselves more fully in the Atlantic battle as the U-boat offensive intensified; even though neutral, Roosevelt declared, the United States had a right to protect its own shipping. Thus US air units from Argentia, Newfoundland, and US destroyers began to patrol the sea lanes in the late summer of 1941.

The United States Navy was just getting its sea legs in the Battle of the North Atlantic when Japan attacked Pearl Harbor on December 7, 1941. The United States now officially joined the United Kingdom and the USSR (which Germany had attacked the previous June) in a full global war against the Axis. That was good because eventually the industrial might of the United States would tip the scale against the Axis. But the immediate result for the Royal Canadian Navy was that the USN virtually pulled out of the Battle of the North Atlantic as it redeployed its destroyers to the Pacific. For most of the next year, the RCN would fight the western Atlantic battle virtually alone.

That battle was merciless; it was a fight not only against the German enemy, but against the sea itself. On December 12, 1941, a Canadian escort group of seven ships, led by *Restigouche*, sailed from Hvalfjordhur to pick up a westbound convoy and bring it to the Canadian coast. Early that afternoon, radio messages from the convoy revealed that it had run into heavy weather and was considerably behind schedule. *Restigouche* raced ahead, tried to locate the merchantmen, failed, then returned to the corvettes. All seven ships proceeded in line abreast lest they miss their charges. The next morning, the glass began to fall precipitously; in the afternoon, the storm broke in all its fury. *Restigouche*, the corvettes and the convoy were in the middle of a hurricane. The official report is graphic:

> It was still daylight but the wind-driven spray had reduced the visibility to practically zero. The seas were mountainous, the wind was a thing of indescribable power. The stubby corvettes bobbed up and over the sea. The thin-plated destroyer, with her long, narrow hull, knifed into them and was slugged unmercifully. Worse still was her tendency to fall off into the trough . . . Within half an hour . . . all the destroyer's canvas covers, splinter mats and carley floats had been ripped off or torn to shreds and her boats reduced to matchwood. At 1700 the foremast split, with a tremendous crack, below the crow's nest. The upper section broke off and the steel lower section bent back . . . To the eerie shrieking of the wind was added the wail of the ship's siren; aerials and halliards from the mast had been borne down on the siren wires.

The ship was badly damaged and had to make port, but heading back to Halifax (where the repairs could be done) was out of the question. Instead, *Restigouche* headed for the Clyde. On the afternoon of December 16, *Restigouche* steamed up the Clyde and into the harbour at Greenock. With a marked list to port and heavy structural damage topside, she was bent but not broken. As the destroyer slipped alongside the quay, the "dockyard mateys" gave them a rousing cheer. It was a fitting end of the year for this hard-working destroyer, and symbolic of the state of her sister ships still plying the North Atlantic run because after more than two years of war, they, too, were bent but not broken.

As 1941 slipped into history, the Royal Canadian Navy turned with fresh determination to face the remains of another North Atlantic winter. It was obvious that the long nights in cold northern waters and the murderous torpedo fire of the wolf packs would further test this raw young navy in the year ahead. But few could anticipate that the next stage of the RCN's battle would be fought not in the mid-ocean, but at the navy's very doorstep—in the home waters of the Gulf of St. Lawrence itself.

CHAPTER 3

CANADA AGAINST JAPAN

Hong Kong Island: December 19, 1941. As dawn began to lighten the fog-shrouded peaks that dominated the eastern portion of Hong Kong Island, small parties of Japanese infantry advanced toward the strategic Wong Nei Chong Gap. The gap, or pass, was the key to the centre of Hong Kong Island; the main north–south road from Victoria Harbour to Repulse Bay and Stanley passed through it and intersected with an east–west road from Aberdeen to the Ty Tam Tuk Reservoir. The gap was where Canadian Brigadier J.K. Lawson had established the headquarters of West Brigade, a mixed force of Canadian, British, and Indian troops, and Hong Kong volunteers, charged with the defence of the western part of the island. The rest of the island was defended by East Brigade, another mixed force commanded by British Brigadier C. Wallis. The defenders were under the overall command of British Major-General C.M. Maltby.

From Stanley in the south and Victoria in the north, artillery fire poured down on the advancing Japanese. They took heavy casualties but pushed ahead and around Lawson's headquarters. A First World War veteran, Lawson had remained with the Permanent Force after the war and was Director of Military Training at National Defence Headquarters in Ottawa in the fall of 1941 when the government decided to accede to a British request and send a small force of Canadians to help garrison Hong Kong. Now he and that force were in mortal danger in a faraway place where Canada seemed to have no real interests.

As the Japanese advanced, the circle around Lawson's headquarters grew tighter. A small group of Canadian reinforcements managed to reach Lawson before the ring closed completely, but there were not nearly enough men to make any real difference. The Japanese infiltrated around the high ground overlooking the gap and poured rifle and machine gun fire at Lawson's headquarters. Snipers were spotted on the roof of the aid station, only 30 or so metres away. Lawson telephoned Maltby to report that "his headquarters was virtually over-run and that the Japanese were firing into his position at point blank range."[16] He and his men were going to go outside to fight it out "rather than be killed like rats."[17]

Lawson and several others destroyed the telephone exchange, then charged out and ran for cover. Lawson never made it; he crumbled and fell as Japanese machine gun fire decimated the remainder of his headquarters group. Despite his death, the Japanese had no easy time of it; they suffered heavy casualties, and the fighting for the gap raged for three more days before they secured the position. When they did, they honoured Lawson as a brave adversary and buried him with full military honours. He was the first senior Canadian formation commander to be killed in action in the Second World War.

* * * *

The attack against Pearl Harbor was the opening blow in a whirlwind Japanese offensive aimed initially at the Philippines, the Malay Peninsula, and Hong Kong. Since Canada was not a Pacific power and had had nothing to do with the long train of events leading to the Japanese assault, many Canadians then and since have wondered why 1,973 Canadian soldiers organized primarily in two battalions—the Royal Rifles of Canada and the Winnipeg Grenadiers—lay in the path of the Japanese juggernaut. The questioning that began as early as 1942 intensified after the war, when Canadians discovered that until the summer of 1941, the British military had basically considered Hong Kong indefensible, and that no less a person than Winston Churchill had declared at the beginning of 1941 that it would be the height of foolishness to reinforce the men already stationed there.[18]

Hong Kong had first come into British possession in the nineteenth century. The colony consisted of the island, a settlement on the Kowloon Peninsula to the north of it, and what became known as the New Territories on the mainland. The area is small—some 35 kilometres from the southern tip of the Stanley Peninsula on the island to the border with China to the north. The island itself is only approximately 16 kilometres wide at its widest point and is separated from the mainland by Victoria Harbour and Lye Mun Passage; the passage is less than 500 metres across. The island and the Kowloon Peninsula are mountainous; the island's western end is dominated by Victoria Peak and its eastern section by a small mountain chain consisting of Mount Parker, Mount Butler, Jardine's Lookout, and Violet Hill. In 1941, the New Territories were mostly flat, with part of the landscape heavily treed and part covered by scrub.

In the 1930s, a defensive line consisting of linked fortified positions had been built across the mainland, north of the Kowloon Peninsula, from Gin Drinkers Bay on the west to Port Shelter on the east. The line was known as the Gin Drinkers Line; the most important position in the line—Shing Mun Redoubt—lay on the western edge of Smugglers Ridge and consisted of a twelve-acre network of defences, including pillboxes, fire trenches, shelters, and artillery observation posts. There were no fall-back positions between the Gin Drinkers Line and Victoria Harbour and no defence in depth on the mainland. Around the circumference of Hong Kong Island were pillboxes designed to house machine guns. There was no defence in depth here either. Before the Canadians arrived, these defences were manned by four battalions of regular troops: the 1st Battalion, the Middlesex Regiment, a machine-gun formation; the 2nd Battalion, the Royal Scots, an infantry battalion; and the 5th/7th Rajputs and the 2nd/14th Punjabis, both infantry battalions of the Indian Army. In addition, there were about 2,000 militia—the Hong Kong Volunteers. Given the distance between Hong Kong and the major British naval and air base at Singapore, the lack of air cover at Hong Kong, the colony's proximity to major bodies of Japanese troops in China, and the terrain, there was almost no chance that Hong Kong could hold out for any significant length of time against a determined Japanese assault. In fact, Britain had concluded that Hong Kong was a mere "outpost" of the Empire rather than a basic strategic asset like, for example, Singapore. Thus it was worth defending as long as possible, but there was no realistic chance of holding off a determined Japanese assault against it. That was why, until mid-1941, the British refused to reinforce it.[19]

Then, they changed their policy. As tensions mounted in Southeast Asia and the Japanese launched their offensive in Indochina, the British shifted ground. Some British strategists came to the conclusion that should war with Japan break out, Hong Kong might serve them well as a forward base for operations against the Japanese in southern China. Others saw it as a potential replacement for the military supply route known as the Burma Road that ran from Lashio in Burma to China's interim capital at Chungking, situated well inland. That route was under constant land and air attack from the Japanese. Perhaps the Chinese could be supplied from Hong Kong. Two other more political goals bore on British attitudes toward strengthening Hong Kong: First, it was believed that Chinese nationalist leader Chiang Kai-shek's military position in south China could be bolstered if additional British or Commonwealth troops might be sent to Hong Kong. And second, after Nazi Germany's attack on the Soviet Union on June 22, 1941—and the apparent obliteration of the Russian armies—some thought that Hong Kong might even be a potential base from which to threaten the Japanese rear and ease the pressure on the Russians.[20] Even Canadian prime minister William Lyon Mackenzie King appeared to believe that. Some British military leaders, including Maltby and his predecessor Edward Grasett, a Canadian serving in the British Army, believed that reinforcing Hong Kong might even deter war. After all, the United States had moved its Pacific Fleet from California to Pearl Harbor, Hawaii, and was sending new heavy bombers to the Philippines, while the Royal Navy had dispatched the new Royal Navy battleship *Prince of Wales* and the older battle cruiser *Repulse* to their Singapore naval base at the tip of the Malaysian peninsula to demonstrate British resolve to Japan.

In August 1941 Grasett visited Canada on his way back to the United Kingdom from Hong Kong and shared his views with H.D.G. Crerar, an old classmate from RMC who was then Canada's Chief of the General Staff. There is controversy to this day as to what was actually said at the meeting and what assurances Crerar gave Grasett, but the latter certainly arrived in the United Kingdom believing that Canada would send troops to help garrison Hong Kong if asked.[21] That request was made in mid-September 1941 and Canada agreed. It is important to point out here that neither Crerar nor his British counterparts believed that those troops would actually have to fight—at least not any time soon—trusting, rather, that their presence in Hong Kong might deter a Japanese attack. Although conspiracy buffs have declared ever since that Britain knowingly sent young Canadian soldiers to be sacrificed in a place they themselves had no intention of defending, there is not a shred of evidence to back up this view. On the other hand, there is now a mountain of evidence that Japanese military moves of some kind were afoot in the region, due mainly to the impact of the sanctions the United States had imposed on her. Canada had no independent means of forecasting possible Japanese moves in Asia, but the Canadian government, including Mackenzie King and Minister of National Defence J.L. Ralston, seem to have had no idea of the high-stakes manoeuvres that the United States, Britain, and China were engaged in when they agreed to send Canadian troops to Asia. In September 1941 war in the Pacific was definitely moving closer—even Ottawa could sense that—but it was still not inevitable; the Japanese were planning for the possibility of an attack against Pearl Harbor but did not actually decide to launch that attack until November 5, when they judged that their last-ditch efforts to arrive at a negotiated lifting of US sanctions would fail.

There is no doubt that the two battalions Canada sent to Hong Kong were not ready for war. The Winnipeg Grenadiers had recently returned from Jamaica, where they had been engaged in garrison duty; the Royal Rifles had performed similar tasks in Newfoundland. The only other formations that might have been sent were units earmarked to join the 4th Canadian Infantry Division in the United Kingdom, and National Defence Headquarters (NDHQ) had no wish to disrupt the buildup of that formation. The fact that these two battalions had had nothing like the intense training that units destined for battle ought to have received (as those sent to Sicily or Normandy underwent in the United Kingdom prior to their deployment) is beside the point, since no one thought they were going to war. Both units had been mobilized for some considerable period and were considered "of proven efficiency"—good enough for what they were intended to do. The truth is that none of Maltby's units were adequately prepared for battle; even if they had been, Japan's air and sea strength in the area would have been difficult to overcome. Here is the real disconnect, and it points to a significant Canadian policy mistake: Hong Kong was to be reinforced as part of a larger pattern of forward deployment by the Royal Navy and American air and fleet units. These moves at least implied a threat of conflict, yet Canadians—and Crerar among them—continued to believe that the Canadian troops would not likely see action. Thus the two battalions, who had both spent months in garrison duty and had been reinforced upon their return to Canada in large measure by green troops, were considered ready enough for the task at hand.

The Canadian Hong Kong force, consisting of the two battalions, reinforcements, a detachment from the Signals Corps, and two nursing sisters, gathered in British Columbia in late October and sailed for Hong Kong aboard the cargo ship *Awatea* on October 27, escorted by the armed merchant cruiser HMCS *Prince Robert*. Before departure, Lawson, who had helped select them, was promoted to brigadier and placed in command of the force. Most of the vehicles assigned to the two units were put aboard the US cargo ship *Don José*, due to take a more circuitous route to the Far East, even though there was still space on the *Awatea*. The Canadians arrived on November 16 and disembarked the next day, but the *Don José* never reached them. It was still at sea when war broke out, and US military authorities refused to allow it to leave Manila; the Hong Kong vehicles ended up in the hands of the United States Army (with Canadian permission).

Maltby's plan for the possible defence of the colony was to divide his 13,000-man force into two brigades, one under Wallis to defend the mainland and particularly the Gin Drinkers Line, the other under Lawson to be stationed on the island to guard against an invasion from the sea and to reinforce the mainland garrison if necessary. The former brigade was made up of the Royal Scots and the two Indian battalions with the Canadian signallers. The latter consisted of the two Canadian units and the Middlesex battalion. Although destined for the island, the Canadians were barracked at the Sham Shui Po camp on Kowloon, where they began active training as soon as they settled in.

* * * *

At 0800 on the morning of December 8 (December 7 in Canada), some six hours after the Pearl Harbor attack, Japanese aircraft struck Kai Tak Airport, wiping out the tiny contingent of obsolete British aircraft stationed there, and also bombed Sham Shui Po. Three regiments of the Japanese 38th Division then began to infiltrate across the Hong Kong–China border, forcing the Punjabis to blow up a bridge over the Sham Chung River and withdraw to the Gin Drinkers Line. The Japanese plan of attack was simple: force the defenders back to the Gin Drinkers Line, break through it, clear the mainland area, then assault the island itself. Although they did not greatly outnumber the defenders, they enjoyed the advantages of air and artillery superiority and their troops were tough, well trained, highly motivated, and had seen combat in China. They knew how to fight as a cohesive force. The defenders were a motley and uneven group by comparison, and help was a long way off.

At first the Japanese thought they would encounter serious difficulty with the Gin Drinkers Line defences; they originally gave themselves up to a week to organize a proper assault. But on the night of December 9–10, a Japanese battalion assaulted the Shing Mun Redoubt, the high point on the defence line and the key to the line's western sector. The redoubt overlooked the Jubilee Reservoir to the north and commanded a key ridge just to the south. The British defenders were taken by surprise; after a few hours of fierce fighting, the Japanese took the position. A counterattack was out of the question because the nearest defenders were too far away and the ground between them and the redoubt too broken and rocky. The mainland defence line had been compromised almost immediately, and there were almost no viable fallback positions for the defenders. Maltby first ordered a company of the Winnipeg Grenadiers to counterattack the redoubt, but changed his mind quickly and on the morning of December 10 ordered an immediate fallback and evacuation to the mainland under cover of darkness. The Rajputs were to stay at Devil's Peak Peninsula, on the north side of the Lye Mun Passage, to cover the withdrawal. On the morning of December 13 they, too, pulled back, taking a number of artillery pieces with them.[22]

With the mainland lost to the Japanese, Maltby set about reorganizing his defending force. Again he created two brigades: West under Lawson and East under Wallis. Lawson had under his command the Royal Scots, the Punjabis, and the Winnipeg Grenadiers, along with a number of Hong Kong Volunteers. Wallis commanded the rest of the defending forces. Although it was obvious that the main Japanese thrust was coming from landward, Maltby was still concerned about a possible landing to seaward and positioned the Royal Rifles in the southeast part of the island to counterattack a Japanese landing.

On the morning of December 13, the Japanese sent a small delegation across Victoria Harbour in a motor launch to demand the surrender of the garrison. Hong Kong governor Sir Mark Young refused. A party of Japanese infantry then tried to gain a foothold across from Lye Mun Passage on the night of December 15–16 but were beaten back. On the 17th came another demand for surrender and another refusal. The defenders were in a hopeless position, but they were determined to delay the Japanese as much as possible.

The Japanese came across the water after dark on December 18. Under cover of heavy shellfire, three regiments in line abreast crossed the harbour and Lye Mun Passage in small boats pulled by ferries, and poured ashore. The Rajputs held the pillboxes that dominated the Lye Mun Passage landing ground; they cut down hundreds of attackers with their machine guns, but the Japanese pushed past them and almost wiped them out. The Japanese then made for the gullies and valleys that led into the centre of the island. They dispatched one regiment to take the walled redoubt on Sai Wan Hill, while the rest of the regiment rapidly climbed Mount Parker and seized its summit. In fog, rain, and mud, the Royal Rifles of Canada attempted to counterattack the advancing Japanese and succeeded in inflicting heavy casualties with automatic weapons, but they could not take Sai Wan Fort back and were forced to withdraw.

Throughout the night of December 18–19, the Japanese pushed to the centre of the island and across it. Their intention was to seize the main passes, especially the Wong Nei Chong Gap, take control of the centre of the island, and split the defenders. By dawn on the 19th, Japanese infantry had reached Repulse Bay and were closing in on Lawson's brigade headquarters. Among the defenders, all was confusion. Through the night there had been no solid information as to how many Japanese had landed, exactly where they had come ashore, or what in direction the main body of their troops was heading. The darkness was made darker by smoke from oil fires burning in Victoria. Japanese sympathizers and fifth columnists cut telephone wires to disrupt the defenders' communications. When Lawson learned that two Japanese regiments were closing in on the summits of Jardine's Lookout and Mount Butler, he first ordered three platoons, each acting as a "flying column," to stop the attackers. They were outnumbered by about six to one, and the results were predictable: the Canadians were pushed back, and two platoon commanders were killed. Lawson then ordered A Company of the Winnipeg Grenadiers to counterattack the Japanese on Mount Butler.

The men of A Company were last seen climbing up through the dark and fog to meet the enemy; most were never seen alive again. Survivors later described how part of A Company, under Company Sergeant Major J.R. Osborne, took the peak of Mount Butler with a bayonet charge and held it for three hours. They were then forced to pull back toward Lawson's position but ran into a Japanese ambush and were virtually wiped out. Osborne himself was killed when he threw himself on a Japanese grenade to save his men; he was posthumously awarded the Victoria Cross when the story became known after Japan's surrender. As the Japanese closed in around Lawson's position, Maltby ordered a group of naval ratings to go to his aid. They rushed forward on trucks but ran into a Japanese roadblock; a small number managed to get through, but the rest were forced back. It was then that Lawson decided to try to break out and was killed.

In the east, Wallis decided that he could not mount any sort of effective defence with his troops scattered among the hills and sought Maltby's consent to withdraw southward toward Stanley. He intended to defend a line across the peninsula, then counterattack. Permission was given and, by nightfall on December 19, Wallis's troops had pulled back south of the Ty Tam Tuk Reservoir. This left the bulk of the island's fresh-water reserves in Japanese hands and also resulted in a break in communications between the west and east brigades. On the morning of December 20, Wallis tried to re-establish contact with West Brigade by sending the Royal Rifles northwest between Violet Hill and Repulse Bay toward Wong Nei Chong Gap. But the Japanese had already taken up positions in the path of the Canadian advance; a company of the Royal Rifles managed to dig in around the Repulse Bay Hotel but could make no further headway. Wallis tried again the next day, sending another company of the Royal Rifles to the south edge of the Ty Tam Tuk Reservoir. Although the Canadians were able to reach the south edge of the reservoir, they could not hold. Toward evening, the company that was entrenched at the Repulse Bay Hotel moved north and made contact with a British unit just south of the Wong Nei Chong Gap. The Japanese counterattacked and inflicted heavy casualties, but the Canadians held on until the night of the 22nd, when they were forced to pull back.

In the western sector, the Royal Scots and the Winnipeg Grenadiers made the Japanese pay dearly for every square centimetre of the Wong Nei Chong Gap. The Japanese held the police station in the gap for most of this time, but D Company of the Grenadiers occupied a position dominating the north–south road and killed and wounded large numbers of Japanese who tried to dislodge them. The fight for the gap finally ended on the morning of December 22 after the last defenders had withdrawn into a shelter behind steel doors, taking their wounded with them. The Japanese brought up a light gun and blasted the doors in; further resistance was useless, and the officer in charge of the remains of D Company surrendered.

Throughout the 23th and the 24th, the Japanese consolidated their hold on the centre of Hong Kong Island. They pushed the remainder of the West Brigade back to a line between Victoria in the north and Aberdeen in the south, and forced Wallis's men to withdraw to the vicinity of Stanley Prison. On Christmas Day the Japanese tried once again to secure a surrender, but once again they were refused, even though the position was clearly hopeless. In the early afternoon, Japanese attacks resumed on both fronts, and casualties among the defenders mounted as ammunition and other stores dwindled. In mid-afternoon, Maltby finally decided that further fighting was useless; the white flag was hoisted and a small party was sent to Wallis to confirm the order to lay down arms.

Although all fighting ended in the early hours of December 26, the killing did not stop. In various parts of the island, Japanese soldiers embarked on a killing frenzy, bayonetting and machine-gunning prisoners, wounded men, and medical staff in hospitals and aid posts. That was not the end of the ordeal for the Canadians or for the other survivors of Maltby's force. Kept in appalling conditions in prison camps and forced to work as slave labourers for almost four years, many more died in captivity of disease, malnutrition, savage beatings, and summary executions. Of the 1,973 officers and men who left Canada in October 1941, 555 never returned, and many of those who did were so broken in body and spirit that they died premature deaths in the years that followed.

* * * *

Although the Battle of Hong Kong marked Canada's most significant role in the war against Japan, it was not the only one. Three squadrons of the Royal Canadian Air Force served in Southeast Asia. No. 435 and No. 436 were both transport squadrons that flew Douglas C-47s (Dakotas) in support of the British Fourteenth Army in Burma. The third RCAF squadron to take part in the Pacific war was No. 413, a general reconnaissance squadron attached to the RAF's Coastal Command flying

Consolidated Catalinas. The squadron moved to Ceylon (Sri Lanka) from the United Kingdom in March 1942. As aircraft and crews arrived, they were pressed into service flying reconnaissance missions over the Indian Ocean, on the lookout for a possible Japanese carrier strike. At 1600 on April 4, 1942, Squadron Leader L.J. Birchall sighted Japanese Admiral Nagumo's fleet, including aircraft carriers, some 560 kilometres south of Ceylon. As the radio operator tapped out news of the discovery, Birchall ducked into cloud cover to try to avoid the inevitable combat air patrol that the carriers most certainly had aloft. His signals were picked up at home and by the Japanese, who directed their fighters toward his aircraft. The warning was heard in Ceylon, but the Japanese also found Birchall and shot him down. Birchall and his crew were retrieved and beaten, then sent to prison camp where they survived the war. The feat earned Birchall the nickname Saviour of Ceylon. No. 413 was involved again in searching for Nagumo's force in the next few days as the Japanese carriers roamed the southern reaches of the Indian Ocean mounting raids on Colombo and Trincomalee, on the north side of the island. For the rest of the war, No. 413 flew anti-submarine reconnaissance but saw no further action.

Canadians were also involved in the campaign to expel Japan from the Aleutian Islands. On June 3 and 4, 1942, Japanese carrier aircraft attacked the US base at Dutch Harbor, on Unalaska Island, about 1,400 kilometres from Anchorage. The air attacks were followed on June 7 with landings on Attu and Kiska, at the western end of the Aleutian chain. By the spring of 1943, Japan had been put on the defensive throughout the Pacific. The United States began to lay plans to retake Attu and Kiska and sought Canadian help. Ottawa agreed and authorized a brigade group under Brigadier Harry W. Foster to take part in the attack on Kiska. A Permanent Force officer, Foster was brought back to Canada from the

United Kingdom to oversee the organization and training of the force. The fighting edge of the Kiska contingent was to be provided by the Winnipeg Grenadiers (re-formed after Hong Kong), the Rocky Mountain Rangers, le Régiment de Hull, and the 24th Field Regiment, RCA. Since the Aleutians were considered part of North America, NRMA (National Resources Mobilization Act) conscripts were used. The force was virtually re-equipped with US weapons and other *materiél* to keep supply problems to a minimum.

The estimated strength of the Japanese on the two islands by May 1943 was 2,500 on Attu and 5,400 on Kiska. On May 12 US troops landed on Attu, beginning a bloody fight for the island that ended two weeks later with a Japanese banzai charge; only eleven Japanese survived from the entire garrison. Then, plans were laid to assault Kiska. A force of 34,000 men was assembled for the operation, 4,800 of whom were Canadian. On the morning of August 15 the assault began, led by the First Special Service Force, an elite Canadian-American commando unit that was later labelled the "Devil's Brigade" and that would eventually see extensive action in Italy. To the surprise of the invaders, the Japanese were gone. A small Japanese task group had slipped past US surveillance aircraft and vessels—something easily done in these fog-shrouded waters—and evacuated the garrison. The Canadians remained on the island for some three months, then withdrew to British Columbia. Foster returned to the United Kingdom, where he was given command of a brigade in the 3rd Canadian Infantry Division prior to the Normandy landings.

The Canadian contribution to the naval war in the Pacific was minimal. As the Battle of the Atlantic wound down in late 1944 and the need for the Royal Canadian Navy's by-then-sizable Atlantic fleet diminished, plans were laid for a Pacific fleet of some sixty ships, including two light fleet carriers, two cruisers, and a large number of escort vessels. The first of this contingent to sail for Pacific waters was *Uganda*, a light cruiser built for the Royal Navy and transferred to the RCN in October 1944. Crewed by 700 officers and men, the cruiser's main armament consisted of nine 6-inch guns. Commanded by Captain Rollo Mainguy, *Uganda* joined a Royal Navy task force in the western Pacific in April 1945 and served as an anti-aircraft screening vessel during carrier strikes at the Japanese home islands and the Japanese naval base at Truk, in the Caroline Islands. The main danger to the task force came from kamikaze pilots determined to smash their bomb- and fuel-laden planes into Allied ships, killing themselves in the process. The two British carriers, *Victorious* and *Formidable* were main targets for the kamikazes, so *Uganda* was not hit. *Uganda* left the Pacific theatre, and the war, in July. That resulted from the King government's determination—announced in April 1945—that all Canadians serving in the Pacific theatre would be volunteers. Thus the crew of the *Uganda* was given the opportunity to vote on whether or not to continue to serve in an active theatre of war and chose not to. That was surely the strangest vote ever held aboard a Canadian warship.

Canada played only a small role in the war against Japan, but the sacrifices of those who gave their lives in that struggle is not lessened by the size of the overall contribution. The Canadian headstones in the Sai Wan War Cemetery overlooking Sai Wan Bay on Hong Kong Island is evidence enough of that. And evidence, too, of the soft-headed British thinking that the presence of fewer than 2,000 Canadians might help deter Japan from its aggressive intentions in Southeast Asia.

CHAPTER 4

THE AGONY OF DIEPPE

Dieppe, France: 0550, August 19, 1942. Captain Denis Whitaker of the Royal Hamilton Light Infantry was pinned down with his men in front of the seawall separating the stony Dieppe beach from the broad, grassy promenade that lay in front of the town. Although the Canadian landing was barely twenty minutes old, German bullets and shells had transformed the beach into a maelstrom of fire. Whitaker's battalion was in the first wave of the attack and in trouble from the very start. He knew that he and his men had no chance where they were: "As I lay there, one tank a few yards to my right had its six-pounder gun shattered by an enemy solid-shot shell. I was determined to get my men off [the beach] before the enemy artillery, mortars and M[achine] G[uns] annihilated us."

Whitaker spotted the partially demolished and burning casino about 50 metres to his right and led his men there in a desperate charge to get into cover. The casino was filled with German defenders but Whitaker and his men fought with an intensity born of desperation and within minutes cleared the position and a number of slit trenches on the building's east side. They then jumped through a window, headed through the slit trenches, and ran toward a low wooden building. As they arrived, a German mortar barrage began to explode around them. They dove to the concrete floor of the shelter and discovered that it was a German latrine: "It was impossible to move, as the mortaring continued without interruption; we lay in this crap for twenty or thirty minutes, feeling great revulsion for every German alive."[1]

Whitaker survived the hell of the Dieppe beach; he was the only Canadian officer to return to the United Kingdom untouched on what became one of the most tragic days in the history of the Canadian military; he was awarded the Distinguished Service Order (DSO) for his leadership. Lieutenant-Colonel Joe Menard, the Commanding Officer of the Fusiliers Mont-Royal, a French-speaking regiment from Montreal, was not so lucky. When Menard hit the beach his immediate objective was a pillbox on top of a 2-metre parapet some 100 metres in from the beach. He took two or three steps and was hit by a piece of shrapnel. He later recalled:

"You say a bullet or a piece of shrapnel hits you but the word isn't right. They slam you the way a sledgehammer slams you. There's no sharp pain at first. It jars you so much you're not sure exactly where you've been hit—or what with. This piece of shrapnel hit me in the right shoulder and knocked me down. I felt confused and shaken up, the same feeling you get on the football field after getting tackled from behind. Stunned, surprised, frustrated." Menard managed to get to his feet and started to bandage himself up but was soon hit again, this time in the cheek. His cheek "felt raw, as though someone had ripped a fish hook through it."[2]

Menard crouched and kept moving toward the pillbox. A close friend was hit in the gut, right beside him. Menard gave him some morphine and moved on; there was nothing else to do. Up to that point bravery and adrenaline kept him going, but then he got mad: "Now, with my friend lying there, I was so blind angry that it seemed to push everything else out of my head. All I wanted was to kill, to get even." As he got close to the pillbox, Menard was hit a third time, this time by a bullet. It went clean through his right arm above the wrist, and he fell back on a steel picket, badly hurting his back. He kept on and reached the pillbox, which other Fusiliers had cleared, then tried to direct his battalion from there by radio. He tried to reach higher ground for a better view, and was hit again by shrapnel in the right leg. He managed to stay on his feet for a while, but was bleeding profusely. He fell, tried to get up, then passed out. His men carried him to the beach to await evacuation.[3] Most of the Canadians who landed that morning were not so fortunate: of the 4,963 officers and men who had embarked for the landing the night before, only 2,210 returned. There were a total of 3,367 casualties: 907 were killed in action, and 1,946 were taken prisoner. Of the Canadians who were killed at Dieppe, 770 are buried in the Dieppe Canadian War Cemetery in the little town of Hautot-sur-Mer, 5 kilometres south of Dieppe itself.

* * * *

As the fall of 1940 gave way to the winter and the German bombers returned night after night to pound London and other British cities, the Canadian presence in the United Kingdom continued to grow. France had fallen, the United States and the USSR were not yet in the war, and Canada, with its 11.5 million people, was Britain's largest ally. Prime Minister William Lyon Mackenzie King's dream of a limited liability war effort had evaporated with the collapse of the French armies, and Canada was now determined to devote all it could to help Britain survive. During June, July, and August 1940, close to 78,000 Canadian men joined the Canadian Active Service Force. As the Battle of Britain raged, the main body of the 2nd Canadian Infantry Division (CID) arrived in the United Kingdom, while the 3rd CID was concentrated in the Maritime provinces. Then it, too, was transported to the United Kingdom, arriving for the most part in late July and early August 1941. The 1st Canadian Army Tank Brigade, Canada's first armoured formation, arrived just ahead of it. Later renamed the 1st Canadian Armoured Brigade (it would eventually fight as an independent brigade), it was the first unit of the Canadian Armoured Corps, formed in August 1940. The 1st Canadian Army Tank Brigade was followed, in November 1941, by the 5th Canadian Armoured Division and, in the late summer and early fall of 1942, by the 4th Canadian Armoured Division. The 2nd Canadian Armoured Brigade, also an independent brigade, was organized in the United Kingdom in the first half of 1943. To command this field army of five divisions and two independent armoured brigades, Canada established the Canadian Corps (later renamed 1st Canadian Corps) in July 1940; the 2nd Canadian Corps in January 1943; and the First Canadian Army, commanded by A.G.L. McNaughton, in April 1942.

Over the winter of 1940–41 and for the rest of the year, the Canadians were engaged almost exclusively in training and mounting a defence against a possible German invasion of the United Kingdom. For the latter role, the 1st Division was stationed in Surrey, the 2nd in barracks at Aldershot. Units from both divisions rotated in and out of defensive positions on Britain's south coast throughout this period. Not until Hitler attacked the Soviet Union in June 1941 did it became obvious that Germany was no longer interested in or capable of invading the United Kingdom.

The war widened dramatically in 1941; the struggle for North Africa, which had begun in September 1940 with an Italian attack from Libya against the British in Egypt, took a dramatic turn in March, when the newly arrived Afrika Korps under General Erwin Rommel opened its first offensive, sweeping all before it. In the Balkans, German troops came to the aid of the floundering Italians, who had sought an easy conquest of Greece, defeated the Greek army and their British allies, and followed through with a costly but victorious parachute invasion of Crete. In the desert, the British Eighth Army counted among its troops Australians and New Zealanders, but no Canadian formations (though individual Canadian officers served there). The only action the Canadian Army in Europe saw in 1941 took place in August and September. That was when a small Canadian force took part in a joint Canadian-British-Norwegian expedition to destroy mining and communications facilities on Spitsbergen, less than 1,000 kilometres from the North Pole, and to evacuate its population. For the most part, the Canadian Army, growing stronger by the day, sat in Britain and trained.

When Canadian divisions left Canada or arrived in the United Kingdom, there was invariably much crowing in the press of both countries about how these formations were fine bodies of fighting men ready to take on anything the Germans could throw at them. But they were not. Although the men had usually been taught the rudiments of marching, drilling, and the other basics of military life, along with how to handle and fire the standard infantry weapons, they knew little else. They did not know how to coordinate an attack or a defence. They did not know how to work with artillery, mortars, or armour in advancing against an enemy position. They did not even know the elementary requirements for moving a battalion by truck from one place to another. They had to be taught virtually everything that an infantryman ought to know before setting foot in a battle zone. That was what training was for.

In general, training proceeded from the individual fighting man to the highest formations. Men had to be taught how to fight in sections, platoons, and companies. Then companies had to be taught how to fight in battalions, battalions in brigades, brigades in divisions, and so on. While individual soldiers learned elementary infantry skills, the formations they were part of engaged in ever-larger exercises that covered more and more of the English countryside. Month after month the men left their barracks, climbed aboard trucks and took part in exercises such as Waterloo, Bumper, Beaver, Maple, or Tiger, as officers and men tried to learn the ways of modern war. They acquired much technical know-how, but was it enough?

In early 1942 British General Bernard L. Montgomery began to visit each and every Canadian formation training in the United Kingdom, examining the state of their training and commenting on the effectiveness of their leaders. Whatever may be said of Montgomery as a tactician—and there is still controversy about the way he organized his battles—he was a superb trainer of men. His comments were as incisive as they were cutting. He found much of the training inadequate and many of the leaders lacking, from divisional commanders on down. In May, he observed the Canadians on Exercise Beaver IV and concluded, "The weak point in the Canadian Corps at present is the knowledge of commanders in the stage-management of battle operations, and in the technique of battle fighting generally, on their own level."[4] Although he found Hamilton Roberts, GOC 2nd Division, acceptable as a division commander, he concluded that George Pearkes, GOC 1st Division, and C. Basil Price, GOC 3rd Division, were "no good . . . Pearkes would fight his Division bravely till the last man was killed; but he has no brains and the last man would be killed all too soon. Price not only has no military ability, but he is not a fighter by nature and has no 'drive.'" Both men were replaced soon after.

Although training was clearly necessary in an army that was militia based and manned almost entirely by volunteers with no military background, the men grew bored and angry as the war raged elsewhere; morale plummeted with each passing week and each new exercise. As Strome Galloway, serving with 1st Division, put it, "Barrack square routine and large scale manoeuvres . . . had started to turn us into a fed-up, browned-off, disillusioned band of volunteer warriors."[5] A strange paralysis of will regarding the use of the Canadian Army seems to have gripped Canadian military and political leaders in the wake of the fall of France. Here was a relatively large force, well equipped, consisting of men who had volunteered to fight, sitting in Britain, training and training, and training some more. Part of the problem undoubtedly lay in McNaughton's insistence that the Canadians stay together. That meant that if the British wanted to use Canadian units in, say, North Africa, they would have had to use all of them at once. That was not possible because the British did not want to leave themselves with virtually no defence and because transporting the entire Canadian Army to North Africa would have caused massive transportation difficulties. Thus Canada's military leaders were reduced to grasping at straws; one of those straws was a cross-channel raid on the French resort town of Dieppe that the new head of Combined Operations, Vice-Admiral Louis Mountbatten, was beginning to consider in March of 1942.

* * * *

Combined Operations was essentially a planning organization responsible for mounting military operations such as cross-channel raids, which combined land, naval, and air forces. In October 1941 the head of Combined Operations, Admiral Lord Keyes, was replaced by Captain Louis

Mountbatten of the Royal Navy, a well-connected member of the royal family whose military experience to date had consisted of having three ships sunk under him. Mountbatten had been urged by Churchill to put some life into Combined Ops, and Mountbatten responded by increasing the tempo of cross-channel raiding with escapades such as the British commando raid on the German submarine facilities at St-Nazaire, France, in late March 1942. Churchill continued to push for more and larger raids after St-Nazaire, but now he also considered two additional strategic-level reasons for these raids: to placate the Soviets, who were pressuring for strikes against the Nazis in the west, and to appease the Americans who were insisting, even this early in their participation in the war, on a cross-channel attack into France. General George C. Marshall, US Army Chief of Staff and Roosevelt's principal military advisor, thought the best way to end the war as quickly as possible was to attack Germany directly. He hoped to mount Operation Sledgehammer—a full-scale cross-channel invasion of France—by the end of the year. The notion was completely unrealistic, given Germany's defences in France and the weakness of US and British forces. It was apparent to most Allied political and military leaders that an invasion of France would come at some point, however, and a large raid on Dieppe might just provide experience in how to take a French port intact.

To this day, the source of the idea and the planning for the raid have been the subject of much controversy. Montgomery's official biographer, Nigel Hamilton, has summed up Dieppe this way: "The Dieppe operation bears the traces of hasty planning, of obtuse enthusiasm on the part of those units desperate to see 'action,' and of amateur, even tragic, overambitiousness . . ." His view of Mountbatten is even more harsh: "As Chief of Combined Operations [Mountbatten] was a master of intrigue, jealousy, and ineptitude. Like a spoilt child he toyed with men's lives with an indifference to casualties that can only be explained by his insatiable, even psychopathic ambition."[6] But if Mountbatten was ultimately responsible for the fiasco of Dieppe, it was the Canadian commanders McNaughton and Crerar (who was the corps commander), who were directly responsible for selecting this mission to be the baptism of fire of the Canadian Army in the United Kingdom and, in Crerar's case, approving the final plans for the raid.

Dieppe is a small resort town on the Channel coast, some 100 kilometres from the English coast at Sussex. It was close enough to be in fighter range of the United Kingdom, but not so close as to be an obvious target for a raid. Besides, there was really not much there that the Germans might have thought to be of strategic value other than a German radar station. The port was small and quite incapable of being a major supply base. Besides, the town was an attacker's nightmare. To the east and west rise high, dominating cliffs. Between the front of the town and the seawall is a wide, flat promenade offering no cover to advancing troops, and the beach itself is narrow, steep, and covered with chert: smooth round stones varying in length from about four to ten centimetres. Chert is hard on the feet and even harder on both wheeled and tracked vehicles. Small pieces of it can easily foul tank treads and bogey wheels, rendering these vehicles immovable.

Dieppe was strongly held by well-equipped German troops of the 302nd Infantry Division. German strongpoints on the cliffs on either side of the town dominated the beach. The Germans were lavishly equipped with automatic weapons, large- and small-calibre artillery, anti-aircraft guns, anti-tank guns (though these were not particularly effective against the Churchill tanks), and mortars. They had large reserves to hand, including the 10th Panzer Division at Amiens. Most importantly, their numbers and weapons strength were badly underestimated by British intelligence. One explanation for this German strength was that German spies in the United Kingdom had unearthed information about the raid and warned their superiors. Another is that the Germans had tapped the secret undersea cable that Roosevelt and Churchill used to talk to each other and had solved the Allied scrambler—a system developed by Bell Telephone and labelled the "A-3"—so that they were now able to decipher the conversations between these two leaders.[7] Claims that German intelligence had discerned British plans for Dieppe have circulated for years. Although the evidence remains inconclusive, there is no question that Combined Operations were dead wrong about the weakness of German defences.

The plan for the Dieppe operation evolved through a number of stages until the Combined Operations staff decided that a strong frontal assault of about 5,000 men, aided by tanks, would constitute the main thrust. It would be supported by landings on each flank. The frontal assault would be supported by air bombing, then by a low-level attack by Hurricane fighter bombers equipped with cannons, against the front of the town. The troops were to seize the port, penetrate through the town to take and destroy the radar station and other important facilities, and, if possible, secure the German divisional headquarters, seize prisoners, and capture any important documents that might be located there. At the same time, parachute troops were to attack and destroy the airfield at St-Aubin-sur-Scie just south of Dieppe.

Crerar was the main Canadian proponent of including Canadian troops in Mountbatten's cross-channel raids. Quite simply, he wanted his men to get combat experience and he was worried by increasing signs that the morale of the Canadian troops was suffering due to inaction. He did not want the Canadians to engage in large raids, but raids large enough—say ten to twenty from all ranks—for his men to get true fighting experience. At one point he wrote to Montgomery that "the reputation of the [Canadian] corps was at stake,"[8] and he continued to press for Canadian inclusion in these raids over the winter of 1941–42. Mountbatten was reluctant to include Crerar's men, because the raids were being conducted mostly by specially trained British commandos, not by regular troops such as the Canadians.

In late April 1942, Montgomery approached Crerar to suggest Canadian participation in a large operation then in its planning stages: Operation Rutter, a raid on Dieppe. Montgomery was to be in overall command, since the raid would be launched from his operational area in the United Kingdom. Monty preferred to use an all-Canadian force for the main invasion rather than a composite British-Canadian one, and Crerar was eager to accommodate him since this, finally, was his chance to get his troops into action. He suggested the 2nd Division, and Montgomery agreed. Monty believed the division's commander, Major-General Hamilton Roberts, was "the best Divisional Commander in the [Canadian] Corps."[9] Since McNaughton was still in overall charge of the Canadian Army in the United Kingdom, his approval was sought and given on April 30. Roberts then selected the 4th and 6th Brigades for the landings; they were to be accompanied by the 14th Canadian Army Tank Regiment (the Calgary Tanks) and a small force of engineers. The raid was eventually scheduled for July 4, and the units destined to take part embarked on intensive training in landing and assault operations. The Canadian staff played almost no part in drawing up the overall plans for the raid but accepted them as sound, despite some reservations about the use of tanks on the Dieppe beaches. After pressing so hard for a Canadian role in Combined Operations attacks, McNaughton and Crerar could hardly have done otherwise.

On July 2 and 3 the troops embarked and were fully briefed; the weather deteriorated on the night of July 3, and the sailing was post-poned repeatedly until it was decided to launch the attack on July 8. But on the morning of July 7, the Luftwaffe attacked the small fleet lying just west of the Solent. It was obvious that the Germans knew something was up because of the concentration of shipping. That, and the failure of the weather to improve, prompted Montgomery to cancel the operation. The disappointed troops were disembarked and, since the plan was no longer a secret, everyone assumed that the attack would be permanently shelved.

But it was not. For reasons still not clear, Rutter was revived not long afterward as Operation Jubilee. Brian Loring Villa's book *Unau-thorized Action* claimed that Mountbatten went ahead at his own ini-tiative and without the approval of the British Chiefs of Staff.[10] John Rickard's wartime biography of McNaughton shows that Crerar was aware of the operation's resurrection even before McNaughton was, but that McNaughton knew precisely why the raid was back on. On July 25 he wrote, "It appears that Stalin had cabled the Prime Minister asking what was being done to distract the Germans by raiding. The Prime Minister had been very pleased to be able to reply indicating action was in hand and in consequence he had approved the highest priority in preparation for JUBILEE."[11] The official historian of the Canadian Army in the Second World War wrote that the initial cancellation of Rutter came at virtually the same time as a suspension of supply convoys from the United Kingdom to the Soviet Arctic—due to effective and intense German opposition—giving Churchill even further reason to assure Stalin that a major raid was coming. Most of the original plan was to be kept, but some important differences were introduced.

Instead of concentrating the landing force at one port on trans-ports, much of the infantry would cross the Channel on the same LCIs (infantry landing craft) that would take them right up to the Dieppe beach. This was done to preserve the element of surprise. The parachute landing was discarded as too complicated, and landings by British commandos to silence German batteries flanking the beaches were laid on instead. Thus the assault would be spread out over some 16 kilometres of coastline, with the flanking attacks scheduled to begin thirty minutes before the main landing. The heavy air bombardment was done away with. Since the Royal Navy would not risk cruisers or battleships in Channel waters while the Luftwaffe was still a very powerful force, the Bomber Command aircraft were the last means of heavy support that the landing was to have. However, Bomber Command chief, Sir Arthur Harris, would not allow his heavy bombers to attack after dawn, and a precision night attack was virtually impossible anyway. The net result would have been the destruction of the town and the deaths of large numbers of French civilians with little effect on the German positions atop and at the base of the cliffs. The almost complete lack of impact that heavy bombings had on German positions on the morning of D-Day provides some indication that bombing German defences at Dieppe would have proven just as ineffective. Thus, in essence, the plan for Operation Jubilee was that the attackers would emerge from the sea in the early dawn, rush ashore before the Germans could react, and seize their objectives by surprise; there was absolutely no room for error. As hazardous an operation of war as the Dieppe Raid was, both McNaughton and Crerar bear responsibility for signing off on the final plan. In the original Rutter planning, they had been excluded from the chain of command, although they had been consulted. But when Rutter was reborn as Jubilee, McNaughton was placed in the chain of command, although he delegated the task of actually helping to plan the raid to Crerar. Crerar was, therefore, fully aware of how the first plan had evolved into the second and final plan, and how hazardous it really was. The landing force embarked late on August 18 and slipped into the English Channel as the dusk melted into a beautiful clear night. The little fleet, accompanied by British destroyers, formed up and made for the French coast.

* * * *

Things began to go wrong just before 0400; a small German convoy proceeding from Boulogne to Dieppe came across several British vessels on the left flank of the attacking fleet and a short, sharp sea battle ensued. On the French coast the sound of guns rolled in from the sea; in the German gun positions on the coast, the defenders rushed to their posts, eyes and ears straining out to sea. A part of the invading force—that carrying the British commandos destined for the landing on the far left flank—was scattered. The commander of the group that had run into the Germans was unable to report the extent of the battle because of damage to his radio equipment but even if he had, it was probably too late: the transports carrying those troops due to make the flank attacks had already lowered their landing craft. That had been done in the hope that the smaller craft could slip into shore undetected by German radar.

The scattered contingent of British commandos was due to assault the coastal battery at Berneval, about 8 kilometres east of Dieppe; only seven of the twenty-three landing craft put their troops ashore. The Germans had been fully alerted by the noise of the sea battle, and most of the commandos who did land were quickly killed or captured. One small group managed to infiltrate close to the battery and keep the German gun crews away from it for some two and a half hours until they managed to escape to the beach and were evacuated.

The Royal Regiment of Canada came ashore at Puys, about 2.5 kilometres east of Dieppe. The plan was to have the battalion land in three waves with a contingent from the Black Watch (Royal Highland Regiment) of Canada, from the 5th Brigade, in the last wave. The beach here was narrow, dominated by high cliffs, and with only one exit up a brick path commanded by a German pillbox. The Royals' attack depended on surprise; they didn't get it. They came in late as dawn was breaking; the Germans were on the alert and the Royals ran into heavy fire even before they hit the beach. Private Steve Michell's experience was all too typical; he had to push his way through a pile of bodies just to get out of his boat. As he waded through the chest-deep water he found one of the younger men trying to stuff his intestines back inside his body. Michell reached shore but found only about a dozen men of his company still standing out of 120.

A handful of men managed to get over the seawall but could accomplish nothing. The second and third waves should not have come ashore but did, due to faulty communications. The Germans had less than a single company guarding the exit from the beach, but it was all they needed. Those Canadians not killed were pinned down all morning and part of the afternoon until forced to surrender; there was no way to get them off. Of 554 Royals who had embarked, 227 were killed in action, died of their wounds, or died in captivity, and 33 of those who did return were wounded. The rest—264—were taken prisoner. Only 65 returned to the United Kingdom. The Black Watch suffered only 4 fatalities, but only 44 men returned to the United Kingdom of the 111 who had embarked.

The disaster at Puys had a direct impact on events at Dieppe itself, because the Royals had been given the task of clearing the headlands that dominated Dieppe from the east. Their failure to do so allowed the defenders to pour fire down onto the Canadians as they came in to the beach. That took place under the cover fire of the guns of four Hunt Class destroyers at about 0520; the landing was preceded by a low-level strafing attack by five squadrons of cannon-firing Hurricanes. Then the Essex Scottish on the left and the Royal Hamilton Light Infantry (RHLI) on the right hit the beach. The tanks should have landed at the same time but the LCTs (tank landing craft) carrying them were delayed by navigational errors.

On the right flank of the main beach, German fire from the cliffs near the radar site, the casino, and the large stone castle that nestled against the cliff engulfed the beach and the RHLI men on it. Despite the storm of shot and shell, Captain Denis Whitaker's men managed to clear the casino while another group, led by Captain A.C. Hill, actually got across the seawall and the promenade and penetrated about two blocks into the town before withdrawing to a position near the casino. But on the left, the Essex Scottish got nowhere at all; German gunners on the east headland and in the buildings that fronted on the promenade kept them pinned down and exacted a heavy toll. One small group of about twelve men got across the promenade but were forced back.

About ten minutes after the main landing, the tanks came ashore. One by one the LCTs approached the beach to land their tanks. Most were hit before they could do so, some immediately after. Some of the tanks never made it out of the water, some were hit by shellfire as they churned over the seawall; about half seem to have got onto the promenade itself, but none made it into the town. That was a blessing in disguise because the 14th Canadian Army Tank Regiment (the Calgary Tanks) had had no training whatsoever in street fighting, let alone in the narrow streets of a Norman fishing village. Many tanks were disabled by shells exploding in their tracks but were not destroyed, because the bulk of the German anti-tank guns at Dieppe were 37mm and could not penetrate the Churchill's frontal armour. (There is controversy to this day as to whether their tracks broke on the chert: in some places, it was so deep that vehicles simply bottomed out as wheels and treads spun uselessly.) Most of those tanks that were immobilized but not destroyed continued to give covering fire to the infantry to the very last. One historian writing on the Calgary Tanks at Dieppe has concluded, "The idea of sending a tank cavalry charge through the narrow streets of an enemy defended town, and out into the surrounding countryside, holding a defensive perimeter and then withdrawing through the town, all in the matter of five and a half hours, was ridiculously foolhardy and reckless. It also showed gross ignorance on the part of [Combined Operations] planners and senior Allied commanders of the capabilities and limitations of tanks."[12]

The right flanking attacks were the only part of the operation that seemed to go at least partially according to plan. The British troops of No. 4 Commando got ashore as scheduled. One party landed at Vasterival and moved overland to attack a coastal battery about 750 metres inland; the other landed about a kilometre farther west and swung behind the battery. The South Saskatchewan Regiment and the Cameron Highlanders of Canada ought to have come ashore astride the mouth of the River Scie at Pourville. This would have allowed the South Saskatchewans to climb the high ground between Pourville and Dieppe and attack the radar station. Instead, the two battalions were landed on the beach to the west of Pourville, about 2 kilometres from the main Dieppe beaches. The beach there was also dominated by high cliffs, but somewhat wider and longer than that at Puys.

To gain their objective, the South Saskatchewans had to cross the Scie on a bridge in the centre of Pourville and move up the main road toward Dieppe. But the Germans, stationed on the heights protecting the radar station and in the hills behind, firing into the town and onto the bridge over the Scie, were fully alerted by the time the Canadians started their push, and they could make no headway; the bridge was soon covered with dead and wounded. At that point Lieutenant-Colonel Cecil Merritt walked toward the bridge waving his helmet and shouting to his men to follow him across. They did (and Merritt won the Victoria Cross for his feat), but they still could not gain the heights. Off to their right, the Camerons landed late and on both sides of the Scie, but managed to push inland despite the death of their Commanding Officer; they reached the hamlet of Petit Appeville, where they were stopped short of the airfield, their ultimate objective. Then they too fell back to the beach. George Gouk, Company Sergeant Major in the Camerons, described the moments when these young Canadians truly learned about war, seeing their comrades cut down by German fire: "Well, there was no stopping the boys then. They were seeing their pals for the first time being killed and wounded . . . and the only thought . . . was to have revenge. It was sure great to see the boys with blood all over their faces and running from wounds in their arms and legs not worrying about getting first aid but carrying on in a systematic manner, clearing out the 'Nazis' from the houses."[13]

As the battle ran its course on the ground, German aircraft rushed to the sky over the blazing beaches and were met by the fighters of the Royal Air Force's No. 11 Group. Charged with command of the raid's air operations, Air Vice-Marshal Trafford Leigh-Mallory ensured that from three to six squadrons of fighters were kept over Dieppe at all times, in addition to the cannon-firing Hurricanes attacking Dieppe itself and the aircraft charged with dropping smoke on the headlands. This guaranteed intensive air action as RAF and Luftwaffe planes tangled time after time. The air battle was more intensive than anything seen since the Battle of Britain. At the end of the day, the RAF had been bested, losing 106 fighters to the Germans' 48 destroyed and 24 damaged.

Aboard command ship HMS *Calpe*, Major-General Hamilton Roberts was unaware of the full extent of the unfolding disaster. Radios on ship and shore were malfunctioning, signallers on the beach were being hit, officers were lying low trying to avoid being hit. At about 0610 a message was received reporting that the Essex Scottish were "across the beaches and into the houses," a gross exaggeration. Roberts decided to send in his reserves. He ordered the rest of the Royal Regiment (but there was no "rest"; the entire contingent had gone ashore at Puys) and the Fusiliers Mont-Royal to land on the left beach behind the Essex Scottish.

The craft carrying the FMRs approached the maelstrom at about 0700 and were met by heavy, accurate, and deadly fire. The current pushed their vessels to the right and they put ashore virtually under the high cliffs on the west side of the main beach. When the boats were about 75 metres out, the Germans opened up: "Every gun and mortar in Dieppe seemed to open fire on the ill-fated Fusiliers Mont-Royal. Two boats were immediately blown out of the water. The remainder were badly holed and many of the men killed and wounded while still at sea."[14] Most of those who did get ashore were unable to move past the headland into the area of the main beach. Because Roberts still had no clear idea of how events were shaping up, he sent another contingent of Royal Marines to land in front of the casino. Their Commanding Officer, Lieutenant-Colonel Joseph Phillips, came ashore with a group of about seventy men; he saw what was happening and stood up to wave off the craft following him. He was killed, but some 200 of his men were saved as a result of his quick thinking.

The Royal Regiment survivors at Puys had already surrendered when Roberts received a message from the FMRs at about 0900 declaring that they were in severe difficulty and would be wiped out if they were not immediately evacuated. Five minutes later, they radioed that they were totally surrounded. Most surrendered shortly after, just as Roberts issued an order to evacuate the beaches by 1100. Across the beach, now littered with burned-out or crippled tanks, damaged landing craft drifting on the swells, and dead and wounded men, those still alive tried to scramble to the water's edge. Some huddled in the shelter of immobile tanks. Those who were too severely wounded to move lay where they were, comforted by comrades, or by Padre J.W. Foote of the Royal Hamilton Light Infantry, who chose to stay behind and accompany his men into captivity. The Royal Navy destroyers, *Calpe* included, came dangerously close to shore to cover the withdrawal with their guns; overhead the fighters of No. 11 Group tried to keep the German bombers and fighters from attacking the evacuating men. Immobilized tanks kept up their fire with 6-pounders and machine guns as long as they could so that the infantry could get away. By 1400 the last Canadians were either off the beaches or had surrendered; the survivors limped back to the United Kingdom.

Dieppe was Canada's greatest disaster in the Second World War. More Canadians were taken prisoner there than in all the rest of the campaign in northwest Europe. Canada suffered more killed in action in the half day of fighting at Dieppe than on any other day of fighting in the war. The casualties were horrendous—that much was clear—but were they worth it in lessons learned? There is still great controversy over this question, but it is hard to escape the conclusion that whatever was learned at Dieppe—that it would be hard to take a port in a direct assault, and that a landing must be proceeded by careful planning and heavy fire—ought to have been known anyway, or could have been figured out in a tactical exercise. It ought not to have taken any great stroke of military genius to figure out that men coming ashore in boats in daylight would be extremely vulnerable to heavily armed, well-protected, and well-supported men on shore who wanted to do them great harm. Of course, the men were not supposed to land in daylight, but then a successful landing in total darkness, near enough the intended objectives to allow the infantry to seize them without resistance, on a distant shore, with boats subject to the vagaries of current, would have been almost impossible anyway—and the planners ought to have known that before they even began. They might also have taken into account the very real danger that the cancellation of Rutter and its remounting as Jubilee might well have created significant security breaches.

In his otherwise authoritative history of the Canadian Army in the Second World War, Canada's official historian, Colonel C.P. Stacey, observed that although the Canadian military could have sidestepped the operation, they were loath to do so because of "how violently resentful the ordinary Canadian soldier would have been had an enterprise like the Dieppe raid been carried out at this time without the participation of the Canadian force which had waited so long for battle."[15] That is an explanation of why McNaughton and Crerar accepted the mission, but it is not an excuse. At bottom, the success of Dieppe depended on two factors: first, absolutely everything had to go right so that the men could rush ashore, on schedule, out of the dark, and seize their objectives before the Germans could react; second, once the Germans did react, they would forget how to function as trained soldiers. The whole history of warfare made both assumptions extremely unlikely, and the Canadian generals ought to have known that.

* * * *

Our Finest Hour

One of the most important exercises in the process of preparing the Canadian Army for war was Spartan, mounted in the first two weeks of March 1943. For the first and only time in the war the entire Canadian field force took part in a single exercise; it was the first real test for McNaughton as army commander and for his First Canadian Army Headquarters. Exercise Spartan revealed McNaughton's real weakness as a field force commander. General Sir Bernard Paget, Commander-in-Chief of the British Home Forces, was especially critical of McNaughton. In his words the Canadian was guilty of "a lack of confidence [which] resulted in missed opportunities, delayed decisions, changes of orders and frequent and conflicting short moves of units and formations."[16] Paget was right; much of the Canadian "battle" suffered from confused and contradictory orders, poor movement planning, and a lack of direction from McNaughton's HQ. As usual, he seemed more interested in tinkering with minor problems than tackling the major difficulties that plagued his forces.

Major-General J.H. Roberts lost his job after Spartan. Although he was awarded the Distinguished Service Order (DSO) for his leadership of the Dieppe raid, Crerar engineered his removal after Spartan, ostensibly for his performance in that exercise. In a letter to McNaughton written in early April 1943, Crerar claimed that he had not had time to assess Roberts's performance in the field "until recent months" but now that he had, he had found him wanting: "I have examined the actions of 2 Cdn Div [in Spartan] . . . My conclusion is that there was, in fact, very considerable confusion, loss of time and inadequate co-ordination of effort . . . It is also to be remarked that 2 Cdn Div suffered very heavy losses by umpire decision." No one should have expected otherwise less than eight months after Dieppe. So Roberts got the chop that Crerar so richly deserved.

CHAPTER 5

THE DEADLY SKIES

In February 1942, Sir Arthur Travers Harris was appointed Air Officer Commanding-in-Chief of Bomber Command. Harris, known as Butch to the aircrews of Bomber Command, had conceived a bold stroke to bring the RAF bombing campaign against Germany to new heights of power and destructiveness. He would marshal a force of 1,000 planes, drawing on operational squadrons, operational training units (OTUs), and virtually anything else he could get his hands on, and send the entire force to bomb a single German city on a single night in just a few hours of elapsed time. His superior, Sir Charles Portal, Chief of the Air Staff and a former commander of Bomber Command himself, strongly supported the scheme and helped Harris win over Prime Minister Winston Churchill. As historian Randall T. Wakelam has written, "Such a raid would show, if successful, what Bomber Command was capable of and also do much to instill confidence in both the crews and . . . doubters in the other Services." Of course if it went wrong, it would be a disaster. He himself favoured Hamburg. It was on the north German coast and thus easy to locate by night, and his aircraft would approach it over the North Sea, thus minimizing risk to themselves. But Harris had great respect for the scientists who worked with Bomber Command's Operational Research Section and Dr. Basil Dickens, the head of the OR section, in particular. Dickens and others recommended Cologne instead. It would be even easier to find because it was in range of Gee, a new UK-based electronic target-finding system first used successfully in March 1942. Harris relented and on May 30, 1942, orders went out from his headquarters at High Wycombe. The target for that night was Cologne. Hamburg would meet its even more terrible fate thirteen months later.[1]

Within a few hours, 1,046 bombers took off in the gathering gloom and headed for Cologne; 68 aircraft of the Royal Canadian Air Force's bomber squadrons were among them. The bombers proceeded to Cologne on a single track; each aircraft's time of arrival over the target had been carefully calculated to produce the utmost devastation in the shortest possible time. The first bombs fell at 0047, the last at 0225. In the intervening ninety-eight minutes, some 898 aircraft dumped their loads (the remainder either returned due to mechanical difficulties or were shot down before the raid began), a rate of one bombload every 6.5 seconds. The fires from the heart of the ancient city were visible to approaching crews from as far as 240 kilometres out. One Canadian pilot later described the scene: "There are other aircraft around us as Ole [the bomb aimer] gives me directions until the moment when he shouts, 'Bombs gone!' . . . As I drop a wing to turn away, I get a full view of the target area. Immense fires are raging now, and bomb flashes are practically incessant."

When aerial reconnaissance photos were taken early the next morning, the damage to Cologne seemed extensive. More than 5,000 houses were destroyed or badly damaged, over 7,000 were partly damaged, more than 45,000 people were made homeless. Thirty-six factories were permanently put out of action, and seventy more were forced to curtail production. There were fewer than 500 deaths, but there were more than 5,000 injured. The Royal Air Force Official History later concluded that Cologne's total war production loss from this one raid amounted to about one month—it was much harder to destroy a factory than Harris and many of his experts yet realized. But then, destroying factories was only a part of what Bomber Command was trying to do in its "area" offensive against Germany.

* * * *

In the early months of the war, it had been anticipated that the Royal Canadian Air Force would keep the bulk of its strength in Canada for home defence and send only three squadrons overseas. One of those squadrons—No. 1 Fighter Squadron (later No. 401)—had participated in the Battle of Britain. Other Canadians had taken part in the Battle flying for the Royal Air Force. As late as March 1941, there were still only three RCAF squadrons in the United Kingdom: Nos. 401 and 402 Day-Fighter Squadrons, and No. 400 Army Cooperation Squadron. Then, over the next twenty or so months, the RCAF's presence in the United Kingdom increased tenfold to thirty-two squadrons including eleven bomber, eight day-fighter, and three night-fighter units. RCAF squadrons could be found in Bomber, Fighter, and Coastal Commands of the RAF, and RCAF pilots daily performed duties as varied as torpedo bomber attacks on enemy shipping to night intruder missions against German airfields. It was not only the size of the mid-war RCAF that was so stunning compared to its immediate prewar establishment, it was also the range and the complexity of its operations.

The Royal Canadian Air Force's wartime role and size was largely determined by the British Commonwealth Air Training Plan. When the original BCATP agreement was signed in December 1939, it contained provision that an indeterminate number of RCAF squadrons would be formed overseas (primarily in the United Kingdom), manned by Canadian graduates of the plan. Further negotiations ensued and, in January 1941, Canada and the United Kingdom reached an initial agreement that twenty-five RCAF squadrons might be formed (in addition to the three already in the United Kingdom), to be paid for by the United Kingdom to balance the fact that Canada paid for the bulk of the BCATP. In addition, Canadians serving with the RCAF would wear their own uniform and, most important to the men, be paid according to the RCAF rank scale, which was considerably higher than that of the RAF. These "Article 15" squadrons formed the backbone of the fighting RCAF, which, by war's end, would expand its overseas strength to forty-eight squadrons. That expansion began soon after the Canadian-British agreement with the formation of No. 403 Squadron on March 1, 1941 (initially as an army cooperation, then as a day-fighter squadron); No. 405—Canada's first bomber squadron—in April 1941; and Nos. 404 and 407 with Coastal Command in May 1941. On March 1, 1941, Canadian squadrons in the United Kingdom and other theatres of war were assigned numbers in the 400 block, beginning with No. 400, to distinguish them from RAF squadrons. Thus No. 110 became No. 400, No. 1 became No. 401, and No. 2 (formerly 112) became No. 402.

Article 15 of the BCATP gave Canada the basis under which the process known as Canadianization could go forward—and under which an RCAF group would eventually take shape as part of Bomber Command—but the implementation of the agreement was far from smooth, especially in its early years. Minister of National Defence for Air C.G. Power was a strong Canadian nationalist, representing a francophone riding in

Quebec City, and consistently pushed the RAF to place Canadians in Canadian squadrons within the framework of both Article 15 and the agreement reached between London and Ottawa in January 1941. Power would later write in his memoirs that he and the minister of national defence, Norman Rogers, believed that "Canadian public opinion would never tolerate the disposition of airmen [into the Royal Air Force]. The public would want to know at all stages what had happened [to these Canadians], and what part Canadian boys were taking in the air war. It would not be sufficient for them to read in the press dispatches that an R.A.F. mission composed of five hundred or a thousand aircraft had bombed Cologne or Berlin . . . There must be some representation of Canada as a nation in the air war." To add to the problem, some Canadians who had been assigned to fly in RAF squadrons felt cut off from their countrymen, while the RAF itself seemed unaware of, or uncaring about, the fact that Canadians in the United Kingdom were far from home—unlike their RAF counterparts—and held different beliefs about class distinctions in general and command and leadership style in particular.

The problem, as Power saw it, was that the British were dragging their heels on assigning Canadian personnel to Royal Canadian Air Force squadrons, not necessarily because they opposed the notion but because the matter was not a high priority for them. In June 1941 he wrote to the prime minister to describe the delays in Canadianizing the RCAF squadrons; he proposed strengthening the RCAF's command in the United Kingdom and pushing the British to take Canadianization seriously. Power flew to London at the end of June and met with his British counterparts to explain the Canadian position as clearly as possible: "Members of the RCAF were well-educated citizens of the Dominion, and the Canadian government had a moral responsibility in regard to their general conditions and welfare while serving with the RAF. They remained members of the Royal Canadian Air Force, and the connection between them and their Home Government must be more than a gesture." Power wanted more Canadians in Canadian squadrons, more RCAF say in promotions, more publicity regarding the accomplishments of RCAF units and eventually, when there were enough Canadian bomber squadrons, a Canadian group in Bomber Command.[2] The trip was not a complete success, but an important step in relaying to the British Canada's refusal to fight the air war with a status any less than full independence.

It was always the case, from the beginning of the war to the end, that a majority of Canadians served either directly in the Royal Air Force or as members of the RCAF in RAF squadrons. One of the most famous was George Frederick Beurling of Verdun, Quebec, a fighter pilot who earned the nickname Screwball from his fellow pilots and Buzz from an admiring public when he became Canada's highest-scoring fighter ace of the war with 31 1/3 kills. Beurling had tried to join the RCAF at the outbreak of war, but even though he had more than 100 hours of solo flying time in his log book he was rejected, apparently because he was not considered to have had enough formal education. He then made his way to the United Kingdom and joined the RAF. After a stint with the RCAF's 403 squadron (though still with the RAF), he was assigned to the RAF's No. 41 Squadron and shot down his first two German fighters. Beurling was a brilliant pilot and fighter tactician with very good eyesight, who trained himself in the art of deflection shooting (shooting at an enemy aircraft from the side by aiming ahead of it). But he was also moody, temperamental, and difficult to get along with, and he earned a reputation as a troublesome lone wolf incapable of bending to the discipline of squadron flying. Not long after he joined No. 41 Squadron, he transferred out and found himself aboard an aircraft carrier sailing to the besieged island of Malta.

In the late spring of 1942, the British were locked in mortal combat with the Germans and the Italians in the battle for North Africa. The British used Malta as a base to attack enemy shipping bringing supplies and reinforcements to North Africa; the Germans and the Italians relentlessly attacked Malta to stop the British attacks on their shipping. The only way the British could reinforce Malta was by sea from Gibraltar, but the resupply convoys invariably took a terrible beating from Axis aircraft and submarines. If new fighters were going to be sent to the besieged island, they'd have to be flown there, but Spitfires did not have the range to reach Malta from Gibraltar. Thus the fighters were brought as close to Malta as possible on board Royal Navy aircraft carriers, then flown on one-way missions to the island. Beurling made the hop from HMS *Eagle* on June 9, 1942 and landed at Takali, a small fighter strip not far from Valletta, the capital.

At first Beurling had trouble here too; he insisted on breaking formation and hunting on his own. But under the stern discipline of P.B. Lucas, his squadron commander, he settled down and soon began to shoot German and Italian aircraft out of the sky at a furious pace. Beurling knew that the pilot who survived air-to-air combat was not the better flyer, able to do aerobatics in a whirling dogfight, but the one who spotted the enemy first, positioned himself above and behind, then pounced, closed the range as quickly as possible, and fired only when too close to miss. After barely two months on Malta, Beurling's confirmed kills had climbed from two to sixteen.

Even in the Second World War, the press tended to depict air-to-air combat as somehow gallant and chivalrous. Men like Beurling knew better, as he later recounted in a description of one of his victories over an Italian pilot: "I closed up to about thirty yards . . . I was on his port-side coming in at about a fifteen-degree angle . . . it look[ed] pretty close. I could see all the details in his face because he turned and looked at me just as I had a bead on him . . . One of my can[non] shells caught him right in the face and blew his head right off . . . The body slumped and the slipstream caught the neck, the stub of the neck, and the blood streamed down the side of the cockpit."[3]

Beurling stayed on Malta and his tally continued to mount, but the strain of constant flying against invariably larger numbers of enemy air-craft took its toll. He began to exhibit unmistakable signs of combat fatigue. In Canada, his exploits had made him a legend—the Knight of Malta—and an asset too valuable for the government to allow to be destroyed. At the end of October 1942, with twenty-nine enemy aircraft to his credit and a chestful of decorations, Beurling was pulled out of action and sent back to Canada to help with recruiting and the sale of war bonds. He was not to meet his end until May 20, 1948, when he was killed at Rome's Urbe airfield. He and another man were in the pro-cess of flying a single-engine, Canadian-built Norseman to the fledgling State of Israel, then in the midst of its War of Independence, to volun-teer for the Israeli Air Force when they crashed and were killed. Buzz Beurling now lies buried in the Holy Land.

* * * *

Although the Royal Canadian Air Force made an important contribu-tion to Fighter and Coastal Command, its most significant contribution to the war effort up to the end of 1942 was in the form of its eleven bomber squadrons. The first of these—405—flew its first operational mission as part of the RAF's No. 4 Group of Bomber Command on the night of June 12–13, 1941, when its Vickers Wellington twin-engine medium bombers attacked Schwerte, southeast of Dortmund. In the remaining war years, No. 405 Squadron would go on to have an illustrious career with Coastal Command, with No. 6 Group (RCAF) and with No. 8 Group (Pathfinders) of Bomber Command.

No part of the Allied war effort was as technically complex, as destructive to Germany's cities, and as controversial as the night area bombing campaign waged by the RAF's Bomber Command from late 1940 to virtually the end of the war. German statistics gathered after the war indicate that more than half a million German civilians were killed in this campaign and more than three million dwellings were destroyed, but the verdict is still open as to how effective the area bombing campaign was in shortening the war. To this day there is considerable controversy about the aims, methods, and results of the Bomber Command offensive against Germany.[4]

The night area bombing campaign was rooted in the experience of the First World War. In that war, both sides initiated long-range bombing operations ostensibly designed to destroy "strategic" targets such as key rail junctions, aircraft factories, munitions plants, etc. The Germans used both lighter-than-air Zeppelins and bombers, and they usually came at night, bombing not only factories but also neighbourhoods. Given the extreme difficulty of hitting anything with a bomb from a high altitude, especially in the dark, that was not surprising. Nor was it unwelcome to the attackers because of the potential impact it might have on civilian morale. The British and French, using bombers only, did likewise. For all intents and purposes, air defence against this sort of bombing was non-existent. Anti-aircraft guns were crude and inaccurate; fighters usually did not have sufficient warning time to reach a high enough altitude to intercept the raiders. Although there was nothing like wholesale panic in the streets of London, many civilians were demoralized by the feeling of helplessness they had as the Zeppelins droned above them in the dark. The Royal Flying Corps and the Royal Navy transferred a large number of fighter squadrons to the United Kingdom from the fighting front in France to bolster the air defences of the capital.

In the interwar years a number of air-power theorists speculated that long-range strikes at so-called strategic targets would not only impair the enemy's ability to fight but would also create mass panic among civilians, shorten wars, and eliminate the need for large armies. One of the most important of these men was Hugh Trenchard, the first Chief of the Air Staff of the RAF, who was responsible for what became known as the Trenchard Doctrine. That doctrine held that an independent air force, mounting a "strategic" bombing offensive, would do incalculable damage to an enemy and might even win a war by itself. The bombing of civilians by the Japanese in China and the Nationalists in Spain in the late 1930s seemed to bear these theories out. The RAF was closely wedded to these notions in any case, since the independent war-fighting role that Trenchard and others envisioned for the RAF gave it a raison d'être as a force independent of the army and navy, with its own command structure, and drawing separately upon the resources of the nation. Thus, as war clouds gathered in Europe in the 1930s, the RAF intended to embark on an ambitious program of bomber development and construction, all for the purpose of the "strategic" bombing of Germany, should war occur. The government of Prime Minister Neville Chamberlain, in the person of Thomas Inskip, minister for coordination of defence, had other ideas. Inskip was convinced of the importance of building up Britain's air defences, including expanded production of the new Spitfire and Hurricane fighters, so that the United Kingdom might survive an initial German onslaught. Only then might the bombers go to work.

But what was strategic bombing anyway? To some theorists, especially in the United States Army Air Corps, strategic bombing involved pinpoint attacks against important industrial targets whose destruction would hurt the enemy war effort. Such targets would include factories building weapons, or factories supplying parts, such as ball bearings, that were vital to modern weapons systems. Civilians would most certainly be killed in these attacks, but they were civilians whose labour directly aided the enemy war machine. For the Americans, it was not civilians who were the targets, it was the factories they worked in. The problem with this theory was that it assumed great accuracy on the part of the bombers as well as the technological capacity to drop bombs from a high altitude (weather permitting) and concentrate the bombing on specific buildings, factories, rail yards, or oil installations. As the experience of war was to prove, that was a very large assumption, even for daylight bombing. Later in the war, when fleets of US daylight bombers sometimes arrived over targets they could not see, they bombed through the clouds anyway or resorted to radar bombing, which was a form of area bombing. In the first four years of the war, it would prove well-nigh impossible at night.

As for the Royal Air Force, its early bombing campaign was a disaster. RAF bombers, such as the single-engine Fairey Battle light bomber and the twin-engine Hampden, Whitley, and Blenheim, were too slow and lightly armed to successfully fend off fighter attack during daylight raids. The twin-engine Wellington was much the best of the RAF's medium bombers and was kept on operations long after the others had been removed from service, but it, too, was extremely vulnerable to fighters. It simply did not have enough gun armaments, the guns were not positioned to cover all points of the aircraft, and the guns were too small and light (303 calibre) to do much real damage to attacking fighters. These bombers suffered frightful losses when used to attack enemy installations, naval bases, or troop concentrations during daylight. After the Battle of France, the RAF began to switch almost exclusively to night bombing, which brought a whole new set of problems.

Just as the darkness hid a bomber from defenders, it also hid the target and the route to the target from the bomber crew. The Germans had partially solved this problem by using the *Knickbein* system of radio beams to guide their bombers during the London Blitz and the other night attacks on British cities in the late fall of 1940 and the winter of 1940–41. The system was simple in conception: two different radio signals from two different stations were arranged to cross over the intended target. When German bombers flew at night they listened to one of the beams and when it crossed the other, they simply dropped their bombs. But although the Germans could locate large cities using such devices, there was no way to pick out individual targets within those cities. Thus German night bombing had amounted to area bombing—the bombing not of specific targets but of whole areas of cities with their houses, apartment blocks, hospitals, and schools, as well as factories, dockyards, government buildings, etc.

When the RAF began its night bombing campaign in earnest in May 1940, with attacks on the industrial Ruhr, it had no target-finding system at all. The campaign essentially consisted of RAF crews trying to pick their way over the blacked-out European countryside, find multiple targets scattered across mostly northwestern Germany in the pitch dark, usually in bad weather, hit something, and get home before dawn. The bomber force was small, and too many targets were usually attacked in one night to allow any real concentration of effort. The crews were often unable to locate, let alone bomb, their targets. When they did, little damage was done, because accuracy was virtually impossible. The RAF bombed fields and forests, lakes and rivers, peaceful farming villages and city neighbourhoods; it even, occasionally, bombed something important, but not very often. On many occasions, the Germans had a hard time trying to figure out just what the RAF had been trying to hit. RAF bomber losses were lower than in the previous daylight raids, but there were still losses from enemy night fighters, anti-aircraft fire, mechanical failure, collisions, and crash landings in the United Kingdom, especially when morning fog hid runways from the tired eyes of fatigued pilots. In August 1941 D.M. Butt of the British Cabinet secretariat issued a report on the effectiveness of the RAF's bombing, concluding that of the two-thirds of RAF bombers that had actually claimed to have attacked their assigned target on any given night (the other third had returned early, gotten lost, etc.), only half came even within 8 kilometres of their targets. When the Ruhr was attacked, only one crew in ten came close. On dark, moonless nights, the average was one crew out of fifteen. The Butt Report brought debate about the future of the air offensive within the RAF and the Cabinet to a head. There was clearly no point in continuing to do the same thing. Either the bombing campaign would be wound down and the precious resources currently devoted to bomber production reallocated to better use, or ways had to be found to make bombing far more effective than it had been so far. Given both that the British public wanted to hit Germany with all the fury to which they themselves had been victim, the decision was almost a foregone conclusion. But it was also true that the United Kingdom had no means of waging a serious war against Germany on the ground or at sea. Therefore, RAF bombers simply had to carry the offensive against Germany and, at the same time, substitute for the army divisions that Stalin was crying for to divert German attention from the eastern front. For now, bombing would be the "second front." Thus the search for more effective bombing techniques intensified.

The Germans were not idle either. Under Night Fighter General Josef Kammhuber, they developed a system of night-bomber interception, which used early-warning Freya radar and Würzburg interception radars working in conjunction with night fighters. The system worked in this fashion: The German costal defence belt was divided into territorially defined boxes. In each box ground radar guided a single night fighter to its target. Searchlights were supposed to illuminate the enemy bombers to allow the night fighters to home in on them. German anti-aircraft fire within these boxes was also radar controlled. In early 1942, the night fighters began to be equipped with airborne Lichtenstein radar. Thus a bomber was tracked from the ground, the night-fighter pilot was guided to the bomber by a ground controller, the radar operator aboard the night fighter then detected the bomber on his own set, the fighter bore in from below, as close as possible to the bomber and opened fire, usually aiming at the bomber's wing roots, where the gas tanks were located.

In the United Kingdom, a number of developments from early 1941 to early 1942 marked an intensification of the RAF's bombing campaign and a dramatic escalation in Bomber Command's ability to find and attack targets. In February 1941, the four-engine Short Stirling entered RAF service. It was the first of what would eventually prove to be a massive fleet of heavy bombers. The Stirling suffered from too low an operational ceiling and was largely removed from front-line service by the start of 1943, but it was replaced by two other mainstays of the heavy bomber force, the Handley Page Halifax and the Avro Lancaster, both four-engine types, which began to enter service with Bomber Command in early 1942. The Lancaster was by far the better of these two aircraft; the Halifax suffered from a large number of serious design flaws, which afflicted most of its marks until late in the war, while the

Lancaster could fly faster, higher, and carry a heavier bombload in its massive bomb bay.

In late February 1942, Arthur Harris took over Bomber Command. A dedicated follower of the Trenchard Doctrine, he aimed to knock Germany out of the war by air bombardment alone. He was a strong supporter of area bombing and scorned what he called panacea targets: factories that produced strategic materials or weapons systems. He believed that intensive bombing of German cities—area bombing—would not only kill and wound the civilians who worked in the war plants, it would also destroy their homes and their morale at the same time. At that time in the war, this view was strongly supported by Sir Charles Portal, Chief of the Air Staff, and Churchill, who both thought of the bombing campaign as the "second front." But later in the war, when Bomber Command's ability to hit specific targets at night improved dramatically, Portal would urge Harris to end area attacks and focus on strategic targets, specifically oil production and storage facilities. Churchill disavowed area attacks after the bombing of Dresden in 1945, when the war was clearly coming to a close. One recent historian of the bombing campaign believes Churchill was never a Trenchard zealot; he was just a man intent on doing Germany the greatest possible damage for the sole purpose of winning.[5]

The introduction of the Gee navigational device and the bomber stream seemed to provide Harris with the means of achieving his objective. Gee consisted of linked ground stations in the United Kingdom sending out three simultaneous, side-by-side radio beams toward the target. In the aircraft, the navigator picked up these signals and was able to guide the pilot to a small diamond-shaped area where the target was located. The problem with Gee was that its beams radiated on a straight line from transmitting stations; the farther the bomber flew, the more the earth's curvature caused the beams to be at heights that the bomber could not reach. Thus the closer to the target the bomber was, the more effective Gee was; but when Bomber Command aircraft began to attack targets deep in Germany, it was much less useful—if it was useful at all, given German jamming. Later in the war, Gee would be replaced by Oboe—another radio navigation device—which used a "cat" and a "mouse" signal from stations as close to the coast of the United Kingdom as possible. When the bomber followed a signal to the target and intercepted the other signal, the bombs were dropped. But Oboe, too, was increasingly ineffective the farther from the stations the aircraft flew. H2S was the code name for early airborne targeting radar installed in a bulge underneath the fuselage, forward of the tail assembly, which bounced radio signals off the ground and gave a very rough topographical image on a radar screen, showing various ground contours, rivers, large bodies of water, and urban topography. H2S was improved throughout the war, giving Bomber Command much improved accuracy for night bombing or bombing through heavy cloud cover.

The bomber stream was a method of concentrating the main bomber effort of any given night on a single target and hitting that target with all available aircraft in the shortest possible time. It was also a way of overwhelming the German night defences by putting many more bombers through the German defensive boxes than the Würzburg radars and night fighters could possibly handle. Harris was very keen on the bomber stream concept, but less so about a proposal made to him by one of his group captains to take the best crews out of each of his groups and create an elite "pathfinder" force equipped with the latest target-finding technologies. Their job would be to lead the bomber stream to the target, then drop a series of target-marking and illumination flares to guide the bombers that followed. Harris didn't like the concept of an elite force within Bomber Command, but he relented under pressure from the Air Ministry, urged on by Sir Henry Tizard, one of Britain's most influential wartime scientists, and other Operational Research scientists. The Pathfinder Force was first tried out in August 1942. Despite early failures, it soon proved effective. In January 1943 No. 8 (Pathfinder) Group was formed, consisting of some of the best squadrons in Bomber Command. One of these was the RCAF's No. 405 (City of Vancouver) Squadron.

Harris's determination to destroy as much of Germany's cities as possible prompted a change in Bomber Command bombloads. Each of the heavy bombers—the four-engine Stirling, Halifax, and Lancaster bombers—usually carried a single 4,000-pound "cookie"—a massive bomb that looked like a large barrel and had almost no aerodynamic qualities whatsoever—and dozens of clusters of small incendiary bombs. The explosive bombs were used to blow the roofs off buildings and open them up to the incendiaries, and also to destroy gas and water mains, thus rendering emergency response measures ineffective. The first time these techniques were used together in a raid was in March 1942, when 234 bombers were sent to attack the German port city of Lübeck; 191 aircraft pressed home the attack, dropping about 300 tons of bombs, including 144 tons of incendiaries. Only 312 people were killed, but more than 15,000 were made homeless.

★ ★ ★ ★

The first of the RCAF's bomber squadrons, No. 405, took part in these attacks, as did the other RCAF bomber squadrons as they became operational. No. 405 began flying the four-engine Halifax in April 1942, while the rest of the RCAF bomber squadrons stayed on twin-engine aircraft for some time after; No. 419 converted to Halifaxes in November 1942, and No. 408 did the same one month later, but the other RCAF bomber squadrons continued to fly Hampdens or Wellingtons until well into 1943. The Canadian squadrons were placed with existing Bomber Command groups—No. 419 Squadron with No. 3 Group; No. 405 with No. 4 Group; and Nos. 408 and 420 with No. 5 Group, generally considered the best all-round group in Bomber Command. An all-French-Canadian unit—No. 425 "Alouette" Squadron—went operational in June 1942 with No. 4 Group.

A typical night mission was a harrowing experience for the young men of Bomber Command. After the crews were briefed in late afternoon, they were taken out to their aircraft in the gathering dusk to wait for final word as to whether the mission was to go ahead. This usually depended on last-minute weather updates received from high-flying reconnaissance aircraft that had been sent out over Germany earlier in the day. Lolling under the wings, they would smoke, or talk, or just daydream as they tried to keep their minds focused on anything but the dangers they were about to face. Everyone was nervous; no one wanted to show it. Then, when word came that they would go ahead, they each urinated on the tailwheel for good luck before squeezing into their respective crew positions. Equipment was checked, lucky charms and talismans were stored away, and engines were started and run up for instrument checks before the wheel chocks were pulled away and the aircraft began to roll toward the perimeter track. As each bomber reached the takeoff point, the pilot stood on the brakes and ran up the throttle; then, when the signal was given, brakes were released, the heavily loaded bomber gathered speed, and, if all went well, pulled away from the runway and into the darkening sky over southern or eastern England. Sometimes all did not go well, and several tons of metal, bombs, gasoline, and human flesh hurtled off the runway and crashed into power poles, or trees, or low hills, creating a massive explosion and leaving a funeral pyre to mark the way for the aircraft that followed. And follow they did, climbing out in silence over the burning wreckage that had once borne friends and comrades.

Once airborne, the bomber began the long climb to its assigned altitude as the navigator guided the pilot into the bomber stream. At their crew stations, the men in their electrically heated suits tried vainly to keep warm in the freezing night air. When the bomber reached 10,000 feet, all were ordered to put on their oxygen masks. If deprived of oxygen over 10,000 feet, they would quickly lose consciousness and possibly die. As engines droned away, each man performed his assigned task. The wireless air gunner (WAG) monitored the radio and peered out into the dark to try to spot German night fighters. The bombers kept radio silence, but sometimes signals were sent from the United Kingdom, and the WAG had to be alert for them at all times. The navigator watched his Gee set or his Oboe (later in the war his H2S) or took star shots. The pilot, sweating to keep the aircraft flying straight and true in the night air usually made turbulent by the passage of hundreds of other bombers, tried to see if he was too near other aircraft in the bomber stream.

If there was moonlight, the crew could sometimes see other bombers and there was less chance of collision but there was also a better chance of being spotted by night fighters. If there was no moon, or if the bomber was flying in cloud, then the men felt as if they were trying to move about a room blindfolded, never knowing when they were going to crash into some dangerous obstacle. In an instant, the tailwheel or the propellers of another bomber could come smashing through a windscreen or into the top of the fuselage. Or worse, a night fighter could sidle up underneath and blast away with cannon fire at the wing roots, setting gas tanks ablaze or exploding bombloads in one terrifying flash. Throughout the bomber war, the crews of American bombers, flying in daylight, could easily see incoming fighters and had time to bail out if their aircraft were stricken. The majority of them escaped their crippled bombers and survived. Flying in the dark, most of the crews of Bomber Command had little or no warning before they were attacked and not enough time to make their escape; the great majority died in their aircraft. So crew members, especially rear gunners, strained to catch a glimpse of an approaching night fighter in time to warn the pilot to go into the stomach-wrenching corkscrew dive that offered the one reasonable chance of survival. Rear gunners often had the rear-facing Perspex plate on the turrets removed so they could see into the dark more clearly even though they endured great cold for most of the flight.

The standard defensive armament of all the RAF/RCAF heavy bombers was the .303 machine gun. These were usually located in a rear turret, a mid-upper turret, and a nose turret; but the lack of a belly turret of any sort on virtually all production models left a dangerous blind spot underneath the aircraft. Early Lancasters, including the pattern Lancaster flown to Canada to serve as a model for the production of Canadian-built Lancaster X bombers in Malton, Ontario, near Toronto, had a small gun mount underneath the aircraft that could be cranked down in flight, but most didn't. The lack of defensive guns and the small calibre and limited range of the guns they did have severely handicapped the bomber crew's ability to defend themselves. In fact, Bomber Command air gunners were instructed to hold their fire unless they had a very good chance of hitting an enemy fighter. In other words, shooting with the .303 machine gun was considered more dangerous to the bomber—in that it might attract the attention of a nearby night fighter—than withholding fire. This was in sharp contrast to the American heavies, which were each defended by some ten .50 machine guns, heavy armament compared to those in the RAF aircraft. Harris argued long and hard for the .303 guns to be replaced by the heavier .50s, and even to install 20mm cannon in the tail, but the cannon were too large for the rear turret, and the Air Ministry was somewhat puzzlingly apathetic about installing .50s in the nose and mid-upper turrets.[6]

If the bomber crews made it across the North Sea, across occupied Holland or Belgium, and into Germany, they then approached the target, a confusing maze of searchlights, tracer, flares, and coloured target markers cascading down from the pathfinders. As one pilot later remembered, "Gun flashes, photoflashes, bomb bursts, streams of tracer of all colours, and everywhere searchlights. Our target runs were like the weavings of a demented bird. With bombs away, we would turn breathlessly into the waiting darkness; sometimes we left fires behind us that could be seen for a great distance." Always, they left comrades behind too. Often the passage of the bomber stream was marked by the flaming wreckage of shot-down bombers, some destroyed by night fighters, others by flak. Sometimes bomber crews flying on dark, moonless nights would see huge explosions in the sky. These were bombers blowing up after being attacked by night fighters, but a story circulated on the bomber bases that these explosions were actually "scarecrows"—pyrotechnics set off by the Luftwaffe—to scare bomber crews into thinking real aircraft were exploding. Loss rates climbed steadily as more and more German targets were attacked and the crews' chances of completing their allotted thirty missions shrunk. The night fighters did not let up as the bombers left the target area, but if the crew survived its run up to the target, it had a better than even chance of coming home. Occasionally they arrived to clear skies in a breaking dawn; often they came back to fog-shrouded runways. Thousands of crew members made it back to England only

Our Finest Hour

to die near their own airfields. The ones who did return, body and soul intact, were debriefed, ate a hearty breakfast of bacon and eggs—scarce in wartime Britain—tried to sleep, then prepared to do it all over again.

Although Harris mounted two more thousand-plane raids after Cologne, on Essen and Bremen, the results were not nearly as spectacular, because in both cases the bombers failed to achieve sufficient concentration to do extensive damage. It was clearly not possible to carry on scraping enough aircraft together to continue these operations. There were too many losses in the Operational Training Units, both of crews and instructors, and Harris was in danger of mortgaging the future in exchange for a dubious advantage in the present. For the remainder of the year, Bomber Command sent smaller forces to attack targets at night and even during the day when there was sufficient cloud cover to hamper day-fighter defences. The search for means of improving accuracy at night also continued as British target priorities shifted from area attacks to industrial targets such as oil facilities, or aircraft plants. Overall, however, RAF bombing policy throughout the war always returned to area attacks against German cities as first priority.

As the Butt Report pointed out, night bombing was very inaccurate in the early days of the bombing campaign. But accuracy improved throughout the war. In part, the improvements were technological and tactical. Gee, Oboe, H2S, and improved H2S all helped, as did the practice of sending master bombers to the target to guide pathfinders in target marking and to instruct bomb aimers on what portions of the target they should aim at or which markers they should bomb. Introducing the bomber stream and pathfinders also helped. But accuracy was also improved by the increased use of operational research teams at Bomber Command, who studied the effects of the raids using high-resolution photos taken by fast and well-equipped photo reconnaissance aircraft.

These boffins, as they were nicknamed, were essentially forensic-like analysts who critiqued bombing altitude, approach routes, bombload, use of target-finding instruments, and other aspects of the attack. British aerial photo analysis improved dramatically, as did the ability of RAF analysts to see through the elaborate camouflage ruses that the Germans used to hide airfields, key industrial facilities, and oil installations. As the science of bombing evolved, the RAF's accuracy improved dramatically as, presumably, did its ability to flatten strategic targets at night.[7] Why then did Harris insist on returning to area bombing whenever he could?

It is this aspect of the bombing campaign that has drawn the most controversy, because attacking the morale of German civilians was clearly tantamount to attacking the civilians themselves and killing as many as possible. Harris never made any bones about this. And if this was done as the deliberate and sole objective of a campaign that actually contributed little or nothing to the war—which Harris, Churchill, Portal, and others knew, or ought to have known—as some historians have alleged, then the campaign was at best immoral and at worst plain murder. The popular version of this argument was most spectacularly advanced in a television program entitled "Death by Moonlight" first broadcast on the CBC in 1992. The conclusion reached by the authors of *The Crucible of War*, Volume III, of the official history of the RCAF, also reflects this view to some extent, though in a more scholarly fashion. One of the more recent works to reflect these allegations is Randall Hansen's *Fire and Fury*, published in 2008.[8]

There is no doubt that area bombing targeted civilians; but in doing so, did it help bring the war to a victorious conclusion as speedily as possible? Did it seriously damage the German war effort and did it undermine German morale and contribute to the victory? Because if area bombing did contribute significantly to the Allied victory, then the killing of

German civilians was an unfortunate but necessary component of the Allied war effort, a war effort intended to defend against Nazi aggression and bring about the collapse of one of the most immoral and murderous regimes in modern history. It is important to this discussion to point out that Hitler started the war, that the Nazis waged a "total" war from start to finish, and that the Nazis aimed for not only the domination of Europe but also the wanton murder of millions of civilians.

Harris forecast many times that the RAF bomber offensive would win the war and that the Allied ground forces would need only to occupy Germany after it surrendered due to heavy bombing from the air. That was fantasy. The RAF never had the capacity to defeat Germany from the air; it could have done so easily with a fleet of American-built B-29 Superfortresses and, say, a score of atomic bombs, but such a bomber force was still almost a decade in the future. On a small number of occasions (which I will address later on), bombing attacks were mounted under conditions that allowed Bomber Command to achieve both accuracy and concentration and to wreak havoc on a German city, greatly damaging its capacity to produce war *materiél*, at least for a time. But for the most part, the results of the bombing campaign were mixed, if the attacks are to be judged solely by their impact on war production; Cologne, for instance, suffered great damage, but industrial production was back to normal a short time afterwards. That was primarily because there were few factories in the centres of German cities; most were located in the suburbs, which usually suffered only marginal damage from Bomber Command attacks.

American historian Williamson Murray, who has written extensively on the air war, did not discount the damage Bomber Command did to industrial targets, but he did point to another important Bomber Command contribution to victory: "The night bombing campaign's greatest contribution to the winning of the war was precisely what Harris claimed and what the conventional wisdom has so often discounted: The 'area' bombing attacks did have a direct and palpable effect on the morale of the German population, and the German leadership, in response to that impact, seriously skewed Germany's strategy." He points out that scholarship in Germany itself shows that, as early as 1942, the night bombing was seriously impacting German morale and that, in 1943, it caused "a dramatic fall off in popular morale." Reports of the *Sicherheitsdienst* (SD), the secret police, showed that the German people were increasingly restive, bitter, and angry at their leaders and blamed them for the tribulations of the bombing campaign. In Murray's view, this growing feeling of despair and anger forced German leaders to continue to waste resources on offensive weaponry in order to placate the demand for revenge: "The SD reports, reflecting the popular mood, explain the leadership's demand for retaliation weapons, (the V-1 and V-2), its willingness to waste the Luftwaffe's bomber fleet over the winter of 1944 even though faced with the threat of an Allied invasion, and its refusal to provide the necessary support needed to the fighter forces until military defeat was obvious and inescapable."[9]

* * * *

In May and June 1942 the representatives of fourteen nations met at Ottawa to review and revise the British Commonwealth Air Training Plan. The Canadian government had already decided to push for the establishment of an all-Canadian bomber group to operate under the overall direction of Bomber Command. The British were less than ecstatic about this decision, fearing it might set a precedent for other Commonwealth countries and break up the operational unity of

Bomber Command. The UK government knew, however, that it had little choice, given the Canadian government's contributions to the war, Canada's independent status, and the precedent already set as to an independent Canadian army and navy. This did not mean that the RAF was especially happy about the decision, which was particularly opposed by Bomber Harris. The RAF dragged its heels on this "Canadianization" until the Canadian government decided that it would pay for the full cost of what was to become No. 6 Group (RCAF) Bomber Command, as well as the other RCAF squadrons in the United Kingdom. After that, there was no excuse for delay. The Group was to consist of the Canadian bomber squadrons then in England and whatever new ones would be formed, and was eventually supposed to be composed of Canadian ground and aircrew, commanded by Canadian officers and even flying Canadian-built aircraft (the Lancaster X). As we shall see (in Chapter 9), that goal was a distant one and was, in fact, never fully achieved.

On January 1, 1943, No. 6 Group went operational with its headquarters at Linton-on-Ouse. Its order of battle consisted of eight bomber squadrons located at six bases in counties Durham and York; two other Canadian squadrons were still attached to No. 4 Group, and one was on loan to Coastal Command at that time. At its peak, it would include thirteen squadrons (with No. 405 being attached to No. 8 Group [Pathfinders]). It was a proud day for Canada, but it was also a day that ushered in a year of grave difficulties for No. 6 Group, high casualties, and the near defeat of the overall night-bombing offensive.

CHAPTER 6

THE RCN ON TRIAL

October 14–15, 1942: approximately 65 kilometres southwest of Port aux Basques, Newfoundland. The passenger ferry SS *Caribou* was on the last leg of its usual run between North Sydney, Nova Scotia, and Port aux Basques. It had departed the Canadian coast at 1900 the previous evening and, escorted by the Bangor Class minesweeper *Grandmère*, headed across the Cabot Strait with its 237 passengers and crew. The ship was the sole link between the Canadian National Railways railhead in North Sydney and the Newfoundland Railway railhead in Port aux Basques. For seventeen years the *Caribou* had carried passengers and freight across the Gulf of St. Lawrence and on this night, as on most others, many of the passengers and crew were part of a closely knit Gulf community that had sent its men to the sea in ships for generations.

The night was clear and cold with a brisk breeze, no moon, and a faint glow from the aurora borealis. The *Caribou* and the *Grandmère*, keeping station to the rear as current regulations for night escort of a single vessel dictated, zigzagged through a slight swell. Most of the passengers aboard the darkened ferry were asleep. It was approaching 0221 Atlantic Standard Time; less than one kilometre away, Oberleutnant

Ulrich Graf and the crew of U-69 waited for the two-ship convoy to pull into torpedo range. With the *Caribou* silhouetted against the faint northern glow, Graf could not miss. Lookouts on the *Caribou* and the *Grandmère* saw no hint of the low-lying submarine. The minesweeper carried no radar, and its position astern of the ferry gave it no chance of detecting the German on asdic. As the *Caribou* pulled into range, Graf gave the order to fire; moments later a single torpedo exploded amidships and the *Caribou* began to list. Then came a second explosion, as the ferry's boilers blew up. The ferry settled quickly then, its guardrails almost to the water within a few short minutes. From below, the engine and boiler room gangs tried to scramble to the open deck. Passengers and crew made for the lifeboats amid the sounds and sights of their vessel breaking up. Some of the lifeboats had been shattered by the exploding torpedo; the rest were quickly jammed with fleeing people. Rafts and Carley floats drifted in the wake of the still-moving ferry, carried forward now only by its own momentum. Then, in less than five minutes, *Caribou* was sucked under; 136 of her passengers and crew perished in the cold waters of the strait.

The communities that ring the shores of the Gulf of St. Lawrence were shocked by the heavy loss of life in the sinking of the *Caribou*, but by the fall of 1942 they had grown used to U-boat attacks ranging far upriver in the Gulf of St. Lawrence. The U-boats had been hunting in Canada's inland waters since May of that year and had already accounted for many sinkings and much loss of life. The Battle of the St. Lawrence, as it would soon be known, came amid a year of great trial for the Royal Canadian Navy, which was suddenly thrust from its primary task of escorting convoys from Halifax and Sydney to the mid-Atlantic, to escorting oil tankers from Nova Scotia to the Caribbean, providing a strong anti-aircraft contingent for the Allied landing in North Africa in November, and finally assuming responsibility for roughly half of all Atlantic convoys from Canadian to UK waters. Because of these new and very important tasks, the navy struggled to meet its commitments in Canada's own waters, not because of a lack of will or even ships and men but due to the low priority of the assignment compared to the navy's other duties.

The Battle of the St. Lawrence also occurred at a time of great sensitivity for the Mackenzie King government, which was wrestling with a backlash in Quebec against the overwhelming endorsement of conscription by Canadian voters in a national plebiscite held by the government on April 27, 1942. As the government prepared Bill 80 to give itself authority to implement conscription, ships sinking along the shores of the St. Lawrence River, and government intentions to keep the sinkings as secret as possible, gave rise to claims from politicians and the press in Quebec that the defence of the province was being neglected. The news of these sinkings could not be totally suppressed from a country at war, and the matter was even raised in the House of Commons and debated in a rare secret session, but the fact that U-boats operated in Canada's internal waters in 1942, 1943, and 1944 somehow escaped the attention of most Canadians for decades after.

★ ★ ★ ★

The Battle of the St. Lawrence had its roots in the Japanese attack against the United States Pacific Fleet at Pearl Harbor on the morning of December 7, 1941. That attack prompted the United States to declare war on Japan and to pull virtually all of its destroyers out of the Atlantic battle and send them to shore up the now dangerously weakened Pacific Fleet. It also brought the United States into the war against Germany, when Hitler committed the second of his two greatest mistakes of the war (the first was his attack against the USSR) and declared war on the United States on December 11, 1941.

In the long run, the US entry into the war was the crucial difference between either a Nazi victory (or a Nazi-dictated stalemate in Europe) and an Allied victory. In the short run, it added to the already tremendous burden on the Royal Canadian Navy. The US Navy had been steadily building up its presence in the North Atlantic since early 1941. As a result of a presidential directive, US Navy ships began to escort US merchant vessels, first to roughly mid-Atlantic waters, later almost all the way to the United Kingdom. The United States even began to build a major destroyer base at Londonderry in Northern Ireland. US anti-submarine warfare doctrine held that only fast, well-equipped destroyers should be used to escort merchant convoys; the United States refused to use smaller, more makeshift anti-submarine vessels such as Canada's corvettes, minesweepers, or Fairmile motor launches. Thus when the US Navy began to transfer much of its escort fleet to the Pacific, it had few other ships to replace the destroyers. A handful of US destroyers and Treasury Class Coast Guard cutters (roughly equivalent to corvettes in size, speed, and armament) stayed in the Atlantic fight, but that wasn't nearly enough to provide the additional escorts that the three North Atlantic allies needed. The largest share of the burden of filling the gap was undertaken by the Royal Canadian Navy, which had to throw its still small and under-equipped navy even more fully into ocean escort work.

The RCN's biggest problem, as always, was too little of everything. True, corvettes were now being launched in large numbers from Canadian shipyards on both coasts and in the St. Lawrence basin and even the Great Lakes, but there were not enough of them to allow the RCN to cover its ever-expanding role. Ideally, there should have been enough corvettes and destroyers to give escort groups sufficient time in port for rest, recuperation, and replenishment between convoys, but there were not. There were not enough to allow the RCN to set up permanent support groups, as the RN was doing in 1942, not dedicated to escorting convoys but trained to hunt submarines and positioned at sea to come to the aid of the escort groups of hard-pressed convoys. Canadian escort groups were chronically overworked, usually short one or two vessels, and often contained at least one untrained and untried new ship with no prior experience working with its consorts. And although an escort group was supposed to have at least two destroyers by mid-1942, Canadian groups sometimes did not have even one. Admiral Nelles and the rest of the professional navy dreamed of Tribal Class destroyers, but the core of the Canadian destroyer fleet through most of 1942 was still the River Class fleet of the 1930s augmented by the four-stackers obtained from the United States in September 1940. There weren't nearly enough of them, and the older ones were either prone to breakdowns or too limited in range, or both, to be relied on. Refueling at sea would eventually overcome part of this problem, but it was not yet standard operating procedure for Canadian convoy escorts in 1942.

For most of 1942, Royal Canadian Navy destroyers and corvettes remained at least a generation behind those of the Royal Navy in both design and equipment. As RN corvettes began to receive the excellent 271-centimetric radar, capable of detecting a surfaced U-boat at up to 10 kilometres, the Canadians were installing the SW1C—a Canadian-designed and -manufactured variant of the British 286-metric radar—which was good for not much more than convoy station keeping; it could almost never detect a surfaced U-boat except when it was already too close to be avoided. Canadian corvettes eventually began receiving 271 radar during refits in the United Kingdom, but not until late

1942. Even then, they could expect no more than ten sets installed each month. Nor did the Canadians have the latest in gyrocompasses, asdic equipment, or shipborne anti-aircraft weapons. Since this newer equipment was in short supply, it was natural that the British would install it on their own vessels first.

In 1942 Canadian corvettes were also overwhelmingly of the original short-forecastle type first commissioned in 1940. Almost all British corvettes were being retrofitted with lengthened forecastles and better guns, but the Canadians were not. This was due to failures of both the government and the navy. The former kept contracting for the original type of corvette to expedite construction, while the latter did not seem to realize that the war ahead was going to be lengthy and would give the navy plenty of opportunity to upgrade its ships. Thus the navy too was eager to get as many escorts as it could handle, even if they were of the original obsolete type.

These problems of growing obsolescence were also reflected in the weapons and anti-submarine gear carried by the Canadian ships. The British and Americans were installing Hedgehog, a new anti-submarine weapon that threw mortar bombs ahead of an attacking vessel, enabling it to keep asdic contact as it approached its target in a high-speed attack. Hedgehog also had the advantage of exploding only on contact, unlike depth charges, which always exploded at their pre-set depths. However, for most of 1942 the Canadians did not have enough corvettes to be able to pull more than a handful of individual ships out of service for any length of time in order to make these and other modifications and improvements.

As a solution to the shortage of destroyers and the limitations of the single-screw corvettes, the RCN looked forward to the arrival of UK-designed and -built River Class frigates and newer, larger corvettes such as the Castle Class. These ships were not built to strict naval standards—and the frigates had an awful tendency to simply blow up when torpedoed in the engine room—but they were newer, larger, and faster, and they had more room for better submarine detection gear and improved weaponry. However, the RCN would have to wait until 1943 before the first of these frigates began to enter Canadian service.[1]

Well into 1943, most Canadian captains continued to command their vessels from bridges that were almost totally exposed to wind and sea, protected only by a canvas "dodger" hung from the bridge railing. When mounting an attack against a submarine, however, they had to jam themselves inside the asdic hut at the rear of the bridge platform because it housed the only compass on the bridge. In the early Canadian-built corvettes, that compass was a magnetic compass, which—unlike a gyrocompass, such as the Royal Navy used on its corvettes—could not give the ship's exact location. Aboard the corvette *Sackville*, Alan Easton found the task exceedingly difficult: "It was a bit of a squash inside the asdic house . . . Once wedged in alongside the compass it was a job to get yourself out. And to be able to make an exit was important. It was almost better to crane your neck in from outside through an open window. But that would have given you a distorted view of the compass card, and you would have needed the sight of a seagull to read the degrees."[2]

Despite these obvious shortcomings, the Royal Canadian Navy took on a more expanded role in escorting North Atlantic convoys in February 1942, when the Newfoundland Escort Force was terminated and replaced by the Mid-Ocean Escort Force (MOEF), which consisted primarily of Canadian and British ships with the handful of US Navy destroyers and US Coast Guard vessels that remained in the Atlantic. The change was a direct result of the US shifting destroyers. Put simply, the remaining ships had to shoulder the burden that the Americans left behind. Hence the need to shorten the route across the Atlantic. The revised convoy scheme operated this way: fast merchant convoys would depart Halifax (New York after mid-September 1942) and slow ones Sydney, Nova Scotia (later Boston), as before. They would be escorted to the Western Ocean Meeting Point (WESTOMP), southeast of St. John's, Newfoundland, by the largely Canadian ships of the Western Local Escort Force (WLEF). But now, at WESTOMP, the WLEF would hand its charges to the MOEF, which would escort the convoys across the entire ocean to meet UK-based escorts at the Eastern Ocean Meeting Point near Northern Ireland. Iceland was largely eliminated as an escort base. In the meantime, the WLEF would proceed to St. John's for refueling and provisioning before heading back to sea to pick up a westbound convoy for Halifax or New York. The route travelled by the WLEF was dubbed the "triangle run."

The Mid-Ocean Escort Force's new eastern terminus was Londonderry, Northern Ireland. From there, they would return to sea to meet a westbound convoy, which they would escort to WESTOMP before heading back to St. John's. As this system was inaugurated, the main convoy routes were also shifted south, away from Iceland, to shorten the convoy track. The shorter track required fewer escorts, but it also put the main convoy track more squarely into that area of the mid-ocean that could not be reached by shore-based patrol aircraft and that was known as the "black hole." That was where the wolf packs waited for the convoys. SC 47, sailing in early February 1942, was the first convoy to follow the new routing; it was accompanied by six RCN corvettes, including the corvette *Spikenard* as the escort commander's vessel. The RCN had no destroyers to spare for this group of ships. On the night of February 10, 1942, the U-boats attacked, sinking *Spikenard* and a tanker; the corvette went down so fast that no distress call was possible. It was only after she could not be raised by radio that her consorts noticed her missing; a search for survivors turned up only eight men clinging to a Carley float in the bitterly cold water.

Londonderry, or Derry, as it became known, was a great improvement over Hvalfjordhur, Iceland. The westernmost port in the United Kingdom, it had been chosen by the Admiralty in the summer of 1940 as a major base for anti-submarine operations in the North Atlantic, but little was done to actually make Derry the eastern terminus for the North Atlantic Run until the US Navy arrived in the summer of 1941 and began building refueling facilities, repair shops, dry docks, warehouses, and administration buildings. The RN and the RCN were to be allowed the use of the US facility as long as the USN had first call on it. When US escorts largely disappeared from the North Atlantic in early 1942, the base virtually became a Royal Navy facility.

Entering Londonderry after a storm-tossed crossing of the North Atlantic was balm to a weary sailor's soul. In the words of James Lamb, "To arrive at Derry after a hard east-bound crossing was a little like approaching the pearly gates."[3] As the little rust-streaked corvettes entered the mouth of the River Foyle, the deep green of the Irish countryside engulfed them; each kilometre they sailed upriver was one step closer to respite and one farther from the brutal war at sea they never became inured to, no matter how many merchantmen they saw blown up or how many human remains they spotted drifting in oily waters. The quaint old town welcomed them and offered them succour. But too often they had little time for anything more than a quick turnaround and back out to face the grey Atlantic; for most of 1942 there were still too few escort vessels to afford the luxury of a week or so in port to heal minds, as well as bodies, and to fix up ships. There was always another westbound convoy to shepherd and another escort group whose ranks needed strengthening by the addition of one or two more corvettes.

The withdrawal of most of the US Navy's destroyers from the North Atlantic and the enlarging of the theatre of the sea war increased the strain on the Royal Canadian Navy. By mid-1942 almost half the escort vessels and a quarter of the aircraft patrolling the Atlantic sea lanes north of New York were Canadian. From December 1941 to July 1942, Ottawa also effectively administered the shipping system in the western Atlantic north of the equator, even though the western Atlantic was still technically under the overall command of the USN. Naval control of shipping, as the Royal Navy first called it, was actually initiated even before Canada officially declared war on September 10, 1939. The system essentially consisted of rules and regulations, enforced by law, that governed ship movements from east-coast Canadian ports to the United Kingdom. Among other activities, it allocated ships to the SC and HX convoys, scheduled the convoy cycle, assigned escorts to the convoys, and dictated which ships could sail unescorted (those capable of at least 15 knots). Royal Navy officers were loaned to the RCN to help inaugurate and administer the system in Canada.

The slaughter of shipping off the US east coast and in the Caribbean (which began in mid-February 1942 with submarine attacks on tankers bringing Venezuelan crude to refineries in the Dutch Antilles and Trinidad) caused immediate problems for the Royal Canadian Navy in eastern Canada. The submarines concentrated on tankers, causing the US Navy to constantly interrupt east-coast tanker traffic, including those that brought fuel oil to the main RCN bases at Halifax and Sydney in Nova Scotia and St. John's in Newfoundland. At one point, RCN stocks were reduced to fifteen days' reserve. In May 1942, Admiral Nelles declared, "To hell with that, we'll get our own," and sent seven precious corvettes from the Western Local Escort Force to escort tankers directly from Trinidad to Halifax. As historian Roger Sarty observed, "It was a brilliant success; the convoys got through without loss, even as the U-boats moved into the Caribbean and the Gulf of Mexico and destroyed eighty-one vessels in these waters during the month of May."[4] The British and the Americans even agreed to allow Nelles to withdraw seven more Canadian escorts from the all-important North Atlantic Run to allocate to his new Halifax Force, with which he also intended to shore up RCN vessels in the Gulf of St. Lawrence. The warm sun of the semi-tropics, the blue of the Caribbean, and the lure of exotic islands was like balm to the Canadian sailors lucky enough to be assigned to the southern tanker routes, but the loss of these escorts to the Western Local Escort Force and the Mid-Ocean Escort Force was serious.

* * * *

The initial foray of the grey sharks into the Gulf of St. Lawrence came on May 8, 1942, when U-553, commanded by Korvettenkapitän Karl Thurmann, slipped through the Cabot Strait into the Gulf and took up station about 80 kilometres north of the Gaspé coast; in the early hours of May 12, Thurmann torpedoed and sank the steamers *Leto* and *Nicoya*. The sinkings were not unexpected; both the government and the RCN had believed for some time that U-boats would inevitably penetrate the Gulf and even the river estuary itself, and had prepared defensive plans based on the scarce air and surface resources then available. There was not much. The RCN's Gulf strength in the spring of 1942 consisted of five Bangor Class minesweepers, three Fairmile motor launches, and a handful of armed yachts, while Eastern Air Command was able to deploy perhaps a dozen twin-engine Douglas Digbys, Lockheed Hudsons, and Consolidated Catalinas at a number of main bases and small airstrips around the Gulf.

Canada's Gulf defence forces were severely limited in both numbers and capabilities. The Bangor Class minesweepers were twin-screw vessels built to naval specifications, but they were small and overcrowded, and had very limited offensive capabilities. The Fairmiles were not much better, and the yachts were just that—civilian pleasure craft purchased by the RCN and adapted to perform a variety of inshore naval duties. The aircraft were excellent for providing air cover when used properly, but Eastern Air Command had a lot to learn about how to deploy aircraft to seek out and destroy submarines. In the beginning of the Gulf campaign, the aircraft were the wrong colour and carried depth charges that were not only too small but also equipped with too weak an explosive to do much damage to a submarine. These forces would eventually adapt to the challenges of protecting shipping in the Gulf and in the river estuary; by the end of the 1942 shipping season, U-boat captains were finding it harder and harder to track and attack Gulf and river shipping.

Although the Royal Canadian Navy and the government believed it was important to keep the Gulf open to ocean-going ships, there were only so many anti-submarine resources to go around. It was decided even before the Battle of the St. Lawrence broke out to resist stripping escorts from Canadian ocean escort groups to protect Gulf or river shipping; to have done that, it was believed, would have weakened those escort groups doing the most important job and given the Germans an advantage out of all proportion to the effort they put in. The fact was that virtually all the important war cargoes that crossed the Gulf in ship bottoms for shipment to the United Kingdom could have been sent to

Halifax or Sydney or any number of US ports by rail. It was true that the rail network in eastern Canada and the northeastern United States was already heavily burdened, but at least cargoes sent by rail would not end up at the bottom of the Gulf, even if they were delayed. This was not true of Canadian bulk cargoes, such as grain and lumber, which were best shipped from the port of Montreal. In the case of these cargoes, the Royal Navy continued to press the Canadians not to send them by rail but to ship them directly from the river.

Though Gulf waters were shallower than those of the North Atlantic, anti-submarine operations there were more difficult than they were at sea. That was because the mixing of the cold fresh water from the St. Lawrence River with the warmer salt water of the Gulf, compounded by the tricky tides and currents, layered the water into different zones of temperature and salinity that bent asdic beams. Submarine captains quickly learned to take advantage of these water conditions to hide both before and after attacks.

The two sinkings on May 12 sparked off intensive air patrol activity and led the RCN to inaugurate cross-Gulf convoys for ships carrying strategic goods. These measures, plus heavy fog, effectively prevented Thurmann from scoring any more kills and, on May 22, he slipped out of the Gulf to hunt elsewhere. A little over a month later, U-132 took his place with orders to attack Gulf shipping and scout the eastern end of the Strait of Belle Isle. Commanded by Korvettenkapitän Ernst Vogelsang, U-132 proceeded up the Gulf virtually to the mouth of the St. Lawrence. Late on July 5 Vogelsang attacked a Quebec–Sydney convoy, sinking three ships before dawn. Depth-charged by the minesweeper *Drummondville*, U-132 sustained minor damage but escaped to resume its war patrol in the Gulf. This latest attack shook Naval Service Headquarters from its previous policy of holding the line in the Gulf, and six corvettes were taken off North Atlantic duty and assigned to the Gulf Escort Force until the close of the Gulf shipping season. This move did not prevent Vogelsang from scoring one final sinking off Cape Magdalen on May 20 in a daylight periscope attack. Then he, too, escaped.

The third incursion of German submarines into the Gulf in 1942 was by far the most serious. Toward the end of August, U-517 and U-165 slipped through the Strait of Belle Isle; on August 27 U-517 torpedoed and sank the US Army transport *Chatham* in a daylight periscope attack just at the western end of the strait. Later, toward evening, it and U-165 sank the US freighter *Arlyn* and badly damaged the *Laramie*, another US merchantman. Less than a week later, U-517 struck again, slipping past two escorting corvettes to attack a small convoy and sink the Canadian freighter *Donald Stewart*. Eastern Air Command now concluded that two submarines were operating in the Gulf and increased its air patrols over the Gulf convoy routes, but on the night of September 6–7, the two U-boats sank the armed yacht HMCS *Raccoon* and four freighters. Four days later, U-517 torpedoed the corvette HMCS *Charlottetown*, which sank in four minutes. Most of the crew escaped into the water, but many were maimed and killed when the corvette's depth charges exploded as the hulk went down; there had been no time to disarm them before abandoning ship.

The choices now facing the navy and the government were stark: reinforce the Gulf Escort Force significantly or close the Gulf to all but local shipping. The former course was out of the question; in August the Admiralty had requested Canadian corvettes to help with anti-aircraft duties in the forthcoming assault on North Africa (Operation Torch) to take place in November. The government was highly receptive to the request, and the RCN decided to allocate seventeen vessels to that task (see Chapter 10). Five of the corvettes were dispatched from the Pacific coast via the Panama Canal; the other twelve were taken from the Western Local Escort Force (WLEF) and Mid-Ocean Escort Force (MOEF). Quite simply, there were no additional escorts of any type for the Gulf. In fact, the contribution to Torch could be accomplished only if the Gulf were closed to ocean shipping and RCN escorts used for that purpose were deployed elsewhere. The fate of ocean shipping in the Gulf for the remainder of the 1942 shipping season was thus decided on September 9 when the order was given to close down the convoy and escort system for ocean-going cargoes. The railways would have to carry the extra burden.

The closing of the Gulf to ocean shipping did not stop local sailings carrying freight and passenger traffic between Gulf ports, especially between Quebec City and Sydney, Nova Scotia. Thus there were still targets for U-boats to shoot at—and shoot they did. U-517 and U-165 sank four more ships and damaged another on the night of September 15–16 before making for the Atlantic. Not long after their departure, U-69 passed through the Cabot Strait to spearhead the last German war patrols inside the Gulf in the 1942 shipping season. It was joined several days later by U-106 and U-43, which set up station in the Cabot Strait. U-69 torpedoed and sank the Canadian freighter *Carolus* early on October 9, and U-106 torpedoed and sank the UK freighter *Waterton* at midday on October 11. The *Waterton* and its cargo of paper sank in eight minutes, and U-69 moved off in search of other targets. It found what it was looking for in the early morning hours of October 15 when the passenger ferry SS *Caribou* hove into view. The sinking of the *Caribou* was the climax of the 1942 Battle of the St. Lawrence. U-69, U-106, and U-43 departed soon after. In mid-November U-518 entered the Gulf to land a German spy on the Gaspé shore, then left the area to begin a patrol off of Halifax. The spy was quickly discovered and arrested; U-518 sank no ships in the Gulf.

The Gulf incursions were certainly daring and, at first, quite successful. In five months, the U-boats sank one corvette, one armed yacht, and nineteen freight or passenger vessels (including the *Caribou*) and heavily damaged two other merchantmen. Over the course of the campaign, the government was forced to divert escorts to the Gulf, even though escorts were in short supply elsewhere. Then, after the Torch commitments and the inauguration of the important Halifax–Trinidad convoys, it closed the Gulf to ocean shipping altogether, causing additional problems for the already overburdened eastern rail network. The Germans paid virtually nothing for the havoc they wrought; in the entire five-month period, not a single German submarine was sunk in Gulf waters; not one was even severely damaged. Historians are divided about the overall results of the campaign. One of Canada's most prolific naval historians, Marc Milner, has pronounced that "the Battle of the St. Lawrence was a German victory."[5] But another prominent Canadian naval historian, Roger Sarty, came to the opposite conclusion in his book *War in the St. Lawrence: The Forgotten U-Boat Battles on Canada's Shores.* Sarty believes that the quick and well-coordinated response of the Royal Canadian Navy and Eastern Air Command to the early 1942 attacks in the Gulf made it almost impossible for the U-boats to operate there and that the sinking of the *Caribou,* tragic though it was, came as a result of the German retreat from the Gulf and not as the climax of a successful campaign.[6]

★ ★ ★ ★

In the larger scheme of things, the Gulf of St. Lawrence was not an important theatre of war; the North Atlantic was. Shortly after Pearl Harbor, Churchill and his staff travelled to Washington to begin to lay joint plans with the United States for the future conduct of the war. He and Roosevelt agreed that their first priority was to knock out Germany, then turn to Japan; they also agreed that an invasion of occupied Europe was the only way that Germany could eventually be defeated. Before they could even begin to think seriously of launching that invasion, the United States would have to build up its land and air forces in the United Kingdom to the point where a combined Allied assault against occupied France would stand a reasonable chance of success. That buildup was dubbed Operation Bolero; it would not succeed if the slaughter at sea continued. The RCN, responsible for the protection of the convoys in the western Atlantic at that point (and for almost half of all convoys after March 1942), would play a vital role in the success or failure of Bolero. Although the Royal Canadian Navy was never capable of winning the Second World War in Europe by itself, it was certainly now capable of losing it if it failed at this new and vital task.

* * * *

By early 1942, U-boat wolf-pack tactics had become tried and true and even predictable. A line of U-boats would take up station across the usual convoy routes and try to make visual contact with a convoy. The Germans had broken key Admiralty codes early in the war and generally had an excellent idea of when convoys were departing the US or Canadian East Coasts and what tracks they were assigned to. When one submarine made contact it would shadow the convoy, usually on the surface, from as far astern as possible, and constantly radio its position to the *Befehlshaber der Unterseeboote* (BdU), the U-boat central command, which would then direct the rest of the pack to the appropriate place to make an attack. The U-boats preferred to attack at night when they could fight on the surface and use their diesels to work their way in between the escorts and the merchantmen. When enough wolf-pack members reported themselves to have made contact with the convoy, the attack signal was given.

The RCN's lack of adequate radar during this period of the war meant that Canadian escort groups were, for all intents and purposes, fighting blind when trying to counter these night attacks. By day they would sweep the flanks of the convoy to the limits of visual range. As night began to fall, the SOE (Senior Officer of the Escort)—the escort commander—usually sailing in a destroyer, would leave his position at the head of the convoy and sweep both flanks and far astern, trying to force any shadowing U-boats to dive. This routine but vitally necessary operation could be carried out only by a destroyer that was fast enough to circle the convoy and then assume its night station. A corvette could not. That would usually be combined with a convoy course change to throw any shadowers off. As darkness enveloped the ships, the escorts would move in close and sweep with asdic. In late 1942, some escort groups began using what was dubbed the "major hoople." When the SOE suspected that surfaced U-boats were lying in wait on the fringes of a convoy at night, he would order his escorts to carry out a "major hoople" to port or starboard. Then all the escorts on either the right or left flank of the convoy would quickly do a 45-degree turn out from the convoy track and begin firing star shells 90 degrees to the course of the convoy. The hope was that lurking U-boats would be illuminated and driven under. It was innovative, but no substitute for radar.

The Royal Navy, by contrast, was relatively well equipped to fight this kind of war. By late 1942, virtually all of its escort vessels carried high-frequency direction-finding (HF/DF) gear, as did the convoy rescue ships. Thus U-boat transmissions could be intercepted while at sea and the positions of shadowers or wolf packs plotted by the SOE. Ultra intercepts were always helpful, but in early 1942 the Germans modified their naval code machines to use a fourth rotor; this deprived the Allies of U-boat Ultra intercepts for almost a year. Still, even if the U-boat signals could not be understood, their intentions could usually be discerned from their positions, giving the RN escorts a chance to spot them at night with their 271 radar.

The Royal Canadian Navy's shortage of ships and modern anti-submarine equipment was made worse by the continuing shortage of trained personnel. As new corvettes were placed in commission, existing crews were stripped of men to crew them. The navy reasoned that it was better to have a lot of ships with mixed crews of veterans and untried men than to have new vessels manned by crews with almost no veterans at all. And although with each passing month more and more incompetent officers were weeded out of ocean-going service, a large enough contingent remained in 1942—even as captains—to continue to impair the overall efficiency of the fleet.

These difficulties trapped the RCN in a vicious cycle. Prior to the US entry into the war it had been decided that if the United States entered the war, its destroyer-heavy anti-submarine force would shepherd the fast convoys (the HX series) to the Mid-Ocean Meeting Point, where they would be handed over to the Royal Navy, while the RCN, with its largely corvette fleet, would escort the slow convoys. That was partly because a corvette's top speed was 15 knots—virtually the same as that of a surfaced U-boat—and partly because of the overall state of training and equipment in the RCN. What this meant in practice was that the RCN was given responsibility for convoys that were more likely to be attacked (because of their slow speed they found it more difficult to evade wolf packs), would remain in danger longer, and would spend more time in the "black hole"—the mid-ocean air gap. What it also meant was that the loss rates of RCN-escorted convoys would invariably be higher than those of the RN convoys, apparently "proving" to the British that the Canadians were incapable of doing the job properly.

These problems put RCN escorts at a serious disadvantage once at sea. In mid-May the nominally American Escort Group A3 was escorting the slow westbound convoy ONS 92 when it was intercepted by wolf pack *Hecht*. A3 actually consisted of the American destroyer USS *Gleaves*, the US Coast Guard cutter *Spencer*, and four Canadian corvettes—*Algoma*, *Arvida*, *Bittersweet*, and *Shediac*. Spotted by U-569 on the morning of May 11, the convoy was attacked after dark with the almost immediate loss of five cargo vessels. Although the two US escorts ranged far ahead of the convoy the next day, forcing down at least two submarines, two more ships were torpedoed and sunk in the early morning hours of May 13. Thus seven merchantmen were lost at no cost to the Nazis—a US and Canadian failure.

The RCN's performance seemed to improve in a number of convoy battles in the summer of 1942. While shepherding eastbound convoy ON 113 toward the end of July, *St. Croix*, leading Escort Group C2, sank U-90; two of the convoy's freighters were sunk and one was damaged. Within days, ON 115, escorted by Group C3, produced similar results. Though the convoy was constantly shadowed by as many as six U-boats, it lost only two merchantmen but accounted for U-588 sunk (by *Wetaskiwin*) and one or two other submarines badly damaged. One of the latter was attacked by *Sackville*, whose captain, Alan Easton, later described the moment of sighting: "The gun went off and I opened [my eyes] again. After what seemed like a long wait the star shell burst. There she was. A U-boat silhouetted against the falling ball of light. I had no need of my binoculars now. The U-boat lay broadside on, about fifteen degrees on the starboard bow, less than four hundred yards away. Her bow was pointing directly across our course and I saw a short boiling wake at her stern." Easton tried to ram but the submarine crash-dived just in time to avoid the onrushing bow of the Canadian escort. As he passed over the turbulent water left by the diving boat, Easton called for depth charges. The submarine was blown to the surface, its bow pointing to the stars, before it disappeared once again, but it was not sunk.[7]

For a time in the late summer of 1942, it might have appeared that a combination of better tactics, improved battle management, and more skilled crews and commanders was finally pulling the Royal Canadian Navy even with the Royal Navy in anti-submarine performance. Although merchant ships were still going down at a rapid rate, U-boat kills were also climbing, and of the five submarines destroyed since May, four had been sunk by the RCN.[8] In the battle for SC 94 in early August 1942, for example, the Germans sank eleven freighters but lost two U-boats, a rate of exchange they could not afford. Still, the real key to victory in the North Atlantic lay in closing the air gap in mid-ocean, something that was still far beyond the capabilities of the RCAF's Eastern Air Command. That failure would become jarringly apparent as the summer of 1942 slipped into fall.

* * * *

Eastern Air Command had come a long way since 1939. The armament carried by its aircraft improved greatly in the first two years of the war; by mid-1942 they were using more powerful depth charges, specifically designed for air dropping, which utilized detonators that could set off the explosives at much shallower depths. That was important because the nature of airborne anti-submarine warfare was that attacks on

U-boats invariably took place while the boats were either just diving or just under the surface. Through trial and error, and with the new equipment, Eastern Air Command crews also began to patrol at higher altitudes, where they were more likely to catch a U-boat without being spotted and still have sufficient time for a well-planned attack.

Still, two major problems remained. The first was tactical. As Canadian naval historian Roger Sarty and German U-boat historian Jürgen Rohwer have written, "Eastern Air Command responded to the German offensive with a wasteful and largely futile effort to fly close cover over as many convoys and independently sailed ships as possible. U-boats, easily evading these rigidly organized and widely dispersed defences, were able to press into and sink scores of ships in the heavily travelled coastal shipping routes and near approaches to harbours." [9] The RAF's Coastal Command had learned the hard way that while positioning aircraft to orbit over convoys might well keep shadowing U-boats down, it accomplished little else. So Coastal Command kept the coastal waters near the United Kingdom relatively U-boat free with offensive tactics; its aircraft swept far ahead of convoys, catching any waiting U-boats on the surface. It sent aircraft to patrol only over convoys that were definitely known to be threatened (i.e., by Ultra or HF/DF).

Eastern Air Command Squadron Leader N.E. Small, Commanding Officer of No. 113 Squadron based at Yarmouth, Nova Scotia, was a great believer in these Coastal Command tactics. He ordered white camouflage paint applied to the bottoms of his aircraft—a camouflage scheme already in use by the RAF's Coastal Command—to make them harder to spot from a surfaced U-boat, and he urged his crews to use intelligence reports to pinpoint likely spots where submarines might be lurking on the surface. On July 31 he himself caught U-754 on the surface southeast of Cape Sable and sent it to the bottom. Despite Small's success (the first U-boat sunk in the war by Eastern Air Command), it was not until late 1942 that EAC began to follow Coastal Command's approach to convoy protection. It was then that improved tactics and a good dose of luck produced one of EAC's best days of the war. On October 30, 1942, while returning home from patrol duty with convoy ON 140, a Digby of No. 10 Squadron, based at Gander, Newfoundland, spotted U-520 on the surface and sank it in a quick attack with four depth charges. That same day, a Hudson of No. 145 Squadron, based at Torbay, Newfoundland, attacked and sank U-658 while on a routine air patrol about 510 kilometres east of Newfoundland.

Eastern Air Command's other major problem was with the aircraft it was forced to use. Its fleet was composed primarily of twin-engine, medium-range Douglas Digbys, Lockheed Hudsons, and Consolidated Catalinas (PBYs). The PBY was probably the best of these aircraft, but it was agonizingly slow; when German submariners spotted the lumbering Catalinas from the bridge of a surfaced U-boat, they usually had ample time for a crash-dive before being attacked. None of these aircraft was in the same league as the major types coming into service with the RAF's Coastal Command: the long-range, four-engine Short Sunderland (a flying boat) and the American-built Consolidated B-24 Liberator.

The Liberator was the aircraft of choice. Designed as a strategic bomber, it was designed to carry a crew of ten and was armed with tail, dorsal, and ball turrets; waste guns; and machine guns in the nose (later models carried a nose turret as well). It had a range of approximately 3,500 kilometres when carrying its normal 2,268-kilogram load of bombs. When field-modified as the VLR (Very Long Range), it was stripped of most of its machine gun armament and other equipment not needed for anti-submarine warfare and had extra fuel tanks installed in the bomb bay. In this configuration, the aircraft range was virtually doubled. Had sufficient numbers of VLR Liberators been stationed on both sides of the ocean and in Iceland in early 1942, the mid-ocean air gap would have been eliminated.

The Royal Air Force began to fly VLR Liberators out of Iceland as early as late 1941, but the Royal Canadian Air Force was denied these aircraft even though it tried desperately to get them. Everybody else seemed to want them, too, and Canada was low on the priority list. The B-24 was one of two heavy bombers (the other was the B-17) that equipped the heavy bomber squadrons of the United States Army Air Force. Thus the USAAF had first call on all the B-24s it needed to build its heavy-bomber strength in the United Kingdom, the Pacific, and other theatres of war. The RAF also wanted B-24s, both as bombers (although few RAF B-24s were ever used in this way) and as anti-submarine aircraft. It was Coastal Command's firm belief that the best time and place to attack U-boats was when they were transiting the Bay of Biscay on the surface at night to exit from or enter their bases on the Biscay coast. Coastal Command demanded and received B-24s to be converted into radar-carrying, Leigh light aircraft even though the statistics proved conclusively that, on average, it took more than 300 hours of air patrolling to sight one U-boat in the Bay of Biscay but only 30 or so hours of air patrolling to sight a U-boat when escorting ahead of convoys. The simple fact was that heavy bombers were a rare and valuable war-fighting commodity in 1942, and none were to be spared for Canada. Thus Eastern Air Command would continue to push its twin-engine aircraft as far out to sea as it dared, knowing that the "black hole" beyond was going to continue to swallow up large numbers of merchantmen and their crews until it was eliminated by long-range aircraft.

* * * *

On September 5, 1942, the Royal Canadian Navy's Escort Group C4, consisting of the destroyers *St. Croix* and *Ottawa*, the RN corvette *Celandine* (equipped with a 271 radar that worked only intermittently), and the RCN corvettes *Amherst*, *Arvida*, and *Sherbrooke* slipped their berths at Londonderry, sailed down the Foyle, and joined westbound convoy ON 127 (consisting of thirty-two merchant ships) just before noon. Acting Lieutenant-Commander A.H. "Dobby" Dobson aboard the *St. Croix* was SOE; Dobson's C 4 Group was as experienced a coterie of RCN escort vessels as could be found in the late summer of 1942.

Unknown to Dobson or anyone else in ON 127, the convoy was spotted by a U-boat one day out of Londonderry; at BdU, U-boat central command, Dönitz mobilized his charges for an attack. Thus, although ON 127 sailed peacefully toward mid-ocean for the next five days, thirteen U-boats from two packs, *Vorwärts* and *Stier*, began to form a patrol line across the convoy lanes out of range of shore-based aircraft. ON 127 was spotted by the Germans on the night of September 9, lost, then spotted again on the morning of the 10th. Then the U-boats moved in. The submarines worked in pairs as they approached the convoy; they came in from ahead during daylight, then dove under the lead escorts to deliver their first attacks from periscope depth.

The very first sign the escorts had that ON 127 had run into a wolf pack came at 1430z (zulu or Greenwich Mean Time) on the 10th, when torpedoes fired by U-96 slammed into the sides of the *Elisabeth van Belgie*, the *F.J. Wolfe*, and the *Svene*. The *F.J. Wolfe* survived the attack, but the other two sank. By the time the convoy reached its destination, a seasoned escort group had lost *Ottawa* and nine merchantmen without taking any toll at all from Dönitz's submarines. The RCN thought that the Canadian escort commander had done a competent job, but the British and the Americans had serious doubts. They began to question the ability of the RCN to carry out its assigned tasks in the mid-ocean; the RCN's reaction to the defeat was to mount an immediate effort to replace its lost destroyer and accelerate the installation of the 271 radars on its vessels.

As early as mid-December, the Admiralty had started pressuring Churchill to request that Ottawa pull the Royal Canadian Navy out of the North Atlantic battle and take over the UK–Gibraltar run under decent air cover. They were becoming convinced that the important North Atlantic convoys could not be left in the hands of the C groups any longer—or not until the C groups had been properly trained and their equipment brought up to a par with that aboard Royal Navy ships. They were all too aware that the vast majority of ships being lost at that point in the war were being escorted by Canadian groups. Nelles and the senior RCN staff bitterly resented the suggestion that the RCN was not up to par and they were not entirely wrong. The Canadians, after all, had the short end of the stick with the slow convoys; no one will ever know if Royal Navy escort groups might have done any better. But then, the Canadians had the slow convoys because of the calibre of their training and equipment.

After ONS 154, the Royal Canadian Navy could no longer deny that its contribution to the battle left much to be desired. Nelles gave in and, on January 9, 1943, the government at Ottawa acceded to the British request. For the hard-pressed RCN, the withdrawal from the mid-Atlantic battle was the lowest point of the war.

CHAPTER 7

ROLL UP OUR SLEEVES
FOR VICTORY:
THE HOME FRONT

By August 1943 William Lyon Mackenzie King had been in power for eight years—through the last half of the Great Depression and the first four years of the Second World War. In the 1940 federal election, he had humbled the opposition, winning one of the largest majority governments in Canadian history. He had challenged the electorate to give him a mandate to lead Canada through war and had received it. But in a mere nine days in August 1943—"black week" the Liberal Party called it—all those accomplishments seemed to be on the verge of evaporating. On Wednesday, August 4, 1943, the Liberal government of Ontario was swept from power and replaced by the Conservatives under the leadership of George Drew, who had no love for Mackenzie King and who believed that the federal government was simply not doing enough to move ahead with the war. The shock was not that the Liberals lost— former Liberal premier Mitchell Hepburn had virtually run Ontario into the ground—but that the Cooperative Commonwealth Federation (CCF), the forerunner to today's New Democratic Party, increased the size of their contingent from zero to thirty-four seats, becoming the official opposition. Five days later, King's own federal party lost four by-elections in ridings they had carried in 1940; the CCF won two of the seats, the Communists won another, and the Bloc Populaire, a Quebec nationalist party, took the other.

The Ontario provincial election and the four federal by-elections were only the first and most obvious signs that Canadians were growing increasingly unhappy with King's war leadership. From roughly December 1942 to June 1944 the rising popularity of the CCF (which gained power in Saskatchewan under Premier Tommy Douglas on June 15, 1944) and the leftward swing of the Conservative Party of Canada (which selected Manitoba Progressive Party premier John Bracken as leader in December 1942 and changed its name to the Progressive Conservative Party of Canada) showed significant voter disaffection with King's Liberals. One national poll during this period even showed that the CCF was leading both the Liberals and the Conservatives in voter preference.

What had happened was simple enough to explain, but harder for King to respond to. The war had changed Canadians as much as it had changed Canada. As the nation did all it could to meet the military demands for war—more and more advanced ships, planes, tanks, radios, radar, and other military gear—its people began to change, too. The role of government transformed overnight. Canadians put their shoulders to the wheel—at least most of them did—but grew increasingly dissatisfied with the political status quo. In Europe, Canadians were dying and being wounded in large numbers, while Canadians at home were being rationed and taxed virtually everywhere they turned. Most were willing to undergo the sacrifices necessary to support the war, but they did not want to return to the status quo when the war was over. King had adamantly refused to consider postwar reform until the war was won; his opponents slipped by him to the left in 1943–44, and the Liberal Party was nearly left in the dust. But in one of the fastest and most politically astute transformations in Canadian political history, the King government, pushed by a number of progressives in its own caucus and Keynesian-thinking mandarins in the burgeoning civil service, shoved the Liberal Party and the government to the left. The process began with the September 1943 meeting in Ottawa of the Advisory Committee of the National Liberal Federation—which adopted sweeping recommendations on issues ranging from national health care to family allowances and compulsory collective bargaining. It progressed in January 1944 with the adoption by King's Cabinet of family allowances and continued with the January 27, 1944, Speech from the Throne, which promised Canadians sweeping changes, including a number of key veterans' benefits. Political fox that he was, King promised the implementation of almost all of these measures after a Liberal victory at the first postwar election (which was held in June 1945). But the promises, backed by a modern and sophisticated advertising and public relations campaign, were enough to give the Liberals a wide margin of victory in 1945 and launch the welfare state in Canada.[1]

* * * *

Whereas Mackenzie King's government was slow off the mark in setting war aims for Canada's military (other than that the country's war effort should be identifiable both to Canadians and to Canada's allies), it was rather quicker in taking steps to organize society and the economy for war. Naturally enough, the process began with the War Measures Act, which had been initially used in the First World War and which was actually anticipated on August 25, 1939, when the government declared

Our Finest Hour

a state of "apprehended war," initiated the mobilization of the navy, and designated army reserve units. The Defence of Canada Regulations, a set of emergency security measures set up under the War Measures Act and put in place on September 3, 1939, allowed the waiving of jury trials and *habeas corpus*, the interning of enemy aliens and those hostile to participation in the war, the prohibition of subversive publications and organizations, and the censoring of media (especially bits of information that could be useful to the enemy or damaging to Canadian morale or recruitment). These were just first indicators of the degree of federal government control over the lives of Canadians; by the end of the war, it would be heavily pervasive.

To enforce these measures and the literally thousands to come, federal civil service appointments began to grow rapidly from approximately 9,000 in 1939 to nearly 53,000 in 1946. Many appointments were temporary, and those who fulfilled them were housed in Ottawa in clapboard "temporary" buildings, many of which were still standing decades later. (Appointment figures are not the same as the number of persons in the service, a number that is difficult to ascertain since people moved in and out of the civil service throughout the war.) But in all, the Civil Service Commission oversaw some 300,000 assignments from 1939 to 1946.

The government established more than fifty independent organizations during the war, some industrial, some regulatory, which hired their own personnel and set their own pay scales. In fact, some people regarded working for the federal government as part of their civic duty. Minister of Munitions and Supply C.D. Howe enlisted a group of business executives to volunteer their services to help set up and manage some of these new organizations. They became known as "C.D. Howe's dollar-a-year men," or "Howe's boys," whose salaries were paid by the corporations they had been employed by prior to the war but who worked full-time for the federal government.[2]

The most important of the new federal agencies established at the outset of the war was the Wartime Prices and Trade Board (WPTB), created on September 3, 1939, to control inflation, set prices and wages, license businesses selling consumer goods, prosecute hoarders, and manage the distribution of scarce items. The WPTB's powers derived directly from the War Measures Act, which gave it a mandate to interfere in virtually every aspect of the war economy, setting aside for the duration the distribution of powers between the federal and provincial governments that had been laid out in the British North America Act, Canada's constitution at the time. The WPTB's mandate was simple: take any measure necessary to avoid the runaway inflation that had plagued the economy in the First World War and set aside free enterprise for the duration, where necessary, to control the national labour and commodity market. Chair Donald Gordon quickly oversaw the issuance of order-in-council PC 7440, which limited wage increases to 1926–29 levels. The move was very unpopular with Canadian workers, whose grievances began to show up with increases in the number of strikes and other industrial actions—even in war industries—within twenty-four months. About 16,000 woman volunteers working for the board's Consumers' Branch kept a close watch on price increases and possible profiteering by local businesses across Canada. The board also tried to control rents across Canada; the influx of rural Canadians into the cities in pursuit of war-industry jobs and the significant burgeoning of military personnel and their families in garrison towns also pushed rents up very quickly. In fact, wartime housing was one of the greatest challenges the federal government faced.[3]

The board also set maximum prices for coal, butter, sugar, and wool by mid-1940, and eventually a sweeping ration system was instituted that allocated virtually all consumer products, from fabric for clothing to meat, gasoline, and fats and oils. The aim was to stifle consumer demand so as to keep prices reasonable—thus also stifling upward pressure on wages—but most importantly to make sure strategic materials were available for the equipping, feeding, clothing, and housing of the burgeoning military forces and the production of the weapons and munitions they would fight with. Under the Combined Boards regimen first established by the Americans and the British in Washington at the end of December 1941 and the beginning of January 1942 (referred to in Chapter 8), Canada also had Allied production quotas to fill—from the assembly of army trucks to the shipment of bacon and almost everything in between. Thus the board was even responsible for controlling prices on many second-hand goods, such as civilian vehicles, which were not produced during the war. For the most part, the board did a more-than-adequate job, keeping inflation over the course of the war to just under 20 percent for the whole six years, with much of that coming in the first year of the war before the board had greatly broadened its own mandate.

* * * *

The Second World War can be considered the most expensive public works project in Canadian history, and, like all government projects, it had to be paid for. In order to do so, the government raised income and corporate taxes severalfold, put a limit on earnings by taxing back virtually all income over fixed amounts, and borrowed heavily from the Canadian people.[4] The borrowing was done through the issuance of Victory Bonds and War Savings Certificates, which promised to pay

Canadians a good interest on the money they were investing in the war effort after the war was over. Investment in Victory Bonds and War Savings Certificates was, strictly speaking, voluntary, but the ongoing public bond and certificate drives, usually featuring well-known personalities and the occasional Canadian war hero, created much moral pressure on Canadians to save. Campaigns were carried on in schools and factories, churches and community associations. Schoolchildren were encouraged to contribute pennies that would eventually add up to quarters and, eventually, entire certificates. Rallies were held in war industry factories. The War Savings Certificates alone eventually covered half the cost of the country's war. There were ten Victory Bond campaigns, with bonds mostly purchased by businesses. Canadians bought bonds and certificates for two primary reasons: it was a way of supporting the war effort, and they had little else to spend their money on. And despite very high taxes, the unemployment of the Great Depression disappeared quickly once war and farm production was in full swing, and people had more money in their pockets than at any time since 1929.

* * * *

C.D. Howe and the Department of Munitions and Supply was the orchestra leader; Canadian factories, shipyards, universities, the National Research Council, and the many new government corporations established to produce goods that Canadian factories couldn't were the orchestra. The department was established in the spring of 1940 to retool industry for war and, without scandal or major problems, set in motion a second "industrial revolution" in Canada. Investment in industry doubled during the 1939–43 period. Howe took Canada from bust to boom and from a nation that made light bulbs to one that built advanced radars and communications equipment, not to mention heavy bombers, sophisticated anti-submarine vessels, trucks, tanks, ammunition and small arms of all sorts, and other advanced military gear. One of the best examples is the way the nation's shipbuilding developed from the start of the war to the end.

By the fall of France, when it became increasingly important to secure shipping and replace lost ships, Canada had just started to build corvettes for the protection of its own coastal shipping. Britain soon placed orders for twenty-six 10,000-tonne cargo ships and orders for more corvettes and minesweepers. This was just the beginning, as Britain made clear it needed Canada to build as many naval and merchant ships as it possibly could. The practically non-existent Canadian interwar shipbuilding industry (three shipyards employing fewer than 4,000 men) expanded to ninety shipyards on the East and West Coasts and the Great Lakes. More than 126,000 men and women were employed. Overall, Canadian shipyards built 4,047 naval vessels, 300 anti-submarine warships, 4 Tribal class destroyers, 410 cargo ships, and 348 Park merchant ships (10,000-tonnes, slow but reliable, and able to handle all kinds of cargo). Shipyard workers got faster and production times dropped significantly by mid-1942.[5]

* * * *

In July 1940 a new Department of National War Services (DNWS) was established to mobilize the civilian population, find every last male eligible for military service, and coordinate and supervise volunteer efforts. Its portfolio of concerns was unmanageably large, so it underwent some changes beginning in 1942, but it always retained responsibility for the supervision of voluntary work. One of the key things the DNWS did was set up local citizen committees to optimize the effectiveness of volunteer groups. Some private organizations such as the YMCA, the Knights of Columbus, the Salvation Army, and the Canadian Legion were given funds and a mandate to provide comforts to training soldiers and those overseas. These groups eventually came under the purview of the Directorate of Auxiliary Services within the Department of National Defence.

The most important step taken by Ottawa to place the national economy and national man- and woman-power under its direction for the duration of the war was the National Resources Mobilization Act (NRMA), passed in June 1940 to secure public safety, defend Canada, maintain order, and exert control over employment.[6] The act's ultimate mandate was within its title. Any resource—human, agricultural, or industrial—was henceforth to be at the call of the nation, to be deployed and or regulated as necessary to assure that the nation's total war effort was fully utilized for the common good. The National Resources Mobilization Act was the umbrella legislation first used to begin military training for home defence for Canadian men who had not volunteered for overseas service.[7]

The national war effort had a profound impact on Canadian women, though the extent to which it was a lasting impact is still the subject of considerable debate among historians. The initial impact was greatest in the voluntary sector, where women employed in traditional occupations—housewives and others—could make a contribution to the war without significantly changing their daily lives. In the fall of 1940, the government created the Women's Voluntary Services Division, which directed woman volunteers into dozens of jobs that they could do while maintaining their traditional ways of life. But it soon became obvious that women could and should play a significant role in replacing men in

Our Finest Hour

tasks such as the Air Raid Protection Program (ARP), which called on them to maintain blackouts in Canadian communities, but also trained them in blackout, air raid, and emergency drills and first aid. Two hundred thousand women volunteered for air raid service.[8]

Women also began to volunteer for the military in large numbers and in military occupations far more diverse than the nursing services in which they had played such an important role overseas in the First World War. Nursing was a long-established traditional war role for women, but in late June 1941 the government established the Canadian Women's Army Corps (which eventually attracted about 22,000 women); this was followed in early July 1941 by the establishment of the Royal Canadian Air Force Women's Division (which eventually took in some 17,000 women) and, at the end of July 1942, the Women's Royal Canadian Naval Services (with an eventual complement of about 6,800 women). These women received rudimentary military training, were issued uniforms, conformed to military rank structure, and largely performed administrative jobs that had once been filled by men. About half of the women who signed up were married, supplementing family incomes as their men went into the military services or earning a steady wage for the first time themselves; mothers, however, were not allowed. Recruitment depended on the idea that these measures were only temporary and would not in any way compromise the femininity on which women's traditional gender role was based. The recruitment message was conflicted, however, because society itself was: on the one hand women were absolutely necessary for the war effort, but on the other hand they were supposed to conform to traditional male notions of chastity, deportment, dress, and conduct.

It's a sad truth that the work women did in the military was often traditionally "female" or women's work—they were bat women, waitresses, cleaners, clerks, etc. Only about 10 percent went overseas to serve, though an increasing number of women were recruited to fly bombers and transport aircraft over the northeast staging route, mostly to replace men who were being sent into the bomber war over Europe. Female personnel were often harassed, discriminated against, and always paid less than men. Instead of tackling these systemic problems, government, industry, and the military bided their time, certain that all would return to normal when the men came home and the women went back to their housekeeping and knitting. Women were being utilized to win the war, not to change their role in society.[9]

In fact, many women's lives remained basically the same throughout the war. The question was, were changes going to be permanent for those women who signed up or went out to work? Historian Ruth Roach Pierson says that gender stereotypes and biased government policies allowed only minor breakthroughs for women, and those breakthroughs were clawed back in the postwar years (because they caused such desperate social anxiety).[10] Postwar, women in uniform (excluding nurses) were seen as a menace to the traditional family and a moral threat. But the good part was, those wartime experiences created a climate of broadened expectations and a sense of confidence, self-respect, and pride that really boosted women's general outlook. Still, there were many changes within wartime households. With the men away, women had greater responsibilities for family finances and household maintenance. They had to fend for themselves in dealing with the coal salesman, the man who changed windows twice a year, or the plumbers and electricians who came to make repairs. And those in the upper classes had less domestic help in doing so. They all had to deal with rationing and shortages, and essentially hunting for the best available grocery bargains on foot or on public transit. Meal planning around shortages and allotments was difficult. They had to learn basic repair and maintenance work around the house (e.g., in plumbing and heating), while money problems in some cases forced women to work outside the home whether they wanted to or not. Overall, the term "housewife" was invested with a higher status during the war.

The women's division of the National Selective Service was created in May 1942.[11] It was very careful to initially recruit only single women, approaching wives and mothers only after the invasion of Sicily. Childcare services and tax breaks were offered as an incentive to work. Generally, women's participation in the paid workforce was greater during the war years (they could work even after marriage and could get higher-status jobs). There were a larger number of the people in better jobs of a wider variety. Men still held workplace authority, but increasingly women claimed that they deserved equal pay for equal work. A lot of effort was put into reassuring people that not much was changing and that by working for wages during the war women were only being patriotic. Childcare was a huge problem only partly addressed, and child neglect was often blamed on or attributed to working mothers—sending a contradictory message that women must work to advance the war effort but that women with children shouldn't work, lest the kids be neglected or even go bad.

By June 1941 the number of women workers was 100,000 more than in 1931, and the demand for women to take up paid labour only got stronger after that, as the pool of male civilian workers dried up. Mackenzie King stated that the most important aspect of the 1942 National Selective Service program was to recruit women. The peak of female employment occurred in the fall of 1944, when more than a million women were working full-time (many others worked part-time only and about another 800,000 were working on farms). Almost half of the full-timers were in the service sector, with just slightly less than that in manufacturing positions; 180,000 were in trade and finance, 31,000 in transportation and communication, and 4,000 in construction. Women's numbers in the civil service went up significantly from the prewar years. As the military situation improved for the Allies, consumer groups began the campaign to encourage women to go home after the war and put the needs of the male breadwinner veterans first. Some were glad to get back to their old lives. But few had any real choice.

It is difficult to connect the advances women made in the Second World War to the rise of feminism in the early 1960s; the drive for equal opportunity for women in colleges and universities, the professions, the civil service (in fact all manner of public and private employment); and the campaign for equal pay for equal work. Women in wartime were asked, coaxed even, to leave stereotypical roles and to take on new responsibilities, but only for the duration of the war, after which everything was supposed to go back to where it was before. Postwar women, at least those in the middle class, were supposed to play an auxiliary role in society, supporting males by raising children, keeping the floors and the laundry clean, and welcoming their husbands home after a day at work. They were materially much better off than they had been in 1939, but their role in society had changed little.

* * * *

It is impossible to generalize about what life was like for the eleven million or so Canadians who did not go off to war between 1939 and 1945. For many, record taxation, war savings, long work hours, few wage increases, high rents, rationing, shortages of certain foods and consumer products, and overcrowding in cities added to the emotional strain of bad war news and—for those with husbands, boyfriends, or fathers overseas—constant worry. In today's world of ubiquitous instant communication—where even soldiers at war get frequent opportunities to phone, Skype, or email their loved ones (sometimes even on a daily basis)—it is very difficult to imagine that couples in the Second World War were often separated for years. Their only means of communication was mail—letters and parcels, and sometimes individually recorded phonographs—that took weeks to cross the ocean by military mail services. In some instances, as historian Jeff Keshen has pointed out, the distance and the emotional strains it precipitated allowed for greater infidelity. Men at war were men at war, after all, and far away for long periods—and the link between war and sex is as old as war itself—while some women who were awakening to their own importance and self-worth, not as extensions of male society, but in their own right, seem to have taken greater licence when it came to fidelity.[12]

The popular music people listened to and danced to—blues, big band, swing—was dominated by themes of loneliness, distance, separation, pleas for fidelity by both men and women, hope for better times after the war. The runaway hit of the war was "White Christmas," from the movie *Holiday Inn* with Bing Crosby, Fred Astaire, Marjorie Reynolds, Virginia Dale, and Walter Abel, which was released in August 1942. Written, ironically, by American Jewish songwriter Irving Berlin, it quickly topped the charts for months in both Canada and the United States at a time when the Allies were still struggling to turn back the Axis tide in almost every theatre of war. Canadian musicians, such as the big band Guy Lombardo and His Royal Canadians, wrote, sang, and played the same sort of music at home. Every major hotel in every Canadian city had its Saturday night dances in the hotel ballroom, with most of the men in uniform and the women doing their best to be attractive despite the many wartime restrictions on nylon for stockings, cosmetics, fabric for clothes, leather for shoes.

Wartime marriages were risky and their numbers boomed when war broke out.[13] There were many reasons to marry: incomes were better, the government offered dependents' allowances for servicemen's families, a commitment could help get people through tough times, intense feelings were generated in wartime, and some married men could get out of military service entirely.

Although divorce was still a relatively difficult process, the number of divorces went up during the war, as did the number of desertions and abandonments. Some groups, religious and military, existed to help mediate problems between spouses.

Separation from loved ones was presumed to create loneliness and depression, and a whole industry grew up around keeping people in touch with loved ones, neighbours, and even acquaintances. Letters were the most important component in this, but there were also photographs, phonographs (of a loved one's voice, made in-store), and radio shows. When it came to infidelity, suspicion was often worse than reality, but while women at home had to appear behaviourally in line or risk getting their allowances cut off, servicemen abroad sowed their wild oats.

Some servicemen overseas or in Canadian towns and cities burgeoning with BCATP airfields, naval bases, or new army barracks, became like debauched tourists, and many took advantage of the unique circumstances of war to conduct themselves in ways they would not normally have. Key to this was the assumption that these actions could be left behind when they were transferred, or the war ended, and there would be no consequences. And it seemed logical to believe that life was short and no opportunity for adventure should be passed up. The prevalence of gambling, booze, sex, female "camp followers," prostitution, and VD outbreaks (especially in Quebec, where they finally generated franker discussion and better treatments) contributed to widespread concern that the war had created terrible permanent changes. Despite many raids on brothels in the bigger cities, the sex trade persisted. Demand was too high!

About 48,000 war brides came to Canada during and after the war, most of them in 1945 and 1946. The majority of them were from Britain, but they also came from Belgium, Germany, Italy, France, and the Netherlands. The Canadian Army officially discouraged these unions but accepted the inevitable marriages—the Canadian government paid for the women to travel to Canada. The outcomes of these marriages varied widely: Some war brides were immediately abandoned, and between 5 and 10 percent of the brides returned to their home countries (with no help from the Canadian government). Of those who stayed, many had a difficult transition to married life in Canada, due to isolation, language issues, climate, unfriendly in-laws, different food and customs, infidelity, inflated expectations, and discrimination. Many were successful in their marriages, and others stayed because with children and no money, they had few options. But the majority soon adjusted and became staunch pillars of the communities they settled into.[14]

* * * *

The Canadian Broadcasting Corporation may have experienced its finest hour in the Second World War. War correspondents such as Peter Stursberg and Matthew Halton filed their reports—short-wave broadcasts—on the Canadian fighting forces from as close to the front as safety would allow, in sound trucks that were miniature recording studios. One CBC announcer, Lorne Greene, became known as the "Voice of Doom" both because of the deep cadence of his voice and because he began his announcing career early in the war, when much of the CBC's news from the front was bad. Canada also produced a corps of new war correspondents such as Ross Munro, Gregory Clark, and Charles Lynch, whose postwar careers would stretch over many decades. In the manner of the day, many of these men felt a patriotic duty to tell Canadians that the glass was almost always half full—instead of half empty, as they knew from the evidence before their own eyes. Munro's early reports from Dieppe stressed accomplishment, rather than the terrible tragedy he had seen unfold.[15] This was not the result of official censorship, but of self-censorship. In this global war against the unspeakable horror of the Axis enemy, they, too, were soldiers. Very few British or American correspondents did otherwise.

Despite the emotional strains of war, the standard of living of most Canadians definitely improved over the course of the war, and they were much better off at the end of it than at the beginning. Salaries rose from prewar levels and, with tight government controls over prices, increased more than the price of consumer goods. People had more available cash, and even though retail and grocery costs were up, there were few "big ticket" items to buy and many more incentives to save through Victory Bonds and War Certificates. When the war ended and hubbies and boyfriends returned to start families, savings poured into new homes, household goods such as stoves, electric refrigerators, radios, and—eventually, by 1946 and 1947—new cars. The buying spree caused huge problems for the federal government because most of the products wanted by consumers were manufactured in the United States; but it also marked the beginning of a rapid enlargement of the middle class, which was also helped along by veterans' benefits that sent hundreds of thousands of veterans to schools, colleges, and universities and helped them obtain loans for new homes.

The number of unionized workers doubled during the war, as men and women flooded into war plants, mines, shipyards, and other industrial facilities such as steel, aluminum, and nickel factories, and the mines that produced the ores out of which the guns and bullets and bombers were made. Organizing drives always produce labour militancy, and no less so during wartime, especially when many workers were convinced that government war policies—particularly limits on wages—unfairly discriminated against them. At the start of the war, federal labour laws were completely outdated. Far more liberal reforms had been introduced in the United States with the 1935 National Labor Relations Act (The Wagner Act) that gave workers the right to organize collectively, outlawed unfair labour practices, and compelled employers to bargain with unions that had been freely chosen by workers in government-managed certification votes. Canadian workers, most of whom were affiliated with international unions that spanned the Canada-US border, demanded the same thing. Labour unrest gave way to strikes even in industries directly related to the war effort. Some government officials and politicians saw these strikes as the products of unpatriotic agitators, but cooler heads eventually prevailed, and in February 1944 the government issued order-in-council PC 1003, which adopted the Wartime Labour Relations Regulations and essentially grafted the major provisions of the US Wagner Act onto Canadian labour law.[16] After the war, the provisions of PC 1003 were extended in peacetime legislation but covered only workers in federal jurisdictions and federally owned Crown corporations (since labour legislation in peacetime is largely within the provincial domain).

Most Canadians tolerated rationing and controls and did what they could to support the war effort in what they reused, recycled, or purchased second-hand. Had they not, there was no way that the government's various boards and agencies would have been able to enforce the strict rationing and consumption regimes that they did. The enforcers were too few, and the jails were not large enough. Thus the war showed an example of civil society banding together to face a common threat. But in a country of almost 13,000,000 people, there was bound to be cheating around the edges. Hoarding was unpatriotic at the least, and black marketeering was simply illegal, as were price fixing, skimming, failure to report excess profits (which were heavily taxed), or stealing salvage to sell to the government at exorbitant prices. It was easy for a grocer to hoard cans of fruit cocktail to sell, under the counter, to the highest bidder and fail to collect the appropriate ration coupon, for example. Or for counterfeiters to distribute fake ration booklets. Black-market activities included trading ration coupons or commodities, outlawed in September 1943; using the coupons of others via theft, impersonation, etc. (shopkeepers were in charge of making sure the person and name on the coupons matched); and offering or accepting cash bonuses or coupons for guaranteed availability or better quality than the standard. Illegal sales of meat were apparently the biggest area of cheating the ration rules, as many Canadians felt plentiful meat was their due, given all the hard physical work they were doing.

* * * *

Not everyone in Canada was a "happy warrior" in this effort to create a united home front in support of the war. There was some political opposition to the war by religious pacifists and conscientious objectors, such as members of the Mennonite community. The National War Service Regulations of 1940 recognized two categories of conscientious objectors (COs): 1) Mennonites and Doukhobors, who had entered

Canada decades earlier with specific promises of exemption from any compulsory military service and 2) other conscientious objectors (such as Seventh Day Adventists) prohibited by their religion from bearing arms. Mennonites and Doukobors both received postponements of military training, though not exemptions, but even those postponements were subject to cancellation. All COs were eventually required to perform non-combatant military service. Application for postponement for those persons was dealt with through an autonomous local board; thus there was disparity in recognition of COs, depending on where they lived, and differences in the way applications were accepted or rejected.

There was certainly more support for this war in French Canada than there had been for the First World War, and many more volunteers for the military services, but not nearly enough to fulfill government hopes for more than a relatively small number of all-French-speaking regiments in the army or squadrons in the air force. The Wartime Information Board (WIB) tried to deal directly with the conscription "crisis" of 1942 and the bad publicity surrounding it, creating propaganda that spelled out the anti-Christian nature of fascism and confronting rumours about French-Canadian soldiers getting the worst of it in actions such as at the Dieppe Raid. But the significant lack of francophone participation in the prewar militia, and decades of mistrust from the 1885 Riel Rebellion to the First World War conscription crisis in 1917, gave the WIB little purchase in Quebec. Many prominent Quebecers, such as future prime minister Pierre Elliott Trudeau, opposed the war, as did many who had developed strong sympathies for the Vichy regime, which Canada continued to recognize until late 1942. Until then, Vichy continued to reach out to Quebec for support, and did indeed have the attention of some of the Quebec intelligentsia as well as members of the clergy. It did so because it stressed values such as work, religion, rejection of state liberalism, and authoritarian (read Roman Catholic Church) control, which closely paralleled major objectives in rural Quebec society.

Perhaps the most egregious example of Ottawa suppressing suspected "enemy aliens" was the exile of Japanese-Canadians, most of whom were citizens, born in Canada, from the West Coast to the interior of British Columbia, the eastern slopes of the Rockies, and as far east as Ontario. The Japanese had already been discriminated against for decades before the war, but the Japanese attack on Pearl Harbor, the Japanese navy's romp across the Pacific, and the Japanese army's stunning victories in Southeast Asia and China ramped that discrimination up to incredible levels. From the time of the bombing of Pearl Harbor, government policy (opposed by the CCF members) supported and institutionalized what had been a more informal hatred for the Japanese. With no trials or charges, the Japanese were uprooted from their homes and neighbourhoods in early 1942, and sent to refugee camps far from the coast, often to do forced labour. By September 1942, 22,000 Japanese-Canadians had been forced inland. Their homes, businesses, fishing boats, and personal property were confiscated and sold, without their receiving any compensation. As the war came to a close, King set up "loyalty commissions" to interview Japanese-Canadians and determine who was "faithful" to Canada; those who didn't pass or who refused to be interviewed were deported (about 4,000 people in all). The restrictions on Japanese-Canadians lasted until four years after the war (1949) and a formal apology and cash compensation offer was made only in 1988.[17] Internment was not limited to the Japanese-Canadians: 660 Germans and 480 Italians were also interned for the duration of the war.

* * * *

Canada was simply not the same country in 1945 as it had been in 1939, partly because of the rapid changes within society itself, partly because of the years-long anxiety of the war, partly because of the changing relationship between men and women both inside and outside families, and partly because Canadians had become used to the idea that an activist government could smooth out inequalities and aspire to social justice. It is clear from the by-election and provincial election results of August 1943 and the year that followed that these deep-seated changes were beginning to manifest themselves through the political process. The civil-service mandarins began to see it early in the war; the CCF, Conservative Party, and Liberal intellectuals and backbenchers took a bit longer but were on board for significant changes in the role of the federal government by the late summer of 1943. Eventually the prime minister, too, saw it, and his old, almost buried social activism, combined with his innate sense of political survival, awakened him to action. The revolution in how the people related to the government and vice versa was truly launched by the beginning of 1944; even the wily old Mackenzie King preferred to "gift" these sweeping new programs to the people of Canada after the Nazis had been defeated, rather than while the war was still grinding on. But the tactic worked. On June 11, 1945, King's Liberals won a majority government, taking 125 seats to the Progressive Conservatives' 67, while 28 went to the CCF, 13 to Social Credit (almost all in Alberta), and 12 to independents, many of whom were actually Quebec Liberals. In the first peacetime budget, many of the promised changes were put in train. The government had not entered the war with a strategy for social change, but it was intent on avoiding the near chaos that had marked Robert Borden's domestic leadership of the First World War and then, when it saw that Canadians would no longer tolerate the status quo ante bellum, it placed itself at the head of the drive for change in Canada. In these ways, it was far more successful in providing national leadership than it was unsuccessful in achieving significant leadership in Canadian war strategy.

CHAPTER 8

FIGHTING AS
A COLONY: CANADA'S
WARTIME STRATEGY

August 18, 1943: This was to be a very big day for William Lyon Mackenzie King. King was staying at The Citadelle, in Quebec City, a fortress built by the British between 1820 and 1831, which incorporated parts of the old French fortifications and which had been used as the residence of the Lieutenant-Governor of Quebec since the 1870s. The fortress had also become the official residence of the Royal 22nd Regiment after the First World War. It afforded a magnificent view of the St. Lawrence River, which flowed past it at the foot of a tall escarpment toward the old city just a few kilometres to the west. King was in Quebec City to host a conference—dubbed Quadrant—between President Franklin D. Roosevelt and Prime Minister Winston S. Churchill, their military staffs and the Combined Chiefs of Staff, which effectively ran the military aspects of the war in the West. The Combined Chiefs had been formed at the Arcadia Conference between Churchill and FDR, which took place in Washington in late December 1941 and early January 1942 to coordinate the military forces of the two nations and all their allies. No other member of the United Nations coalition was represented on the Combined Chiefs, and although Mackenzie King had, by this time, had several one-on-one meetings with Churchill and Roosevelt to discuss various aspects of the war, he had never been a participant in any joint strategic discussions with them. Nor would he this time. He was to host the two commanders-in-chief, but in the words of historian Charles P. Stacey, "So far as the Quebec Conference proper—the meetings of the Combined Chiefs of Staff—was concerned, the Canadians had no more to do with it than if it had been held in Timbuctoo."[1]

Mackenzie King first heard of the possibility that Churchill and Roosevelt would meet in Quebec City on July 11 in a telegram from Churchill. He discussed his possible response with Under Secretary of State for External Affairs Norman Robertson and UK High Commissioner to Canada Malcolm MacDonald. King was most anxious to take advantage of an opportunity to hold an important war strategy conference in Canada, but was unsure of what his own position would be with respect to the meetings between Churchill and Roosevelt. Robertson pointed out that if the two leaders met at Quebec, Mackenzie King would have to "be with them as an equal . . . the people of Canada would expect [him] to be in full conference with both Churchill and Roosevelt." Mackenzie King "saw the force of this but felt embarrassment in the matter" because he did not want to lay down any conditions for the meeting, especially ones he knew Churchill and Roosevelt would not agree to. As he recorded in his diary, "To try to get Churchill and Roosevelt to agree to this would be more than could be expected of them. They would wish to take the position that jointly they have supreme direction of the war. I have conceded them that position." The answer, then, was to very publicly host the two men in such a way as to give Canadians the impression that Canada's prime minister was very much a part of the conference "without having the question raised too acutely or defended too sharply." Malcolm Mac-Donald undertook to clarify Mackenzie King's position to Churchill, and several days later, Churchill's reply showed clearly that he completely understood what Mackenzie King wanted. King wrote, "Telegram was most satisfactory and made quite clear Churchill saw the need of the conference appearing to be a British-American-Canadian conference. Malcolm and I laughed very heartily as we read Churchill's words 'Anglo-American-Canadian' . . . Whole message most buoyant and cheerful . . . When I become host to the P.M. of Great Britain and President of the U.S. at a conference with them both at Quebec in the Old Capital of Canada, it will be a pretty good answer to the Tory campaign of 'our leaders Churchill and the President.'"[2]

Mackenzie King sometimes deluded himself that Roosevelt was a closer colleague, and more sympathetic to Canadian aspirations in the war, than was Churchill, the old imperialist who had even opposed the Statute of Westminster in 1931, which gave the dominions of Canada, Australia, New Zealand, the Irish Free State, and South Africa formal constitutional independence. In fact, Roosevelt strongly opposed Canadian participation in this or any other high-level meeting between himself and Churchill or representation on the Combined Chiefs of Staff. As Churchill wrote in his memoirs, "The President, while gladly accepting Canadian hospitality, did not feel it possible that Canada should be formally a member of the Conference, as he apprehended similar demands by Brazil and other American partners in the United Nations. We also had to think of the claims of Australia and the other Dominions. This delicate question was solved and surmounted by the broadminded outlook of the Canadian Prime Minister and Government. I for my part was determined that we and the United States should have the Conference to ourselves in view of all the vital business we had in common."[3]

Thus on August 18, 1943, Mackenzie King rose to readings and prayer before breakfast, then turned his attention to the arrangements for a formal dinner to be held that evening. He had "considerable discussion" with one of his staff regarding the question of serving cocktails—he had sworn off alcohol for the duration of the war; Churchill and Roosevelt had done no such thing! Then he lay down for a short rest before attending a lunch at the Château Frontenac hotel, given by Churchill in honour of the Governor General Lord Athlone and his wife, Princess Alice. After lunch, the three leaders retired to the terrace for photographs. Mackenzie King smiled for the cameras, captured for posterity sitting with Churchill and Roosevelt. Canada's newspapers reported the event as if he were conferring with the US and UK leaders over war matters, an impression reinforced by Mackenzie King himself in a radio address to the nation. It was all a grand show for the cameras, because while from the very start of the war, Mackenzie King and his government aimed to demonstrate to Canadians that Canada was fighting as an ally alongside first the United Kingdom and then the USSR and the United States, Canada's major war effort on land, at sea, and in the air—and in factories and on farms—was in fact really more that of a colony than an ally.

* * * *

In his sweeping study of both the interpersonal and professional relationships of Roosevelt, Churchill, General Sir Alan Brooke, and General George C. Marshall, British historian Andrew Roberts writes, "It is surprising how little influence Canadians enjoyed in the higher direction of the Second World War. They had the world's third largest navy at one point, pushed furthest inland of any of the armies on D-Day, were fabulously generous to British coffers throughout the war, contributing much more than the Americans per capita, and provided the only two armed and trained divisions standing between the south coast and London after Dunkirk. Yet they had virtually no say on the various bodies that ultimately decided when and where Canadians would fight."[4] The question is an intriguing one, especially in light of the government's consistent policy, from the very beginning of the war, of ensuring that Canada's fighting forces be recognizably Canadian, serve together, and serve under Canadian commanders. The explanation for the almost total lack of Canadian participation in the making of higher Allied war strategy that Andrews points out must ultimately begin with William Lyon Mackenzie King himself.

When war loomed in late summer 1939, Mackenzie King had almost no international experience at all. As prime minister since 1920 (with a five-year Conservative interregnum from 1930–35), virtually all King's international experience focused on Imperial affairs with the overall objective of pushing the cause of Canadian autonomy forward whenever possible and as cautiously as necessary. In key Imperial conferences in the 1920s, Mackenzie King acted with his usual reticence in seeking to loosen the constitutional ties of Empire and to push for further definition of the vague commitment that Britain and the rest of the Imperial War Cabinet had made at their meeting in 1917 to create a postwar Empire of equal dominions.

In this regard, Mackenzie King was a firm nationalist. But when it came to international affairs—and in particular the growing international crises of the 1930s that eventually led to war—he showed interest but no particular expertise and no desire to intervene politically or diplomatically. Part of his reason was very personal. He was both a religious man and a man who believed that mediation and moderation were the only effective means of solving international disputes. But he was also very conscious of the religious, linguistic, and ethnic divisions that had nearly torn Canada apart in the First World War, particularly in the aftermath of the Conscription Crisis of 1917. He had thus come to the conclusion that if Canada attempted to stick its nose into international issues that had no apparent direct bearing on Canada, those divisions would re-emerge. King's most important objective in both domestic and international policy (and military affairs, for that matter) was national unity pure and simple. And he believed that the more active Canada was on the international stage, the more that unity would be threatened. Thus he himself was content to follow the lead of the British and the French in the interwar years, hoping that opportunities might also arrive when he might act as a lynchpin between the British and the Americans. The simple truth is that even with a handful of active and brilliant diplomats in its fledgling Department of External Affairs (and they were mostly trade experts), he and his government simply did not have the know-how to participate in higher strategic decision making.[5]

Not that he wanted to, either. If national unity was the chief war aim of the Mackenzie King government, second only to the overall Allied defeat of Hitler, of course, avoidance of conscription was its corollary. King believed that if he were to participate in the formulation of Allied strategy, he might well be called upon by Allied leaders—the prime ministers of Britain and France (until the French defeat in June 1940)—to raise substantial forces, particularly on the ground, in accordance with that strategy. This, combined with his real lack of understanding of geopolitics and military matters and his personal distaste for violence, meant that he seemed at the start of the war to have never given any thought to even expressing his views to Chamberlain or the French about how the war should be conducted, or how and where Canadian military resources might be used. That certainly suited Chamberlain and the French. Even before the start of hostilities, they had formed a rather loose Supreme War Council, fashioned after the body that had coordinated Anglo-French strategy in 1917 and 1918, which could have included representation from other Allied nations but never truly did. As far as Mackenzie King was concerned, the presence of an able and distinguished Canadian High Commissioner in London—Vincent Massey—along with a small but accomplished diplomatic corps and with Malcolm MacDonald in Ottawa, he would know everything he needed to know about the conduct of the war and could intervene directly with the British prime minister whenever he needed to. After all, as Adrian W. Preston has pointed out, conditions were quite different in 1940 than they had been in the First World War, when Prime Minister Robert Borden had gone to the United Kingdom twice to present his views on the war (and the shortcomings of British generals) directly to the British government. Now, "communications were multiple, expeditious, and dependable; and brought governmental scrutiny and influence directly to bear on the very field of battle."[6]

In the spring of 1940, Canadian Military Headquarters was set up in London as a direct representative of National Defence Headquarters in Ottawa to coordinate Canadian military issues overseas and to liaise directly with the British military. (Later in the war, a Canadian Joint Staff mission was also established in Washington.) Thus Ottawa and Mackenzie King did receive a constant flow of general and even secret information about events in the war, as did other Commonwealth prime ministers, but not at the highest levels and certainly not including the immensely important discussions and decisions between Churchill and Roosevelt. The information Canada regularly received never told of higher Allied war plans, nor were invitations extended to Canada to communicate Canadian desires to the United Kingdom regarding the use and deployment of its military forces. Mackenzie King was okay with that. For example, when 1st Canadian Infantry Division arrived in the United Kingdom in mid-December 1939, they immediately became part of a larger British formation. The division was first commanded by Major-General George Pearkes, a First World War Victoria Cross winner, but his operational commander was a British Corps commander. As in the First World War, Pearkes was responsible to the minister of national defence in Ottawa for administrative matters, but to the British for operational issues. As the war evolved and Canada's contribution grew, Canadian higher formations such as 1st and 2nd Canadian Corps and even First Canadian Army (stood up in France at the end of July 1944), all remained responsible to Ottawa for administrative matters but to their British higher-formation commanders in operations.

* * * *

Mackenzie King's executive for the running of the war was the Cabinet War Committee. Formed at the end of 1939, the committee was nominally supposed to coordinate Canadian defence policy, but in fact it operated in as wide a mandate as Mackenzie King wished it to. On May 27, 1940, the membership of the Cabinet War Committee was set at six—Mackenzie King himself, with the leader of the Senate and the ministers of national defence (Norman Rogers), finance, justice, and mines and resources. When the Department of Munitions and Supply (under Clarence Decatur Howe as mentioned) and the Ministries of National Defence for Air and National Defence for Naval Services were created, their ministers also became members of the Cabinet War Committee, as did the minister for national war services. The latter department was set up in the summer of 1940 to administer the National Resources Mobilization Act. As mentioned, the act was passed on June 23, 1940, to coordinate manpower, organize national selective service, and run conscription for home defence, among other key responsibilities. The Cabinet War Committee was dominated by Mackenzie King from first to last, even after it became a more formal body with the appointment of A.D.P. Heeney as clerk of the Privy Council, first secretary of cabinet, and secretary of the Cabinet War Committee in March 1940. This was no accident. Even in war, Mackenzie King saw military policy as having a high potential to create political crises, and he was determined to dominate military policy making.

The two most dominant members of the Cabinet War Committee after the death of Norman Rogers were J.L. Ralston and C.D. Howe. Ralston was thirty-eight when the Second World War broke out. A former battalion commander in the First World War, he was elected to Parliament as a Liberal in 1925 and became minister of national defence in Mackenzie King's government in 1926. He retained his post until the government was defeated in 1930. He was re-elected in 1935 but chose to retire from politics and practise law. When Canada went to war, Ralston felt the call of duty and re-entered the Mackenzie King government as minister of finance. During the first nine months of the war, Ralston resisted the entreaties of the military to increase defence spending, fully supported the prime minister's limited liability war effort, and stood solidly against any rapid expansion of the military. With Rogers's death in June 1940, he agreed to assume the position of minister of national defence. Even after the appointment of Charles Gavan "Chubby" Power and Angus Macdonald as ministers of national defence for air and national defence for naval services, respectively, Ralston maintained direct responsibility for the army but also acted as the senior of the three ministers in charge of overall Canadian military policy subject, of course, to the prime minister himself. Though Ralston had been a soldier, he tended to rely on the advice of civilians in his department more than on the military. His job was infinitely demanding, and once the decision had been made to abandon limited liability and push toward a much more robust mobilization, he guided that process expeditiously. But Ralston had little strategic sense, listened to British advice (and prejudices) too much, and tended to agree with the last person he had discussed a problem with. He had supported conscription since at least late 1941 and resigned over it in the fall of 1944.

C.D. Howe was a US-born engineer and businessman who came to Canada early in his career and made a fortune building grain elevators in western Canada. His reputation as a man who got things done in time and on budget grew rapidly, and he was recruited to run for the Liberals in Port Arthur in 1935. He proved to be as strong a candidate as he was a boss, and with his reputation in the grain elevator business, he was easily elected and retained his seat until 1957. Howe was named minister of railways and canals (which later became transport) in the new government, and one of his first accomplishments was the establishment of Trans-Canada Air Lines as a Crown corporation in 1937. In 1940, Mackenzie King named him to head the new and all-important Department of Munitions and Supply, and Howe quickly got down to work to build a department that was soon in charge of all Canadian war production. As mentioned, to achieve his aims, he recruited dozens of leading industrialists and businessmen from across Canada as "dollar-a-year-men"—their companies paid their salaries but they worked with Howe in various ways as heads of new Crown corporations or within his department for a token government salary of $1 a year. If Howe perceived a need to get the government into an area of war production that private companies could not do, he gave the job to the one of the dozens of Crown corporations established for specific purposes. For the production of Lancaster bombers, for example, the government established Victory Aircraft at Malton airport in Toronto.

Mackenzie King never shied from seeking advice from his military when he felt he had no choice, but he was not eager to seek it out. The Chiefs of Staff met regularly on the Defence Council, but its influence on war policy was nominal.[7] Beginning in June 1942, the Chiefs of Staff began to meet with the Cabinet War Committee every two weeks. Mackenzie King almost never met alone with the Chiefs of Staff except on an informal, ad hoc basis and almost never with all of them at the same time unless it was on ceremonial occasions—such as when Churchill visited Ottawa in December 1941, Quebec City in August 1943, and again in Quebec City for the Octagon Conference in September 1944. The prime minister met with the Chiefs of the General Staff (army), particularly Lieutenant-Generals H.D.G. Crerar, Ken Stuart, and J.C. Murchie, as necessary and almost always in combination with his minister of national defence (Norman Rogers until his death in June 1940 and J.L. Ralston after that). Thus he relied heavily on the advice of his ministers of national defence. And since his ministers of national defence had no information regarding the higher direction of the war anyway, neither did the Cabinet War Committee or Mackenzie King. This remained a constant throughout the war and did not change even with the fall of France in June 1940. As Paul Dickson and Michael Roi write, "The crisis-driven military expansion of the early summer of 1940 was not reconciled to any government defence policy or coherent assessment of what Canada's objectives should be in the war beyond Mackenzie

King's national unity, no conscription agenda."[8] As for direct military input into the policy decisions of either the Cabinet War Committee, the prime minister, or the ministers of national defence, it too was sporadic, episodic, and inconsistent and usually connected to the political implications of military policy. Even after Harry Crerar tried to introduce consistency into military policy making during his time as Chief of the General Staff (1940–41), Mackenzie King's "disdain for his military advisors" remained a major obstacle to the integration of professional military advice into Canadian war policy.[9]

It is hard to overestimate how important this was in the making of Canadian war policy. Mackenzie King and his government made decisions about manpower, production, the financing of the war, etc., without being fully aware of the decisions being made by the British and the Americans regarding where they wanted to drive the war. So, for example, Canada's decision to field an army of five divisions and two independent armoured brigades was a decision rooted in Canadian considerations and decisions about how many able-bodied men should be allowed to serve in the army, as opposed to other branches of the armed services, industry, agriculture, or other endeavours. It was not based on any higher coordination with the British or the Americans on what the Allies might hope to achieve in their drive for victory, or when they might hope to achieve it. The same situation applied to the debate, which started very early, over whether conscription would be needed to bolster voluntary enlistment. When conscription actually evolved into a full-fledged political crisis in November 1944, peak demand for infantry in the Canadian Army had long since passed, though Canada could hardly have known that—because it was not a party to higher Allied decision making and was not brought into the charmed circle of those who shared the results of deliberations at the highest Allied political and military decision-making level.

The Allied war situation changed drastically with Winston S. Churchill's accession to power in London in May 1940 and the French surrender on June 22, 1940. As minister of defence as well as prime minister, Churchill ran the British war effort. He consulted closely with his Chiefs of Staff, relying heavily on Sir John Dill, Chief of the Imperial General Staff until November 1941, and his successor, General Sir Alan Brooke, but as much to try out his own views as to seek advice. Churchill had been an officer in two wars, a war correspondent in two others, First Lord of the Admiralty (naval minister) at the start of the First World War, and minister of munitions after that. He read extensively in foreign affairs, military history, and defence matters and had strongly opposed appeasement in the 1930s. He considered himself a military expert, though he was often wrong in his strategic evaluations and plans, and believed in sweeping strategic moves and taking the offensive wherever and whenever possible. He certainly believed he knew a great deal more about war in general, and this war in particular, than the prime ministers of any of the dominions (even Jan Christiaan Smuts of South Africa, a retired Boer War general whom he actually consulted quite often), and he was right, especially in regard to Mackenzie King. King's reticence and Churchill's extreme self-confidence complemented each other very well. When, in early 1941, Australia pushed for a Second World War version of the Imperial War Cabinet of 1917, King and his Cabinet strongly resisted the idea, even though Australian prime minister Robert Menzies had told King on a visit to Ottawa in August 1940 that Churchill was, in effect, running the war by himself. But then, what possible advice could any dominion prime minister offer Churchill in those dark days after the fall of France? Or even after Hitler attacked the Soviet Union in June 1941? Canadian troops in the United Kingdom came under the command of the British in accordance with Canada's Visiting Forces Act, passed in the early 1930s, and thus the two Canadian divisions, which had been transported to the United Kingdom by the fall of 1940, went and did what the British Chiefs of Staff Committee told them to do, namely, help defend against a possible German invasion.

Although Churchill reached out to the Soviet Union immediately after it was attacked by the Nazis in June 1941, all he could do at that time was to send what little military aid Britain could spare—and that was not much. There was no planning of higher strategy between the British and the Soviets, especially because the USSR was barely hanging on as the Wehrmacht drove inexorably toward Moscow in the summer and fall of 1941. Britain had started higher military planning with the still-neutral United States in early 1941, aimed at determining "the best methods by which the armed forces of the United States and the British Commonwealth, with its allies, could defeat Germany and its allies, should the United States be compelled to resort to war."[10] The talks excluded dominion representatives, who were briefed by the British, setting a pattern that was later set by the Combined Chiefs of Staff when this entity was created after Pearl Harbor. The talks produced a planning document known as ABC-1, which called for continuous cooperation between the high commands of the United States and the United Kingdom in the event of war. Canada was barely mentioned, except insofar as it would cooperate with the United States in North American defence to the extent defined by Canada-US agreements.

The only such agreement at that time was the Ogdensburg Agreement, issued by Mackenzie King and Franklin Roosevelt at Ogdensburg, New York, on August 18, 1940. Roosevelt had invited Mackenzie King to meet him at the town of Ogdensburg on the south bank of the St. Lawrence River to discuss Canada-US cooperation in the defence of the Continent in light of the German triumph over France and the obvious difficulties that both nations would now face in defending the approaches to North America from across the Atlantic. At that meeting Roosevelt proposed the immediate establishment of a new Permanent Joint Board on Defence (United States-Canada), which would report directly to both the president and prime minister. The agreement was the first Canada-US defence arrangement ever and has formed the basis of Canada-US defence cooperation in defence of North America ever since. (The Permanent Joint Board on Defence, or PJBD, exists to this day.) The agreement came about because King was very worried about the defence of Atlantic Canada, given the state of Britain's defences, and Roosevelt was anxious for an opportunity to insert US defence planners directly into that defence. After all, Newfoundland (not yet a part of Canada) and Nova Scotia lay directly alongside the heavily travelled New York–Europe shipping lanes.

King obviously hoped that the PJBD would give Canada a direct say in North American defence planning (though that was often not the case), while Roosevelt hoped that it would place American military concerns directly in front of the Canadian government. Composed of both military and civilian members and chaired by former New York City mayor Fiorello H. LaGuardia, the PJBD began almost immediately to draw up plans for North American defence. The first (Basic Plan No. 1) addressed the question of what might be done in case Britain was forced to surrender or the Royal Navy lost control of the North Atlantic. The second (Joint Operational Plan No. 1) vested the "'strategic direction' of all land and air forces in the Chief of Staff of the United States Army, subject to prior consultations with the appropriate Canadian heads of service."[11] This plan was later supplemented by ABC-22, which provided that should the United States actually enter the war, Canadian-American mutual defence efforts were to be coordinated between the two militaries. That did not settle the matter of which nation would command what and when on the Atlantic coast. Although Newfoundland formally sought Canada's protection just after Ogdensburg, US forces tried repeatedly to take over the defence of the island.

The United States began to get involved in the defence of the North Atlantic after the French surrender. In late summer of 1940, Churchill began to suggest a plan to acquire First World War–era destroyers from the United States in return for ninety-nine-year leases for bases on British possessions located on an arc starting from Argentia Bay, Newfoundland, through Bermuda, and into the Caribbean. To Roosevelt and his commanders, such bases would provide the Americans with an ability to deploy air and naval forces to defend the Panama Canal in the south and the shipping approaches to New York and Boston in the north. The British agreed and the Destroyers for Bases Deal was born. Mackenzie King had played a marginal role in the arrangement, making the British case in a visit to Roosevelt in Georgia, where he very tentatively played intermediary between Churchill and the president on the issue of what Churchill might do with the Royal Navy in the event of a British defeat. Canada also took over seven of the fifty destroyers, which started to be transferred in September 1940.

In mid-August 1941 Roosevelt and Churchill met in Placentia Bay, Newfoundland, to define joint war aims should the United States enter the conflict. The two leaders signed the Atlantic Charter, which laid out joint objectives such as ensuring self-government, freer global trade, democracy, and human rights—which eventually became the basis of the United Nations Charter, promulgated in Washington at the beginning of January 1942 after the United States entered the war. The two men had been in continuing communication with each other from almost the beginning of the war when Roosevelt began a correspondence with Churchill that lasted until Roosevelt's death. King was notified about the meeting but was not invited. Thus the Argentia meeting, as it was called, set the pattern for the unique Roosevelt-Churchill collaboration that began to wither only in late 1944, when Britain's contribution to the war effort started paling in comparison to that of the United States and the Soviet Union.

The course of war shifted dramatically once again when Japan attacked Pearl Harbor on December 7, 1941, and began to run rampant in Southeast Asia, the southwest Pacific, Indonesia, and the Philippines. Churchill seized the opportunity to essentially invite himself and most of his Chiefs of Staff Committee to come to Washington for what became known as the Arcadia Conference—the first wartime conference between Churchill and Roosevelt. Churchill's purpose was to interject himself directly into American war plans before the Americans themselves could firm those plans up. To a degree, much of the discussion that took place in Washington evolved from the Anglo-American staff talks held earlier in the year. But in addition, the two allies decided to fight the war not as allies but as close coalition partners, joining together across a wide spectrum of areas from food production, to shipping assignments, to armaments production, and, of course, to high military strategy. They established a number of joint boards, the most important of which was the Combined Chiefs of Staff, based in Washington, which consisted of the British Chiefs of Staff Committee and the American Joint Chiefs of Staff.[12] They also agreed that in each strategic arena of war, a single commander would hold sway over all land, sea, and air forces in his jurisdiction. No other country was invited to join or even to observe the deliberations of the

Combined Chiefs of Staff, nor even to share the secret deliberations of the CCS. Canada was completely excluded.

The Combined Chiefs of Staff was the most important of the combined US and UK bodies established at the Arcadia Conference and subsequent to it, but it was not the only one. The Combined Munitions Assignment Board, the Combined Shipping Adjustment Board, and the Combined Raw Materials Board were also established. They were followed in 1942 by the Combined Food Board and the Combined Production and Resources Board. The purpose of all these boards was to effectively pool the war resources of the United States and Britain—which to the British meant the British Empire/Commonwealth including the dominions. Put in practical terms, these boards decided what to do with Allied war production, be it Canadian pork or American trucks, and what ships would carry it all.

This served both American and British interests, of course, but the net result for Canada was that the ultimate fate of Canadian food, Canadian-produced munitions, and Canada's armed forces was to be decided by these boards. Their decisions would be made not only without Canadian input but essentially without Canadians knowing anything about them, except what Churchill chose to tell King and what Canadian soldiers or diplomats in London and Washington could harvest from personal contacts and discussions or from the very general summaries of meetings made available after the fact to representatives of Allied governments.[13] The same conditions applied to decisions made in the subsequent wartime meetings of Churchill and Roosevelt and the meetings of these two men with Stalin. What this meant was that decisions made at these highest levels—such as when the cross-Channel attack to retake France and begin the penultimate drive into Germany would take place—were transmitted only vaguely, if at all, to King and the other Allied leaders. Thus key Canadian decisions, such as whether to send an infantry division to Sicily, or when to send another division and a corps headquarters to Italy, were essentially made in the dark.

King learned something about the Washington discussions from Churchill himself when he made a side trip to Ottawa, partly to address the Canadian Parliament and partly to brief him on what was going on at the Arcadia Conference. Churchill was rather vague, even disingenuous in what he told King, downplaying the long-term significance of the Washington arrangements. King was clearly worried, as he wrote in his diary on December 29, 1941: "... said quite openly to him the problem we faced was that while we had been in [the war] during two and a quarter years, things would be so arranged that the U.S. and Britain would settle everything between themselves and that our services, Chiefs of Staff, etc., would not have any say in what was to be done ... He said he thought we should be entitled to representation there, but expressed the hope that we would take a large view of the relationships of the large countries, to avoid anything in the way of antagonisms." Or, as C.P. Stacey pointed out, Canada was being told not to rock the boat in the interests of Allied unity.[14] As far as the higher direction of the war was concerned, King kept his peace. After all, he had decided long before that he would not seek to play any role in the higher strategic direction of the war, and the simple fact of the matter is that by the time of the Arcadia Conference, it was far too late for him to do anything about it even if he had wanted to. Churchill was more than happy to represent the Empire/Commonwealth, and the Americans were more than happy to keep things that way.

As the US and Soviet contributions to the war grew rapidly in subsequent months and years, and the proportion of the UK contribution fell accordingly, Churchill's stature as a leader of one of the three leading Allied countries came to depend more and more on the contributions of the British Empire/Commonwealth. With soldiers, ships, and aircrew of Canada, Australia, New Zealand, etc., under the sway of the British Chiefs of Staff Committee, the purely British contribution of the war was considerably bulked up.

But not everyone in the Canadian government was as sanguine about Canada's lack of participation in all the joint boards as King apparently was about Canadian membership or even effective representation on the CCS. Under Secretary of State for External Affairs Norman Robertson and other External Affairs mandarins believed it was inconceivable that Canada would simply hand its war production over to boards consisting of only British and American representation. They believed that, since Canada was making significant contributions in munitions and food, it ought to be accorded representation on those boards. Though King was reticent, a decision was made in the spring of 1942 to focus on representation on the Combined Food Board. The Canadian rationale was that in an area where a nation was making a significant contribution to the war, it ought to be allowed to join the combined board most concerned. The most obvious target was the Combined Food Board, and efforts began in the fall of 1942 to gain a seat for Canada. Both the British and the Americans pushed back hard. Eventually the Canadians won the British over, and then the Americans, too, and Canada was formally admitted to full membership on the board in October 1943.

* * * *

Mackenzie King's main effort in the war was to maintain national unity, of course, but within that overall aim, to organize the nation for war and to generate the fighting forces that would represent Canada in the Allied coalition. He was challenged on the home front two weeks after Canada declared war when Quebec premier Maurice Duplessis dissolved his provincial parliament and went to the polls. Duplessis never quite declared it, but the election was in effect a provincial referendum on the federal government's assumption of key areas of provincial power in order to manage the war. At first there was confusion and not a little panic in Ottawa. If Duplessis won, what might the impact be on Ottawa's ability to lead a national war effort? And what might Canada's allies in London and Paris conclude if Quebecers effectively said no to federal government leadership in the war? King's Quebec lieutenant, Ernest Lapointe, met the prime minister the day Duplessis called the election and declared that the Quebec premier's election call was nothing less than "straight sabotage, the most unpatriotic thing he knew."[15] Lapointe and the other Quebec ministers decided to intervene in the Quebec election and threatened to resign if Duplessis won. In effect they told Quebec voters that re-election of the Duplessis government would be a vote of non-confidence in them, and that if they did resign there would be no one in Ottawa who might protect them from conscription. King was not happy with their decision and tried to dissuade them but they persisted. The election result on October 25, 1939, was a decisive defeat for Duplessis; his opponent, Quebec Liberal leader Joseph-Adélard Godbout, won 53 percent of the popular vote and took sixty-nine seats in the provincial parliament.

It seemed a perfect time for King to call his own federal election. His government had come to power in the fall of 1935, and unless some special provision were to be adopted with the consent of the opposition to extend the constitutional limit of his mandate (as had been done during the First World War), he would have to dissolve Parliament in the fall of 1940. On January 25, the sixth session of the 18th Parliament was convened by the Governor General and then, in a surprise move, immediately dissolved, with an election called for March 26, 1940. Mackenzie

King had promised Conservative opposition leader R.J. Manion that he would not call an election during wartime, but the prospect of governing with a new majority mandate for the next five years was just too tempting for him. King and his Cabinet effectively turned the election into a referendum on the government's leadership in wartime. The fact was that the war was too young for Mackenzie King to have faced any real challenges, domestic or overseas, and although Canadians were certainly not enthusiastic about entering another European conflict (it was not yet another world war), very few of them thought Canada had had any real choice but to declare war.

Once again, conscription was a major issue, especially in Quebec, where all federal parties pledged not to introduce it, which was easy enough to do at that point in the war. Poland had been subdued by the Nazis, but the German offensive in the west had not yet begun. Canada had sent only a single division to the United Kingdom in late 1939, but was holding the mobilized 2nd Canadian Infantry Division in Canada and had not decided if any more troops would be sent. The government at that point was bent on fighting a limited liability war, which emphasized industrial and agricultural output as Canada's main thrust in the war, in addition to the recently completed agreement to operate and pay for the British Commonwealth Air Training Plan. At the beginning of 1940, therefore, there were, in fact, more men volunteering for service than there were places for those men in the fighting forces. On March 26 the Liberals won a landslide victory, gaining 178 seats against 39 for the Conservatives, 10 for the Alberta-based Social Credit party, 10 for the Cooperative Commonwealth Federation (CCF), with 10 independents. Manion resigned, to be replaced by R.B. Hanson, another ineffective leader who was himself gone within two years.

King now had a safe majority to run the nation's war as he saw fit, but he did not have long to savour his victory—two weeks after the election, Germany attacked Norway in the first of a sequence of events that would include the German conquest of Denmark, Belgium, Holland, and France, and Italy's entrance into the war as Germany's ally. Within three months of the election, Britain stood alone. King's government quickly cast aside the limited liability approach to war. Plans were made to dispatch the 2nd Canadian Infantry Division to the United Kingdom and revive Defence Scheme No. 3—a Canadian Army Headquarters consisting of two corps and the equivalent of six infantry and armoured divisions. It became obvious rather quickly that if Canada was to make a significant contribution to the defence, indeed the survival, of the United Kingdom, it would need to do much more at home to organize a national war effort and mobilize as much of its war potential as possible.

At first, Ottawa hesitated. How much could Canada send to the United Kingdom without stripping itself of the meagre defences it already had? There were several discussions in Cabinet but Mackenzie King, to his credit, argued decisively that Britain was now Canada's last line of defence. Perhaps he realized that in the end, the defence of Canada could be achieved only with the full cooperation of the United States and that it would be useless to try to devote immediate resources to the defence of the Canadian East Coast and Newfoundland while Britain was almost on its knees. Canada was going to go all in and send to the United Kingdom whatever was not immediately necessary for its own defence. Although Canada's war was initially a limited liability effort, it was one thing to declare that Canada would send the products of factories and farms to the UK to aid its war effort, and another to come to terms with the United Kingdom on prices and quantities.

When the French surrendered, that all suddenly changed, of course; now, Britain stood much more ready to pay what the Canadians needed

1. Troops arrive in Hong Kong aboard HMCS *Prince Robert*, November 1941.

2. Disaster on the Dieppe beach, August 19, 1942.

3. Corvette HMCS *Agassiz*.

4. Admiral L.W. Murray presents an award to a *St. Croix* crew member after the sinking of submarine U-90 by HMCS *St. Croix* on July 24, 1942.
PHOTOGRAPHER: H.A. IRISH

5. HMCS *St. Croix* off of Halifax, March 1941. The ship in the distance is HMS *King George V*.

6. The captured German submarine U-190 is escorted from the Bay of Bulls to St. John's, Newfoundland, June 3, 1945.
PHOTOGRAPHER: H.A. IRISH

7. The frigate HMCS *St. Stephen* near Esquimalt, British Columbia, August 14, 1944.
PHOTOGRAPHER: KEN MACLEAN

8. The River Class destroyer HMCS *Restigouche* in Halifax, 1940.

9. Lorne Greene, the "Voice of Doom," broadcasting over the CBC national network.
PHOTOGRAPHER: RONNY JAQUES

10. Commander J.P. Prentice on the bridge of HMCS *Chambly* at sea, May 24, 1941.

11. Veronica Foster, known as "The Bren Gun Girl," poses with a finished Bren gun at the John Inglis Co. plant.

12. A poster for a victory loan drive.
ARTIST: ARCHIBALD B. STAPLETON

13. Rationing was a fact of life for home-makers during the war.

14. Writer Madge Macbeth raising money for war bonds.

15. U.S. President Franklin D. Roosevelt, William Lyon Mackenzie King, and Winston Churchill at the Citadel during the Quadrant Conference.

16. J.L. Ralston and C.D. Howe in front of Canada's 500,000th military vehicle.

17. Winston Churchill and Lieutenant-General A.G.L. McNaughton studying a map at Canadian Military Headquarters in London.

18. The Cabinet War Committee. Back row, left to right: Angus MacDonald (Navy), J.E. Michaud (Transport), C.D. Howe (Munitions and Supply), Louis St. Laurent (Justice and Solicitor General). Front row, left to right: C.G. Power (Air), T.A. Crerar (Mines and Resources), W.L. Mackenzie King, J.L. Ralston (Defence), J.L. Ilsley (Finance).

19. Canadian troops in an assault landing craft during an invasion training exercise in southern England, July 1942.

20. General Dwight D. Eisenhower, followed by General H.D.G. Crerar, inspecting the guard of honour during his visit to the 4th Canadian Armoured Division, November 29, 1944.
PHOTOGRAPHER: HAROLD G. AIKMAN

21. Pilot Officer George G. Beurling on his return from Malta in November 1942.

22. Canadian troops embark for the invasion of the Aleutian Islands, Kiska, Alaska, August 1943.

23. Vice-Admiral P.W. Nelles (*right*), Air Chief Marshal L.S. Breadner (*second from right*), and other officers at the Quebec Conference in 1943.

24. A Sherman tank of the Three Rivers Regiment amid the ruins of Ortona, Italy, December 23, 1943. PHOTOGRAPHER: T.F. ROWE

25. Bomb damage at Pontecorvo, Italy, as Canadians advance through the Hitler Line, May 24, 1944. PHOTOGRAPHER: R. NYE

26. A burnt-out German Tiger tank on the Agira-Regalbuto road, Sicily.
PHOTOGRAPHER: J.E. DE GUIRE

27. A captured German 88-millimetre anti-aircraft gun, without the carriage, at the Royal Canadian School of Artillery, Petawawa, Ontario.

28. A Canadian Regimental Aid Party carrying a wounded soldier, Italy, October 1943.
PHOTOGRAPHER: TERRY ROWE

for their goods. Under Howe, Canada then made a concerted effort to liquidate Canadian debt in the United Kingdom in return for Canadian products, and wrangling over prices virtually ceased.

In early 1941 the president proposed to Congress that the United States become the "arsenal of democracy" by lending military equipment to Britain, as needed, for the duration.

The Lend-Lease Act was signed into law on March 11, 1941; it was a blessing to Britain and a curse to Canada. Britain had started to purchase Canadian war supplies early but quickly ran into the problem of how to pay for the food, munitions, and raw materials. As Britain began to run out of cash, Canada loaned money to it so that it might continue ordering war supplies from Canada. The reason was not because "greedy" Canada wanted to profit from Britain's distress; it was because Canada's own market was so small that if it could not sell to Britain, Canadian production would become prohibitively expensive—possibly too expensive to carry on. That applied to food as well as army trucks and rifle bullets. Lend-Lease gave Britain a means of acquiring war supplies from the United States for no money down and created the possibility that the British would simply stop buying from Canada. King himself soon concluded that the only way to save Canadian war production was to convince the Americans to put Canada under the Lend-Lease umbrella, which would mean that Britain could make purchases in not only the United States but also Canada. The Americans might listen if the case were put directly to the secretary of state and to Roosevelt himself that it was not in the interest of the Allies to lose Canadian war-production capability. A Canadian proposal was drawn up, and King himself took it to Washington to sell it to the United States. In his words, "I stressed the part relating to war materials, pointing out that we had neither gold nor American dollars; that if we became dependent on American [sic] for loans and the like, we would have nationalist policies developing after the war." This, explains Abe Roof, was a reference to protectionism, which the US Secretary of State Cordell Hull abhorred.[16] The plan as eventually presented to Roosevelt included not only Canada being taken under the Lend-Lease umbrella but also a commitment for the two nations to rationalize cross-border war production, as if the border didn't exist. On April 20, 1941, Mackenzie King and Roosevelt signed the Hyde Park Declaration at Roosevelt's retreat in Hyde Park, New York. It was one of the most effective initiatives King made in the entire war, demonstrating that when King deeply believed vital Canadian interests were involved, he could be as assertive as necessary with Roosevelt.

* * * *

On June 21, 1940—one day before the formal surrender of France—Ottawa passed the National Resources Mobilization Act, which gave the federal government sweeping powers to take whatever measures it deemed necessary to mobilize men and women, factories, farms, and other resources for purposes of fighting the war. As mentioned, one of the measures introduced by the NRMA was conscription for home defence. At first the period of service was short—only three months—and the act made clear that no one drafted under the NRMA would be sent to an active theatre of war overseas. Mackenzie King's Quebec ministers were not happy with conscription in any form, but only the most ardent Quebec nationalist could argue a case that Canadians, including Quebecers, should not be called up if Canada were directly attacked by the Axis. Later in the war, military training periods under the NRMA would be extended several times, and four battalions of NRMA conscripts were added to US forces sent to destroy a Japanese base on Kiska in the Aleutian island chain in 1943. (After a dramatic bombardment and landing, the US and Canadian force discovered that the Japanese had already evacuated.) At first the conscripts were received and trained in special new camps, but it was impossible to create soldiers out of them in ninety days. Their initial training consisted of marching, athletics, rifle training, and military discipline, but in 1941, at Crerar's suggestion, conscripts and volunteers began to train together.[17] The volunteers were sent on to active service units for more advanced training, while those conscripts who chose not to "go active" were assigned to reserve units in Canada. The reservists wore an "R" on their uniforms, while the volunteers wore a "GS" for general service. From almost the very beginning, various means of persuasion from the benign to physical abuse was used to "convince" unwilling reservists to go active. It is not known how many Canadian men actually waited until they were drafted before they willingly volunteered to go active, but certainly the numbers were in the many thousands even in the early years of the war.

Conscription for overseas service—Mackenzie King's greatest nemesis—began to be raised in the public arena even before the Japanese attack on Pearl Harbor. Even as the NRMA recruiting program began to take shape in the fall of 1940 and over the winter of 1940–41, demands emerged in different parts of Canada—especially in the West—to go all the way and use conscription for overseas military service as well. Much of the growing demand centred on Arthur Meighen, a Conservative who had been Attorney General under Robert Laird Borden in 1917 (helping to draw up the Military Service Act of that year), and who had succeeded Borden as prime minister in 1919 only to be defeated by King in the 1921 election. Meighen stayed on as leader of the opposition and briefly regained power in 1925, only to be defeated again by King in 1926. Not long after that he left politics, but only for a time. When Manion was defeated in the 1940 federal election, he was succeeded by R.B. Hanson, who resisted pressure from his party to reverse its stand on conscription for overseas military service. By the fall of 1941 this was becoming an increasingly popular position in the Conservative Party, which wrested the leadership from Hanson and thrust it upon the sixty-seven-year-old Meighen in November 1941. Somewhat reluctant to accept it at first, Meighen quickly gave in. He then became the focal point for the gathering pro-conscription sentiment in Canada.

The gathering momentum for conscription for overseas military service ran parallel to plans being made for the expansion of Canada's military contribution to the war. When these plans were presented to the Cabinet War Committee in early December 1941, the prime minister sought assurances that expansion of the overseas army to the equivalent of six divisions could be done without compulsion. Minister of National Defence J.L. Ralston and Chief of the General Staff Ken Stuart assured King that it could. But Chief of the Air Staff L.S. Breadner disagreed.[18] The Cabinet was about to discuss these plans on December 9, 1941, when news of the Japanese attack on Hawaii arrived, dramatically altering the debate nationally and within the government. Now the long-considered question of defence of the West Coast entered the national discussion, and pressure for conscription rose dramatically. As J.L. Granatstein has put it, "Clearly Canada had to do more in a war that was now truly a world war."[19]

King was well aware that Ralston, Macdonald, and Finance Minister J.L. Ilsley all favoured conscription while not a single Quebec minister supported it. As sentiment for conscription rose in English-speaking Canada, anti-conscription sentiment and the pledge the government had made in the 1940 election not to introduce conscription was brought up again and again. King characteristically pinned the blame on Meighen for making the issue a political one—as if it had ever been anything else—and took some comfort from the knowledge that there was, at the time, absolutely no manpower shortage in Canada. But he seems to have underestimated the great fear that Axis military advances had precipitated among many Canadians. The Japanese army and navy were running rampant in the Far East and the Pacific, and the ability of the United States Navy to hold them from the West Coast was in doubt. In fact, Canada had already transferred its small fleet of West Coast destroyers to the Atlantic months before. The panic was so great that a cry arose among British Columbians to "do something" about the tens of thousands of Japanese-Canadian citizens and recent immigrants—who lived in coastal communities and who were feared as a fifth column. The Germans were at the gates of Moscow and helping the Italians push the British out of North Africa. German submarines were taking a terrible toll of shipping in the North Atlantic, particularly right off the US east coast. They were sinking ships right off the beaches! Of course Canadians were apprehensive.

Mackenzie King's answer, announced in the Speech from the Throne opening Parliament on January 22, was to announce that a national plebescite would be held asking Canadians whether they would release the government from its pledge not to introduce conscription but, at the same time, not to introduce conscription until it was absolutely necessary. King knew that a large majority of English-speaking Canada would vote yes, but he also thought Quebecers might trust him enough not to do so and thus also vote yes. He was very wrong; a strong majority (64 percent) of English-speaking Canada did vote yes, but about 72 percent of Quebecers voted resoundingly against. The only thing the government did in the wake of this vote was to amend the National Resources Mobilization Act to give itself the legal power to send NRMA conscripts overseas should a situation arise wherein the government believed that such action had become necessary. Ralston submitted his letter of resignation to the prime minister, who refused to act on it, but kept the letter nonetheless.

* * * *

Until the 1st Canadian Infantry Division landed in Sicily in July 1943, the Canadian Army did not have to face the grim prospect of sustained contact in a ground war against an implacable enemy. Then things changed. The army had forecast how many reinforcements (which is what the British and Canadians called men who were placed into combat units to replace men killed or severely wounded) would be needed based on the casualty rates that the British Eighth Army had suffered in North Africa, which was primarily a war of movement. When the shooting actually started for the Canadians in Sicily, casualty rates were not excessive. The Italians were not a difficult opponent, and although the Germans were, their strategy in Sicily was to hold and withdraw. Sicily was not a war of attrition. But Italy was, especially when the Canadians went into battle along the Moro River and in the fight for Ortona. And it was even more so in the Liri Valley in the spring of 1944. The government's early commitment of Canadian infantry, first in Sicily, then in Italy, with an added armoured division and corps headquarters, played havoc with casualty projections. In addition, significant numbers of neuropsychiatric casualties took literally thousands of men out of the front ranks for days and weeks at a time, if not for the duration. The tough grind in Italy in the late fall of 1943, combined with the terrible weather and the relentless German opposition, pushed those battle exhaustion numbers up. Then, in June 1944, when the 2nd Canadian Corps entered the Battle of

Normandy, a severe shortage of infantry began to manifest itself in the army overall. Ralston saw it after a trip to Italy in late 1943. A very Tory Toronto Maple Leafs hockey club owner, Major Conn Smythe, increased the pressure on the government in September 1944 when he published a claim that the army was receiving neither the number nor the quality of trained men it needed to carry on.

As General E.L.M. Burns revealed in his postwar study *Manpower in the Canadian Army: 1939–1945*, the actual problem was not a shortage of Canadians in the army, as it had allegedly been in the First World War, when conscription was introduced in 1917. It was that the army had too many support troops for each infantryman actually at the front shooting at the enemy. For a variety of reasons, including the desire to provide Canadian products and services to Canadian soldiers whenever possible—a complete Canadian military mail service, for example, or Canadian hospitals in the United Kingdom[20]—the ratio of front-line troops to those in the rear was much lower than in the British or US armies. The military often refers to this as the "tooth to tail" ratio, and it was very small in Canadian divisions. Measured by "divisional slice"— the actual number of front-line troops in a division—the Canadian Army had too few fighting men. And because the heavy fighting in Italy and Normandy in the summer of 1944 was done when the Luftwaffe had already been heavily worn down by Allied air power, there were far more anti-aircraft gunners than were needed. Burns's main conclusion is that if the army had been organized differently, there would have been enough infantry, machine gunners, mortar men, combat engineers, etc., to fight through the war without any need for conscription.

The pressure on the prime minister to now use the changes made in the National Resources Mobilization Act to send members of the reserve army overseas mounted daily. Ralston led the charge in Cabinet. In army camps across the nation, extreme pressure was put on the conscripts, known derisively as zombies due to their status as neither civilians nor general-service soldiers. Many succumbed and went active, but they were too few to meet Stuart's estimate of how many additional infantry would be needed if, as he rightly believed, the war would drag on into 1945 and casualty rates did not dramatically decrease. The Cabinet crisis mounted. Mackenzie King concluded that the army itself had decided to pressure the government into sending the zombies overseas—it was a conspiracy! He acted. On November 1 he fired Ralston in front of a full Cabinet meeting and called on Andy McNaughton to succeed Ralston as minister of national defence. McNaughton was opposed to conscription for overseas military service and believed that, with his great personal popularity among the troops, he might succeed in convincing enough reservists to go active to ameliorate the infantry crisis. In the army at home and overseas, many troops whose jobs were no longer considered essential—for example, anti-aircraft gunners—were remustered into the infantry. But they still had to be retrained as infantry, and although many did reach front-line units in early 1945, the process seemed too slow to the army to make a real difference. As the threat of a full-blown split in the Cabinet mounted, King finally gave way and on November 23, 1944, the government issued an order-in-council sending 16,000 zombies overseas. There was a near revolt at the army base in Terrace, British Columbia, but most of the NRMA men went quietly. At the end of the whole process, only 2,463 NRMA men were ever posted to the front lines, partly because the Canadian Army saw almost no action from the beginning of November 1944 until February 1945, partly because the army's two corps were united once again in March, and partly because German resistance, though stubborn and bloody in the battle for the Rhineland (see Chapter 17), began to dissipate after that.

From beginning to end, the conscription issue in Canada was dealt with entirely as a matter of domestic politics within the larger context of military requirements. But Canada did not have the sort of information about the greater Allied military context, both because it had no representation on the Combined Chiefs of Staff and because the key detailed information generated by the Combined Chiefs and their various subcommittees was not shared with Canada except in the same general terms as it was shared with the other Allied countries. So Canada, with the fourth-largest contribution to the war in Europe—and larger than that of, say, Brazil or Mexico—knew no more about higher Allied strategy than those other smaller allies did. When McNaughton had been commanding First Canadian Army, he had "ardently believed that Canada's decisions should be anchored by a lucid consideration of Allied strategy. Only in this way could he and the government ensure that Canada's army was used in a manner that protected and promoted its national interest."[21] Basically McNaughton's information at that point, in the fall of 1942, came from meeting Sir Alan Brooke, Chief of the Imperial General Staff, every two or three weeks. In Washington, Major-General Maurice Pope, who headed the Canadian Joint Staff Mission there, had similar problems gleaning information from the Combined Chiefs of Staff. When it was established over some considerable American objection in the spring of 1942—the Americans much preferred to deal only with the British, and with the Canadians only through the British—the Mission was supposed to keep Ottawa fully informed about CCS events. But Pope's access to CCS information was limited to reading relevant papers (selected by the British) at the British Mission (which shared the same building) or from personal conversations with US and British officers. As Christine Leppard observes, "Pope was on the outside looking in. Relying heavily on hearsay and off-the-record conversations was hardly a methodical way for Canada to obtain information about grand strategy."[22]

At the Cabinet level, however, no one seemed to be interested in grand strategy. For example, when initial planning began for the Normandy invasion in late 1943, Ralston's most immediate concern was that Canadian Military Headquarters in London, and Ken Stuart, in particular, had only limited access to those planning the cross-Channel attack. He wrote Stuart in February 1944, "I and a few others have been thinking that it would be a very much better working arrangement if there could be established a procedure whereby Canada would be 'in on' the planning at a high level." But he quickly assured Stuart that he was not talking about getting in on deliberations of high strategy, but rather "the tactical dispositions to carry out that strategy."[23] Even this he failed to achieve. On June 6, 1944, hours after the 3rd Canadian Infantry Division and the other Allied troops hit the beaches in Normandy, King was awakened by a loud knock on his door at about half past four in the morning: "Wentzell, one of the Mounted Policemen on duty, coming in and saying: 'Mr. King, the invasion has begun. Mr. Robertson wants you on the phone.' I questioned him as to what information he had. Rang up Robertson immediately. Asked him if he was sure the report was correct. He said he was; that official communiqués had come in."[24] Thus did the Canadian prime minister, with some 800 Canadian paratroopers, 18,000 infantry, dozens of ships and hundreds of aircraft taking part, learn about the Normandy landing.

In the First World War, Canada had been a colony of Great Britain from beginning to end, supplying troops for the British to use. Prime Minister Robert Borden had started to resist that circumstance as early as 1916 and finally succeeded in convincing British prime minister David Lloyd George by 1917 that the status quo ante bellum was no longer acceptable. He brought the other dominion prime ministers with him, and the result was the Imperial War Cabinet meeting convened on March 2, 1917, in London, which passed Resolution IX, moved by Smuts and Borden, which declared that after hostilities ended, the dominions and the United Kingdom would redefine the Empire as a common-wealth of equals. In a sense, Borden's Canada began the First World War as a colony and ended it well on the road to nationhood. Mackenzie King's Canada began the war as an independent nation but fought it as a colony.[25]

CHAPTER 9

BOMBING GERMANY

January 21–22, 1944: somewhere in the darkened skies of northern Europe a Halifax of the Royal Canadian Air Force's No. 419 Squadron, based at Middleton St. George in County Durham, struggled to reach its assigned bomber-stream altitude en route to Magdeburg, a key German rail centre. Staying in the bomber stream was no guarantee of survival, but it certainly increased the odds of returning. Bombers that drifted off track or flew too low were choice prey for the German night fighters; they were easily spotted and just as easily picked off. The pilot of the Halifax was Warrant Officer I.V. Hopkins. He and his crew had heard a loud bang just fifty minutes after takeoff and had discovered that the landing gear would not retract all the way. Something was wrong with the aircraft's hydraulic system. As the fully loaded bomber crossed the Dutch coast, Hopkins could manage no better than 3,900 metres, well below its assigned 6,100 metres altitude inside the bomber stream. Flying alone, they were sitting ducks for German nightfighters. Hopkins ordered his bomb aimer to jettison their incendiaries, which lightened the load, then nursed the Halifax back up into the bomber stream.

Hopkins's bomber was one of 645 dispatched by Bomber Command to attack Magdeburg that night. The target offered some respite from Bomber Command chief Arthur Harris's campaign against Berlin, which had started the previous August with three preliminary raids on the German capital. The main Battle of Berlin had been launched in earnest in mid-November 1943. Harris had fixated on destroying Berlin, especially if the United States Army Air Force would join the campaign. He thought, wrongly, that bringing Berlin to its knees might end the war before the Normandy invasion. Thus began a grueling five-month campaign that came close to breaking Bomber Command itself. No. 6 Group and the other Bomber Command groups had hit Berlin continuously through the late fall of 1943 and through the winter of 1943–44. In effect, Magdeburg was a break from the Berlin raids, the ninth attack on the German capital having taken place just the night before Hopkins took off to attack Magdeburg.

As the attacks on Berlin continued, casualties rose as German night defences improved. The Bomber Command crews were being worn to the nub. Night after night, they endured the gauntlet of flak, night fighters and bad winter weather. They were tired. They saw hundreds of bombers explode in the dark and they saw the empty beds in their barracks when they returned to the United Kingdom. Yet they flew on. The Luftwaffe had introduced a new tactic in its efforts to defend German airspace. Known as "tame boar," it involved radar-equipped night fighters, some designed specifically as twin-engine fighters such as the Me-110, others actually obsolete twin-engine bombers such as the Ju-88, which didn't need to be fast or manoeuvrable at night. They all had to be big enough to hold a pilot and a radar operator, big enough for a fancy array of radar antennas attached to the nose of the aircraft, and big enough to hold radar-receiving equipment in their cockpits. Directed to the bomber stream by ground controllers' large Freya or Würzburg radars, they then entered the stream to seek targets of opportunity. Many of these night fighters were armed with a new weapon—*Schräge Musik* ("jazz music")—20mm cannon mounted to the rear of the night-fighter cockpit, usually at a 60-degree angle, to fire upward into the vital spots of the bombers. Using *Schräge Musik*, a night fighter could sidle underneath an unsuspecting bomber, open fire at wing tanks or bomb bays, and blow bomber and crew to eternity with no warning at all.

Bomber Command was also using different tactics than it had earlier in the war. Spoof raids were now routinely mounted to other cities in Germany (usually by Mosquitos spreading aluminum chaff) to fool the ground controllers while the main force headed to its true target. A new Pathfinder Force had been set up in late 1942, and had then been consolidated in a new No. 8 Group, established in January 1943, to lead the way to the target and to mark it with a variety of coloured pyrotechnics. Harris had initially opposed the Pathfinder idea, but had relented under pressure from Bomber Command's Operational Research Section.[1] A variety of newly developed technical wiles that both sides had been developing throughout the war—radar, radar jamming, spoof raids, radio-telephone transmission interception, IFF (Identification Friend or Foe)—were in use to achieve one of two basic aims. For Bomber Command, it was to bomb Germany long enough and heavily enough to win the war; for the Germans it was to make the British bombers pay so high a price that they would stop their campaign before achieving their objective.

Thus there was much high strategy being played out in the skies over Germany on the night of January 21–22, 1944, but little of that was in the minds of Hopkins and his crew as they approached Magdeburg. All they could see was a rolling plain of cloud; the target was totally covered. This was all too usual for weather over northern Europe in winter. Thus Hopkins's crew aimed for the skymarkers that had been dropped by the Pathfinder Force—coloured flares descending beneath parachutes, hopefully over Magdeburg—then turned for Liepzig, with nose down, trying to pick up more speed for the run back to the coast. A German fighter flashed in front of them from left to right. Hopkins pulled sharply right and dove. He did not hear the fighter's shells strike, but he saw his outer starboard engine burst into flame. He managed to get the fire out, feathered the engine, then resumed course, this time just under 3,000 metres. Then the Halifax was attacked again; raked from below at least three times, probably by *Schräge Musik*. Hopkins would later remember, "Upon starting evasive action the [starboard] inner [engine] burst into flame, cannon-shell hit the selection box and shrapnel hit me in [the] leg and shoulder, also wiping out some instruments." The bomb bay was on fire, the gas tanks were leaking, the port engines were overheating, wind screamed through a hundred bullet holes, and Hopkins's controls were not responding. The Halifax was losing altitude fast; Hopkins ordered his crew to bail out, held the bomber steady as they did so, then jumped himself and watched his plane flip over and dive into the ground.[2] He and his crew were captured and spent the rest of the war in captivity. (One was later killed by Allied fighter bombers.) They were lucky; the vast majority of Bomber Command crews whose aircraft were hit by German night fighters never survived.

No. 6 Group sent out 114 aircraft that night: 13 returned early or aborted the mission due to some sort of mechanical failure; 86 managed to locate and attack the primary target. But 14 bombers with 98 crewmen aboard did not return. That was a disastrous loss rate of 12.3 percent. In total, Bomber Command sent more than 600 bombers to Magdeburg and lost 57—a loss rate of almost 9 percent. The attack was also a colossal failure; most of the bombs fell outside the city and little damage was done. No military force can survive long when its losses are as high as those suffered by Bomber Command, and especially No. 6 Group, that night. And yet, five nights later, Hopkins's comrades took to the skies once more to continue the Battle of Berlin. There would be yet many more losses before the bomber offensive against Germany concluded.

* * * *

No. 6 Group (RCAF) was intended by the Canadian government to be one of the most important and highly visible symbols that Canada was fighting as an ally, and not as a colony. The Group was intended to be composed of Canadian pilots, aircrew, and ground crew, commanded by Canadians, flying a Canadian-built aircraft—the Lancaster X—on bases commanded by Canadians. In administrative and personal matters, it was responsible directly to Minister of National Defence for Air Chubby Power through the RCAF Overseas. But at the same time it most decidedly was not—and was never intended to be—an independent air force, deciding its own strategy, choosing its own aircraft, and selecting its own targets. Nor did the Canadian government make operational air policy. In operational matters—targets, bombloads, aircraft, overall strategy, No. 6 Group was completely under orders of Bomber Command in the same way that the other Bomber Command groups were.

The man appointed Air Officer Commanding (AOC) of No. 6 Group at its inauguration was Air Vice-Marshal G.E. Brookes, forty-seven years of age at that time. British-born, he had come to Canada in 1910 and served in the Royal Flying Corps in the First World War. He had joined the fledgling RCAF when it was established in the early 1920s and had filled a number of posts in the interwar years. Although he had no operational experience on bombers (but then, neither did Harris), he was considered a good trainer of aircrew, something that the neophyte No. 6 Group would definitely need.

Brookes had been one of only three men considered eligible for the job of AOC; in late 1942, there were few Canadians in either the RCAF or the RAF qualified to command bases or squadrons, let alone a group. Thus RCAF Canadians were appointed where available, but RAF Canadians and RAF British were brought in where necessary. Invariably many posts, including squadron leaders, went to British or other Commonwealth officers serving in the RAF. There was simply no choice. But this operational necessity still set off alarm bells in certain quarters in Ottawa, just as the agonizingly slow pace of Canadianization in Article 15 squadrons had in 1942.

There was also difficulty Canadianizing the aircrew themselves. In the United States Army Air Force it was standard practice to form up a heavy-bomber crew in the United States and then have that crew fly a new B-17 or B-24 to the United Kingdom. That was not the case in Bomber Command. Canadian aircrew and others who had graduated from the BCATP's schools in Canada were brought to the United Kingdom and assigned to an Advanced Training Unit (ATU) to learn the basic craft of bombing, then to an Operational Training Unit (OTU), where crews were assembled and trained on actual bombers (usually obsolete or worn-out aircraft). The assembly of crews was done at the OTU in a large room (usually a hangar) in a rather haphazard way that somewhat resembled a high school dance. Most men just stood about eyeing the others, usually in a small cluster of friends, while a few bolder ones went from cluster to cluster, often selecting crew members

Our Finest Hour

on the basis of nothing more than a quick first impression. Thus the crews assembled themselves from all over the Commonwealth. Until the RCAF established its own purely Canadian OTUs, there was no way to guarantee that the crews assigned to it would be all Canadian or even predominantly Canadian. Even then, however, there was a shortage of Canadian flight engineers for most of the war (there weren't enough being trained in Canada), and this meant that in most RCAF bombers there was usually at least one Australian, South African, or Briton flying as flight engineer. This is why most of No. 6 Group's flying personnel and its ground crews were not Canadian during its first year of operations. But then it must be remembered that during the whole course of the war, more Canadians served in the RAF, wearing RCAF uniforms or RAF ones, than served in the RCAF.

The group's problems with Canadianization were minor compared to the major difficulties it experienced in operational efficiency in its first fourteen months or so. One of the most significant challenges No. 6 Group had to overcome arose from the location of its bases in Yorkshire or northern County Durham. Put simply, No. 6 Group was farther from the Continent than all other groups in Bomber Command. No. 6 Group was assigned these bases because it was the last large group to be formed in Bomber Command, and by the time it was formed there was simply no other viable place in the United Kingdom to put it. It was important that all the bases of a particular group be located in the same general area. This made communications, personal travel, shipment of everything from personal mail to equipment, much easier. It was also done to make it easier to service aircraft, since different squadrons sometimes flew dissimilar aircraft types, especially in the middle years of the war. It was, therefore, standard practice to station squadrons flying Hampdens, for example, near other squadrons flying the same aircraft. In the case of No. 6 Group, this consideration was, if anything, strengthened by the desire to keep the Canadians together.

Between the Canadian bases in Yorkshire and northern County Durham and the North Sea, where the bomber stream formed up for raids into north Germany, was a range of hills with a few peaks as high as 450 metres. Fully loaded bombers taking off for a night's mission had to clear these hills, sometimes in fog or low cloud, while bombers returning from long and grueling night flights had to avoid them while searching for their home fields. Returns were especially difficult when aircraft were damaged or when there were wounded aboard, making it necessary for a bomber to come straight in without entering a landing pattern. These bases were so much farther away from targets in southern Germany, France, or Italy that No. 6 Group aircraft sometimes had to land at airfields closer to the south coast of the United Kingdom to top up with fuel on either an outgoing flight or on a return. Statistically, the chances of a bomber being damaged or destroyed climbed with each takeoff-and-landing cycle it made. Finally, the location of No. 6 Group's bases meant that the RCAF bomber squadrons often did not join the bomber stream until they were near the Dutch coast, well within German night-fighter range. This gave them less protection as they neared the coast than bombers joining the bomber stream near the United Kingdom.

For much of its history, No. 6 Group squadrons were also plagued with aircraft that were not the best in the British inventory. In early 1943, that aircraft was the Avro Lancaster, a sleek aircraft that was the happy marriage of the poorly performing twin-engine Avro Manchester and four magnificent Rolls-Royce Merlin engines. The Lancaster could fly higher and faster, and carry more bombs, than its four-engine rival, the Handley Page Halifax. Because it was such an excellent aircraft, it was in high demand and Avro could barely keep up with demand. Harris rightly favoured the Lancaster over the Halifax, which he despised. (He also had no use for its manufacturer.) Over the course of the war he tried several times to convince the air ministry to force Handley Page to cease production of the Halifax and use its facilities to build more Lancasters.[3]

The overly optimistic plans for No. 6 Group called for it to eventually be equipped with the Canadian-built Lancaster X, which was to be manufactured by government-owned Victory Aircraft at Malton, north of Toronto. Equipped with Rolls-Royce Merlin engines, the Lancaster X was a virtual copy of the Avro Lancaster I or III (these two marks were distinguished primarily by place of engine manufacture), but it could not be built quickly enough or in sufficient numbers to equip an entire group. In fact, the first of these Lancaster Xs, named "The Ruhr Express," was not delivered in the United Kingdom until September 1943 and did not actually see action until some time after. Fewer than 500 were built in the whole war—far fewer than the Canadian squadrons needed. In fact, the first RCAF squadron to go operational on these Lancaster Xs, No. 419, did not begin to receive their aircraft until March 1944; at war's end, only six out of the group's fourteen squadrons were flying the Canadian-built bomber. Most of the rest were equipped with British-built Lancasters. However, when No. 6 Group was born on January 1, 1943, only two of its squadrons—No. 408 and No. 419—were actually flying heavy bombers— the Halifax Mark II and Mark V (No. 405 was also flying Halifaxes but was under command of Coastal Command on January 1, 1943). The rest of the squadrons were flying twin-engine Wellingtons. Ottawa wanted No. 6 Group to be an all–heavy bomber group (in fact, an all-Lancaster group), but there were simply not enough heavy bombers available to convert quickly. When the Canadian squadrons did begin to make the change over from Wellingtons, it was usually to the Halifax and not to the Lancaster.

The two versions of the Halifax most used in the first years of the bomber offensive—the Mark II and the Mark V—were inferior aircraft in just about every category save one: they had larger and better-placed escape hatches than the Lancaster. Poorly assembled, with a lower operational ceiling than the Lancaster, slower, and with an inferior bomb-carrying capacity, they were cold and uncomfortable. Worse, they could be highly dangerous to their crews. Their exhaust flames were easily seen at night, they offered poor downward vision, their tail assemblies were badly designed, and their controls were too sensitive for the sort of violent manoeuvres required to evade night fighters. When a pilot of a fully loaded Halifax II or V put his aircraft into the corkscrew turn and dive called for when a night fighter was spotted, the bomber could go into a flat, upside-down spin. Recovery was all but impossible. Loss rates of Halifax aircraft were consistently higher than the Lancasters.

Why was it that No. 6 Group squadrons tended to convert from Wellingtons to Halifaxes while some RAF units, such as No. 5 Group, were converting to the much superior Lancaster? Some observers then and since have chalked it up to Harris's biases against dominion crews and his particular opposition to the forming of No. 6 Group in the first place. He was certainly unhappy at any prospect that the Canadian squadrons would somehow push to the head of the line in converting to Lancasters. In September 1942, when Victory Aircraft was about to be set up in Canada, Harris wrote to Chief of the Air Staff Sir Charles Portal, "I fail to see why we should give people who are determined to huddle into a corner by themselves on purely political grounds, the best of our equipment at the expense of British and other Dominion crews. To rob our own crews of their expectations of Lancasters for that purpose is to add injury to the original political insult."[4]

Harris was not alone in that opposition. In general, the Royal Air Force and the British government would have much preferred to have had Canadians streamed into the RAF. They believed it made for a stronger and more effective RAF, and they were not wrong from the point of view of war-fighting capability; it would have been less disruptive to Bomber Command if all its crews and groups had been mixed in with one another. It would also have enhanced British political muscle to present the RAF as a united Commonwealth fighting force. But there is no evidence that Canadians were actually denied better aircraft simply because they were Canadians. In fact, No. 426 Squadron began to receive the radial-engined Lancaster II as early as July 1943, while No. 408 Squadron, based with No. 426 at Linton-on-Ouse, was equipped with the same aircraft in October of that year. This was a stopgap aircraft, made necessary because of the shortage of the better Merlin engines. When the US-built Packard variant of the Merlin engine was wedded to the Lancaster airframe to produce the Lancaster III, the Lancaster II was withdrawn from service. But most Canadian squadrons flying the Lancaster II received the supposedly improved Halifax III, rather than the Lancaster III; four RCAF bomber squadrons were still flying Halifax bombers at VE-Day.

The Lancaster II was not as good an aircraft as the Lancaster I or III, and new aircraft of the better variants tended to go first to No. 5 Group squadrons. However, that was because Harris believed, and not unreasonably, that his best aircraft should first equip his best and most experienced squadrons until there were enough Lancasters for all the squadrons of Bomber Command. This meant that the seven new Canadian bomber squadrons formed in the last half of 1942 (Nos. 424, 425, 426, 427, 428, 429, and 431) would have to wait in line for their Lancasters behind the more established squadrons of theirs and the other groups. Thus the bulk of No. 6 Group's aircraft were bound to be inadequate for the task at hand for some time to come.

The most serious problem afflicting No. 6 Group in its first seven to eight months of operations was the inexperience of many, if not most, of its crews. The night-bomber war was both a highly technical and a physically and emotionally demanding business. And it grew even more complex in 1943 as it began to rely more and more heavily on electronic measures to find targets, and countermeasures to avoid radar-equipped German night fighters. In January 1943 the British first introduced H2S—airborne target-finding radar. Over the next six months, a myriad of electronic devices was added to the bombers. This was a response to the lessons learned by both sides in their bombing campaigns in the first year or two of the war. Prewar theory had held that a large enough force of "fast" bombers would always get through the enemy defences in sufficient numbers, even in daylight, to inflict heavy damage on the enemy. It had soon become apparent that this was not so; day bombers needed fighter escort to survive. In other words, they needed to have air superiority to, from, and over the target in order to carry out their mission with a reasonable chance of survival.

Night bombing was supposed to solve the air superiority problem for the RAF by hiding the bombers in the dark. But radar was rapidly stripping the dark away, and night-fighter defences were beginning to inflict heavy damage on unescorted night bombers, though not as heavy as that wreaked by German day fighters on unescorted American bombers: they lost seventy-four aircraft shot down, damaged beyond repair, or crashed on landing out of 291 sorties—25.4 percent—in a October 14, 1943, raid against the German ball bearing–manufacturing centre of Schweinfurt. Harris might have called for the creation of a large force of radar-equipped night fighters and intruders to aid his bombers—

the excellent twin-engine Mosquito fighter/fighter bomber nicely filled the bill—but he resorted, instead, to evasion to gain the upper hand. In other words, he did not make much effort to defend his night bombers with night fighters. Instead he tried to hide his night bombers by attempting to blind or deceive the enemy in a variety of ways. At the same time, he tried to increase the chances that his bombers would do the job assigned to them in finding and hitting their targets in the dark. This task would have been hard enough in ideal conditions, but was made even more difficult by the poor weather that usually prevails over northern Europe during the long nights of winter. Summer weather was better, but the nights were not long enough for deep-penetration raids.

Harris is often depicted as somewhat of a technical troglodyte who eschewed the theories and ideas of egghead scientists trying to tell him how to run his bomber war. Nothing could be further from the truth. By early 1943, Harris had become a convinced believer in operational research and air intelligence. Operational research was conducted into many aspects of the bombing campaign by "boffins," as the scientists were called, who examined the results of raids in minute detail and teased out lessons that greatly improved operational success. It was the boffins, for example, who guided Bomber Command policy on the height and speed of the bomber stream, the least hazardous ways of approaching targets or avoiding night fighters, aircrew morale, mission aborts, accuracy, survival rates with different types of aircraft, and dozens of other key parts of the missions. Randall Wakelam, who has written the standard work on operational research in Bomber Command, writes that "Harris was almost effusive about the contribution of OR section."[5]

Air intelligence combined the science of photographic reconnaissance and the art of photographic interpretation. Also referred to as "bomb damage assessment," the process was an extension of ordinary photo reconnaissance, which grew more precise and sophisticated as better aircraft, cameras, and film increased Bomber Command's capacity to understand exactly what its aircraft ought to target and, after a raid, what they had accomplished and what remained to be done. This was especially important in the case of strategic targets such as aircraft plants, transportation hubs, or synthetic oil facilities, and less important in area bombing. Aircraft with great range, such as specially modified Spitfires and Mosquitos, flew missions deep over enemy territory to capture images on film that were quickly processed on return to the United Kingdom, giving Bomber Command the best possible picture of exactly what the enemy was doing. By the end of the war, colour film was regularly employed, which greatly increased the ability of Bomber Command analysts to understand what they were looking at. The interpretation of those photographs took great skill and patience, and the use of stereoscopic equipment to detect new structures; distinguish real targets from spoof runways, hangars, factories, etc.; and determine just how much of a target had actually been destroyed and what had not. The combination of operational research and newer target-finding equipment, such as H2S, greatly increased Bomber Command's ability to find, hit, and destroy particular targets at night through 1943 and 1944.[6] The RAF got so good at air intelligence that the USAAF learned as much as they could from the British when they began their bombing campaign in earnest in 1943.

The Germans were well aware of Bomber Command's efforts to hide their aircraft or to hit their targets more effectively at night and tried to neutralize every new device and technique that the British came up with. Thus the night-bomber war became a highly technical war of measure and countermeasure. There was Naxos, a night-fighter device that homed in on H2S; Monica, bomber-borne radar to detect night fighters; Boozer, another bomber-borne radar device to detect fighters; and many others. The Germans also improved their main airborne radar, the *Lichtenstein*, and their ground radar and air control systems.

In the summer of 1943, the war of jamming, radar detection, electronic countermeasures, spoof raids, and ghost raids, became even more complex. In fact, Bomber Command established a special electronic warfare unit—No. 100 (Bomber Support) Group—in November 1943 to jam German radio and radar, broadcast fake ground-controller instructions, and carry out other highly technical tasks in aid of the bombers. It should not be surprising, then, that "sprog" (i.e., green) crews who had not even honed basic skills, such as how to stay in the bomber stream or how to search for night fighters, were disadvantaged in the night-bomber war. Statistics showed clearly that sprog crews were far more likely to be lost on operations than those who had served at least half of their normal thirty-mission tour of duty. The large number of sprog crews in the new Canadian squadrons was a key reason why No. 6 Group's performance was so poor through much of 1943 compared to that of the rest of Bomber Command.

No. 6 Group's inferior performance showed in just about every category: fewer sorties per aircraft due to poor maintenance, a higher rate of aircraft returning before reaching the target, a lower percentage of aircraft placing their bombs within 5 kilometres of the aiming point, and higher loss rates. The high rate of early returns was partly due to poor maintenance, but there can be no doubt that it was also partly due to fatigue, low morale, and unwillingness to press on. Too many times a crew would return complaining of some malfunction in their aircraft, only to have the bomber check out in perfect working order. There was a clear correlation between low morale in No. 6 Group squadrons, as measured by Bomber Command's Operational Research teams, and mission aborts due to alleged mechanical failures that were not subsequently discovered by ground crews.[7]

One of the most difficult issues that the RCAF had to deal with was the phenomenon the Royal Air Force had already labelled LMF, for "Lack of Moral Fibre." In the army, soldiers who suffered from this condition were assessed as having shell shock, combat exhaustion, or battle fatigue. LMF was the catch-all phrase that referred to aircrew who simply could not continue flying. Whether the cause was a close shave in air combat, the loss of a close crew member, witnessing or being in a crash, or simply the inability to carry on night after night watching the "scarecrows" in the sky, feeling the turbulence, seeing the angry red flash from nearby exploding flak, or being under attack from night fighters but surviving—it all amounted to the same thing: intense aerial combat produced the same sort of battle exhaustion as did prolonged ground combat. Although the RAF's methods of dealing with LMF varied according to rank—far fewer commissioned officers were labelled LMF than non-commissioned aircrew—the ultimate punishment was immediate removal from all flying duties, transfer off base, stripping of rank, and in some cases, forced labour in mines or on docks.

As historian Allan D. English has observed, there was "a major rift between the RAF and the RCAF in their attitudes toward LMF."[8] Put simply, the RCAF treated Canadian LMF cases in a "more lenient" fashion than did the RAF and the Canadian government came to strongly object to some of the practices of the RAF in dealing with LMF, such as stripping an airman's rank in front of the rest of the squadron. The Canadians saw LMF as a far more complex phenomenon than simply cowardice or insubordination. One major difference was that the Canadians in Britain were thousands of kilometres away from home, friends, and family. The UK airman usually, with little trouble, found succour just a bus or train ride away. In any case, the RCAF Overseas and Chubby Power insisted on handling LMF among Canadian crews in a Canadian way, using Canadian medical personnel to evaluate Canadian aircrew.

LMF in No. 6 Group, quite naturally, grew more serious as the night-bomber war intensified. The group was learning the art of night aerial bombardment by doing it, and this guaranteed a host of serious problems and a casualty rate higher than that of other groups. This was the ultimate price for Canadianization. Sprog crews were sprog crews in any squadron, RCAF or RAF, and thus subject to higher casualty rates. But if Canadians had been mixed in with other crews in mixed squadrons and groups, they would probably have at least learned the skills necessary for survival from other more skilled crews and commanders and had a better chance to complete their thirty-mission tours of duty. At the same time, however, Ottawa's key war objective of being seen by Canadians and Canada's allies fighting the war as an independent nation and not a British colony would have been seriously undermined. Such was the price of fighting as an ally.

* * * *

Bomber Command's assault on Germany's industrial cities was intensified on the night of March 4–5, 1943, with the opening attack of the Battle of the Ruhr. Located in western Germany, the Ruhr was (and still is) one massive industrial basin, home to steel works, manufacturing facilities, munitions factories, and synthetic oil and rubber plants, all fed by a large rail and canal network. The cities of the Ruhr were jammed with industrial installations and with the workers who laboured in them. The Ruhr lay at the heart of the German war effort.

The Ruhr was easy enough to find in the dark, but bombing a

particular target or even a particular city was not easy to do. In Essen, the sprawling Krupp works so dominated the city that it was almost impossible to miss even from a good bombing altitude, but Essen was the exception. The cities of the Ruhr were jammed together, hard to distinguish from one another at night, even with H2S, and often obscured with industrial smoke and haze. They were also defended by a formidable array of radar-guided searchlights and flak guns, while the route from the North Sea coast to the Ruhr was dominated by night-fighter fields and night-fighter beacons. No. 6 Group took part in the opening Battle of the Ruhr and in most of the raids against the Ruhr that followed throughout the war.

On the night of July 24, 1943, Bomber Command launched 791 aircraft at the German port city of Hamburg in the opening attack of what Harris had labelled Operation Gomorrah. No. 6 Group dispatched 78 aircraft. The bombers were carrying a new weapon in the night air war against Germany: millions of strips of aluminum foil cut to precise lengths designed to jam the German radar with a fog of blips. Fed down the flare shoots of the bombers at timed intervals, the aluminum strips, called Window, registered on German radar screens as if they were aircraft. Both ground and airborne radar was rendered useless. German night-fighter pilots and ground controllers filled the dark with radioed cries of frustrated anger. German flak guns and searchlights went blind. Flight Leader G.F. Pentony, flying a Wellington from No. 429 Squadron, later remembered, "The master searchlights and all the others were waving aimlessly about in the sky . . . My crew were delighted. My bomb aimer said that his bloody hands were frozen with dropping Window but that it was well worth it . . . he asked if we could do as many trips as soon as possible and finish our tour before the enemy found a solution."[9]

Hamburg began to die that night; in three subsequent raids on July 27–28, July 29–30, and August 2–3, Bomber Command mounted 3,095 sorties against the city with about 2,500 aircraft actually bombing the target. On July 25 and 26 the Americans bombed by day. Close to 50,000 people were killed, another 40,000 were injured, and some 61 percent of the city's living accommodations were destroyed. The worst damage was inflicted on the second night, when a combination of concentrated bombing, hot weather, and an almost complete lack of fire-fighting equipment (water mains had been destroyed) resulted in an immense firestorm. To the aircrews it seemed as if the heart of the city was in flames; smoke billowed up over 7,000 metres into the night sky. One member of No. 427 Squadron recalled, "It was incredible. The place was a great mass of flame. Halfway home we could still see the smoke rising from Hamburg."[10] In all, Bomber Command lost 86 aircraft (2.8 percent of the attacking force) with another 174 damaged (5.6 percent). It was not a high price for the result. Hitler's minister of war production, Albert Speer, warned the Führer that six more attacks such as the one on Hamburg would "bring Germany's armaments production to a halt."[11] But Bomber Command could not easily replicate the results of the Battle of Hamburg; the combination of conditions that had caused the firestorm were rarely duplicated. More to the point, the Germans quickly devised means to counter Window.

Hamburg epitomized the type of war that Arthur Harris meant to wage against Germany. He strongly believed that his crews were incapable of precision strikes against specific targets. He also believed that such strikes were useless. He scorned suggestions that attacking industrial "choke points"—synthetic oil plants, ball bearing factories, etc.—would shorten the war. He called these "panacea" targets, and those who advocated attacking them "panacea merchants." As mentioned, he believed that burning the heart out of Germany's major industrial cities, killing as many Germans as possible, and destroying their houses and places of work would win the war virtually by itself. Thus he stubbornly resisted attempts to harness Bomber Command to specific campaigns against strategic objectives.

On June 14, 1943, the Pointblank directive was issued by the Combined Chiefs of Staff, directing the USAAF and the RAF to stop their virtually independent bombing campaigns of Germany and to instead coordinate attacks against German industrial production, particularly the aircraft industry. But the directive was loosely worded and gave Harris all the leeway he needed to continue to focus his growing force on area attacks against German cities. So although Bomber Command did, in fact, launch many attacks at industrial and war industry targets, Harris always returned to area attacks, which he pursued relentlessly for the rest of the war whenever he could.

Harris had wide popular support for his position. By all measure, the civilian populations of the United Kingdom and Canada supported this endeavour of making the German people reap what they had sown in Warsaw, Rotterdam, Coventry, and London. Many political leaders also backed Harris's area offensive. One British MP probably put it best in 1942 when he wrote: "I am all for the bombing of working class areas of German cities. I am Cromwellian—I believe in 'slaying in the name of the Lord' because I do not believe you will ever bring home to the civil population of Germany the horrors of war until they have been tested in this way."[12]

The Canadian government had no say in the making of Royal Air Force bombing policy; it was interested strictly in the administrative control of the RCAF Overseas, not operational control. But the prime minister, for one, had no regrets about Harris's way of waging war against Germany's civilians. This was, after all, total war, and one forced on the world by the German nation. And although there were some voices raised in moral outrage at these attacks against German civilians, it was inconceivable to most people in Britain and Canada that the population of Germany should be spared in any way from the horrors of a war they had so brutally inflicted on everyone else.

* * * *

Bomber Command's area bombing campaign has remained controversial right into the twenty-first century. Harris himself actually dismissed the words "area bombing" as a euphemism. He was out to destroy German cities and kill the people in them. In the course of this campaign he intended to destroy Germany's willingness and its ability to wage war. At least one recent Canadian author has concluded that Harris's single-minded focus on killing Germans was little more than a war crime.[13] An earlier, more serious study by British military historian Max Hastings, makes the point that the tremendous cost of Harris's area bombing campaign in men—over 79,000 killed—and *matériel* did not bring about the defeat of Germany, as Harris hoped it would, nor was it even particularly effective in throttling the German war industry. The British and American governments both commissioned studies of the bombing campaign after the war. These studies—the United States Strategic Bombing Survey, under the direction of economist John K. Galbraith—and the British Bombing Survey, both concluded that the bombing campaigns had certainly been effective in wearing Germany down, but not decisive.

Were they correct? It is an important question, because if the tremendous sacrifices of the bomber war were essentially in vain, then so were those sacrifices—and the large loss of German civilian life that attended it. Perhaps the great resources and manpower that were devoted to city bombing could have been used more effectively to win the war earlier. The British Admiralty, for example, certainly believed that the use of four-engine bombers would have greatly aided them in winning the Battle of the Atlantic much earlier, but the aircraft were not made available because Harris and his US counterparts hoarded them for their attacks against Germany.

More recent scholarship—such as *Why the Allies Won* by Richard Overy (1995), *How Effective Is Strategic Bombing?* by Gian P. Gentile (2001), *The Strategic Bombing of Germany, 1940–1945* by Alan J. Levine (1992), *The Bomber War* by Robin Neilands (2001), *America's Pursuit of Precision Bombing, 1910–1945* by Stephen L. McFarland (2004), *Air Power* by Stephen Bodiansky (2004), and last but not least *The Wages of Destruction: The Making and Breaking of the Nazi Economy* by Adam Tooze (2006)—disagree with the earlier works (and Hansen) and came to essentially the same conclusions: Allied bombing began the systematic destruction of the Luftwaffe by early 1944. Allied bombing destroyed the German synthetic oil industry by the fall of 1944. Allied bombing wreaked havoc on the German rail transportation system by mid-1944 and the canal system by the fall of 1944. German war industry was dead by the start of 1945. All from bombing.

Adam Tooze, whose primary sources were largely drawn from the Third Reich's own statistics or from German wartime industry records, discusses some of these impacts in minute detail. He shows how bombing literally cut the Ruhr off from the rest of Germany, and warped the already overstretched German war economy to such an extent that virtually every kind of economic activity in Germany was dedicated to war production and everything else was stamped out by the Nazis. He shows

Our Finest Hour

that the impact of the bombing on fighter production, for example, was to force the Germans to keep on building more and more obsolete aircraft like the Bf-109. He concludes that "it was not territorial losses that paralyzed the German economy but the onset of a campaign of aerial bombardment, of completely unprecedented intensity."[14] It can be argued that it was really the US bombing that did most of that damage; Speer certainly declared that to be so.[15]

Harris was the commander of Bomber Command, and in the RAF's peculiar administrative set-up, virtually master of all he surveyed. His immediate superior, Chief of the Air Staff Sir Charles Portal, had no authority to tell Harris what targets to bomb or not bomb. But Harris, like all commanders, was capable of being swayed, persuaded, and brought on side when necessary. Thus Bomber Command, and No. 6 Group, attacked much more than the built-up centres of German cities. They also assaulted industrial, transportation, and military targets, sometimes with great effectiveness. One such attack was on the German experimental rocket installations at Peenemünde, on the Baltic Sea coast, on August 17–18, 1943, when Bomber Command sent 541 aircraft (57 from No. 6 Group) to destroy or delay the German V-2 effort. The attack was a reasonable success, forcing the Germans to disperse V-2 production and delaying that production by several months, but No. 6 Group suffered grievous losses—12 aircraft, representing 19.7 percent of the total dispatched—compared to the total attacking force (6.7 percent). Part of the reason was that the Group's aircraft bombed toward the end of the raid when German night fighters had been fully alerted and had congregated near the target. But part was also due to poor discipline among the crews. Martin Middlebrook, whose book on the raid remains the standard account, wrote, "Canadian Main Force crews were not notoriously rigid followers of flight plans and timetables, and a study of the records of the 6 Group squadrons reveals a characteristic spirit of independence."[16] It was clear that the problems that had plagued the RCAF bomber group from the start were troubling it still.

As the summer gave way to fall and longer nights, Harris launched the preliminary phase of what would later prove to be a prolonged assault on Berlin. Between August 23–24 and September 3–4, Bomber Command attacked Berlin three times. No. 6 Group sent 129 aircraft to the target (only 3 on the last raid); 96 actually bombed Berlin, 19 returned early, and 12 were shot down for an overall loss rate of 9.3 percent over the three missions. Bomber Command did not return to Berlin until the night of November 18–19; in the meantime, it and No. 6 Group attacked a variety of other targets, concentrating on the Ruhr. From September 3–4 to November 18–19, the RCAF mounted twenty bombing attacks and eight minelaying operations. Hanover was the most frequent target—attacked four times—and the object of No. 6 Group's first sortie of 100 aircraft or more on the night of October 8–9. Its losses that evening were 6 aircraft (6 percent), still too much for sustained operations.

Harris truly believed that Bomber Command could destroy Berlin and win the war without the need for an Allied attack across the English Channel. In early November he penned a memo to Churchill, which has since become famous either as an example of his gross over-estimation of the abilities of Bomber Command or of his enormous ego: "We can wreck Berlin from end to end if the USAAF will come in on it. It will cost between 400 and 500 aircraft. It will cost Germany the war." The USAAF did not come in on it—its emphasis was on bombing strategic industrial choke points, not in area campaigns—and Bomber Command never had the capability of winning the war by itself. Thus the Battle of Berlin was a long shot from the very beginning. In the early winter of 1944, many

Bomber Command crews came closer to cracking than at any time in the war. And yet they did not crack. Somehow, they dragged themselves to their aircraft night after night, took off into the gathering gloom, and did their best to fulfill their missions. It was their greatest time of testing. However, despite the persistence and the courage of the crews, the Battle of Berlin was an unmitigated defeat for Bomber Command. The heavy losses of bombers were not nearly balanced out by the destruction visited upon the city. There were many reasons for this. Berlin was far from the United Kingdom, and it was difficult for the crews to keep to the main path on so long a trip. The winter weather over northern Europe was usually bad; high winds, cloud, and icing of aircraft control surfaces made navigation a nightmare. Once the aircraft were over Berlin, the size of the city and the almost perpetual cloud cover, not to mention the heavy concentration of searchlights and flak, made accurate marking all but impossible. The primitive H2S sets carried by most of the Pathfinder Force could not pick out any distinguishing features of the city; Berlin was all just a great splotch of white light on their radar screens. Even the newer and better H2S sets helped little. And the main force crews often failed to bomb the markers properly. The intense flak and usually heavy concentration of night fighters exacerbated the problem of "creep-back" (i.e., bombing short of the markers in order to get away from the target area more quickly). Thus many tons of bombs fell in forests and fields.

Harris's preoccupation with Berlin did not stop him from ordering attacks on a host of other targets in the early months of 1944. He even sent his bombers to participate in the so-called Big Week, a planned combined bomber offensive (i.e., Bomber Command and the USAAF Eighth Air Force) designed to destroy German aircraft factories. But Berlin was his main target. He knew that the long-expected cross-Channel invasion of France was looming, and he feared that his bomber force would be pressed into pre-invasion preparatory attacks on defence installations and communications facilities. He was desperate to complete his self-appointed task of destroying Berlin before that happened.

At the end of the Battle of Berlin, Portal and Harris had perhaps the most serious of many disagreements that had started to crop up in early 1943. This time it was over Harris's demand for squadrons of Mosquito night fighters to protect his bombers. At one point Harris made a serious threat to resign, and Portal backed down. Leo McKinstry has since concluded, "If Portal had accepted Harris's resignation, the course of the European war might have been different. It would probably have been several months shorter, given that Bomber Command would have concentrated on targets of real military and economic value [which Portal wanted to do at that point in the war and which Bomber Command had become quite proficient at] instead of relentlessly aiming for nothing more than urban devastation."[17]

* * * *

Although No. 6 Group's performance had been improving steadily by the end of 1943, as Brookes tightened up on training (and as the survivors of the early disasters became more experienced), it was still not up to that of the other groups. Thus on February 12, 1944, Brookes left his post as Air Officer Commanding No. 6 Group and was replaced by Air Vice-Marshal Clifford "Black Mike" Mackay McEwen. A genuine First World War ace with twenty-seven enemy aircraft to his credit, McEwen had become an RCAF career officer in the interwar years, AOC of the RCAF's No. 1 Group based in Newfoundland, and a base commander in the United Kingdom before assuming command of No. 6 Group. McEwen was determined to make his new command one of the best in

Bomber Command. A hard taskmaster and a stickler for discipline on the ground and in the air, he made sure his crews lived up to his high standards of performance. He especially stressed good navigation and the maintenance of as high an altitude as possible both to and from the target. He ordered his crews into the air for extensive training flights whenever operations and weather allowed, and he even snuck aboard his aircraft to fly missions as an air gunner on a regular basis. That was strictly forbidden by Bomber Command, but he did it anyway, making sure his boys knew he was taking the same risks they were. Under his leadership, No. 6 Group would eventually become one of the best groups in Bomber Command in almost all areas of performance from early returns to accurate bombing of the target.

Harris had one more chance for a massive area attack on a German city before coming under US General Dwight David Eisenhower's command on April 1, 1944; he chose Nuremburg as his target. On the night of March 30–31, 795 bombers took off for Nuremburg, flying most of the way in a clear, moonlit sky. Gordon W. Webb was one of the No. 6 Group pilots flying that night: "The moon . . . was the brightest moon any enemy night fighter could have asked for. Visibility was virtually unlimited for a night sky. At our altitude cloud cover simply did not exist. What cloud there was hung low to the ground providing a perfect back drop, silhouetting the bombers."[18]

Webb saw that the bombers flying at his assigned altitude were leaving vapour trails, ghostly white in the night air, that no German pilot could possibly miss. He decided to climb as high as he could in the hope that the colder air would dissipate his bomber's vapour trail.

Given the moonlight and the visibility of the bomber stream, Bomber Command's usual deception tactics did not work. German air controllers determined the direction of the bomber stream early in the night and the German night fighters had little difficulty spotting the bombers; 95 were shot down—almost 12 percent of the attacking force. No. 6 Group put up 118 aircraft and lost 13, or 11 percent of the total. Webb saw one destroyed: "We were at 21,000 feet and our air speed just over 200 mph . . . Suddenly, a Lancaster dived across from right to left directly ahead and just below us . . . Right on the Lanc's tail was a ME 110. The fighter closed quickly and fired both his cannon and machine-guns. The shells hit across the fuselage of the Lanc and entered the starboard outer engine. The coolant released from the engine burst into flames and trailed a long line of fire." The fighter turned, fired again, and a wing tore off the bomber. It went into a "twisting, spiraling dive" and crashed. Webb saw no parachutes.[19]

In April the bomber offensive was harnessed to the needs of Operation Overlord, the invasion of Normandy; Although there would be attacks on German cities in the months that followed, the main effort was over France and the low countries both in aid of the D-Day landing and the ground battles that followed June 6. In March 1944, 70 percent of the bombs dropped by Bomber Command had been against German targets; that number fell to less than 25 percent in May and almost none in June. The switch of targets was reflected by dramatic falls in loss rates both for Bomber Command and for No. 6 Group. The respite would prove to be temporary for Germany's cities; when Eisenhower relinquished control of the British and American heavy-bomber forces on September 25 the bomber offensive against Germany resumed. In fact, the last seven months of the war would see some of the heaviest raids of any phase of the RAF/RCAF bomber campaign.

CHAPTER 10

VICTORY AT SEA

By the start of the fourth year of war in the North Atlantic, HMCS *St. Croix* had become one of the stalwarts of the Royal Canadian Navy and the Mid-Ocean Escort Force. Despite repeated problems with minor equipment failures, the old four-stacker had put to sea time and time again to help guard the vital convoys that made up the Allied lifeline to the United Kingdom and the supply line for the eventual invasion of the Continent. After several refits, *St. Croix* was about as well equipped as could be expected of a quarter-century-old ship; as mentioned, she and her crew had themselves destroyed U-90 in late July 1942 and assisted the Canadian corvette *Shediac* in the destruction of U-87 in early March 1943.

In August 1943 *St. Croix* was transferred from the Mid-Ocean Escort Force (MOEF) to the Royal Navy's Western Approaches Command, along with the RCN Town Class destroyer *St. Francis* and the RCN corvettes *Chambly*, *Morden*, and *Sackville*, to become part of Escort Group 9, a support group for North Atlantic convoys. These support groups were designed to reinforce the close escort of endangered convoys or to hunt submarines in mid-ocean and kill them. Unlike regular escort groups, support groups could stay in one locality long enough to sink a trapped U-boat while the convoy sailed on. The work of escort groups was invariably defensive—protecting convoys—but the role of support groups was inherently offensive—finding U-boats and destroying them.

On September 15, 1943, Escort Group 9 sailed from Plymouth to carry out an anti-submarine patrol in the Bay of Biscay when it was diverted to rendezvous with convoy HX 256. When it was clear that HX 256 was in no danger, Escort Group 9 was ordered to reinforce Escort Groups B 3 and C 2, which were guarding the westbound convoys ONS 18 and ON 202, respectively. The slow convoy—ONS 18—had sailed from the United Kingdom on September 13; the faster ONS 202 had departed several days later on a similar track and was now coming up behind the first convoy. At sea, a patrol line of U-boats awaited. On September 20, after the Admiralty picked up increasing signs of a German submarine concentration, they ordered the two convoys to merge. The merchantmen would be easier to defend in one large group, especially because they would be protected by more than twice as many escorts.

Escort Group 9 took up outer screening positions ahead and astern of the gaggle of merchantmen, on the port (south) side of the convoy. The weather was deteriorating, with fog and rain, as the motley collection of escorts and their charges headed west into a weather front. On the late afternoon of September 20, *St. Croix* was on station to the rear of the merging convoys when the Senior Officer of the Escort (SOE) ordered it to proceed farther astern to check out a possible U-boat sighting reported by an orbiting Coastal Command aircraft. At that point, the combined convoys were about 640 kilometres southeast of Greenland.

In the gathering gloom, *St. Croix* turned eastward and headed back along the convoy track, zigzagging at 24 knots. As it approached the spot where the sighting was reported her captain, Lieutenant-Commander

A.H. Dobson (Royal Canadian Naval Reserve) ordered the *St. Croix* to begin an asdic sweep. The ship was just settling back when two massive explosions detonated just near her port propeller. *St. Croix* glided to a stop and almost immediately took on a heavy list. The warship sent out a signal, but as the crew took to the sides, a third torpedo tore into the ship's stern. Within three minutes, *St. Croix* was gone; eighty-one members of her crew remained on life rafts and Carley floats, clinging to whatever they could. When the *St. Croix's* signal reached the escort commander, he dispatched the RN corvette *Polyanthus* to pick up the *St. Croix* survivors. On the way to the spot where *St. Croix* had gone down, the British warship was also torpedoed. It sank rapidly with the loss of all hands save one.

The next day, the RN frigate *Itchen*, another member of Escort Group 9, searched back over the convoy track and found the lone survivor of the *Polyanthus* and the eighty-one crew members from *St. Croix*. All were hauled from the cold sea some thirteen hours after the two sinkings. The next night *Itchen* was pursuing a surfaced U-boat when an "ear-shocking explosion" tore across the water. Apparently hit by a U-boat shell in its magazine, *Itchen* blew up in a spectacular display of pyrotechnics. Only three men were rescued, two from *Itchen* and one from the *St. Croix*.

St. Croix was the thirteenth RCN ship lost in the Second World War and the one that produced the heaviest loss of life—only one man survived out of a crew of 147. It was likely the first Allied warship sunk by a deadly new German device, the acoustic homing torpedo (Gnat), which homed in on the propeller noises of a target vessel and was especially designed to sink escort ships. One of the dead from the *St. Croix* was Surgeon-Lieutenant William Lyon Mackenzie King, nephew of the prime minister.

* * * *

On January 14, 1943, Churchill and Roosevelt met at Casablanca, Morocco, to decide key questions on the future course of the war. One of the topics covered was the war at sea; the conclusion they reached was that the defeat of the U-boat menace must have absolutely top priority, or else an invasion of the Continent could not be mounted. In fact, the high Allied losses at sea meant that no invasion would be possible that year. There were simply not enough merchantmen crossing the ocean from North America to both feed Britain and bring it sufficient men and weapons to mount a successful cross-Channel attack. It was decided that the Americans would have to return to the Atlantic battle in sufficient numbers to allow them and the British to form support groups, with escort carriers wherever possible, that could hunt and kill U-boats at sea. Escort carriers, or CVEs, also referred to as "baby flattops," were created from large merchant-ship hulls and improvised flight decks. HMS *Audacity* was the first; it began to escort convoys in the fall of 1941. While sailing with a convoy to Gibraltar, *Audacity*'s aircraft successfully fought off German planes and submarines, but she herself was torpedoed only a few days later.[1] In the war in the Pacific, the Americans began using these small carriers in 1942, and many more would be constructed in 1943. At the same time, enough VLR (Very Long Range) Liberator aircraft were to be diverted to the combined navies to close the air gap. As naval historian Dan van der Vat has put it, "The absolute necessity of providing end-to-end air-cover was thus clearly identified, together with the measures necessary for supplying it."[2]

That was all well and good. The politicians and their staffs made their pronouncements, then departed the sunny clime of North Africa for their cold capitals and let their naval commanders fill in the details.

But Admiral Ernest J. King, Commander-in-Chief of the US Navy, was in no hurry to operationalize the decisions made at Casablanca. He dragged his feet on the buildup of USN escorts in the Atlantic. After all, he had a naval war to fight in the Pacific and growing problems of command and control in his allotted part the Battle of the Atlantic theatre; thus the first US escort carrier, USS *Bogue*, and its accompanying destroyers did not begin operations until March. In addition, the RCAF was still denied VLR Liberators for Eastern Air Command, although the British hinted strongly that they themselves intended to station RAF Liberators in Newfoundland.

A large part of the Allied problem in the battle was lack of unity of command, which had been split between the US Navy and the Royal Navy even before the United States entered the war. The RN's Western Approaches Command was responsible for roughly the eastern half of the North Atlantic, while the USN's Task Force 24, based in Newfoundland, commanded the western half. Thus the Royal Canadian Navy was under the operational control of either the Americans or the British, depending on which part of the North Atlantic it was operating in. Yet by the late winter of 1943, the RCN supplied just about 46 percent of all the escort vessels available in the theatre and the United States only 4 percent. Vice-Admiral Nelles, for one, began to question this arrangement in the fall of 1942, hinting strongly that it was time for his British and US counterparts to let the Canadians into the overall command process. At the same time, however, RCN assets were themselves divided between one commander in Halifax and another in St. John's, Newfoundland. And Canada's ships were all over the place—seventeen corvettes in the Mediterranean, four escort groups in the North Atlantic (soon to be temporarily reassigned to the United Kingdom and the Gibraltar run for training), more in the Western Local Escort Force in Halifax, and at least half a dozen escorting tankers from the Caribbean to New York or Halifax. As to the question of which nation should assume command of the entire theatre, no one could come up with a satisfactory proposal just yet.[3]

* * * *

In January 1943 the RCN Escort Group C1 accompanied a fast HX convoy to the United Kingdom, then remained for rest, refitting, the installation of newer anti-submarine equipment, and the beginning of a long training regimen. They arrived at Londonderry on January 22. The other three Canadian groups followed in February. In agreeing to allow the C groups to be pulled from the North Atlantic, Mackenzie King had insisted that they were to be "returned to the North Atlantic Convoys as soon as they have reached a satisfactory state of efficiency and in any case not later than May, 1943."[4] The Canadians received concentrated instructions on how to do escort work correctly—or "properly," as the Royal Navy would have it. First the crews were retrained ashore in basics such as gunnery, signalling, asdic tracking, depth charging, and damage control. Officers were sent to the Western Approaches tactical unit in Liverpool for tabletop exercises and other tactical training. Then the entire group sailed for Tobermory, Scotland, where the Royal Navy had its extensive work-up and training facilities for its own escorts—HMS *Western Isles*—and where the Canadians received hands-on training at sea, aided by a "tame" British submarine.

The Gibraltar run, and the convoy route from there to North Africa in support of the Torch landings that had taken place the previous November, was thought to be a good training ground for the refurbished RCN crews and ships. There were fewer convoys, allowing more time for rest and repair between sailings, and virtually all of the route to Gibraltar was under land-based air cover. In addition, the Canadian escort groups could continue their training whenever they were back in the United Kingdom and could, if necessary, reinforce the seventeen RCN corvettes that had been sent to the Mediterranean for the Torch landings in the fall of 1942. Those vessels were doing yeoman work accompanying merchant ships to and from North Africa, particularly in the face of German and Italian air attacks. Between January 13 and February 8, 1943, for example, *Ville de Québec, Port Arthur*, and *Regina* sank one German U-boat and two Italian submarines. But these victories did not come without loss. On February 6 convoy KMS 8, sailing from Gibraltar to Bone, Algeria, and escorted by six British and nine Canadian corvettes, was hit by a large force of Italian dive and torpedo bombers; *Louisburg* was hit by a torpedo and sank within four minutes, taking half her company with her. Another RCN corvette, *Weyburn*, was lost after hitting a mine as it left Gibraltar for the United Kingdom. In both cases the death toll was higher than it might have been, due to the explosions of the ships' depth charges as they sank below the surface—an ever-present threat when escort vessels went down. C1 got in its licks in the Mediterranean theatre when escorting KMS 10 to North Africa. While still in the North Atlantic, the convoy was attacked by three U-boats, which sank two merchantmen before *Shediac* and *St. Croix* destroyed U-87.

Although the Allies had themselves rebroken the German naval codes in December 1942 (the code produced by the new four-rotor Enigma machine), they temporarily lost their ability to decipher them in early February 1943 as the Germans made one of a number of periodic adjustments to their encoding machines. In fact, through much of mid-1943, decoding of the new German code was sometimes painfully slow, and messages arrived at Western Approaches too late to be of any use in fighting off submarine attacks.

Qualified success was better than the unmitigated disaster that had marked the war at sea in 1940 or 1941, but it was still not good enough by far to sustain Operation Bolero. What was needed were more convoys, more frequent sailings, and reduced losses. That meant more and better-equipped escorts, among other things. Thus C3 was scheduled to return to the Mid-Ocean Escort Force (MOEF) by March 11, with the three other Canadian groups following in short order. Remaining temporarily under RN control and commanded by Royal Navy SOEs (Senior Officers of the Escort), they were assigned to their old role of close escort, while the job of seeking out and attacking the wolf packs was taken up by the new British and American support groups then being deployed to the battle.

The Canadians returned to the North Atlantic better prepared and, in many cases, better equipped with new radar, asdic, anti-submarine weapons such as Hedgehog, and gyrocompasses to replace their old magnetic compasses. But the ships themselves were still a generation behind British corvettes, which the Royal Navy had been improving since mid-1940, and did not compare to new US Destroyer Escorts, which were purpose-built to escort convoys or kill submarines. Canadian escort groups were also still desperately short of destroyers. They were thus fast enough to escort convoys, especially the slow ones, but not nearly nimble or heavily armed enough—as the British and Americans were—to take on the job of dedicated U-boat hunting. Thus the Royal Canadian Navy continued to plod the convoy routes while the Royal Navy and the US Navy set out to win the war against the U-boats.

One of the most important but little-known gatherings of the Second World War opened in Washington on March 1, 1943; the Atlantic Convoy Conference brought together representatives of the US Navy, the Royal Navy, and the Royal Canadian Navy to discuss command organization, tactics, and the equipment needs of the three navies in the Battle of the Atlantic. The meeting was called and hosted by Admiral Ernest J. King, the US Chief of Naval Operations, but it was the brain-child of Vice-Admiral Percy Nelles, Chief of the Canadian Maritime Staff, who was determined to carve out a recognized operational role for the RCN, which was contributing almost 50 percent of the convoy escorts but was still under the command of the US Navy's Task Force 24 when operating in the western Atlantic and that of Western Approaches of the Royal Navy when operating in the eastern Atlantic. While the RCN still suffered from shortages of the most up-to-date equipment, including destroyers, its capacity to fight off the U-boats had increased consider-ably since the first year of the war. It had a large fleet of corvettes, it was about to begin to receive the new River Class frigates, and its ability to generate and share intelligence with the Royal Navy and the US Navy had grown exponentially. The RCN had established its own Operational Intelligence Centre, or U-boat tracking room, in Ottawa[5], where the latest signals intelligence from radio intercepts and RCN-controlled high-fre-quency direction-finding stations, combined with information from its two North Atlantic Allies, gave the RCN a very clear picture of what was happening in the war at sea and the ability to instruct its escort groups on course changes to avoid gathering wolf packs. Since the United States had almost no ships escorting convoys, Nelles believed the time had come for the Canadians to emerge from the shadows of the RN and the USN. Admiral King had initially rejected the notion of such a meeting—and what the request clearly implied—when it was first raised by Nelles in the fall of 1942, but changed his mind, in part because of the Casablanca directives and in part because he was coming to the conclusion that the United States Navy would do well to be rid of the task of escorting North Atlantic convoys anyway. The Royal Navy's Western Approaches

Command, under Sir Max Horton, was at the same time anxious to expand its area of operational control right to the shores of Maine. Nelles was greatly aggravated by this prospect.

The conference opened against the backdrop of an approaching climax at sea; the Germans were launching more U-boats in larger packs than ever and were determined to reprise the "happy times" of earlier in the war. The Allies were equally determined to pour more and newer ships, aircraft, and anti-submarine warfare technology into the Atlantic campaign to break the U-boat packs and greatly increase the convoy tonnage moving to the United Kingdom. If they could not do so, the war in the west might degenerate into stalemate.

The conference opened on a sour note. Admiral King, never happy about US escorts sailing in mixed groups (such as A 3) but still unable to commit large numbers of destroyers to the North Atlantic battle, threatened to pull the US Navy out of the fight altogether. This coincided with a renewal of Canadian demands to take over full command responsibility for naval and convoy operations in the northwest Atlantic. In the end, the conferees decided that the position of Commander, Task Force 24, would be abolished—thus eliminating USN control of Royal Canadian Navy escort groups in the western Atlantic. Instead, the US Navy would take general responsibility for southern convoy routes (from the Caribbean to the Mediterranean) but would leave one support group in the North Atlantic. The United Kingdom's Western Approaches would continue to be in charge of the anti-U-boat war in the eastern Atlantic, with an even larger area of control than before. At the same time, Canadian Rear-Admiral Leonard W. Murray would become Commander-in-Chief, Canadian Northwest Atlantic Command. He assumed this new post on April 30, 1943, taking responsibility for all Allied convoy and naval operations north of latitude 40 and west of longitude 47. He thus became the only Canadian to command an entire theatre of war in the Second World War, while the Royal Canadian Navy gained operational control of its own ships—and those of the US Navy and Royal Navy—in the waters near Newfoundland and maritime Canada, and on the approaches to Boston and New York.

Then forty-seven years of age, Murray had been born in Nova Scotia and had entered the Royal Naval College of Canada in 1912, when he was just sixteen. Like all interwar career officers, Murray put in his time aboard Royal Navy vessels, making important connections and learning the ropes of a big-ship navy. But he never affected the British accent that so many other Canadian officers did after serving with the RN. He loved sports, particularly hockey, and with the ordinary seamen of the RCN he cultivated the common touch that reflected his roots in rural Nova Scotia. Soon after the outbreak of the war, he was appointed to command the Newfoundland Escort Force, then promoted to Commanding Officer, Atlantic Coast in 1942. By all accounts, he was a popular leader with a good grasp of the essence of the anti-U-boat campaign.

The Atlantic Convoy Conference marked a significant change in the Allied approach to the war against the U-boats. There were to be more escorts, more escort groups, more support groups, and more escort carriers; eventually the United States would increase its contingent of support groups—all of which were formed around baby flattops—from one to four. This allowed for larger convoys and more frequent sailings. And the Royal Canadian Air Force was finally going to get two squadrons of the long-sought-after VLR Liberators to fly air cover over the western Atlantic and help the British and the Americans close the air gap.

Operating with the aid of Ultra intelligence, the support groups were especially effective in destroying the U-boat supply system that Dönitz had built up since the start of the war. That system depended on the

1,700-tonne Type IX "milch cows," which rendezvoused with U-boats on war patrol and provided them with fuel, food, mail, and spare parts. The meetings were arranged through coded radio transmissions. Once the Allies were able to decipher the German naval codes again, it was easy to arrange ambushes. Of ten such milch cows operating in the spring of 1943, only two were still afloat by the end of the summer. The impact on U-boat operations was immediate and dramatic; war patrols had to be shortened, and it became necessary to arrange meetings of several U-boats at the same time—a dangerous move. Former U-boat captain Peter Cremer later recalled one such resupply operation in August 1943: "We were five boats dawdling away the time without fuel or food. The situation was not only grotesque, it was desperate . . . here we were, five of us confined in the narrowest space, a prey to anything that might happen."[6]

The Canadians, too, acquired new escort vessels in mid-1943. First came a second generation of River Class destroyers, ex-RN vessels, which were more heavily armed than the original prewar River Class types. The first into commission, in March 1943, was the *Ottawa II*, which became the nucleus for a new Canadian escort group, C5, formed partly from the disbanding of the mixed Canada-US group A3. Eventually six of these destroyers were acquired and all were assigned to the Mid-Ocean Escort Force (MOEF) to give the Canadian groups more punch. In June the Royal Canadian Navy also took delivery of the first of what would prove to be a fleet of more than seventy River Class frigates, virtually all of which were built in Canada. The frigates were built to merchant-shipping, not naval, specifications and had a disturbing tendency to simply blow up if torpedoed in the engine room.

However, most of the new frigates would not be ready until 1944. Until then, the Royal Canadian Navy was still a largely corvette navy—

and its original-pattern corvettes were simply inadequate for the job of hunting submarines. Thus the RCN played almost no role at all in the Allied offensive against Dönitz's wolf packs, which peaked in May 1943, when forty-seven U-boats were destroyed in one month. As Canadian naval historian Marc Milner has put it, "Canadian groups were back in the mid-ocean, but British groups were doing the fighting."[7]

That month, Dönitz lost his own son, a watch officer serving aboard U-954. The tide had clearly turned to the point where heavy U-boat concentrations now invariably meant heavy U-boat losses. The mid-Atlantic air gap had finally been closed, and the Allies now had enough high-quality escort vessels, escort carriers, and aircraft to shepherd large convoys safely to their destinations with small loss. On May 14 Dönitz told Hitler, "We are facing the greatest crisis of the U-boat war: The enemy are making it impossible to fight." It was time to rethink tactics and to re-equip his submarines with advanced new weapons and detection gear to give them a fighting chance. At the end of May he pulled his U-boats out of the North Atlantic for the first time since the start of the war and assigned them to the area west of the Azores.

* * * *

Although it was the British and American navies that bore the brunt of the offensive against the U-boats in the spring of 1943, they could not have been successful without the Royal Air Force and the Royal Canadian Air Force. Most historians who have written about the Battle of the Atlantic are agreed that the Allies could have closed the mid-Atlantic air gap much sooner than they did had the bomber barons of the RAF and the USAAF not fought tooth and nail to keep all the heavy bombers for themselves and deny them for anti-submarine operations. Their success in hoarding these large and long-range aircraft until mid-1943 remains one of the great enigmas of the war. By all measure, the Combined Chiefs of Staff surely realized that the greatest U-boat victories always occurred beyond the reach of aircraft, and that long-range aircraft were of inestimable value not only to sink U-boats, but to keep them down and render them virtually blind while the convoys manoeuvred around them. They ought to have realized all this, but either they did not—even though the long-range aircraft and the submarine-hunting technology had been available at least since the start of 1942—or they simply lacked the will to compel the air force chiefs to comply.

The RCAF's contribution to turning the tide against the U-boats was made at both ends of the Atlantic. No. 10 Squadron of Eastern Air Command, based at Gander, began to receive VLR Liberators on April 22, 1943; by the end of May the entire squadron had converted to the new aircraft. No. 11 Squadron, located at Torbay, Newfoundland, began to convert to the Liberators in July. As mentioned, No. 10 Squadron had already sunk one submarine (U-520) the previous October when a Douglas Digby had spotted it on the surface as it was returning from patrol over convoy ON 140. The squadron's new Liberators would account for two more sunk U-boats before the end of 1943. Its first victim was U-341, spotted and sunk on September 19 as the aircraft was returning to Gander from Iceland after escorting HMS *Renown* (which was carrying Winston Churchill back to the United Kingdom after the first Quebec Conference). The second victim, U-420, was destroyed on October 26. No. 11 Squadron made ten sightings and mounted eight attacks but did not sink any U-boats.

At the other end of the transatlantic lifeline, five RCAF squadrons served with the RAF's Coastal Command in the United Kingdom at various times during the war, including No. 405 and No. 415, both of which later reverted to Bomber Command. Nos. 422 and 423 Squadrons, which flew Sunderland IIIs out of Castle Archdale, Northern Ireland, together (and in combination with other Allied units) accounted for four U-boats during the war. The most successful anti-submarine squadron in the RCAF was No. 162, which flew Canso patrol bombers. Originally based at Yarmouth, Nova Scotia, the squadron was loaned to the RAF's Coastal Command in January 1944 and transferred to Iceland. Its first victory came on April 17, 1944, and by the end of the war it had accounted for five submarines sunk, one shared sinking, and one U-boat damaged. On June 24, 1944, a No. 162 Squadron Canso flown by Flight Lieutenant D.E. Hornell attacked U-1225 and sank it but was hit by return anti-aircraft fire in the course of the engagement and crashed. The crew spent nine hours in the water before being rescued (seven were rescued, one had drowned). Hornell died shortly after rescue and was posthumously awarded the Victoria Cross.

From the beginning of 1943 to the end of the war, RCAF squadrons sank or shared in the sinking of seventeen U-boats. It was a solid performance, aided by the fact that from early 1943 on, the RCAF was no longer the stepchild of the Allied anti-submarine air forces but began to receive the newest in an ever-lengthening list of high-tech anti-submarine devices. For example, Eastern Air Command's Liberators were equipped with the newest US-designed anti-submarine radar, a ten-centimetre radar that could detect a surfaced U-boat from about 20 kilometres away but could not be picked up by the U-boats' Metox radar-detection receivers. EAC also received the newest US-built homing torpedoes, designed to be used in conjunction with airdropped sonobuoys. The system was intended to detect prowling U-boats and radio their location to patrolling aircraft, which would then drop the homing torpedoes to hunt the submarines down. A highly technical and temperamental system, it never worked properly during the war but became the mainstay of anti-submarine weaponry in the years afterwards. That was also true of the new magnetic anomaly detector (MAD) gear, designed to detect submerged submarines from changes in the earth's magnetic field caused by the passage of large metallic objects. The Germans were not standing still while the Allies improved their submarine-hunting techniques and technology. They designed and began to build newer boats, the Type XXI and the Type XXIII, which were streamlined and much faster underwater than the old Type VII and Type IX. They even planned to develop a hydrogen peroxide–fuelled engine to drive the submarines underwater—which could keep the submarines submerged for many days at a time. It is sometimes said that if they had been able to put these submarines into full production (only a handful of the conventionally powered Type XXIIIs were built) the tide of the North Atlantic battle might once again have turned in their favour. That may have been so, but the Allies were not asleep either, and the new anti-submarine devices (such as sonobuoys and homing torpedoes) and fast-escort vessels then in experimental stages or on the drawing boards would undoubtedly have helped restore the balance in the fight to keep the sea lanes open.

One of the most perplexing mysteries of Canada's war at sea is the fate of Vice-Admiral Percy Nelles, who in January 1944, was kicked upstairs; he was removed from his post as Chief of the Maritime Staff in Ottawa by Minister of National Defence for Naval Services Angus L. Macdonald and dispatched to London as Senior Canadian Flag Officer Overseas (SCFO [O]), a largely administrative position with little involvement in naval operations. He was replaced by Vice-Admiral G.C. Jones in January 1944. The reason given by Macdonald was that Nelles had been responsible for RCN vessels "putting to sea inadequately equipped as compared to British ships ... over an unduly long period of time."[123] In fact, however, Nelles was Macdonald's and the government's scapegoat for a situation that had been developing since before the war and that was in large measure the direct result of both circumstances beyond his control and government policy.

The political story of Nelles's demise began in early August 1943 when Macdonald received a private memorandum from Captain William Strange, Director of Naval Information at Naval Service Headquarters, which made a singular point: the RCN was not equipped to fight an anti-U-boat offensive in the North Atlantic because most of its vessels (particularly the corvettes) still lacked basic modern equipment such as gyrocompasses and Hedgehog. Strange was a reserve officer who had joined the Naval Information Branch of the Royal Canadian Naval Volunteer Reserve (RCNVR) from a position at the CBC. His job was to write about the war at sea, and in the summer of 1943 he decided that to do that job properly, he ought to cross the ocean with a Canadian escort group and see what the Battle of the Atlantic was like from a Canadian perspective. It was then that he discovered the appalling conditions aboard RCN corvettes and their ineffectiveness as submarine hunters. Conversations with Royal Navy officers in the United Kingdom added to the evidence he was gathering that the RCN needed significant improvements in equipment before it would be able to join the campaign to destroy German submarines in the mid-Atlantic.[8]

Strange's report may have been news to Macdonald, but anyone who knew anything about the war at sea in late 1942 and early 1943 knew these stark facts already. The British had tried to remedy the situation as much as they could by fitting up-to-date anti-submarine equipment onto some Canadian vessels when they were in port in Londonderry, but the best British kit naturally went to Royal Navy ships first. The underlying problem could not, however, be solved by adding radar here or bolting on a new anti-aircraft gun there. The original corvettes were too slow, too lively at sea, and too uncomfortable for their crews to engage in sustained submarine hunting. They needed to be modernized, primarily through the extension of their forecastles and rebuilding of their bridges, as the Royal Navy had done to virtually all of their corvettes by mid-1943. Nelles and the navy knew that and started the rebuilding job with the corvettes *Edmonton* and *Calgary* but were hampered by a lack of space in Canadian shipyards and by the constant use of Canadian vessels in the Western Local Escort Force, the Mid-Ocean Escort Force, the New York–Trinidad tanker run, and the assignment of seventeen corvettes to the Mediterranean. The root cause of the problem, however, was a government decision made early in the war to keep contracting for the short-forecastle corvettes instead of incorporating design changes into each new batch ordered, as the Royal Navy had done. Nelles had certainly accepted too many assignments for the navy, too quickly, thus exacerbating equipment and training issues. But his political masters—notably Mackenzie King and Macdonald—had given little thought to the crisis they themselves were helping to create in the navy. Besides, in a total naval war for which Canada was completely unprepared in 1939, what else was Nelles to do?

Macdonald was minister in charge of the navy. He ought to have been aware of this problem—it had, after all, plagued the RCN for at least two years. And letters, reports, and memoranda regarding this "equipment crisis," as it came to be known, had reached his office—if not his desk—several times prior to the Strange memorandum. In fact, a petition had been sent to him in the summer of 1942 by Lieutenant-Commander Andrew Dyas MacLean, RCNVR, and a group of anonymous reserve officers, and while it focused mainly on regular navy discrimination against reserve officers, it also mentioned inadequate equipment and training. It was almost always reserve officers such as MacLean and Strange who brought these matters directly to the minister because, for the most part, the RCNVR had joined up to fight the war and go home, while the "pusser" navy had careers to think of.

Upon receiving the Strange memorandum, Macdonald ordered a behind-the-scenes investigation of the equipment situation while trying to get written answers from Nelles to the questions posed in the memo. Not surprisingly, Nelles defended his and the navy's record, but to no avail. News was already beginning to reach the public via press reports that all was not well at Naval Service Headquarters, and Nelles's head was on the block. Macdonald's real choice was either to resign and admit that both he and the government had made several poor choices regarding the war at sea, or fire Nelles. In this way, the man who had single-handedly done so much to shoulder aside the powerful Royal Navy and United States Navy and to carve out an RCN area of operational command in the war at sea was unceremoniously dumped.

* * * *

No one was more aware of the impact of the battle of new technologies on the war at sea than Dönitz. He was determined to re-equip his submarines before sending them back into the mid-Atlantic, and between the end of May and the beginning of September 1943, he did just that. The long-run answer to the Allies' new ships and equipment was to be the Type XXI and XXIII U-boats. Until they were available, however, Dönitz relied on improving his conventional submarines. This was done by supplying them with additional anti-aircraft guns, new radar detection equipment, and the snorkel device, which allowed the U-boat to use its diesel engines while travelling just under the surface, thus attaining higher speeds and giving it the ability to recirculate stale air, recharge batteries, and stay under water for much longer periods than previously. Each submarine was also allotted four *Zaunkönig* homing torpedoes (Gnats) intended especially to destroy escort vessels. Fired in the direction of the intended victim, the Gnat was designed to circle until it picked up the appropriate propeller noise, then home in on it.

In early September the re-equipped U-boats returned to the mid-Atlantic. Group *Leuthen* with twenty submarines intercepted ONS 18 and ON 202 about 640 kilometres southeast of Iceland and inflicted heavy damage; six merchantmen were destroyed, under cover of night and bad weather, and three escorts—*St. Croix, Polyanthus,* and *Itchen*—went to the bottom with heavy loss of life. When the skies cleared on the afternoon of September 22, RAF and RCAF VLR Liberators were there, orbiting the convoy, ready to provide cover; the RAF's No. 120 Squadron then accounted for one U-boat sunk.

The battle of ONS 18 and ON 202 was, without a doubt, a German tactical victory, but it was also one of the last they were to have and was a clear exception to the general trend of events in the North Atlantic in the last months of 1943. Within weeks the Royal Navy and the Royal Canadian Navy began to equip their escorts with towed decoy devices to counter the homing torpedoes—the British used Foxer, and the Canadians utilized the simpler and lighter CAT gear—thus effectively neutralizing one of Dönitz's most important new innovations. In one convoy fight lasting from November 18–21, for example, the Germans threw twenty-three U-boats and twenty-five long-distance Focke-Wulf 200 Condor bombers at a convoy of twenty-eight escorts and sixty-six merchant ships, but sank only one merchantman while losing three U-boats. One of the submarines destroyed was U-536, which fell victim to the

RCN corvettes *Snowberry* and *Calgary* and the RN corvette *Nene*. In the first six months of 1943 the U-boat fleet had sunk 1.7 million tons of Allied shipping; in the last six months its total dropped to 500,000 tons, while it lost 142 submarines. Many more merchant vessels and escorts would be sunk and several thousand more merchant seamen and naval personnel would lose their lives before the end of the war, but the tide of the war at sea had clearly turned.

* * * *

On November 30, 1942, the Tribal Class destroyer *Iroquois*, built in the United Kingdom, was commissioned into the Royal Canadian Navy. It was the first of four Tribals built for the RCN in the United Kingdom during the war; the other three were *Athabaskan* (commissioned in February 1943), *Huron* (commissioned in July 1943), and *Haida* (commissioned in August 1943). The Tribals were by far the most advanced and most powerful of the destroyers acquired by Canada during the war. Designed for Royal Navy fleet service in the late 1930s, these ships displaced close to 1,800 tonnes, had a top speed of 36 knots, were manned by fourteen officers and 245 ratings, were armed with six 4.7-inch guns and four torpedo tubes as main armament, and carried a large complement of medium and light anti-aircraft weapons. In every sense, the Tribals—sometimes described as small, light cruisers—were designed for fleet action and not for escort duty.

In 1941 the Canadian government, at the urging of the Royal Canadian Navy, had decided to build four modified Tribals in Canada, even though the RCN's Chief of Naval Engineering and Construction, Rear-Admiral George Stephens, opposed the move as extravagant and unnecessary. The Canadian-built Tribals were not commissioned until after the war, and it is clear from the historical records that the RCN saw them as the backbone of a modern and moderately sized postwar fleet, rather than as ships to help win the current war. The acquisition of the British-built Tribals was but the first step in the RCN's effort to build a small, modern, balanced fleet of destroyers, cruisers, and light aircraft carriers—a small "big ship" navy. This sort of navy had been the dream of virtually all the regular RCN officers from the very beginning of the navy in 1910. Now, with a global war to fight, Nelles and the rest of the navy's high command saw their opportunity. The British-built Tribals were followed by two light cruisers, also British-built. The first was HMCS *Ontario*, built in Belfast, Northern Ireland, as a Minotaur Class light cruiser and transferred to the Royal Canadian Navy in July 1944. *Ontario* was completed and commissioned in late May 1945 and sailed for the Pacific to join a Royal Navy cruiser squadron, but arrived after the Japanese surrender. The second was HMCS *Uganda*, commissioned into the Royal Navy in early January 1943 and transferred to the RCN in October 1944 (see Chapter 3). This focus on building a small "big-ship" navy while the real war the RCN was fighting was the Battle of the Atlantic was yet another source of friction within the navy between the regular "pusser" navy and the volunteer navy, who sailed and eventually commanded the "sheep dog" navy of corvettes, Town Class destroyers, and eventually River Class frigates.

The RCN Tribals were based in Scapa Flow in the Orkney Islands for much of 1943 and performed a variety of duties, from anti-submarine patrols in the Bay of Biscay to anti-aircraft escort on the Arctic convoy routes from the United Kingdom to Murmansk, USSR. There were trials aplenty for these destroyers, ranging from equipment failures and a short-lived mutiny on the *Iroquois* to the damaging of *Athabaskan* by a German glider bomb off the coast of Spain in late August. *Athabaskan* was part of a five-ship support group attacked by Dornier 217s carrying Hs 293 glider bombs in the early afternoon of August 27. A new weapon, the Hs 293 was a winged, radio-controlled missile with a 600-pound warhead, capable of speeds of up to 375 miles per hour. As the aircraft approached, the Canadian destroyer opened fire at 1303; soon the sky was filled with flak from the guns of the five warships. One of the ships, HMS *Egret* was hit almost immediately and sank quickly with heavy loss of life. Then, five aircraft attacked *Athabaskan*, three releasing their glider bombs at the same time; one missile tore into the destroyer and out the other side before exploding—its fuse improperly set. But it did tremendous damage; five men were killed or died of their wounds, twelve were injured, and the ship was left down at the bow, on fire, and with a significant list. Escorted by the remaining ships in the group, *Athabaskan* limped back to port, arriving at Plymouth late on the 30th; the dead had already been buried at sea.

By the end of 1943 the RCN was beginning to complete its transition from a built-from-scratch navy operated primarily by reservists to a modern, well-equipped fighting force. In the last year and a half of the war, it would face the U-boats on better-than-equal terms and acquit itself at least as well as its larger Allies. It was a long struggle, and there was much war yet to come, but by 1944 the Royal Canadian Navy was clearly out of the woods and ready to assume a full share of responsibility for what would soon prove to be the Allied victory at sea.

CHAPTER 11

SICILY

The small Sicilian town of Nissoria sits astride Highway 121 connecting Leonforte and Assoro to the west with Regalbuto and the Catania Plain to the east. About 5 kilometres east of Nissoria, and higher up, lies Agira, which dominates the peaks of Mount Gianguzzo to its southeast, Mount Campanelli to the west, and the road to Troina to the north. Both Nissoria and Agira sit like eagles' nests, perched on high peaks, and reachable only by narrow roads that twist and climb over the hills and mountains dominating the centre of Sicily. They were built there long ago, because armies from time immemorial have fought over Sicily, and the Sicilians long ago learned the hard lesson that it is easier to defend hilltops than valleys. From Nissoria to Agira, the two-lane blacktop that is Highway 121 passes over three ridges, which the Canadians referred to as Lion (about a kilometre to the east of Nissoria), Tiger (another 2 kilometres on), and Grizzly, just on the western edge of Agira. On the morning of July 24, 1943, this otherwise unexceptional place was the initial objective of a major attack mounted by the Royal Canadian Regiment (RCR) of the 1st Canadian Infantry Brigade, 1st Canadian Infantry

Division. The ultimate goal of the attack was Agira on the outer ring of the defences that the Axis forces—German and Italian—were forming to protect the northeast corner of Sicily from the British, Canadian, and American forces, which were pushing toward Messina.

The assault plan, conceived by divisional commander Guy Granville Simonds, was designed to use the massive firepower and air resources available to the Canadian division to clear the way for the RCR attackers. Under cover of a massive air and artillery bombardment, the RCR's four rifle companies were to leapfrog astride the highway through Nissoria and then make the long, hilly climb into Agira. They would be followed in due course by the other troops of the 1st Canadian Infantry Brigade, the Hastings and Prince Edward Regiment, and the 48th Highlanders, accompanied by the 12th Canadian Tank Regiment (Three Rivers Regiment). Before the attack began, RCR Commanding Officer Lieutenant-Colonel Ralph Crowe took his company commanders forward to reconnoiter the ground over which they would advance. One of them later described the scene: "Ahead lay undulating ground covered with olive orchards and grapevines while Nissoria looked white and deceptively clean in the burning sun."[1]

The barrage and the airstrike began, and the ground ahead of the advance was covered with smoke and literally shook with the shock of exploding bombs and shells. Then the infantry began its advance. The RCRs tried to follow the creeping barrage, but the inevitable delays that accompany any infantry advance slowed them down and the barrage moved on, the men falling farther and farther behind. As soon as the shelling passed over, the German defenders on Lion clambered out of their slit trenches and bunkers, sited their mortars and machine guns, and waited for the Canadians to draw within range. At about 1630, they opened fire. The RCR regimental history tells what happened:

"Just as [the RCR] began emerging from the eastern edge of [Nissoria] heavy fire was brought down upon them. At the same time the rear companies were breaking from cover, provided from orchard lands west of the town. Some of the troops were actually eating apples as they moved forward, when suddenly a terrific mortar barrage fell upon them and a low ridge they must of necessity cross was swept by machine gun fire."[2]

D Company was chewed up and the survivors pinned down. The other three companies took cover in a gully south of the highway, advanced up it, and found themselves behind the German ambushers and in sight of Agira. Despite the best efforts of Lieutenant-Colonel Crowe, the RCR could not advance, due to heavy German fire and constant failure of their radios. Crowe himself and a party from his tactical headquarters were killed trying to scramble up Lion. Cut off from their battalion headquarters and unable to use their radios, the three company commanders in the gully remained where they were until dawn the following day and then withdrew to rejoin the rest of the battalion. Subsequent attacks by the other battalions of 1st Brigade also failed. One historian of the brigade would later write that Lion was the brigade's "most bitter and fruitless fight in Sicily."[3]

The campaign to capture Agira was supposed to be over in two days or less. It was not. The heavy casualties suffered in the initial attack by D Company of the RCR were just the beginning; it would be five more days before Agira was taken by the 2nd Brigade, and the cost to the division was high: 438 killed, wounded, missing, or taken prisoner. The Canadian war cemetery at Agira is the largest in Sicily. Canadian military historians have recently written a great deal about 1st Canadian Division's war in Sicily and with good reason.[4] It was the first sustained Canadian Army operation of the Second World War, and it was a triumph for the division, which had been assigned a marginal role at the start of the

Our Finest Hour

campaign but which was then called upon to play a significant and successful part in the overall Allied victory. But the most peculiar part of the story of Canada's participation in the Sicilian operation was how and why almost one-sixth of the Canadian Army was split away from First Canadian Army and sent to a faraway theatre of war, not reuniting with the rest of the Canadian Army until the spring of 1945.

* * * *

While the battles for North Africa raged back and forth over desert sands and coastal blacktop roads, and from wadi to oasis to seaport, the Canadian Army in the United Kingdom—the "dagger pointed at the heart of Germany"—trained and trained and trained some more. By the spring of 1943 it had assumed the basic shape it would retain for the rest of the war—an army headquarters (then commanded by A.G.L. McNaughton), two corps headquarters, five divisions (three infantry and two armoured), and two independent armoured brigades. In addition, the 1st Canadian Parachute Battalion was being made ready to join the 6th British Airborne Division in July. Altogether, that was a formidable force, whose main purpose was to provide the United Kingdom with an effective defence so that British divisions could be sent elsewhere—the Balkans and North Africa, for example—without leaving the United Kingdom open to attack. The fact that Hitler's campaign in the Soviet Union, which he had attacked on June 22, 1941, rendered the possibility of any new German campaign to invade the United Kingdom completely moot, is beside the point. The United Kingdom could not denude itself, and the British Chiefs of Staff Committee believed that for the moment British divisions would do better fighting the Axis than Canadians would. That, and the major difficulties posed by trying to move the entire Canadian Army—some 120,000 men—by sea to some fighting front, and then insert them into an ongoing campaign, discouraged any effort by the British to use the Canadian Army. Best to keep them in the United Kingdom and use them when the time came to assault France.

Much has been written about the role of General A.G.L. McNaughton in insisting on keeping the Canadian Army together, thus making it difficult for Britain to use any portion of the army in places such as North Africa.[5] And it is most certainly true that McNaughton, an avid follower of Canadian Corps Commander Arthur Currie in the First World War (he was appointed in June 1917), believed both that Canadians fight best when they fight together and that Canada's political interests were best served when its troops formed one concentrated expeditionary force. Yet there were other key reasons why the Canadian Army was still sitting in the United Kingdom in the spring of 1943. Chief among them was that, although the government of William Lyon Mackenzie King had effectively placed the Canadian Army under the British Chief of the Imperial General Staff (Sir Alan Brooke since December 1941), there was little effort to coordinate the growth or shape of the Canadian Army with the British ministry of defence (headed by Churchill himself). The Canadian Army was evolving along the lines of Defence Scheme No. 3, with new divisions being inaugurated, filled up, and sent to the United Kingdom, and corps and army headquarters being set up. Canada was thus acting as the independent nation it was and devoting its resources and manpower to the war effort as it saw fit and believed would help the greater Allied cause. But by late 1942 and early 1943, it was also building a far larger force in the United Kingdom than the British could practically use in the only active theatre of war in which it was then fighting: North Africa. And that fact had nothing to do with McNaughton.

Despite the disastrous outcome of Dieppe, Lieutenant-General H.D.G. Crerar, Minister of National Defence J.L. Ralston, and Chief of the General Staff Ken Stuart remained as eager as ever to get Canadians into ground-combat action. On October 15, 1942, for example, Brooke recorded in his diary, "After lunch Ralston (Defence Minister of Canada) with Vincent Massey [Canadian High Commissioner to the UK] and Stewart [sic] came to see me as regards the possible role of Canadian forces in 1943! Not an easy matter to lock them into any of our proposed offensives."[6] One good reason was that Brooke himself did not know what Churchill and Roosevelt were planning for 1943 and would not know with any real certainty until after the Casablanca Conference in January 1943 and the Trident Conference in Washington in May 1943. He did know that the Torch landings were in preparation and would take place in November, but by October, it was far too late to insert any sizable Canadian formations into the Allied order of battle.

Whether Brooke realized it or not, Ralston, Stuart, and Massey's visit to him in October 1942 was actually a sign of the significant lack of unity within the Canadian government and its high command regarding how and where Canada's army ought to be deployed. That lack of unity was an inevitable result of how Mackenzie King chose to run Canada's military effort—or rather, not to run it. From the earliest days of the war, Mackenzie King had chosen not to seek any significant role in the higher strategic direction of the war. This does not mean that the government had no military aims. Those aims, signified by the drive for Canadianization in the war in the air and Nelles's campaign for a separate operational area for the Royal Canadian Navy at sea were to keep Canadian units together wherever possible and to ensure that Canada's military contribution be as visible as possible. Both principles were designed primarily to demonstrate to Canadian voters that their government was ultimately responsible for their war, that it was "Canada's war," as historian J.L. Granatstein pointed out in the very title of his history of Mackenzie King's war policies. In fact, however, the government eschewed almost entirely its prerogative—a prerogative enshrined in its military cooperation agreement with the United Kingdom—to intervene in the British command of Canada's forces. Thus Ottawa was not ultimately responsible for the decision as to where and when the Canadian Army was to be deployed; Brooke and the high command of the British army were. In early February 1943, for example, when fighting was raging in North Africa, Stuart was informed that "two divisions of the Canadian army might be sent into action very soon . . . [either] to North Africa [or] in the attack on Italy."[7] That particular deployment did not come about, but it is interesting that Mackenzie King's diary shows no remonstration at the fact that the British were choosing what to do with the Canadian Army. Under those circumstances, the rather peculiar situation arose that Stuart, Crerar, and Ralston were lobbying the British to use the Canadian Army as soon as possible, whereas McNaughton, the army commander, wanted to keep the army together, and Mackenzie King agreed with McNaughton. But as to the general principle of how the Canadian Army was to be used, Mackenzie King told British Admiral Sir Percy Noble, a member of the Combined Chiefs of Staff then visiting in Ottawa, that the Canadian government "was ready to have our men go anywhere so long as it was in accordance with the wishes of the combined Chiefs of Staff. It was not due to any word of ours that men were being held back in Britain."[8] That statement was somewhat ingenuous but basically true. The Canadian government would have the ultimate say, but the real decision would be Churchill's and Brooke's.

Throughout March, as the Germans poured reinforcements into Tunisia in a vain attempt to put off the inevitable, Stuart, Ralston, and

Crerar continued to push in Ottawa and in London, trying to convince Brooke to send a Canadian division to North Africa or to the looming campaign in Sicily. McNaughton pushed back—with King's blessing and with Churchill and Brooke's initial backing as well. As late as mid-March, the British Chiefs of Staff and Churchill himself did not want a Canadian division sent to the Mediterranean. But within weeks, Churchill relented, possibly because Brooke had convinced him that McNaughton would be a hopeless army commander when First Canadian Army eventually entered battle and that splitting the Canadian Army might be a means of forcing McNaughton's retirement. Brooke thus proposed to McNaughton on April 23 that a Canadian division (and a Canadian armoured brigade) be substituted for the 3rd British Infantry Division, which was already in the Sicily order of battle, thus not adding significantly to the number of Allied troops to fight there.[9] McNaughton reluctantly chose the 1st Canadian Infantry Division and the 1st Canadian Army Tank Brigade to go. The Canadians were to be attached to the 30 Corps of the British Eighth Army under General Bernard L. Montgomery. The rest of the invading force consisted of the United States Seventh Army under US General George S. Patton. Overall ground commander was British General Sir Harold Alexander, while overall commander of air, land, and naval forces was US General Dwight David Eisenhower, who had been in command of the Torch landings.

Mackenzie King thought it was "a pity to see McNaughton's force broken up," but relented due to the growing public demand in Canada to see the army in action. He recorded in his diary "perhaps it is all for the best. I can see that the Canadian people and perhaps the Americans, Australians and New Zealanders and others would wrongly construe Canadians remaining out of action for another whole year."[10] King also feared another Dieppe if the Canadian Army were to be kept in the

United Kingdom until the invasion of France, and was thus no doubt relieved that one division, at least, would escape a possible slaughter. But was it all for the best? Later that year Canada would successfully press the British to accept an additional armoured division (the 5th Canadian Armoured Division) and 1st Canadian Corps Headquarters into the order of battle for the campaign in Italy. The Canadian Army would remain divided until the last months of the war and the very existence of First Canadian Army would be called into doubt by the British, who always chafed at having dominion higher headquarters to deal with. After all, they had learned in the First World War how inconvenient it was to have all four Canadian divisions fighting under a Canadian Corps headquarters because it made it so much harder for them to order the Canadian divisions about as they pleased, or as they believed the battle situation required. And Canada was ultimately the poorer for the decision to split the army, because Ottawa's already self-limited leverage over Canada's fighting forces was undermined even more, while any political leverage Canada might have had with the British or the Americans as a result of putting the equivalent of six full divisions ashore in Normandy slipped away.

* * * *

The first Canadian division to be mobilized and dispatched to the United Kingdom, the men of the 1st Canadian Infantry Division, wore the "old red patch" on their shoulders, the same divisional insignia worn by the 1st Canadian Division in the First World War. The division included the three prewar Permanent Force regiments: the Royal Canadian Regiment, the Princess Patricia's Canadian Light Infantry, and the Royal 22e Regiment—one in each of its infantry brigades—and six militia battalions.

Under the command of Major-General H.L.N Salmon, it was assigned a landing zone at the extreme left flank of the British invasion force, but Salmon and much of his staff were killed on April 29 as their Tunis-bound plane crashed after takeoff from the United Kingdom. Guy Simonds was assigned to take Salmon's place. Born in the United Kingdom in 1903, Simonds came to Canada as a tot with his family before the First World War and settled in Victoria. He entered Royal Military College in 1921 and graduated in 1925. He then joined the Royal Canadian Horse Artillery to begin a long and distinguished career in the Canadian Army, which ended only upon his retirement in 1955. Simonds was one of the best of the small corps of professional officers that kept the Canadian Army alive in the interwar years, and one of the few Canadian officers who thought systematically about the craft of war, publishing articles on armour-infantry tactics in 1938. He went overseas with the 1st Canadian Infantry Division in 1939 and was noticed early for his brains, his devotion to his task, and for his no-nonsense approach to soldiering.

Simonds is a controversial figure in Canadian military history. He was British born, learned much from the British, and was admired by no less a man than Monty himself as the best of the up-and-coming Canadian officers. Never loved by those who served under him, he was respected by the British as a man who they believed understood war and the requirements for winning battles. Non-Canadian military historians today generally believe him to have been the best field commander Canada produced in the Second World War. Simonds tried to be a teacher as much as a leader; as commander of the 2nd Canadian Corps from early 1944 to the end of the war, he constantly sent memos to his officers, advising them on subjects as diverse as German defensive tactics and on the importance of properly integrating reinforcements (i.e., replacement personnel) into their battalions. He was a devotee of the set-piece battle, and his battle plans were invariably long and complicated and based on major applications of firepower. He firmly believed in the maxim, born of bitter experience in the trenches of the First World War, that it was better to waste shells than the lives of men; he seemed not to pay much heed to another maxim, that of the nineteenth-century German commander von Moltke, that no battle plan survives first contact with the enemy.

* * * *

The Allied plan finally came together in May at the Trident Conference in Washington, but only after a long and fierce debate among British and American commanders as to what objectives, roles, and portions of the island were to be assigned to what forces. In the end, a compromise plan evolved that was to have the British land on the island's southeast coast, south of Syracuse, on a front of some 60 kilometres, while the Americans were to land at Gela, on a front only slightly smaller, on the south coast. The Allies were then to attack northward, cut Sicily in half, pivot eastward, and then destroy the enemy forces between them and the east coast. The Canadians were assigned a benign sector of the landing beaches near the southernmost tip of Sicily, opposite the town and airfield of Pachino. D-Day was set for July 10.

On June 19 the first transports carrying the Canadians from the United Kingdom directly to Sicily left Scotland; a second group of transports sailed five days later. This was known as the Slow Assault Convoy. A second convoy, known as the Fast Assault Convoy left the River Clyde on June 28. Both proceeded to Gibraltar. The men did not know for certain where they were going, but the fact that they had traded their Canadian-built Ram tanks for American Sherman medium tanks (the standard battle tanks used by both the British and the Americans in North Africa) must have given them a clue. They were also equipped with Thompson .45 submachine guns (also the standard submachine guns in the theatre), rather than the British Sten guns used by Canadian and British troops in northwest Europe. The voyage to Sicilian waters took many days, and after they had passed through the Strait of Gibraltar, enemy aircraft and submarines posed a serious threat. On July 4 three ships from the Slow Assault Convoy were torpedoed and sunk; fifty-eight Canadians were killed, thirty artillery pieces and more than 500 vehicles were lost, as well as the radios to be used by divisional headquarters.

In the pre-dawn darkness of July 10, American and British paratroopers assaulted the southern and southeastern coasts of Sicily. The mixed force of glider-borne troops and parachutists was badly scattered, and there were heavy casualties. Then the naval support force opened up, and the sounds of heavy gunfire and the flash of the long-range naval guns tore through the night. The Canadians' beach, code-named Bark West, was on the southwest side of the Pachino peninsula. The 1st Brigade was assigned to the right flank of the beach—"roger"—and the 2nd Brigade to the left flank—"sugar." The landing on the left went well, and the troops were quickly ashore with no opposition, but on the right there were delays due to the late arrival of the landing craft. Then, when they did nose toward shore, they grounded on a sandbar about a hundred metres from the beach. Platoon commander Farley Mowat was there: "This was the moment toward which all my years of army training had been building . . . Revolver in hand, Tommy gun slung over my shoulder, web equipment bulging with grenades and ammo, tin hat pulled firmly down around my ears, I sprinted to the end of the ramp shouting 'follow me, men!' . . . and leaped off into eight feet of water."[11]

All along the beachheads, the Italian defenders offered little or no resistance; British, Canadians, and Americans were quickly ashore and then pushed inland. The 1st Canadian Division easily captured the airfield at Pachino. Then the business of unloading the supplies and equipment began as the battalion and company commanders huddled at Brigade O (Orders) Groups to look at maps and aerial photographs and to plan the next move. As the sun climbed higher, the flies and mosquitos were everywhere, the vehicles produced thick clouds of dust and grit, and the heat increased by the minute. Since most of the Canadian vehicles had been lost at sea, the men would have to walk. Makeshift mule teams were organized to carry the heavier equipment, the animals "requisitioned" or hired from the locals. After a night near the beach, the 1st and 2nd Brigades started out, the 1st on the right, moving overland through the hills to the village of Giarratana, the 2nd on the left, marching by road toward Modica and Ragusa, where they were to effect a junction with the US 45th Division. That first day set the pattern for most of those that followed: the men walking up steep roads or making their way over rocky hillsides under a broiling sun in unbearable heat, with water rationed and clouds of mosquitos and flies to torment them every time they stopped for rest. As the division moved inland, it was accompanied by the Three Rivers Regiment of the 1st Canadian Army Tank Brigade; the rest of the brigade remained behind with the armoured reserve of the British Eighth Army (the designation of this unit was soon changed to 1st Canadian Armoured Brigade, a pattern that was followed for all similar formations).

The Canadians encountered virtually no opposition for the first five days and took the headquarters of Italian General Achille d'Havet in Modica on July 12 without a struggle. Simonds went there personally to accept d'Havet's surrender. Riding in a jeep, CBC war correspondent

Peter Stursberg was just back of the troops as they advanced beyond Modica: "We passed columns of Italian prisoners, who had fallen into our hands with the capture of General d'Havet's headquarters at Modica. There were thousands of them, and they were only too willing to cheer and raise their fingers in the V sign for the photographers."[12] This seemed to be the attitude of the great majority of Italian troops in Sicily: happy to resign from the war. It was a different story with a handful of crack Italian troops and, of course, with the Wehrmacht.

To the right of the Canadians, the bulk of Montgomery's Eighth Army drove ashore easily and began to advance north. On July 12 Montgomery approached Alexander with a new plan for the capture of the island. The British would proceed north along the narrow coastal plain east of Mt. Etna directly to Messina to cut off the German and Italian escape route to the mainland. The Americans would protect the British left flank. This meant that the US 45th Division would change its axis of attack from northeast, virtually alongside the 1st Canadian Division, to northwest, and that the main north-south highway in that sector would be given to the Canadians for their use in their advance toward Leonforte. To the consternation of the Americans, Alexander complied. Thus the Canadians were fated to run into major concentrations of German troops offering stiff resistance, while the US 45th Division, close on the Canadian left, had a rather easier time of it. In the words of US military historian Carlo D'Este, "So ludicrous was the situation that once the orders were issued transferring the disputed boundary and Route 124 to Montgomery, the Canadians encountered stiff resistance while the 45th Division stood helplessly by, unable to come to their aid even though their artillery was within one mile of the highway."[13]

Thus was the Canadian Army finally committed to the battle. No doubt Crerar, Ralston, and Stuart were satisfied with their efforts;

Mackenzie King, however, was not. One of the major reasons why he had reluctantly consented to adding a Canadian contingent to the Sicily campaign was to address popular and political complaints in Canada that the army wasn't doing anything to defeat the Axis. Now that it was about to join ground combat in Europe, the prime minister wanted to make certain that everyone knew about it as soon as the event took place and that he, as Canada's leader, should have an opportunity to make his own announcement about it. On July 8, however, Mackenzie King learned that the British were taking great steps to ensure that Montgomery's role in the campaign be kept a secret and that nothing was to be given out "as to the extent of Canadian troops employed." Mackenzie King was indignant and made a special point of complaining both in Parliament and in the press. He openly blamed the British and strongly implied that Roosevelt was far more sympathetic to Canada in matters like this. Eventually the issue was allowed to rest, but King's temper tantrum does show how much he had grown to resent Canada's exclusion from the higher councils of Anglo-American decision making that had first been established in December 1941 and January 1942, right after Pearl Harbor when Churchill had quickly rushed off to Washington to impose himself and his Chiefs of Staff into American war planning. At the same time, however, and almost from the start of the war, Mackenzie King had refused any suggestion that Canada try to inject itself into higher Allied war planning. Thus from the United States' entry into the war on December 8, 1941, Mackenzie King's main effort in the area of high policy was directed at ensuring that Canada be recognized for what it was doing, even though what it was doing was being decided by Roosevelt, Churchill, and their high commands, without reference to the Canadian government.

On the Sicilian battlefront, the Canadians ran into their first firefight at Grammichele, about 65 kilometres northwest of Pachino as the crow flies, on July 15. It was a short fight—the Canadians suffered only twenty-five casualties—and the village was taken by noon. Then it was on up the climbing, twisting road to Caltagirone and beyond that to Piazza Armerina, which the division reached on July 17. The firefight at Grammichele set a pattern for most of the skirmishing that took place in the following few days. Not strong enough in men or heavy weapons to permanently block the Canadian advance, the Germans used the terrain to set up ambushes manned by rearguards, who were under orders to withdraw as soon as their positions appeared to become untenable or as soon as ordered. Thus, most of the time, the Germans would put up stiff resistance for several hours, then use the cover of darkness to withdraw to their next defensive position, usually at the next village, a few kilometres up the road. German engineers effectively used explosives to blow up bridges and culverts, increasing the difficulties Canadians were already having traversing the rough terrain.

With the almost total collapse of the Italian forces on the island, the Germans rushed the 29th Panzergrenadier Division to Sicily and began a concerted counterattack against Montgomery's positions south of Catania. The British advance north to Messina was stalled by fierce German resistance at the Primosole Bridge spanning the Simeto River; the road to Catania and beyond ran over that bridge.

The German strategy was no longer to try to drive the Allies off the island but, to the contrary, to hold a main defensive line of resistance running northwest roughly from Mount Etna on the east coast to the north coast near San Stefano. In this way they could keep Messina out of British or American hands as long as possible and prepare for an orderly withdrawal from Sicily to Calabria via the Strait of Messina. (In the event, the decision to eventually evacuate was made around July 23.)

On July 17, as the Canadians were moving up the highway beyond

Piazza Armerina toward Valguarnera, General A.G.L. McNaughton, who had arrived in Algiers on July 10 with the intention of visiting the Canadian troops in Sicily, was told by Montgomery that "no visitors will be allowed on the island" as long as the fighting continued. McNaughton appealed to Alexander who backed Monty; McNaughton returned to the United Kingdom without seeing the Canadians and lodged a stiff complaint with Sir Alan Brooke, Chief of the Imperial General Staff. Monty never liked visitors on the battlefield, no matter who they were, and was the operational commander of the Canadians in Sicily, but McNaughton was the General Officer Commanding-in-Chief of the army, which 1st Canadian Infantry Division was a part of. Monty later claimed that Simonds had not wanted to be bothered in the midst of handling his first battlefield command and that, in effect, he was protecting Simonds—and that is entirely possible. But his action created further friction between McNaughton and the British high command, which was already beginning to doubt McNaughton's ability to command an army in the field.

As the Canadians moved toward Valguarnera, the division was still short of artillery and transport, but the battalions seemed to make up for their shortages through innovation. The Hastings and Prince Edward Regiment, for example, used the cover of darkness to infiltrate its rifle companies across country, thereby outflanking the main German defences, which faced west on Highway 117. An even better example of using darkness and terrain to mask movement came a few days later as the lead elements of the division approached Assoro and Leonforte. Simonds decided to advance at night: the 2nd Brigade would head for the town of Leonforte, on the highway, the 1st Brigade for the heights of Assoro, one of the highest peaks in the area located about 3 kilometres southeast of Leonforte. The Germans were strongly entrenched in the region.

The Hastings and Prince Edward Regiment was given the task of leading the 1st Brigade. As they began to form up for their advance, their Commanding Officer was killed by German shellfire as he was attempting to get a good look at the German defences. His replacement, Major the Lord Tweedsmuir, decided on a bold night march and a steep climb up a height known as Castle Hill, which dominated the German positions. All night the men struggled upward over a steep rocky slope, weighted down by packs, rifles, and ammunition, and with the ever-present necessity to keep absolutely quiet. Before dawn they reached the peak, surprised the small German observation party camped there, and took control of the position. All the next day and the next night they called artillery fire down on the German defences. With the Hasty Ps already in their rear, those positions were no longer viable, and the Canadians soon took both Assoro and Leonforte with minimal casualties.

The Canadians had done well thus far. They had used brains and initiative to find the weak spots in the German defences; they had utilized what military theorists call the "indirect approach" to outflank the Germans or to make German forward positions untenable. The Germans were impressed. Their initial assessment of the Canadians was this: "very mobile at night, surprise break-ins, clever infiltrations at night with small groups between our strong points."[14] The Germans undoubtedly admired those tactics because they were so like the ones they themselves used. Emphasizing manoeuvre over firepower as a way to achieve victory on the battlefield, the Germans habitually encouraged officers, NCOs, and men to think for themselves in battle, to find the point of least resistance in the enemy defences, and to exploit those weaknesses to outflank, to infiltrate, to flow through and around enemy strongpoints. The Germans respected firepower (artillery, tanks, tactical air support), but combined firepower with manoeuvre in a flexible manner to ensure that firepower did not dictate the shape of the attack. The Germans eschewed rigid attacks, systems for centralized control of infantry movement, and pre-set fire plans to which the infantry was supposed to adhere. It was the infantry that determined what would happen in a German attack, not the artillery.

As the Canadians consolidated on the Leonforte-Assoro massif, German resistance continued to stall northward movement on the Eighth Army front. Montgomery thus decided to assume an "aggressive defence" south of Catania and switch the main focus of his attack inland, with the Canadians turning their axis of attack eastward, from Leonforte along Highway 121. This was the hinge of the German defensive line. On July 22 Montgomery visited Simonds to update him and direct him to secure advance to Nissoria, capture Agira, and continue on to Regalbuto and, if possible, to the Simeto River.[15]

Simonds began to prepare the attack on Agira. By now most of his lost artillery had been replaced. He knew he was facing formidable German defences somewhere around Agira, and he also knew that the Canadian division's role in the Sicily campaign was now much more important than it had been previously. He decided to abandon the tactics of movement and flexibility that had worked so well up to this point and lay on a full-fledged set-piece attack with air support, armour, and an intricate artillery fire plan. Everything was to be centrally controlled and depend on precision timing.

The forward elements of the 1st Canadian Division attacked toward Agira from the west on the afternoon of July 24, while the British 231st (Malta) Infantry Brigade, under Simonds's command for this operation, attacked from the south. The Canadians were led by the 1st Brigade under Brigadier Howard Graham. Nissoria was easily taken, but (as we

Our Finest Hour

have seen) the RCR, which led the attack, suffered heavy losses in one company. The other three companies unwittingly infiltrated behind the German forward defences but were caught between the Germans on the Lion feature to their rear and the Tiger feature that lay between them and Agira. They were able to fire on German reinforcements moving west along Highway 121 but were unable to move forward and were withdrawn after dawn on the 25th. That night, the Hastings and Prince Edward Regiment tried to follow the RCR assault and outflank the Lion position, but they, too, were beaten back with heavy losses. The 48th Highlanders attacking north of the highway toward Monte de Nissoria had no better luck that day. Then the 2nd Brigade went at it on the night of July 26 behind the strongest barrage yet. Supported by anti-tank guns and the tanks of the Three Rivers Regiment, the Patricias quickly captured Lion and moved onto Tiger, about 1,500 metres to the east. There they waited while the artillery paused for twenty minutes to allow the Patricias to consolidate. This was a constant theme in Simonds-planned attacks. Initial stages heavily supported by firepower of one sort or another, a pause to move up artillery or consolidate, then a second attack coming soon after the first. Unfortunately, the Germans used the breathing space to pull themselves together, and when the Patricias resumed their attack, they ran into stiff opposition at Tiger and could go no farther. Second Brigade commander Brigadier Chris Vokes ordered the Seaforth Highlanders in to stiffen up the PPCLI. The two battalions battled through the night, and by morning of the 27th succeeded in pushing the Germans out of their defensive positions and back toward Agira. One more defensive position remained before Agira: Monte Fronte, just south of the highway and the Grizzly feature to the north. These dominating features lay about 3 kilometres to the east of Tiger. On the 27th, Vokes sent the Seaforths to attack Monte Fronte. One company advanced north of the highway and was rebuffed by strong German defences, but another worked its way overland and outflanked Monte Fronte. Vokes then ordered the Edmonton Regiment to attack Grizzly itself. Advancing over broken ground against stiff resistance, they, too, seemed stymied until one section of men moved into the German rear and so confused the defenders that they began to break. By the next morning, the 2nd Brigade was on its objective and preparing for a heavy bombardment of Agira itself, preceding a PPCLI attack on the town. The bombardment was cancelled when a Forward Observation Officer from the Royal Canadian Artillery failed to spot any Germans remaining in the town and two companies of the Patricias simply advanced into Agira. After two hours of house-to-house fighting and the support of yet another company and the Three Rivers Tanks, Agira was taken.

Three days before Agira was secured, Italian dictator Benito Mussolini was overthrown by Marshal Pietro Badoglio, who formed a new ministry. Badoglio told the world that Mussolini's demise would not affect Italy's allegiance to the Axis, but Hitler did not trust him. Hitler could ill afford an Italian collapse followed by the hurried advance of the Allied armies to the Italian-Austrian border; thus massive German reinforcements were rushed into Italy to virtually occupy the country as the Italians sorted out their political mess. The Germans effectively began to dissolve the Italian army and place their own soldiers in defensive positions throughout the country. Henceforth, it would not matter whether or not Italy surrendered; the Allies would still have to fight and die for every metre of the country.

In the fight for Agira, Simonds's division had consisted of his two Canadian brigades and the Malta Brigade; the 3rd Canadian Infantry Brigade had been attached directly to 30 Corps to aid in the clearing of the valley of the Dittaino River, some 15 kilometres to the south of the

Canadian division. It reverted to Simonds's command in early August, but not before capturing an important bridgehead at Catenanuova on July 30 from the 923rd German Fortress Battalion. Thus Simonds continued his drive toward Regalbuto, about 8 kilometres east of Agira, with a mixed division of two Canadian and one Maltese brigade (commanded by a British officer). The village was strongly held by the Hermann Göring Division, and the Malta Brigade was beaten back in the initial attack on July 31. Then it was the turn of the RCRs. They managed to get as far as a small bridge to the southeast of the town before being stopped by German fire. Throughout the day the RCR men clung to their positions in the heat, baked by the sun, and exposed to German machine-gun fire from two directions. The battalion was in an "unenviable situation," according to its regimental historian.[16] Simonds knew it would be useless to continue with a frontal assault and pulled the RCRs back after dark. But the Germans withdrew also, as they had so many times, and the town was occupied on August 3.

With 3rd Brigade as the spearhead, the Canadians pushed on toward Adrano, crossing the Simeto River on August 6. That was about as far as the division was going to go; on August 7 they were pulled out of action to prepare for the next round of fighting, the assault on southern Italy. On the other fronts, the Americans under Patton had swung wide to the western part of the island, taking Palermo on July 22, then headed toward Messina along the north coast. Montgomery's troops finally broke through the German defences as the Germans withdrew units to try to hold their line against the 1st Canadian and 1st US Infantry Divisions. The Eighth Army entered Catania on August 5 and then also began to push toward Messina. The Germans and those Italians who fought alongside them conducted a skillful defence and withdrawal and pulled both men and equipment back toward Messina, where an elaborate shuttle operation brought them quickly over the strait to the Italian mainland. As the Allies advanced and the Germans withdrew, the front narrowed, and Montgomery decided to pull the Canadians out of the line for a well-deserved rest.

As fighting formations, the previously untried 1st Canadian Infantry Division and the 1st Canadian Armoured Brigade had done well in their first test. The infantry battalions had shown skill and determination under difficult conditions of heat, mountainous terrain, dust, and the continued need to march, rather than be trucked, to the next objective. The Canadian infantry worked well with the artillery and the air force. There were the usual mistakes, foul-ups, and failures of communication made more difficult by the woeful inadequacy of the basic Mark 18 radio in hilly country (it was not much better on flat ground). There were also weaknesses in leadership that did not show up in training but emerged starkly under fire—Simonds always dealt ruthlessly with such situations. But the greatest single problem that the fighting in Sicily pointed to was not so much a failing as it was an inherent part of the thinking of so many Canadian commanders, from Simonds on down: the idea that massive firepower, stepped assaults, and centralized control (i.e., fire over movement) were the keys to victory in battle. Too often, in the months ahead, this way of war produced as much failure as success.

The Allies entered Messina on August 16 and 17; the Germans got clean away. Not a single able-bodied German soldier was left behind, aside from those who had been captured, and masses of armour, artillery and transport vehicles were brought over to Italy as well. Given that the Allies' combined strength was roughly eight times that of the Germans, the campaign had taken far too long, had been too costly in casualties, and had not achieved its ultimate objective of destroying the

German forces there. Sicily had been taken—at a cost of approximately 29,000 Allied casualties, 2,310 of whom were Canadian (562 killed, 1,664 wounded, 84 taken prisoner in the 1st Division)—but that event in itself would have little impact on the outcome of the war. Across the Strait of Messina, Italy, and a formidable German defensive force, awaited.

CHAPTER 12

ORTONA

Ortona, Italy: Christmas Day, 1943. War artist Charles Comfort was still sleeping in the pre-dawn dark when incoming German 88mm rounds shattered his reverie. The shells seemed to be falling behind his position, raising his by then recurrent fears of stray or short rounds: "As I rose, all hell broke loose from our own guns, including the 7.7s whose thundery voice might well 'wake the dead.' The dawn was dark as the grave and chilly and the mud sucked powerfully at my rubber boots as I wandered over in the direction of 'E' mess. Above the man-made thunder I heard myself humming the old traditional carol 'God rest you merry, gentlemen, let nothing you dismay.' 'Let nothing you dismay' seemed to have a special significance this morning . . ."[1]

The words of the old carol would have seemed more than a little ironic to the men of the 2nd Canadian Infantry Brigade and the 12th Canadian Armoured Regiment (Three Rivers Tanks) battling for every metre of the small Italian coastal town of Ortona. The fight for the town had started at nightfall on December 20 when the Loyal Edmonton Regiment, supported by the Seaforth Highlanders of Canada, moved into the western outskirts of Ortona. Some Canadian officers thought the

Germans might evacuate the town, rather than engage in a costly urban fight for a place that had little military significance. Ortona was a small town built on a rocky outcrop poking into the Adriatic, with a small port below it that, by now, had been rocked by shellfire and half destroyed by German engineers. By the time the 2nd Brigade began its assault on the town, Division Commander Major-General Chris Vokes had already ordered his 1st and 3rd Brigades to push northwest of the town with the aim of surrounding it completely.[2] But just as Vokes had his orders to take Ortona, the Germans had orders to hold it. The German paratroopers who defended the town were determined to make the Canadians pay for each building and for every block. "For some unknown reason, the Germans are staging a miniature Stalingrad in Ortona," wrote one war correspondent, a reality that the men in the town knew well.[3] House by house, Ortona was eventually cleared of its defenders as the year 1943 and the first phase of the Canadian campaign in Italy dragged to its bloody conclusion.

It is difficult, if not impossible, to even find the name Ortona in most of the histories of the war in Italy written by non-Canadians.[4] For them, it seems to have been but a skirmish compared to the dramatic near-disasters at Salerno and Anzio or the great Allied drive up the Liri Valley to open the via ad Romam—the road to Rome. But Canadians should long remember what happened at Ortona, because Ortona was the first episode of urban combat—city fighting—in the Italian theatre, and although the Canadian Army was unprepared for combat in a built-up area, it was forced to learn quickly. In a few short days, the Canadians were able to adapt to this most difficult form of warfare and share its lessons with Allies far and wide.[5] The desperate fight in the ruins of that small Italian town showed beyond all doubt that the Canadian Army in Italy had learned how to adapt to modern war against a determined enemy.

Italy is a defender's dream and an attacker's nightmare. Since the Apennine range runs down the centre of much of the peninsula, the water courses from the mountains to the Mediterranean on the west and the Adriatic on the east virtually all flow east–west. Thus for anyone advancing up the coasts of Italy there was, in a very real sense, always "one more river to cross." The land between these rivers was rugged, the few coastal roads were narrow and twisty and easily covered by shellfire or cut by the blowing up of numerous bridges or culverts. Mule trains were as necessary for military transport in the mountains of Italy as they had been in Sicily. There was precious little open ground anywhere suitable for tank warfare, nullifying the Allies' overwhelming numerical advantage in armoured fighting vehicles, and the many small villages, usually built of stone with walled courtyards and narrow streets, were easy to defend. Summers were hot and dry, winters cold and rainy, especially in the mountains.

The German defence was coordinated by one of the best defensively minded German officers, Field Marshal Albert Kesselring. His overall strategy was to withdraw virtually all his troops from Calabria, the southernmost province of Italy, allow the Allies to advance rapidly north through most of southern Italy up to the Sangro River, and then mount an aggressive defence along a series of fortified lines anchored in the mountains. In the opening stages of the fight, this strategy would put the main body of his troops outside the range of Allied tactical air power based in Sicily. At his disposal was the German Tenth Army and other veteran units, including most of the troops who had escaped from Sicily. The most important of the major defensive positions, comprising several defence lines strung across the peninsula about 120 kilometres southeast of Rome, was collectively known as the Gustav Line.

The Allies had no real clues as to Kesselring's strategy; General Sir Harold Alexander, who commanded the 15th Army Group, decided on an initial two-pronged landing. The British Eighth Army was to proceed directly across the Strait of Messina on September 3 (Operation Baytown), hopefully to draw the Germans south; then the US Fifth Army (consisting of one British and one US corps) was to land at the Bay of Salerno six days later (Operation Avalanche). Montgomery hated the plan. He later claimed in his memoirs that he had been ordered to take his army into Italy with no clear military objective. It was his view that the Avalanche landing should have gone first, and that if it had then proven successful, his army should have added its strength to it. Then the Germans in southern Italy would have had to retreat north or risk being cut off.

Canada had no say in these strategic decisions, either at the stratospheric political level of Roosevelt, Churchill, and Stalin, or at the Combined Chiefs of Staff in Washington, where US and British military planners oversaw the war against the Axis. As far as the Americans were concerned, the Canadian Army was part and parcel of larger British formations, and there was no need to consult the Canadians about how their troops were to be used. The British agreed, since to agree meant they had no reason to convince Canadian commanders to go along with their operational or strategic plans. Canadian commanders in the field always had the option to refuse assignments that they considered to be particularly dangerous to their troops, but that option was a last-ditch one that was, in fact, never used during the war. Canadians generally saw their war effort as part of a great Allied venture led by the British, the Americans, and the Soviet Union. They would not have tolerated for long a government that seemed to hold back Canadian troops from operations in order to score political points. The overwhelming majority of Canadians backed the war and wanted to see Canadian soldiers fighting it; that gave the Canadian government precious little leverage to try to horn in on the making of grand strategy, even had Mackenzie King been so inclined, which he was not.

* * * *

In the pre-dawn darkness of September 3, 1943, the 13th British Corps under the command of Lieutenant-General Miles Dempsey, led by the 5th British and the 1st Canadian Infantry Divisions, slipped across the Strait of Messina under cover of a massive artillery bombardment of the mostly deserted coast. The Canadian 3rd Brigade headed for Reggio di Calabria, the capital of Calabria, just on the coast, and took it without opposition; the 1st Brigade moved straight into the mountains, pushing over the high Aspromonte range toward the small town of Locri, on the other side of the "toe" of Italy. The weak Italian opposition caused few delays; the Germans were nowhere to be found. The countryside was almost idyllic and mostly untouched by war; as Charles Comfort noted, "The grape harvest was going on everywhere. The principal native traffic of the road was concerned with the harvest and with wine. The grapes were contained in large tubs, carried on low wagons. As we passed, bunches were thrown at us, sweet and lush."[6] Within one week, the Canadians had reached Catanzaro, about 120 kilometres from Reggio as the crow flies.

The Eighth Army landing was the last straw for the new Italian government of Marshal Badoglio. A secret surrender was signed on September 3 and became public five days later. The Allies and Badoglio's government had hoped to keep the surrender secret for as long as possible so as to forestall possible German action to pour more troops into Italy and assume the positions of the Italian army, but the delay was to no avail. All over Italy, German troops quickly surrounded Italian garrisons and forced their surrender. Italian soldiers were forced into prison camps or conscripted as forced labour. Kesselring had Hitler's explicit orders that Italy was to be defended. Thus the Italian surrender had very little measurable impact on the task facing the Allies, although the symbolic withdrawal of one of the Axis powers from the war may have provided some comfort to Churchill. Politically, Italy had indeed turned out to be the soft underbelly of Europe; militarily it was nothing of the kind.

The Eighth Army landing was a cakewalk; the Salerno landings were another matter. Kesselring was well aware that the Bay of Salerno was the northernmost suitable landing place available to the Allies that was within fighter cover of Sicily; the Germans were ready with the 16th Panzer Division: 15,000 men strong with more than 100 tanks and an experienced core of officers and NCOs. The announcement on the night of September 8 that Italy had surrendered to the Allies gave Kesselring ample warning of the invasion. Allied troops going ashore the morning of September 9 knew about the surrender and may have expected a walkover; they were bitterly surprised. It took more than five days of heavy fighting and some 13,000 Allied casualties before the combined British-American force under command of American Lieutenant-General Mark Clark's Fifth Army broke out of the beachhead and headed for Naples, which they entered on October 1.

While the Fifth Army struggled at Salerno, Simonds was ordered to take his division inland to seize the important road junction town of Potenza, about 90 kilometres east of Salerno. Potenza was about

80 kilometres east of the Salerno bridgehead; capturing it would put the Eighth Army in a position to attack westward to relieve the Allies there. Simonds assigned the task to the 3rd Brigade to be led by a scratch unit known as Boforce, commanded by Lieutenant-Colonel M.P. Bogert, Officer Commanding (OC) of the West Nova Scotia Regiment. Boforce consisted of the West Novies, the Calgary Tanks, and other units; it combined armour, truck-mounted infantry, artillery, mortars, and engineers. It was to rush more than 200 kilometres to the northwest to punch through German-controlled terrain and push the Germans out of Potenza. The concept of an all-arms task force designed specifically for a single operation was certainly not unknown in the war up to that point; Simonds had experimented briefly with the concept in Sicily. But it was a novel idea for him; generally Simonds planned for set-piece battles where artillery fire plans and the ability of the guns to move forward dictated infantry and armour tasks. But not this time. Boforce caught the Germans napping as it embarked on its sixty-hour dash to Potenza.[7] On September 19 Bogert's troops approached Potenza; Bogert feared that the many new apartment blocks in Potenza might be well defended and waited for nightfall before ordering his troops in. Three West Novies companies attacked, ran into about 100 German paratroopers, and were soon engaged in a furious firefight. Simonds sent the Royal 22e Regiment (the Van Doos) to outflank the German positions as tanks moved into the town; the Germans decided to pull out. The rest of the brigade moved in quickly to prepare for an expected counterattack that did not materialize. By the time Boforce took Potenza, German resistance around the Salerno bridgehead had started to crumble, but with Potenza in Allied hands, the Germans were forced to withdraw to the north over crowded roads with little room for manoeuvre.

By the end of September the Fifth and Eighth Armies held a line across Italy that ran northeast from just north of Naples on the Mediterranean to the Adriatic. The British 5th Corps had come up from the south to seize the Foggia plain and the strategic airfields located there, but the formidable defences of the Gustav Line lay between the Allies and Rome, and it was becoming more obvious by the day that Kesselring had no plans to abandon Rome (as the Allies had thought he might do once they had broken out of the Salerno beachhead).

The task assigned to the Canadian Division by Miles Dempsey, the British corps commander, was to take the left flank of the 13th British Corps front and drive toward the mountaintop town of Campobasso, while the 78th British Division fought its way north on the right or coastal flank. From height to height, and town to town, the advance was slow and deliberate. At every opportunity the Germans held fast as long as they could, and usually long enough to force the Canadians to redeploy from line-of-march into attack formation, thus causing more delays. Each hilltop seemed to hold another fortified position; every valley road was cut by a blown bridge. Mines were strewn everywhere. The rainy weather and the bad roads made a mess of logistics; the division had to move slowly in order not to outrun its supplies. At the beginning of December Montgomery wrote to General Sir Alan Brooke, Chief of the Imperial General Staff, "I am fighting a hell of a battle here . . . I don't think we can get any spectacular results so long as it goes on raining."[8] Although mud and rain did not deter Canadian mule trains, the mules could not carry enough supplies to support an entire infantry division. That could only be done by trucks on good roads cleared of mines and far from enemy artillery or mortar fire.

Cold nights, rainy weather, and mud plagued the Canadians as they struggled westward from the Foggia plain and upward into the mountains along narrow roads and mountain paths. Their immediate objective was the Fortore River where the Germans were dug in in strength on the north bank. One company of the Van Doos tried to force its way across the river on the night of October 5–6 but were driven back by German shellfire from the 15th Panzergrenadier Regiment. Two days later the West Novies and the Carleton and York Regiment captured Gambatesa on the important Highway 17, which led west to Campobasso. That precipitated a general German withdrawal from the north bank of the Fortore. The race to Campobasso was now on in earnest.

On October 14 the Royal Canadian Regiment finally entered Campobasso, high in the mountains. A small city of some 17,000 people, the town was destined to be a leave and administrative centre. The troops quickly dubbed it Maple Leaf City, as thousands were given short leaves to sample the local culture. Comfort and his fellow war artists put on an exhibition of their paintings and sketches, which was a huge success. For the average infantryman, however, war art was not first on the priority list. As Brigadier Chris Vokes later put it in his memoirs, "The personal view of a private soldier in war is 'I'm here today and gone tomorrow . . .' So, the mentality of a soldier in the field is that he wants to get drunk and he wants to get laid, because these are pleasant things he may perhaps never experience again."[9] The Canadians did their best to get their fill of those simple pleasures in Campobasso.

Because German shells continued to fall sporadically on Campobasso, Simonds was forced to push farther north to the Biferno River, which runs about 9 kilometres to the north and west of Campobasso. The RCR crossed on October 23; the Hastings and Prince Edward regiment followed two days later. Farley Mowat was there: "On a rain-dark night we slipped and slithered down to a roaring river swollen by the endless downpours and spanned by a decrepit power dam over which the waters foamed so fiercely that the Germans must have assumed the dam was impassable and so had failed to defend or even mine it."[10] The 1st and 2nd Brigades stayed in position about 15 kms north of the Biferno throughout November. They engaged in vigorous patrolling to determine the location and strength of the enemy and, if possible, to drive him farther back. But Montgomery had had second thoughts about assaulting the Gustav Line defences inland, on his left flank, and had started to prepare for a new thrust along the coast. His new plan was to advance up the coast to seize the seaside resort town of Pescara, then swing west on Highway 5, cross the mountains, and approach Rome from the east.[11] To cover his intentions, the 3rd Canadian Infantry Brigade advanced beyond the divisional area toward the upper Sangro, reached it, and then mounted a series of limited attacks to try to convince the Germans that the entire division was operating in that vicinity. They remained there until ordered to rejoin the division after it moved to the coast.

* * * *

As Montgomery laid plans to pierce the Gustav Line along the Adriatic, the officers and men of the 5th Canadian Armoured Division began to arrive in Naples. The move to add a second Canadian division and a corps headquarters—1st Canadian Corps—to the Allied contingent in the Mediterranean had been initiated by Minister of National Defence J.L. Ralston and Chief of the General Staff Ken Stuart the previous summer. The decision marked a major turning point in Canada's wartime strategy, namely the abandonment of the ideal that First Canadian Army should fight together, as the Canadian Corps had done in the First World War. There was a chance that it would also bring about the end of A.G.L. McNaughton's command of the army. It would most certainly mean the overall diminution of any real possibility that Canada's government would gain significant geostrategic advantage from the united efforts of its six-division (or the equivalent of six divisions) army during the inevitable fighting in France and the rest of northwest Europe.

The idea of First Canadian Army had its roots in Defence Scheme No. 3, first adopted by the government in the late 1930s for an army of six divisions or so, under two corps and all under a Canadian Army headquarters. McNaughton—a disciple of Canadian Corps Commander Arthur Currie in the First World War—strongly believed that Canadians would fight best when they fought in a Canadian formation and that the achievements of the Canadian Corps had laid the groundwork for Canadian nationhood in the post–First World War era. Mackenzie King had believed that too. Thus McNaughton had strongly advocated keeping the Canadian Army together in the United Kingdom until it could be used, all at once, in some important theatre of war. He wanted the Canadians to lead the cross-Channel attack. He called the Canadian Army a "dagger pointed at the heart" of Nazi Germany. But McNaughton had been forced to yield in mid-1943, when Stuart and Ralston had convinced Mackenzie King to seek to add 1st Canadian Infantry Division to the order of battle for the invasion of Sicily. One of the arguments used by the proponents of sending the division to Sicily was that the Canadian Army needed battle experience, which the Canadian division would gain there. Their assumption was that the division would be returned to the United Kingdom in time to prepare for the landing in France.

What exactly did Mackenzie King and the Canadian high command know about the forthcoming landing in France when the decision was made to send a division to Sicily? Not much. King had not sought to participate in any of the high-level conferences between Roosevelt and Churchill. No Canadian sat on the Combined Chiefs of Staff that met continually in Washington and periodically when Roosevelt and Churchill met. All the major strategic decisions involving US and British Commonwealth forces were made at those meetings and subsequent meetings that involved Stalin. Lack of Canadian involvement meant that King, his defence ministers, and his generals shared a broad knowledge of what the Americans and the British were planning but lacked the necessary detailed information they ought to have had to shape Canadian strategy so as to fit into British and American planning.[12]

In July 1943 Ralston and Stuart began to push in London and Ottawa to send yet another Canadian division to the Mediterranean and one of the two corps headquarters of First Canadian Army to command the two divisions. In part they resurrected the old arguments about sinking morale in the Canadian Army and demands from the public for Canada to play more of a role in the ground war. Ironically enough, they also tried to convince Mackenzie King that Canada would increase its political leverage if it established a corps in Italy, even though sending a corps headquarters and another division would raise major challenges to the continued existence of First Canadian Army. They made some claims that these two divisions might be able to return to the United Kingdom in time for Overlord (the invasion of Normandy), but then they had no firm idea from the British when Overlord might occur. British Chief of the Imperial General Staff Sir Alan Brooke and British General Sir Bernard Paget told them it might come as early as May 1, 1944, or as late as September 1, 1944. The two Canadians were let in on some of the disagreements between the United States and the United Kingdom regarding strategy in the Mediterranean and given some hints that Churchill might win Roosevelt over to an indefinite postponement of Overlord, except in the unlikely event of a sudden German collapse, as had happened in the fall of 1918. One other major reason for splitting the Canadian Army was that Brooke, Ralston, and Stuart agreed that McNaughton was not fit to take the army into combat, had to be replaced, and would resign if the army were split.[13]

Although Ralston and Stuart claimed to be keeping the long-term Canadian objective of fighting as a unified army together, they were not. They surely knew that a shortage of shipping would make such a transfer to and from Italy very difficult and that Italy was slowly being relegated to a secondary front maintained to hold German troops but not to win the war. The decision to do that had initially been made by Roosevelt and Churchill at the Casablanca Conference in early 1943, reiterated at the Trident Conference in Washington in May 1943 and the Quadrant Conference in Quebec City in August. In fact, they knew—or they ought to have known, even with their limited means of knowing what the United States and the United Kingdom were deciding—that seven British and American divisions and one British Corps headquarters were going to be returned to the United Kingdom prior to Normandy. Yet they pushed the idea anyway, against Mackenzie King's initial skepticism and British resistance.

Britain did not want a Canadian Corps headquarters in Italy because it would restrict their freedom to order Canadian divisions to go wherever the British believed they needed them. Instead of dealing with two Canadian divisional commanders, they would have to deal with a Canadian Corps commander, whose duties included keeping Canadian divisions together. They also had a low opinion of high-ranking Canadian officers—McNaughton for one—and worried about who would command the corps. Harry Crerar's name was raised on a number of occasions. As far as Brooke, Paget, and Montgomery were concerned, anyone was better than McNaughton, but Crerar was virtually unblooded. Britain had also made a commitment to the United

States to pull divisions out of Italy, not insert new ones, even though the new Canadian division and Corps headquarters would replace formations the British were withdrawing.

The final argument Ralston and Stuart used to move Mackenzie King to their position was that Overlord and the subsequent fighting in France was going to be a bloodbath. Italy, they reassured him, was not. Indeed, when these decisions were being contemplated, Canadian casualties in Italy were relatively low. The Canadian body count in deaths, physical wounds, and battle exhaustion did not really begin to spike until early December with the Moro River crossing and the Battle of Ortona. Thus the decision was made by Mackenzie King on August 31. He wrote in his diary, "The more of our men participate in the campaign in Italy, the fewer there are likely to be who will be involved in the crossing of the Channel which, as Churchill says, will be a very tough business . . . Churchill does not think the further fighting in Italy will occasion anything like the loss of life that the fighting in Sicily has occasioned."[14] Events would prove Churchill tragically wrong.

There were two major fallouts from the decision to split the army even further. First, it made McNaughton's position untenable. Mackenzie King knew it would but had larger questions to consider. McNaughton did not initially oppose the idea when it was first suggested to him by Ralston, but quickly changed his mind and had an open row with his boss, declaring to him on August 10, "It is clear from the conversations you have been having that you do not care anything about the Canadian Army."[15] By this point McNaughton's constant championing of the aim of a united Canadian Army, his constant push back against British efforts to interfere in what he saw as internal Canadian Army matters, and his alleged failure to lead his army effectively during Exercise Spartan—an army-level pre-invasion exercise in March 1943—at least as far as the

British were concerned[16] made him a marked man. He eventually acqui-
esced in the further transfer of the 1st Canadian Corps and 5th Canadian
Armoured Division, but his credibility had been reduced to virtually
nothing. Crerar was tapped to take over after a brief stint as commander
of the new corps.

The second major issue that had to be dealt with after the decision
to split the army was whether or not to even maintain First Canadian
Army. The British, ever mindful of their belief in the inferiority of colo-
nial leaders and desirous of having as few national headquarters under
their command as possible, were anxious to disband First Canadian
Army. General Ken Stuart strongly supported them. They all proposed
an Anglo-Canadian army, led by a British general, with a British corps
to replace 1st Canadian Corps and at least 50 percent of the staff to
be made up of British officers. This matter was seriously discussed for
several months in the latter half of 1943 and into 1944, as the date for
Overlord drew nearer. But this was where Ralston drew the line. Thus
First Canadian Army was saved, and placed under command of 21st
Army Group, commanded by General Bernard L. Montgomery for the
upcoming invasion. But the First Canadian Army that fought in northwest Europe contained only three Canadian divisions (2nd Infantry,
3rd Infantry, and 4th Armoured), 2nd Canadian Armoured Brigade, a
British Corps, and a Polish armoured division until January 1945, when
many more troops were added for the Battle of the Rhineland.

With McNaughton cowed into submission, Ottawa approached
London with the offer of an armoured division and a corps headquarters. The British were just then in the process of pulling 30 Corps headquarters and their famous 7th Armoured Division (the Desert Rats)
back to the United Kingdom to prepare for the invasion of Europe. An
agreement was quickly worked out. The Canadians would leave their

equipment in the United Kingdom to be taken over by the returning British formations and would, in turn, take over the British equipment on their arrival in Italy. That the British equipment was worn, in need of repair, and often obsolete (while the Canadian equipment left in the United Kingdom was much better and more numerous) seems not to have occurred to Ralston, who engineered the deal. Thus it would be many months before the 5th Canadian Armoured Division was ready for battle, especially since H.D.G. Crerar, the designated commander of the 1st Canadian Corps, diverted part of the new equipment that did arrive in Italy from the 5th Armoured to his own corps command. In fact the new corps and the armoured division did not see significant action until the battle for Rome, which opened on May 10, 1944, less than a month before Overlord. If Ralston, Stuart, and their allies had not pushed to split the Canadian Army, 1st Canadian Corps and 5th Canadian Army would have missed only some four weeks of battle in Normandy—hardly worth the political price of the divided army. In this matter it appears that the only man who consistently maintained a geostrategic view of Canadian war aims was Andrew George Latta McNaughton. As official Canadian historian C.P. Stacey put it, "It seems evident that on this question of policy McNaughton was right and they were wrong; and the government may be said to have recognized this fact . . . when it pressed [in the summer of 1944] for the early return from Italy of the troops whom it had insisted on sending there".[17]

The arrival of the new Canadian formations signalled changes in the Canadian command structure. Simonds was transferred to command of the newly arriving armoured division, Chris Vokes was promoted to command the 1st Canadian Infantry Division, and Crerar was earmarked as General Officer Commanding of the 1st Canadian Corps, scheduled to be activated in January. It would be the first Canadian corps in the field since the end of the First World War, even though it would be roughly half the size of its illustrious predecessor. On November 29 the 1st Canadian Infantry Division began to pull out of the Campobasso area and head for the coast. They were to occupy positions being vacated by the British 78th Division, which had managed to push across the lower Sangro River in heavy fighting and with many casualties. The Canadians were to take over the hard-won British positions and, accompanied by the 1st Canadian Armoured Brigade, assault across the Moro River and capture the small coastal town of Ortona, about 3 kilometres farther on on the way to Pescara. By December 4 the Canadians found themselves in their new positions on a ridge overlooking the south bank of the Moro.

* * * *

Dating back to the ancient Trojans, Ortona is dominated by a fortress, a cathedral, and two massive defensive towers standing on a promontory alongside a small harbour. The streets are narrow, the buildings stone or brick, many of them sharing common walls. There were three large open squares in Ortona, the centremost and largest being the Piazza Municipale, which was connected to the Ortona-Orsogna lateral road to the south by the Corso Vittorio Emanuele. The Germans laid out their defences to make killing grounds of the streets leading to the centre of the town and the piazzas, demolishing buildings and blocking streets to force vehicle and foot traffic through the piazzas—every metre of which was covered by heavy concentrations of automatic weapons, mortars, and even flame-throwers. Mines were laid in abundance, including the infamous Italian wooden mines, which could not be detected by Canadian mine-detection gear. Anything that could be booby-trapped was.

The unwary soldier might easily pull a wire going across a staircase, or open a door, and blow himself and his companions up. German machine guns were protected by other machine guns; entire houses were wired to blow up if the Canadians entered. Ortona was a series of killing zones, and the Canadians would have to pay dearly for entering them. The town could not be approached along the seafront or from the west; there were two roads into the town: the Ortona-Orsogna lateral road from the south and another road from the southeast, parallel to the coast. To reach Ortona, the Canadians would have to cross the Moro River, work their way up the bluffs on the other side of the river, then cross a deep but narrow gully that paralleled the river about 3 kilometres to the west of it before gaining the Ortona-Orsogna road, which ran at right angles to the coast. They would then have to wheel to the right and advance northeast up that road into Ortona. The German paratroopers defending Ortona and vicinity would contest every step of the way.

One question raised by the late Brereton Greenhous, a Canadian military historian of some repute was, Why was Ortona attacked at all? By itself it was not a vital crossroads that the Canadians had to capture in order to push through to Pescara, in accordance with Monty's grand scheme. The harbour was not large and certainly incapable of handling more than two or three small supply ships at a time. But it could be expected that the Germans would demolish the harbour to the fullest extent possible. Greenhous pointed out that the area's most important road junction was located 3 kilometres southwest of Ortona and that, once that junction was in Canadian possession, the town could have been masked off, the German defenders there isolated and bypassed. Greenhous accused Chris Vokes, newly appointed to command the division, of a decided lack of imagination in not doing just that. In Greenhous's opinion, Vokes was determined to drive straight into Ortona, no matter the effectiveness of the German defences, because he and his German counterpart were engaged in a battle of wills: "The struggle for Ortona ... assumed a public relations importance out of all proportion to its military significance."[18] That view fits with Kesselring's Christmas Day message to his Tenth Army commander: "We do not want to defend Ortona decisively, but the English have made it as important as Rome ... you can do nothing when things develop in this manner."[19]

More recent scholarship takes issue with Greenhous. C.G. Case points out that Vokes had been given very definite orders to capture Ortona as part of the plan to push through to Pescara and that Montgomery was pushing very hard for Vokes and his Canadians to take the town as quickly as possible. Case also shows that Vokes's strategy was not nearly as simple as Greenhous made out. Although Vokes ordered the 2nd Canadian Infantry Brigade, then under the command of former Seaforth Officer Commanding (OC) Bert Hoffmeister, to capture the town itself, the 1st and 3rd Brigades were in fact ordered to attack to the northeast of the town and cut it off to force a German withdrawal.[20] A more experienced division commander might have acted with greater leeway in how he handled his brigades in both the approaches to and the taking of the town, but Vokes was completely new in the job, took no opportunities to interpret his orders as he, the man on the spot, might have done, and just went straight at it.

Vokes planned the attack on Ortona in three stages: first, cross the Moro River; second, cross the gully to get onto the Ortona-Orsogna highway; third, advance into Ortona and capture it. In the waning daylight hours of December 5, the three battalions of the 1st Brigade led the attempt to force the Moro crossing. On the coast road the Hastings and Prince Edward Regiment crossed the river near its mouth and set up a defensive bridgehead just atop the bluffs on the west bank of the river.

This was intended as a diversion for the main attack about 1.5 kilometres to the south by the Seaforths. Thus when the Hastings and Prince Edwards ran into stiff opposition, they withdrew back across the Moro. The Seaforth Highlanders moved across the Moro and worked their way up a narrow twisting road toward the hamlet of San Leonardo, perched just near the edge of the bluffs.

Three kilometres farther south, the PPCLI forded the river and stormed the hamlet of Villa Rogatti, taking the Germans by surprise. As dawn broke, the PPCLI was counterattacked by both tanks and infantry. They held on with the help of British armour from the 44th Royal Tank Regiment (which managed to move a number of Shermans across the river and up its steep and muddy sides). The Patricias might have held a firm base at Villa Rogatti for a further advance toward Ortona, but the commander of the British 5th Corps, Lieutenant-General Charles Allfrey (Vokes's commander), moved the Canadian divisional boundary closer to the coast in an attempt to give the Canadians a narrower front. He believed that this would allow them to focus their combat power more effectively to get across the Moro. Thus on the night of December 7–8, the Patricias handed their positions over to troops of the 8th Indian Division and then pulled back over the river.[21]

The Seaforths had made it onto the west bank of the Moro, but were sorely pressed and had no armour support. They were forced to withdraw across the river on the evening of December 6.

Undaunted, Vokes ordered the frontal assault on the Moro to continue. On December 6 the Hasty Ps were sent back across the river. Farley Mowat wrote about that attack years later: "What followed was the kind of night men dream about in afteryears, waking in a cold sweat to a surge of gratitude that it is but a dream. It was a delirium of sustained violence. Small pockets of Germans that had been cut off throughout our bridgehead fired their automatic weapons in hysterical dismay at every shadow. The grind of enemy tanks and self-propelled guns working their way along the crest was multiplied by echoes until it sounded like an entire Panzer army." To top it all off, it began to rain, and a bitter wind chilled the men through and through.[22] Despite the terrible weather and the enemy armour, the battalion held: the only Canadian bridgehead across the Moro.

Vokes now hatched a new plan: the 1st Brigade would attack with two battalions up, the 48th Highlanders moving directly across the river east of San Leonardo, the Royal Canadian Regiment breaking out of the bridgehead held by the Hasty Ps and attacking southwest toward San Leonardo. The attack began on the afternoon of December 8; the 48th Highlanders achieved their crossing, but the RCR ran into a strong German counterattack. The regimental history describes the ordeal:

> Throughout the night of December 8th–9th the RCR maintained its position on the feature which came to be known regimentally as "Slaughterhouse Hill." The fighting was most confused, the enemy appearing on several sides of the perimeter as well as within it. The sound of armoured vehicles moving gave the impression that a counterattack would come in at dawn, and the incessant shellfire from both sides turned the night into pandemonium.[23]

The RCRs beat off the counterattack, but not without heavy casualties. In the meantime, the engineers used the cover of darkness to build a bridge across the river and by the morning of December 9, tanks and anti-tank guns were crossing over to the west side to reinforce the bridgehead. By nightfall on the 9th, the RCRs and the 48th Highlanders had linked up; San Leonardo was in Canadian hands.

The gully was a relatively narrow cut in the landscape that lay just beyond Vino Ridge and paralleled the Ortona-Orsogna road, between the coast and Cider Crossroads, the junction of the old coastal highway and the Ortona-Orsogna road. Overgrown with vines and other brush, it was a natural tank trap. The Germans built dugouts and revetments on the forward slope of the gully (facing east) from which they could fire on the Canadians as they appeared on the eastern lip of the gully. Machine guns and mortars on the western lip of the gully gave ample cover fire to the German defenders in the gully—paratroopers who had taken over from the worn-out infantry. The Canadians were surprised by both the strength and the tenacity of the defenders; they had expected that the Germans would pull back from the Ortona area securing a crossing of the Moro. Not knowing what he faced, Vokes initially attempted to simply storm the German defences and tried to push one battalion after another across the feature. Each of these attacks was repulsed with heavy losses. It was only after several vain and costly attempts that Vokes's attention was drawn to the head of the gully, where the deep terrain rose to meet the coastal plain, allowing the gully to be bypassed altogether, so that the Canadians could gain the vital Cider Crossroads.

The key to outflanking the gully was Casa Berardi, a cluster of walled farm buildings on the west side of the gully, about 3 kilometres cross-country from San Leonardo. The task of securing this vital position was given to the Van Doos; on December 14 C Company, courageously led by Captain Paul Triquet and supported by the Sherman tanks of C Squadron of the Ontario Tank Regiment, battled their way across the head of the gully, through German paratroopers and armour, to the stout walls of the main house. Though down to a handful of men and just six tanks, the small force stormed the house, captured it, and held it until after dark when reinforcements arrived. Triquet was awarded the Victoria Cross for his courage, the first Canadian VC in the Mediterranean theatre.

Now, on the Ortona-Orsogna road, the 3rd Brigade was ordered to take the vital Cider Crossroads southwest of Ortona. Under cover of a massive artillery bombardment that began at 0800 on December 18 the 48th Highlanders and the Three Rivers Tanks began the advance, which was then continued by the Royal Canadian Regiment. But Canadian shells began falling on the advancing troops and the barrage was lifted; once again the Germans had time to emerge from their bunkers and slit trenches, site their weapons, and open fire on the Canadian infantry. In the words of the RCR regimental history, "the slaughter was terrible." The regiment halted short of the Crossroads, unable to continue. The next morning, the advance resumed with closely coordinated tank and artillery fire, and the Crossroads were taken.

The battle for Ortona itself began the following day when the Loyal Edmonton Regiment of the 2nd Brigade, already well below strength, advanced toward Ortona from the newly captured Crossroads. By nightfall they and the Seaforths, who covered their right flank, were into the western edge of the town. The German paratroopers who held Ortona were determined to fight for every metre of ground. Their machine guns were sited for interlocking fire, and they had dug tanks into the rubble, with turrets exposed, as mini-fortresses. Houses were fortified with everything imaginable, with chicken wire attached over windows and other openings to keep out grenades. Virtually every tempting object lying in the street, from full wine bottles to bibles, was booby-trapped.

The Canadians divided the town into sectors, the better to clear each one and secure it before moving on to the next one. They advanced house by house in small actions involving platoons, sections, even half-sections. As two or three men gave cover with a Bren gun, the others eased up to a front door, kicked it in, lobbed grenades inside, then rushed in, Tommy guns blazing, as soon as the grenades had gone off. The Loyal Eddies found a new use for their new 6-pounder anti-tank guns: "We used the anti-tanks in a unique way. The shells could not penetrate the granite walls, sometimes 4 ft thick. So we just put them through the windows [and fired] and they (i.e., the shells) bounced around inside much like they would in an enemy tank doing horrible damage."[24]

Another technique perfected by the Canadian infantry was "mouse holing." The streets were a death trap, so the Canadians moved under cover from house to house by blasting through the walls. Using "bee-hive" (i.e., shaped) high explosives, they would blow a hole from one house to another on the top floor, then clear the neighbouring building from top down. Although the Three Rivers Tanks gave valuable support, the battle for Ortona was primarily an infantry fight. Germans and Canadians were too close together for the Canadians to use artillery, and many streets were too strewn with rubble and mines for armour. Besides, the new German weapon known as the *Panzerfaust* was coming into use—the best infantry-carried anti-tank weapon in the war—making the streets exceedingly dangerous for armour.[25]

As the Canadians inched painfully forward toward the central square (the Piazza Municipale), preparations were completed to give the men Christmas dinner as close to the lines as possible. A sumptuous meal was prepared and tables were set, usually in church courtyards. As the battle roared around them, the men at the fighting front were brought back a few at a time, fed, given Christmas sweets and cigarettes, then returned to action. The Seaforths held their dinner in a parish church near the Piazza della Vittoria. Norman Pope of the Canadian Army Historical Section witnessed the spectacle and later described it to Charles Comfort:

Over the crash and din of the surrounding battle came the skirl of bagpipes and the raised voices of men singing Christmas carols. Through a smoky haze [Pope] saw men seated at tables covered with white napery. Three hundred yards away the enemy had active machine-gun posts, mortar bombs and shells creating a hellish dissonance, as cool young subalterns (in true Christmas tradition) served Canadian turkey with dressing and vegetables.[26]

The Germans prepared a deadly Boxing Day for Lieutenant E.B. Allen and his platoon of twenty-three Loyal Eddies by mining a building near the Piazza San Tommaso. When Allen and his men entered the building, the Germans blew it up. Canadian pioneers rushed forward to dig the men out, but were met by grenades and rifle fire. Only five men were rescued from Allen's platoon, one after being pinned in the rubble for some seventy-two hours.

Two days before Christmas, Vokes had sent the 1st and 3rd Brigades to cut off the German escape and supply routes to the west of the town. At first the Hasty Ps and the 48th Highlanders made it through to the high ground west of Ortona, but they were then cut off; on Christmas night a party of the Saskatoon Light Infantry reached them with supplies and ammunition, and the next day tanks from the Ontario Regiment broke through. The German position in Ortona was now untenable; they had suffered heavy casualties and all their escape routes were about to be cut off. On the 27th, the survivors began to pull out of Ortona; they were gone by the 28th, their unburied dead rotting in the streets.

The fight for the Moro River crossing and the capture of Ortona had cost the 1st Canadian Infantry Division 2,339 officers and men killed and wounded and another 1,617 men taken out of the line due to illness, many afflicted with battle exhaustion. Since hitting the beaches at Pachino,

Sicily, in July, the division had earned a reputation for doggedness and determination. Officers and men had overcome high-calibre German troops mounting highly skilled and innovative defences. The campaign in Italy thus far was more like the battles of attrition fought in the First World War than the blitzkrieg-style warfare that some had expected. By the end of 1943 it was clear that Canadian officers and men could fight the set-piece battle as well as any army and could adapt fairly quickly to new challenges, such as the street fighting at Ortona. What was not so clear was whether or not they could excel at a war of swiftness and manoeuvrability. They would find that out a few short months later in Italy's Liri Valley.

* * * *

As 1943 drew to a close, the Axis was on the defensive everywhere. In the Pacific, the Japanese navy had suffered a stunning blow in June 1942 at the Battle of Midway. This defeat had been followed by the American invasion of Guadalcanal, the start of the US Navy's island-hopping campaign in the central Pacific, and the American-Australian thrust to recapture New Guinea. Mired in China and the jungles of Southeast Asia, the Japanese were being pushed back with heavy losses on virtually all fronts. American submarines were taking a huge toll of Japanese merchant shipping, and American shipyards were turning out new fleet and escort carriers, fast battleships, and modern cruisers and destroyers by the score.

With two divisions and a corps in Italy, and no realistic chance of returning them to the United Kingdom before D-Day, it was obvious at the end of 1943 that the First Canadian Army would, for a good long while, fight the war in northwest Europe in a part-Canadian, part-British, part-Polish formation (though under Canadian command) and not as an all-Canadian unit (as the Canadian Corps had been in the First World War). It was also clear by December 1943 that it would not go into action commanded by A.G.L. McNaughton. The British had lobbied hard for McNaughton's removal ever since the Spartan debacle in March 1943 and had been helped by Crerar, who saw himself as McNaughton's successor. McNaughton's long-held political views regarding the unity of the Canadian Army, and his clash with Montgomery over his plans to visit Sicily, had not helped his position. But McNaughton had relented regarding sending two divisions and a corps to Italy, and thus the foremost reason why the Canadian government was prepared to sack him was the British view that he was not competent to command a field army. William Lyon Mackenzie King liked McNaughton, knew he was popular with the troops, and did not want to fire him. But Sir Alan Brooke and others had convinced Ralston and Stuart that McNaughton had to go, and Mackenzie King had little choice but to accept Ralston's advice. McNaughton was sacked in December 1943—the government claimed that he resigned due to ill health—and replaced by Crerar, who would command First Canadian Army for the duration. Crerar was eventually succeeded at 1st Canadian Corps by E.L.M. "Tommy" Burns. Vokes stayed in command of 1st Canadian Infantry Division, and Bert Hoffmeister took command of 5th Canadian Armoured Division in March 1944. Simonds was brought back to the United Kingdom to become commander of the 2nd Canadian Corps. That corps would be the premier Canadian component of First Canadian Army (the other corps was to be the 1st British under Lieutenant-General J.T. Crocker) until the 1st Canadian Corps was brought back from Italy to rejoin First Canadian Army in the spring of 1945.

On New Year's Eve 1943, the 48th Highlanders captured the hamlets of San Tommaso and San Nicola, a little more than 3 kilometres west of Ortona. An assault on Point 59, a small hill on the coast about

3 kilometres northwest of Ortona, was less successful, and more than fifty Canadians were killed, wounded, or captured. Point 59 was finally secured by the Carleton and York Regiment on January 4, and the Canadian front on the Adriatic then fell quiet. There was no point in trying to go any farther on this coast when the road to Rome, on the Mediterranean side of Italy, was still blocked by the fierce resistance of Kesselring's troops. The Allies now paused to rethink their priorities and their strategy; the hiatus was more than welcomed by the tired, disheveled, and understrength Canadians, who badly needed a rest.

CHAPTER 13

VIA AD ROMAM

May 24, 1944: at the Melfa River in the Liri Valley on the road to Rome. Canadian Lieutenant Edward J. Perkins and his small band of reconnaissance troops struggled across the Melfa River in mid-afternoon to blaze a trail for the lead elements of the 5th Canadian Armoured Division to follow. The riverbanks were steep, but Perkins and his men coaxed their three small General Stuart (or "Honey") reconnaissance tanks up the other side and then captured a small house occupied by eight German paratroopers. Perkins then placed his tanks in a hull-down position and organized his men for the inevitable German counterattack. He expected the infantry of A Company of the Westminster Regiment to follow in short order. Until they did, the Sherman tanks of A Squadron, Lord Strathcona's Horse, would provide covering fire from the other side of the river.

The Melfa River flows from the north to intersect the Liri River some 20 kilometres due west of the Italian town of Cassino. The Liri River is one of the very few south of Rome that flows in a general east-west direction. The river valley has long been used as an invasion route to Rome, and the Germans, in full knowledge of the history and geography of the region, had strongly fortified the eastern end of the valley. If the Allies could reduce or bypass those defences, they would penetrate the Gustav Line and turn the flank of Kesselring's still formidable Tenth Army.

The battle for the approaches to Rome had raged for many months when Perkins and his men crossed the Melfa River. Under fire and alone in their small perimeter for several hours, the Canadians were joined at about 1700 by infantry from the Westminsters. The infantry had taken several casualties crossing the river, but as soon as they arrived on the west bank of the Melfa, they pushed out on the left flank to expand the bridgehead. At dusk, three German Panther tanks and about 100 infantry started to advance toward the Canadian position. Perkins's men and the men of the Westminster Regiment fired everything they had at the approaching enemy, including PIATs (projector, infantry, anti-tank), even though the range was too great for the PIATs to have any effect. Perkins himself was slightly wounded when hit by fragments from a high-explosive shell as he leaped into his tank. There was little to stop the Germans from pushing the Canadians into the river, but the daylight was almost gone and the Germans were thrown off balance by the ferocity of the Canadian fire. They failed to press their attack home. The Canadians held their positions and remained in control of the bridgehead until they were joined by stronger forces the following day. The main body of the Canadian armour then crossed the Melfa as the Allies drove for Rome.

* * * *

After the capture of Ortona and the high ground to the west, the Eighth Army's offensive on the Adriatic coast closed down for the winter. The Allies had hoped to take Rome by the end of 1943, but a skilled and tenacious enemy still held the Gustav Line from the Adriatic to the

Mediterranean. There was no use trying to push farther north when the winter mud, rain, cold, and snow in the high passes made the going even more difficult than it had been before. Thus the 5th Canadian Armoured Division's 11th Canadian Infantry Brigade saw its first limited action at the Arieli River, north of Ortona, only on January 17, 1944. In December Guy Simonds, who had taken command of the 5th Armoured Division, asked that the 11th Brigade be brought into action as soon as possible to get a taste of the enemy while the armoured component of the division was still re-equipping itself. Since the 5th Armoured was not yet fully concentrated, the 11th Brigade was temporarily attached to the 1st Canadian Infantry Division and ordered to mount limited attacks across the Arieli to divert German attention from the Anzio and Cassino areas. On January 17 the Cape Breton Highlanders and the Perth Regiment mounted their first real action against the Germans. The two battalions, each accompanied by a squadron of tanks, "went in across open ground in daylight against well-prepared river defences manned by experienced veterans of the German 1st Parachute Division. The combination of a disjointed plan, inexperienced units and strong defences produced a dismal failure."[1]

The problems that underlay the brigade's failure at the Arieli would plague the 5th Armoured Division for many months. Equipment shortages hampered training, command assignments were changed constantly (for example, the division had three commanders in less than five months), and the units had had precious little practical experience in tank-infantry cooperation, which is the essence of an armoured division. Despite these difficulties, the full division was put into the front lines in the Orsogna sector at the beginning of February, replacing the 4th Indian Division, just eighty-five days after its arrival in Italy. At virtually the same time (January 31–February 1), the 1st Canadian Corps was activated and relieved 5th British Corps in the coastal area. By February 9 Corps Commander H.D.G. Crerar had both Canadian divisions under command. Crerar had been selected to command the corps at the insistence of General Sir Alan Brooke, Chief of the Imperial General Staff, and Montgomery, who knew that his battle experience was very limited. He had already been selected to succeed A.G.L. McNaughton, but only after he gained some experience commanding troops in combat. His experience in Italy was brief and unhappy. Montgomery hounded him constantly on his lack of experience and made it plain that he—Monty—was very unhappy to have yet another non-British corps under his command (the Eighth Army already contained a Polish and New Zealand Corps). Crerar grew restless quickly and sought to be returned to the United Kingdom to begin planning for the Normandy invasion. His wish was granted in early March, and as mentioned Lieutenant-General E.L.M. Burns was named to replace him.

Crerar hand-picked Burns to succeed him in Italy. It was a strange choice. Although Burns may have been one of the most intelligent men to command a higher formation in the Second World War, he was decidedly lacking in human skills, an essential component of successful command. Burns was a First World War veteran who stayed in the army in the interwar years, rising slowly through the ranks—a perennial problem in a small peace-time army. He was an excellent staff officer and thought systematically about how the Canadian Army ought to evolve in an era when horses were fast being replaced by tanks. What was the most effective way to use tanks? How should they be integrated with infantry? During that period, he was one of a small number of Canadian officers (Simonds and Stuart were two others) who wrote professional articles for the new *Canadian Defence Quarterly*, which was started to present a forum for forward thinking on the military issues of the day.

Burns also wrote articles for *American Mercury*, an American political/literary magazine edited by that famed US man of letters, H.L. Mencken. But Burns was a perpetually unhappy introvert who simply had very few people skills. A stickler for dress and comportment, he was referred to by his troops as "smiling sunray"; "sunray" was the radio call sign for a formation commander, and the "smiling" part was pure sarcasm, since Burns constantly gave the impression that he was never happy about anything. He certainly had the brains to command a corps; his command presence was another matter entirely.

In contrast to Burns, the new commander of 5th Canadian Armoured Division, named just after Burns, was a man deeply respected by those who fought under him. Perhaps the best senior Canadian commander in the war, Bert Hoffmeister started his military career in the militia, the Seaforth Highlanders of Canada from Vancouver. In peacetime he had worked in the forestry business with H.R. Macmillan, a then well-known West Coast logging company. Hoffy, as he was called, took the Seaforths to England, where he suffered a breakdown of sorts when he suddenly felt the heavy weight that had fallen on his shoulders as commander of a regiment that was soon going to be called to battle. He was unsure of his ability, lost confidence in his capacity, and was uncertain how he would hold up. He took his own measure and sought help as he worked through his crisis, emerging as a more humble man in his outward appearance, but more certain of himself and determined to provide his subordinates with the most consideration possible in light of their being soldiers in a vicious war. Hoffy quickly became known as a man who did not waste lives, took great risks to share front-line dangers with his troops, and had an unerring grasp for the battlefield and what was unfolding on it in the middle of a fight. The men of his command soon nicknamed the 5th Canadian Armoured Division Hoffy's Mighty

Maroon Machine, due to the maroon shoulder patches they wore and their admiration for their steady commander.

* * * *

From the end of the Ortona fighting to the opening of the Liri Valley offensive, the Canadians took no part in any major operations, and yet the war of attrition in the mountains and on the coast continued to take a dreary toll of casualties. By the start of the Liri Valley offensive, 9,934 Canadians had become casualties in the Italian campaign, 2,119 of them fatal. Many were battle exhaustion casualties, which had started to mount even during the summer fighting in Sicily. Because the Canadian Army had had no truly sustained contact with the enemy until the Sicily campaign, battle exhaustion had posed no especially significant problem. Since then, the nature of the war in Italy and the daily dangers faced by the men had caused battle exhaustion casualties to mount at a rapid pace. There is a wealth of evidence that all soldiers, throughout history, have faced battle exhaustion. Once known as shell-shock or battle fatigue, battle exhaustion generally results from a soldier being too long in a combat zone with too little apparent prospect of survival. It is a phenomenon far more evident in long campaigns, even of relatively low intensity, than in short ones, even ones as horrific as the Dieppe landing.[2]

Any soldier in a line unit, of any rank, can be stricken with battle exhaustion. Men too long under fire watching comrades being killed in the most horrible fashion, getting more and more fatigued from lack of sleep and constant movement, living in mud and dirt with little or no news from home, would eventually crack. Even the bravest of the brave had their limits; no one was exempt; battalion commanders were afflicted no less than riflemen. (Battle exhaustion afflicted the bomber crews as well, and for much the same reason. In the first years of the war, aircrew who refused to fly were labelled as LMF—lacking moral fibre—removed from active service, and treated harshly for the balance of their service. They were sometimes even sent to work in the coal mines.)

The Canadian Army in the Second World War tried to mitigate battle exhaustion in two basic ways: prevention and, where possible, quick cure. Prevention was best served by trying to keep troop morale up with hot food whenever possible, regular mail, mobile baths, and fresh changes of clothes. Most of these amenities were not available at the front during periods of intense action, so units were rotated out of the line and placed in reserve as often as the combat situation would allow. In addition, men would take turns being LOB—left out of battle—to ensure that some men in a platoon or company were always fresh. When in reserve, NAAFI—the Navy, Army, Air Force Institute, a civilian-run organization—provided canteens, movies, and sometimes live entertainment, while the army supplied beer and hearty meals. The more often a soldier could rest, clean up, eat a few good hot meals, and generally recover from the constant pressures of front-line existence, the less chance there was that he would be quickly afflicted with battle exhaustion. High-quality leadership on the part of company and battalion commanders also mitigated the problem.

But no matter how well rested or fed a soldier was, virtually any man was bound to crack in a prolonged campaign. In the Italian theatre, men marched for days on end over bad roads, crossed rivers without apparent end, slept in the open in cold rainy winters and hot dusty summers, endured flies and disease, and witnessed the poverty and misery of the population. When combined with the tenacious and deadly defence of the German enemy, these conditions inevitably produced battle exhaustion in large numbers. Thus treatment was as important as prevention.

Canadian army psychiatry was in its infancy at the beginning of the war, but knowledge about battle exhaustion eventually expanded and, with it, sensitivity to the problem. The key breakthrough was to recognize that anyone could be afflicted, and that those who were were not slackers or cowards but just men who had reached their limits. Also important was the realization that much battle exhaustion was temporary—a good sleep and a few calm days of good food and rest usually restored a man's sense of balance and allowed him to return to his unit. In other cases, reassignment to other, non-combat duties was called for. In very rare cases, complete discharges were necessary. The experiences gained in Italy taught the Canadian Army's medical staff a great deal about battle exhaustion, but it still took some convincing to win over old-line army officers who still thought of battle exhaustion as cowardice and nothing more. Guy Simonds is a good case in point. After weeks of hard fighting in Normandy, he concluded that infantry battalion commanding officers had to be replaced every four months because of the constant strain they were under and the consequent danger of mental breakdown. He also realized that adverse fighting conditions—poor weather, bad food, static warfare—were major factors producing battle exhaustion. At the same time, however, he cautioned army medical officers not to take too lenient a view of battle exhaustion. In a late August 1944 memo to his divisional commanders he warned, "It requires the close attention of commanders to see that malingering is not only discouraged, but made a disgraceful offence and disciplinary action taken to counter it."

* * * *

By January 1944, US General Mark Clark's Fifth Army had reached the Gustav Line at the entrance to the Liri Valley, but every step of the way had been costly. This tough going prompted Generals Alexander and Eisenhower to hatch Operation Shingle, a landing at Anzio, about 50 kilometres south of Rome, which was intended to outflank the Gustav Line defences and establish a base at the foot of the Alban Hills. From there a quick drive to Rome might be mounted. The US 5th Corps, under command of US Major-General John Lucas, was composed primarily of 50,000 American and British troops (and the Canadians of the First Special Service Force, of which more later). The landing took place on January 22; the German defenders were caught by surprise, but although Lucas sent reconnaissance troops to scout out the road to Rome, he delayed his main attack in order to build a firm base on the beach and in the town by bringing more troops and supplies in before attacking. The German defenders quickly rallied. When Lucas's troops eventually began a rather ponderous move toward the Italian capital, they met stiff and determined resistance from the approximately 14,000 German troops already in the Anzio area and another 20,000 or so German reserves near Rome, whom Kesselring immediately ordered to Anzio. In just days, Anzio became a killing zone.

There was a small Canadian contingent at Anzio—the Canadian participants of the First Special Service Force, a mixed American-Canadian commando unit under the command of US Lieutenant-Colonel Robert T. Frederick, which has been immortalized in the movies as the "Devil's Brigade." The force had been activated in Helena, Montana, in July 1942 and had received intensive training in amphibious, parachute, and ski commando tactics. Originally conceived to attack power plants and other strategic installations behind enemy lines in northern Europe (Project Plough), the Force saw its initial introduction to operations during the Aleutians campaign in August 1943 but saw no combat, since no enemy forces were encountered.

The First Special Service Force was then shifted to the Italian front, where it distinguished itself with a spectacular climb up the steep Monte La Difensa to surprise the German defenders and gain control of a key point in Kesselring's Winter Line. In that and subsequent battles, it suffered heavy casualties and was used less and less for commando-style operations and increasingly as a highly skilled and aggressive infantry unit. It was assigned a key sector of the front line on the Anzio perimeter and played an important role in the eventual breakout from Anzio and the pursuit to Rome.

* * * *

The failure to break out of the Anzio perimeter made the Allied position south of Rome worse, not better. With the equivalent of more than three divisions bottled up and taking a daily pounding from artillery and aircraft, it was soon apparent that unless Anzio was abandoned altogether—which would have been an unmitigated disaster on a par with the Gallipoli disaster of the First World War—the Fifth Army was going to have to come to the rescue of the troops in the beachhead. It could do that, of course, only by breaking through the Gustav Line—a formidable task.

It was a man newly arrived from the United Kingdom—Lieutenant-General Sir John Harding, a skilled staff officer with extensive combat experience—who conceived Operation Diadem. Harding had been sent to Sir Harold Alexander's headquarters by Sir Alan Brooke, who believed that Alexander's rather loose control of his army group and his shortcomings as a strategist were prolonging the drive to Rome. Harding produced a plan for a joint Fifth Army/Eighth Army attack through the

Liri Valley. It called for the Eighth Army to secretly transfer the great bulk of its fighting power over the Apennines and mount a massive armoured assault westward, from the area east of the Gari River. At the same time, the Fifth Army would be shifted southward to the left flank of the attack; the French Expeditionary Corps would form the right flank of the Fifth Army. Thus the Eighth Army would make the main thrust—a fact that Mark Clark brooded over. Sir Oliver Leese, GOC-in-C of the Eighth Army, would have three corps under his command—13th British, 2nd Polish, and 1st Canadian.

The attack began an hour before midnight on May 11 with a massive artillery barrage. One Canadian officer described it this way:

> In those few miles between the hills, a thousand guns suddenly let go as one, and then they kept on firing. We'd never seen or heard or imagined anything quite like this. You could see the flashes of nearby guns and you could hear the thunder of dozens and hundreds more on every side and you could only imagine what sort of Hell was falling on the German lines. It damn near deafened you.[3]

1st Canadian Corps was in reserve for the initial assault across the Gari River, but 1st Canadian Armoured Brigade (i.e., the independent armoured brigade) assisted the 8th Indian Division, which had been assigned to effect a crossing, hold a bridgehead, and erect bridging in the Sant' Angelo sector for the armour and vehicles to follow. The Indian infantry, assisted by the Canadian armour, made slow going at first, but by the late afternoon of May 13, they had penetrated through the initial Gustav Line defences to establish a number of bridgeheads across the Gari. Then the tanks and troops of the British 78th Division moved

Our Finest Hour

across and began to advance toward the Hitler Line, the next German defensive position, some 13 kilometres west of the Gari. On the left flank the skilled mountain troops of the French Expeditionary Corps made a wide sweeping advance through rugged terrain south of the Liri; had Leese been prepared to take advantage of the French breakthrough, the Canadian armour might have been used to form a northern pincer to entrap the Germans manning the Hitler Line. But he did not. Never prone to react quickly or with boldness, Leese let the opportunity slip by; the classic set-piece battle would continue as planned.

The Indian breakthrough of the Gustav Line and the rapid French advance south of the Liri rendered the Gustav Line untenable. Those Germans not killed, wounded, or captured withdrew to the Hitler Line. To assault that secondary defence position, Leese called upon E.L.M. Burns and the troops of the 1st Canadian Corps. In typical fashion, Burns prepared for a set-piece attack with heavy artillery support, 1st Division infantry in the lead (hopefully to break through the Hitler Line), to be followed by the 5th Armoured, which would exploit any infantry breakthrough and then advance as quickly as possible up the Liri Valley. The 3rd Brigade was positioned on the right, the 1st Brigade on the left, and the Pignataro–Cassino road was the start line.

The attack began in the early morning hours of May 17. Although the Germans resisted the Canadian advance through the day, they melted away at nightfall, and both Canadian brigades failed to make contact the following day as they advanced to the vicinity of the Hitler Line. It was a different story when the Canadians finally reached the Line itself on the 19th; the Ontario Tank Regiment lost thirteen tanks destroyed and many others damaged supporting an attack on the Line by the British 78th Division, while the Royal 22e suffered heavy casualties in an ill-conceived direct assault on the Line's barbed wire. There would be no penetration of the Line and no breakthrough advance by the Canadian armour that day. The attack had run out of steam.

Burns was ordered to lay on another attack to punch through the Hitler Line at a point about 2 kilometres southwest of the hamlet of Aquino. It began on the hazy morning of May 23 with a heavy bombardment followed by an advance by two brigades from 1st Division: 2nd Brigade on the right, 3rd Brigade on the left. On the right, the 2nd Brigade struggled forward under heavy fire to its first objective and then went no farther. The PPCLI was especially hard hit: The slaughter was indescribable; the North Irish Horse, an armoured regiment supporting the PPCLI, suffered as greatly as did the Patricias. Tanks blew up on mines. Tanks were blown up by anti-tank guns and self-propelled guns. Tanks slithered and twisted to get away from the murderous fire but were trapped by a gully on one side and a raised road on the other. The regiment lost twenty-five Churchill tanks that day. Patricia Commanding Officer Cameron Ware advanced too far ahead of his own headquarters in the thick of the fighting and was out of reach of his regiment. He looked in vain for a radio in working order to at least put him in touch with his brigade. At about 1500 he learned that B Company of the PPCLI were stalled at the wire, taking casualties. Ware would later recall, "It became apparent we were not going to get on to this objective with enough people to be able to do anything . . . In other words, the right flank [attack] was not a success. A glorious failure if you want to call it because there wasn't anybody left."[4]

Things went much better on the left, where there was no German flanking fire; the infantry battalions moved quickly through the German defences and over the Pontecorvo–Aquino road. Vokes decided to reinforce success and threw his divisional reserve into the battle behind the 3rd Brigade. The advance started late in the afternoon in a heavy rain and caught the Germans in the open, preparing to counterattack. The Canadians killed many Germans and widened the breach. To their left, the Princess Louise, a reconnaissance regiment, and the 1st Brigade cleared the town of Pontecorvo.

The next morning, May 24, Hoffmeister sent his tanks through the gap made by the infantry and toward the Melfa River. Three infantry/ tank battle groups of the 5th Armoured Brigade forced a crossing by nightfall and held the bridgehead while the 11th Infantry Brigade began to pass through the next morning (May 25). By midday the division was across the Melfa on a two-battalion front. But then problems arose. The rear area of the division was a confused and tangled mass of vehicles and men; supplies, ammunition, bridging equipment, could not be brought up quickly, and the infantry of the 11th Brigade were forced to curtail their advance toward the Liri. They did not cross that river until May 26, and it was a full day again until they were able to occupy the town of Ceprano, near Highway 6 to Rome. Leese held Burns entirely responsible for the traffic jams and the delay in exploiting Hoffmeister's success in getting the 5th Canadian Armoured Division across the river. But although Burns was at least in part responsible for the delay—the Liri Valley was, after all, his first campaign as a corps commander—Leese, too, was responsible for the mess.[5] Leese was pushing five divisions and two corps (1st Canadian and 13th British) along a single highway in a narrow battle space. He also allowed the British 78th Division to move through the Canadian sector, all the while pressing Burns to get on with the attack. Burns admittedly made mistakes, but he merely compounded the problems that Leese himself had caused.[6]

Of course Leese did not see it that way. Burns was called on the carpet after the battle, while Leese also complained to General Sir Harold Alexander that "[neither] Burns nor his Corps staff are up to the

29. Major-General E.L.M. Burns at Larino, Italy, March 18, 1944.
PHOTOGRAPHER: C.E. NYE

30. Canadian troops before going inland on D-Day, Normandy, June 6, 1944.
PHOTOGRAPHER: F.L. DUBERVILL

31. A member of the Canadian Provost Corps guards the first German prisoners to be captured by Canadian soldiers on the Normandy beachhead, June 6, 1944. PHOTOGRAPHER: F.L. DUBERVILL

32. Some of the underwater obstacles carrying deadly charges that Canadian troops faced on the Normandy beachhead.
PHOTOGRAPHER: F.L. DUBERVILL

33. German prisoners, members of the SS, captured by Canadian troops in Normandy, June 17, 1944.
PHOTOGRAPHER: F.L. DUBERVILL

34. Four Ack-Ack gunners near the front line, with one Junkers 88 to their credit, France, June 17, 1944.
PHOTOGRAPHER: F.L. DUBERVILL

35. Members of the Royal
Canadian Artillery with a
17-pounder anti-tank gun in
Normandy, June 22, 1944.
PHOTOGRAPHER: KEN BELL

36. General H.D.G. Crerar (*right*)
and Lieutenant-Colonel J.C.
Spragge, Commanding Officer of
the Queen's Own Rifles of Canada,
drive through Bretteville-le-Rabet,
France, June 23, 1944.
PHOTOGRAPHER: F.L. DUBERVILL

37. French rescue workers remove
bodies from destroyed buildings in
Caen, France, July 18, 1944.
PHOTOGRAPHER: KEN BELL

38. Members of the Royal Canadian Artillery firing a 5.5-inch Howitzer near Voucelles, France, July 23, 1944.
PHOTOGRAPHER: KEN BELL

39. Bombing on the Caen-Falaise road, Normandy, August 1944.

40. An Avro Lancaster in flight.

41. A Vickers Wellington aircraft in flight.

42. Major David Currie of the South Alberta Regiment (*left*) directs the successful three-day defence of St-Lambert-sur-Dives, France, August 19, 1944. As commander of a mixed force of tanks, infantry, and artillery, he was awarded the Victoria Cross for his part in this action.
PHOTOGRAPHER: D.I. GRANT

43. A Consolidated VLR Liberator provides air cover for a transatlantic convoy.

44. Officers of the 6th Canadian Infantry Brigade watch the warm-up of Hawker Typhoon aircraft of No. 121 Squadron, RAF, Antwerp, Belgium, September 22, 1944.
PHOTOGRAPHER: KEN BELL

45. The Consolidated Canso, a flying-boat of the RCAF, built by Canadian Vickers Ltd. in Montreal, 1944.

46. A Bren gun carrier is ferried across the Afwalnings Canal, the Netherlands, April 7, 1945.
PHOTOGRAPHER: DANIEL GURAVICH

47. Dutch children watch Canadian vehicles cross a homemade bridge in Balkburg, the Netherlands, April 11, 1945.
PHOTOGRAPHER: DANIEL GURAVICH

48. Sherman tanks of the 4th Canadian Armoured Division near a German position at the Dortmund-Ems Canal, Germany, April 8, 1945.
PHOTOGRAPHER: A.M. STIRTON

49. General Kurt Meyer handcuffed to Major Arthur Russel during his exercise period, Aurich, Germany, November 12, 1945.
PHOTOGRAPHER: B.J. GLOSTER

50. Major-General Bert Hoffmeister takes the salute during the march past of the 5t Canadian Armoured Division, Groninger the Netherlands, May 13, 1945. PHOTOGRAPHER: J.H. SMITH

51. A Sherman tank of the Sherbrooke Fusiliers entering Xanten, Germany. PHOTOGRAPHER: KEN BELL

52. Generals of the First Canadian Army, May 20, 1945. Seated, left to right: H.S. Maczek, G. Simonds, H.D.G. Crerar, C. Foulkes, B.M. Hoffmeister. Standing, left to right: R.H. Keefler, A.B. Matthews, H.W. Foster, R.W. Moncel, S.B. Rowlins. PHOTOGRAPHER: KEN BELL

53. Canadian and British prisoners of war who were liberated by a landing party from HMCS *Prince Robert*, Kowloon, Hong Kong, August 1945. PHOTOGRAPHER: JACK HAWES

[British] Army standards."[7] In the weeks following the Liri Valley campaign, Leese sought to have Burns fired and the Canadian Corps broken up. Leese's observations were coloured by at least two other factors, according to Major J.P. Johnston. The two men were polar opposites in personality, and Leese, like his former boss and mentor Montgomery, was strongly resentful of the hard reality that politics—British and Canadian—had left them with an additional corps headquarters to deal with and, worse, that the Canadian government insisted that the two division corps (as opposed to the usual three divisions) were to be kept together as a unit. In addition, British senior officers in general simply refused to accept their counterparts as equal in rank, no matter how many pips (rank badges) they wore on their shoulders. In their view, the British knew how to fight, the Canadians did not, and were thus not equal in competence, no matter what rank they held. There were exceptions—famed British Corps Commander Brian Horrocks most notably—but they were few. Leese's complaints reached Major-General Ken Stuart, then commanding Canadian Military Headquarters in London, who went to Italy to determine whether or not Burns was fit to continue to command the corps. After an investigation that included interviews with Leese, Alexander, Vokes, and Hoffmeister, Stuart concluded that Burns deserved another chance. Alexander reluctantly agreed, and Leese was forced to accept Stuart's conclusions.

* * * *

The Allies entered Rome on June 4, the Canadians of the First Special Service Force among them. But while Mark Clark's Fifth Army seized Rome, he allowed the bulk of the Tenth German Army to slip away to the north. It was a major error, which gave Kesselring ample troops and weapons to man strong defensive positions, such as the Gothic Line that ran from north of Pisa on the west coast of Italy to south of Rimini on the east coast (sometimes referred to as the Pisa–Rimini Line). Thus the Allies would have to continue to slog north through difficult terrain fighting a well-armed and resourceful enemy determined to make them pay for every metre of advance.

In early May, even before the Normandy landings, there were musings in Ottawa and at Canadian Military Headquarters (CMHQ) in London, about reuniting 1st Canadian Corps with First Canadian Army. On May 3 Minister of National Defence J.L. Ralston suggested to the Cabinet War Committee that Ottawa's instructions to Crerar—to be issued before Operation Overlord—should "make reference to the desirability of Canadian formations in western and southern Europe being united and the [First Canadian] Army and that this should not be restricted to the postwar period." Or, as Christine Leppard phrases it in her 2013 PhD thesis, "rather than waiting for the end of the war, 1st Corps should rejoin First Canadian Army whenever possible."[8] Stuart quickly came to agree with Ralston; from his perch at CMHQ in London, he saw Montgomery's "ongoing recalcitrance in respecting Crerar's special position as national commander."[9] Montgomery had no intention of having his hands tied by Canadian political considerations when it came to operational matters regarding First Canadian Army. In fact he had even raised the subject matter directly with Mackenzie King when they met in the United Kingdom in May. Ralston, Stuart, and Crerar were rapidly coming to the conclusion that splitting the army and watering down the Canadian contribution by adding 1st British Corps to Crerar's command to replace 1st Canadian Corps had also undermined Crerar's moral and political authority within 21st Army Group. So now they wanted 1st Corps back when these very same men were responsible for sending 1st Corps to

Italy in the first place. There is no better evidence that Ottawa simply had no idea how to run Canada's war overseas.

Despite the initial success of the Allied forces in gaining a toehold in Normandy on June 6 and in the days that followed, the British—Churchill, Brooke, and Alexander—were determined to push ahead with the Italian campaign. That meant that an assault on the Gothic Line—Kesselring's next major defence position—would be necessary. On August 25, 1944, Operation Olive—Leese's attempt to smash the Gothic Line on the Adriatic coast—began. Of the two Allied armies in Italy, Leese's Eighth Army had been the least affected by the transfer of troops to France for Operation Anvil (the proposed invasion of southern France, to be carried out in August), and he had persuaded Alexander to allow him to move his forces back over the Apennines to attack the Gothic Line at its right anchor. For three weeks the transfer was carried out with great care and secrecy. Kesselring was taken by surprise. Leese's offensive began with three corps up front: 2nd Polish on the right, 1st Canadian in the centre, and 5th British on the left. In command of the Canadian troops, Burns planned a four-stage assault that would take them from the Metauro River, about 16 kilometres east of and parallel to the Gothic Line defences, to Rimini on the Adriatic coast. It took the Canadians four days to clear the ground between the Metauro and the Foglia Rivers, but when they closed up to the Gothic Line on August 30, Hoffmeister quickly realized that the Germans were not present in great strength. From an observation post above the German defences, Hoffmeister was surprised by what he saw: "We could by careful examination pick out the odd concrete gun emplacement, and we could see the barbed wire, and we saw the minefields; but there was no life around the place at all. I didn't expect to see German officers to be swanking up and down but the whole thing looked terribly quiet."[10]

The Canadians had arrived at the Gothic Line just after two German divisions had withdrawn but before two fresh divisions arrived. With Burns's and Leese's support, Hoffmeister ordered a careful gatecrashing using "echelon" tactics: sending in the smallest unit, followed by a larger unit, and so on. The Germans were unprepared.

Fifth Armoured Division broke through the main German defences by the afternoon of August 30 and scrambled to the high ground beyond it.[11] In the words of US military historian Carlo D'Este, "The timing and boldness of the Canadian attack left the Germans in considerable disarray and helpless to prevent an exploitation, provided it was carried out before they regrouped. In fact, if a drive had been mounted . . . Eighth Army might have outflanked the Gothic Line entirely and unleashed its armour onto the plains of the Po Valley."[12] But a drive was not mounted because Burns had no reserve to exploit Hoffmeister's breakthrough, and Leese, not thinking that the Canadians would accomplish much of anything, had not positioned reserves behind Burns to throw into the fight. He had left the 1st British Armoured Division some 160 kilometres to the rear, out of the battle entirely. There wasn't even a chance to catch the German 1st Parachute Division hurriedly withdrawing along the coast to the north to avoid being trapped by Hoffmeister's troops. As William McAndrew has observed of his performance in this battle, "The Canadians were placed on the best ground for movement but lacked reserves to exploit . . . . Leese had [given away] his capability to influence the battle directly. Had he retained control [of his armoured reserve]. Leese could have had it in hand to exploit where and when the decisive breakthrough occurred: on the Canadian Corps' front."[13] Alexander, for one, was very pleased with the Canadians' actions. He awarded Burns an immediate Distinguished Service Order in recognition of the Canadian Corps' performance and told Stuart that Burns had done very well. Even Leese grudgingly admitted that Burns had done a good job.

The Germans recovered; the British and Canadians (minus the Poles who had been "pinched out" on the right) fought their way toward Rimini as the hot dry weather broke and the rains of late summer began to turn the ground into a muddy morass. The infantry of the 1st Division had a particularly difficult time dislodging the Germans from the small village of San Martino, as German shellfire from the San Fortunato Ridge beyond made life hell for the Canadians. That ridge was the key to the German defences in the sector and on the night of September 19–20, it was the objective of an all-out assault by 3rd Brigade, with the Hasty Ps from 1st Brigade under command. The attack began at 0400. By first light two Hasty P companies, supported by tanks, were in position to attack the crest of the ridge. Many of the tanks were hit by anti-tank fire; the German paratroopers on the crest poured machine-gun, mortar, and rifle fire down the slopes at the approaching Canadians. The Hasty Ps were too close to the Germans to call on artillery support, so had to withdraw before shell explosions began to blanket the crest. Then they tried again: "Up through mangled vineyards and orchards the platoons clawed their ways to reach their objectives under the lee of the last slope. Here, engaged in bitter hand-to-hand fighting they dug in to hold the ground."[14] But the battle was not yet over. The other battalions of 3rd Brigade had not done so well, and the Hasty Ps were in danger of being outflanked and cut off. They were forced to withdraw once again to allow the artillery to have its way. Through the remainder of the day and into the night, the shells rained down on the hill, the Germans, and on the men of 14 Platoon of C Company of the Hasty Ps, who had failed to get the word to withdraw. The intense shellfire and a renewed assault finally carried the day; by the next morning the ridge was firmly in Canadian hands. The fighting on the

Adriatic front did not end with the capture of the San Fortunato Ridge. The Eighth Army offensive ground on, and the Canadians with it, across seven more rivers before reaching the Ronco River and going into reserve at the end of October. Even then the interlude was relatively brief, and the Canadians were back in action and driving toward the Senio River in early December. They reached it on the 21st of that month—the farthest north point they would reach in Italy.

* * * *

On November 5 E.L.M. Burns was relieved of command of 1st Canadian Corps and replaced by Major-General Charles Foulkes, who had commanded the 2nd Canadian Infantry Division in Normandy and had been acting Officer Commanding (OC) of 2nd Canadian Corps during the Battle of the Scheldt Estuary (see Chapter 16). This extraordinary turn of fortune for Burns, who had been awarded a DSO three months earlier, was initiated by Leese's successor, Lieutenant-General Sir Richard McCreery, who was dissatisfied with the Corps' performance after the Gothic Line and blamed Burns for the situation. Both Hoffmeister and Vokes had been increasingly vocal in their complaints about how Burns was commanding the Corps, not simply because of his personal characteristics, but also because he had developed the habit of conferring with Hoffmeister and Vokes's brigade commanders without directly engaging the two divisional commanders. Burns had made no friends among his two divisional commanders and was intensely disliked by Vokes, who wrote to a friend at CMHQ, "I have done my best to be loyal but goddamnit the strain has been too bloody great."[15] Both men also knew that Burns had, in effect, been on probation since Stuart's visit to Italy after the battles of the Liri Valley; they were thus in a position to move him far more easily than might have otherwise been the case. Burns had certainly not been among the best of the Allied corps commanders in Italy, but he had performed tolerably well, considering the initial inexperience of his armoured division. The communications foul-ups at the Melfa were at least as much the fault of Leese as they were his, and Leese was surely the more culpable of the two in his failure to exploit Hoffmeister's Gothic Line breakthrough at the end of August. But no matter. A corps commander who did not have the respect of his divisional commanders could not function. That was especially important because, in the words of Sir Brian Horrocks, GOC of the 30th British Corps in the last year of the war, "a Corps is the highest formation in the British Army which fights the day to day tactical battles."[16] That applied equally well to the Canadian Army. At the same time that Burns was relieved, Vokes was sent to Holland to assume command of 4th Canadian Armoured Division, and Major General Harry Foster, who had been in command of the 4th since late August, was sent to Italy to take over the 1st Division.

* * * *

In February 1945 the Combined Chiefs of Staff, meeting in Malta, decided to pull more troops out of Italy to reinforce those about to fight the final battles for Germany. The 1st Canadian Corps was to be among those troops. Beginning that month, slowly, and with as much secrecy as possible, the Canadians pulled out of the front lines, withdrew to the coast, and boarded transports for southern France. They began to form up in northern Europe in late February and early March, too late for the Battle of the Rhineland, but just in time for the final push into occupied Holland.

In all, some 92,757 Canadians served in the Italian theatre of operations, including those in the First Special Service Force. They left behind them 5,764 of their comrades who were either killed in action or died of other causes while on active service. A further 19,486 Canadians had been wounded in the campaign and 1,004 taken prisoner. The Canadians in Italy poked a bit of fun at themselves as Overlord was launched on June 6 and the Battle for Normandy began; they called themselves the D-Day Dodgers. But their role in the liberation of Italy stands among the finest achievements of Canadian arms anywhere.

CHAPTER 14

JUNO BEACH

The English Channel: 0315, June 6, 1944. It was pitch dark when Charles Martin and the other men of the Queen's Own Rifles of Canada began one of the most momentous days in history aboard the pitching transport SS *Monowai*. The men knew that when daylight finally came, they would be among the first wave of Canadian infantry to hit the Normandy beaches in front of the little resort town of Bernières-sur-Mer. It may have occurred to some of those men that behind them stood the combined armies of three nations with millions of fighting men, thousands of armoured vehicles and warplanes, and an invasion armada the likes of which the world had never seen. Some may even have taken some comfort in that thought. But most knew in their guts that when they ran across the sand, each man would be utterly alone with his fears, his courage, and his determination to survive.

Just before 0600, with a faint hint of the approaching dawn on the eastern horizon, the men began the tricky climb down the loading nets into the LCAs (assault landing craft) that pitched below them. The men were heavily laden with extra ammunition, a full pack, extra grenades, shells for the 2-inch mortars, spare barrels for the light machine guns, and the other accoutrements of war. It was not easy to climb down the nets and time their leaps to the deck of the bucking landing craft, which were tied loosely alongside the transport with their motors running. It took time, but if the men were hurried, some would miss their jumps and sink like cannon balls into the cold depths.

The assault boats were finally loaded. As they cast off, they began their long voyage to the breakers about 8 kilometres away. At 0715, as they moved toward the shore, the sky around them was lit by the gun flashes of hundreds of ships and landing craft. Each ship was supposed to be firing at a pre-selected target; the great weight of explosives was intended to ensure that D-Day would not be another Dieppe. The craft moved closer and closer to the maelstrom of fire and explosion that had been a peaceful beach not long before. Then, at 0720, they learned that their landing had been put back by half an hour because some of the specialized assault vehicles, such as the Duplex Drive (DD) tanks, were having trouble in the rough sea. These were waterproofed Sherman tanks with special canvas shielding and propellers hooked up to their engines that allowed them to float. They were designed to be disembarked off-shore to "swim" to the beaches. The lateness of the DD tanks meant that the Queen's Own would land in the full light of dawn; the absence of the tanks meant there would be no close-in covering fire.

Martin peered through the mist and light drizzle and caught sight of Bernières-sur-Mer. Untouched by the barrage, it seemed postcard perfect in the dim morning light. He later remembered, "There wasn't much talk . . . as we came closer, it was the strange silence that gripped us." The landing craft spread out as they neared the beaches. A nervous German gunner opened fire when the boats were still too far out, wounding one of the men. Martin, in charge of the platoon in the LCA, ordered the Royal Navy lieutenant in command of the boat to move ashore as fast as possible. At about 0805, the prow grated on the sand and the ramp at the front of the boat dropped. Mortar and machine-gun fire opened up all along the beach front. "Move! Fast!" Martin shouted. "Don't stop for anything. Go! Go! Go!" They all raced down the ramp, fanned out, and headed for the seawall as fast as they could. The invasion of occupied Europe—Operation Overlord—had begun.[1]

* * * *

Charlie Martin's platoon was one small part of the 8th Canadian Infantry Brigade, 3rd Canadian Infantry Division. That division had been selected to play a key role in the largest invasion in history and had been planning for the assault for nearly a year. The division had been chosen because it was the only one of the three Canadian infantry divisions available for the job: 1st Division was in Italy; 2nd Division was still rebuilding after the disaster of Dieppe. The 8th Brigade with the 10th Canadian Armoured Regiment assaulted the eastern sector of Juno Beach; the 7th Brigade with the 6th Canadian Armoured Regiment assaulted the western sector. The 9th Brigade and the 27th Canadian Armoured Regiment were the floating reserve, not due to land until several hours after the assault brigades had secured the beaches.

Third Canadian Infantry Division was commanded by Major-General R.F.L. Keller, who pointed out to a historical officer some two weeks after D-Day that the division had been taught how to cooperate with the navy and the air forces, how to embark into landing craft at sea, how to cope with heavy weather (many did not and vomited copiously into their landing craft on their way ashore), how to attack beach defences, and how to get over the beach and inland as fast as possible. By May 1944, Foster claimed, the 3rd Division "could well have been described as 'web footed.'"[2] Keller claimed "by and large, the mechanics of the assault and the lines along which we had trained, did work."[3] Keller was certainly correct about some of the preparation, particularly the direct-fire support from the DD tanks and the specialized armoured vehicles designed to explode mines, provide flame-thrower support to the infantry, and bridge culverts and small gulleys. But many of the Armoured Fighting Vehicles (AFVs) in support of the infantry were late, or didn't make it to shore at all. Many of the engineers who were supposed to land immediately behind the infantry to dispose of the mines and other explosives that the Germans had attached to their beach obstacles were also late. Worse, the massive pre-landing bombardment by the huge naval guns of British and US battleships, cruisers, and monitors, and the heavy bombing from USAAF B-17s and B-24s and Bomber Command's Lancasters and Halifaxes roared over the actual beach defences of the Germans, and instead plowed up thousands of acres of farms and villages a kilometre or two inland. Brigadier Harry Foster, commanding the 7th Brigade, remembered that "the terrific devastation which was to have been caused by bombing of the coast defence . . . did not materialize. The only damage visible from the sea was that effected by our own self-propelled artillery fire from [the landing craft].[4]

Along with Martin and his platoon, tens of thousands of other Canadians, British, and Americans landed along a front of some 100 kilometres on the south shore of the Bay of the Seine. Elements of eight Allied divisions (three of them airborne) took part: three British, one Canadian, and five American. The first of them to engage the Germans—the 6th British Airborne Division and the 82nd and 101st US Airborne Divisions—came to Normandy by parachute or glider to begin what the Germans later called "the longest day." Both sides had been preparing for Overlord for at least three years; both sides knew that the outcome of the invasion would have a major impact on the course of the war. Both sides were prepared to commit all the resources at their command to ensure victory.

* * * *

Allied invasion planners were well aware that the Germans had started 1944 with some thirty-eight divisions in France and the Low Countries. These divisions were in various states of readiness and differed in both fighting quality and intended role. For example, there was a major difference between a low-grade infantry division assigned to defend a particular stretch of coastline or one that contained many eastern Europeans and Russians impressed into the Wehrmacht, and a crack SS panzer division such as the 12th SS Panzer Division (Hitlerjugend), a well-equipped, motivated, first-line division. The Allies were also aware that more German divisions were being shifted to France and the Low Countries as the date of a likely invasion drew closer.

The Allies knew their invasion force would inevitably be outnumbered by all the German troops in northern France. They did two things to solve that problem. First, they succeeded in convincing the Germans through a variety of subterfuges that they would land either in Norway, or in the Pas de Calais area north of the Seine, more than 200 kilometres northeast of the landing beaches. Thus the Germans placed their Fifteenth Army near Calais and held much of their armour in reserve there long after the D-Day landings, which they initially thought might be a diversion. Second, British Air Ministry strategist Solly Zuckerman devised the "transportation plan" designed to make the actual landing zones as inaccessible as possible by road, rail, or canal from the rest of France and the Low Countries. The object was to stop the Germans from reinforcing their troops in the landing zone, giving the Allies time to push enough men and weapons ashore to overwhelm the Germans on the beaches and in the lodgement areas immediately behind the beaches.

General Dwight D. Eisenhower, who had been designated Supreme Allied Commander in Europe, assumed control of the heavy-bomber forces on March 27, 1944, and delegated command to his deputy for air, RAF Air Chief Marshal Sir Arthur Tedder. By then the transportation-plan bombings had already started. On the night of March 6–7, 1944, 267 Halifaxes from Nos. 4 and 6 Groups, guided by Mosquitos from No. 8 Group, attacked the marshalling yards at Trappes, near Paris. Of course, there were casualties among French and Belgian civilians, as Eisenhower and Churchill knew there would be. On the night of April 9–10, for example, Bomber Command severely damaged the rail yards at Lille, but at a cost of 456 French civilian casualties. The next night, 428 Belgians were killed and 300 injured when the bombers attacked rail targets near Ghent, Brussels, and other locations. Even though the civilian casualties were lower than had been forecast, Churchill and the Free French minister of the interior, General Marie-Pierre Koenig, agonized over these deaths. Eisenhower knew, however, that there was simply no choice but to carry on with the bombings if the Allied troops were to have a chance of making a successful lodgement and hold their ground. In the rough arithmetic of war, the civilians who died in these bombardments were sacrificed so that the Allies would increase their odds of defeating the Nazis more quickly.

Despite the order to implement the transportation plan, Bomber Command chief Arthur Harris sought every opportunity he could to continue to conduct area attacks on German cities whenever attacks on the French and Belgian transportation networks were not scheduled.

Major raids were mounted against Berlin (March 24–25), Nuremburg (March 30–31), Essen (April 26–27), Friedrichshafen (April 27–28), and other German cities. The great bulk of the missions flown by the British and American heavies, however, were against rail and other transportation targets. That was a blessing to the bomber crews, especially those of Bomber Command. German night-fighter defences were less effective in countering the bombers on these shorter missions because the night fighters had long ago been concentrated in Germany itself.

At the beginning of June the heavy bombers switched targets from rail and transportation centres to coastal batteries and other purely military targets near the French coast. In order to hide the fact that the Normandy beaches had been selected as the landing ground, twice as many sorties were flown to other locations, particularly the Pas de Calais area than to Normandy. On the night of June 4–5, for example, Bomber Command attacked three coastal batteries near Calais and only one located between the designated US landing beaches of Utah and Omaha.

On the night of June 5–6, as the Allied flotilla drew near to the landing beaches, Bomber Command set out to destroy ten strategically located coastal batteries, using some 6,000 tons of bombs. Virtually every serviceable bomber that could be mustered took off into the darkening sky and headed for the French coast. One of the men flying that night was Flying Officer Murray Peden, a Canadian piloting an RAF Flying Fortress with No. 214 Squadron. Peden's mission was to patrol the coast north and east of Dieppe, dropping Window, strips of aluminum foil designed to jam the German radar. Toward dawn, mission completed, Peden headed the bomber back to England: "Suddenly we saw a sight that brought a lump into my throat. A tremendous aerial armada was passing us in extended formation a mile or two on our left side—not bombers, but C-47s: an airborne army. They were going in. We were coming out. For a long minute I watched them sailing silently onward to their date with destiny."[5]

* * * *

The heavy bombers did not bear the total burden of disrupting the French and Belgian transportation network. On November 13, 1943, the Allied Expeditionary Air Force was born. Its dual mission was to attack transportation targets, airfields, and coastal defences in France prior to the invasion and to provide tactical air support for the Allied armies in France after it. The American contribution to the AEAF was the Ninth US Air Force; the British was the 2nd Tactical Air Force, which included the light and medium bombers of No. 2 Group of Bomber Command and the fighters and fighter bombers of No. 83 and 84 Groups. Fifteen of the twenty-nine squadrons in No. 83 Group were Royal Canadian Air Force. They flew Spitfires, Mustang Is, and Typhoon IBs, the latter one of the deadliest Allied fighter bombers of the war.

The primary mission of No. 83 Group was to provide air support for Second British Army. This was ironic since First Canadian Army was to receive its air cover and support from No. 84 Group, which had no Canadian squadrons. To provide air support meant to gain and maintain air superiority over the battlefield, to interdict the flow of enemy men and supplies to the front, to attack designated ground targets, and to strike other targets as needed at the request of the fighting units on the ground. At first the ground attack missions were flown primarily by the Typhoon squadrons, armed with cannon and bombs (Canadian Typhoons did not carry rockets). As the German day-fighter force all but disappeared from the skies over western Europe, the Spitfires were also increasingly used as fighter bombers.

When the AEAF was first formed, Allied airmen believed that the Luftwaffe would pose a serious threat to the invasion and subsequent battles to liberate France and the Low Countries and subdue Germany. In fact, Normandy was, in part, selected as the landing site because it was within easy fighter range of the United Kingdom. When the great day arrived, however, the Luftwaffe barely made a showing, and in the long battle for Normandy that followed, it was hardly a factor except for the odd night bombing of Allied troop encampments or supply dumps. The Allies enjoyed almost total air superiority over Normandy, making it difficult for the Germans to bring up large numbers of troops, armour, or other essential war equipment in daylight. That happened because the battle for the skies over western Europe had been won by the Allies, especially by the Americans, in early 1944, when long-range Mustang fighters began to accompany the US heavy bombers on raids deep into Germany. The US-built Mustangs, which mated the original airframe with a British Merlin engine, was the best-performing propeller fighter of the war and, within months, destroyed thousands of German fighters in the air and on the ground. This wholesale destruction of German aircraft, combined with heavy bomber attacks on German aircraft plants and fuel production, gave the Allies virtually complete control of the air by the time of D-Day.

There is considerable historical debate about the role of tactical air power in the eventual victory of the Allies in Normandy. For example, operational research conducted after the battle revealed that very few German AFVs were destroyed by Allied aircraft. Whether armed with bombs or rockets, Allied fighters usually missed what they were bombing or shooting rockets at—because the target-finding devices they were using were primitive, because they were flying too fast (so as not to be too vulnerable to ground fire), or because the bombs or rockets

Our Finest Hour

they were carrying were too inaccurate to hit vehicles on the ground. Moreover, the command structure used to direct tactical air power to aid the army on the ground was cumbersome and slow to evolve. The situation was not unlike the relationship between Coastal Command and the Royal Navy in the early days of the Battle of the Atlantic; service rivalries were rife, and service pride—not to mention the lack of inter-service training and cooperation—mitigated against the development of close air support that has evolved so far in the late twentieth and early twenty-first centuries.[6] There is no doubt, and the Germans themselves admitted this, that virtually complete control of the skies over Normandy played a major role in the Allied victory. But when the evidence shows that German tanks were, for the most part, rendered inoperable by breakdown, fuel shortage, ground anti-tank weapons, artillery, or just plain abandonment, just how did that tactical air power provide effective close air support?

To begin with, the Luftwaffe was nowhere to be found. German dive bombers did not attack Allied convoys, troop emplacements, or artillery batteries because they never appeared in daylight. German aircraft did not hinder Allied movement or fighting ability. Next, Allied soldiers knew they were fighting under "friendly" skies, even if they were not often directly aided by Allied aircraft. The opposite circumstance held for the German soldiers, who knew that any aircraft they saw and heard were hostile. That surely contributed to a difference in morale. But the real impact of Allied tactical air power was in making German daylight movement very difficult. Aircraft machine guns and cannon destroyed thousands of German soft-skinned vehicles, hindering the movement of troops and supplies. Roaming Allied fighters were a decided advantage in fighting in the Normandy battleground.[7]

In the months leading up to the Normandy landings, the fighters and fighter bombers of No. 83 Group attacked German airfields, coastal defence installations, radar sites, and road and rail targets, especially bridges and rolling stock. Specially equipped Spitfires and Mosquitos flew thousands of aerial reconnaissance missions, taking photos of beach areas, inland defences, tank parks, etc. The fighters also flew escort missions for the medium and heavy bombers that were taking part in the transportation-plan raids. Many squadrons moved to advance airfields along the British coast to be closer to the future battle zone. Still others prepared for quick transfer to France to begin operating from makeshift fighter strips as soon as a bridgehead was secured.

The RCAF's No. 401 Fighter Squadron, which had been the first RCAF fighter squadron to arrive in the United Kingdom in 1940, was now flying the highly manoeuvrable and fast Spitfire IX. Moved to Tangmere airfield for forward operations, the pilots spent the weeks before D-Day flying intercept and search and destroy missions against enemy aircraft, and attacking ground targets, something the Spitfire was not especially designed to do.

* * * *

The men and ships of the Royal Canadian Navy were also destined to play an important role in the Normandy landings and were an integral part of the pre-invasion preparations. The RCN's duties included offensive night sweeps in the English Channel carried out by the four Tribal Class destroyers, minesweeping, escort work, the transport of men and equipment from the United Kingdom to the beaches, and helping the Royal Navy maintain standing anti-U-boat patrols in strategic areas near the entrances to the Channel. When the invasion began, the Canadian Tribals added their gunfire to the other Allied ships supporting the men going ashore. At the same time, RCN frigates, corvettes, and destroyers were still carrying about half of the convoy escort burden in the North Atlantic. By the spring of 1944 the RCN was also putting its own support groups to sea in the fight to sink U-boats.

In January 1944 the four Canadian Tribals were reassigned from Scapa Flow to Plymouth to become part of the Royal Navy's 10th Destroyer Flotilla, operating under the Commander-in-Chief, Plymouth. The Canadian Tribals thus joined their British counterparts in conducting regular offensive night sweeps of the English Channel from roughly Ostend, Belgium, to the Bay of Biscay. The operations were carried out at night to avoid the Luftwaffe and its new remote-controlled glider bombs; they were directed at hunting and sinking German destroyers and other warships, disrupting Channel convoys, hunting U-boats passing through the Bay of Biscay, and acting as screens for British mine-laying operations.

The Canadian and British Tribals fought in four ship divisions. Thus the four Canadian Tribals often sailed with RN ships. They first sortied in January 1944, but did not meet any German naval units until the night of April 25–26, when *Haida*, *Huron*, *Athabaskan*, and the RN Tribal *Ashanti*, combined with the RN cruiser, *Black Prince*, ran into three German destroyers. As the cruiser laid back to fire star shells, battle was joined. One German destroyer was sunk; the others escaped. *Ashanti* and *Huron* suffered minor damage from a collision that occurred as the ships returned to Plymouth.

Three nights later, *Athabaskan* and *Haida* and two motor torpedo boats sortied in support of a Royal Navy mine-laying flotilla. The two destroyers took up station off the French coast in a spot where they would be able to intercept any German destroyers or E-boats (torpedo boats) coming from the east. At about 0200 on the morning of April

29, Plymouth alerted them to two enemy vessels steaming westward at about 20 knots. The two Canadian destroyers altered course to the southwest and went to full speed to intercept. At 0412 two German destroyers were sighted; within moments star shells illuminated the seascape. The Germans were about 7,300 metres away. They fired two torpedo spreads before turning back sharply to the east; the two Tribals opened up with their main armament and chased after the fleeing destroyers, altering course to avoid the torpedoes. The Germans returned the shellfire, shrapnel peppering *Athabaskan*'s decks. Suddenly Captain John H. Stubbs received word that his ship's radar had detected two objects travelling off his port quarter at high speed. E-boats! Then, thirty seconds later, a terrific explosion ripped apart the starboard stern quarter. Whether the explosion was caused by an E-boat torpedo or a torpedo fired by one of the German destroyers was never clear. It did not matter anyway. What did matter was that the explosion caused many casualties and much damage; *Athabaskan* lost headway and began to founder almost immediately. Within minutes the "abandon ship" order was given and moments later, *Athabaskan* disappeared beneath the waves, stern first. Stubbs and 128 crew were killed; *Haida* returned to rescue forty-two survivors, but had to abandon the search just before daybreak because she was less than 10 kilometres from shore and well within range of German guns and aircraft. Nevertheless *Haida*'s captain, Harry DeWolf, left the ship's motor launch behind, and it was able to pick up six more men and make its way back to Plymouth, though dogged by engine trouble and German minesweepers and fighter aircraft.

While the Channel battles began to reach their climax in late April, a fleet of nineteen Canadian corvettes to be used for convoy escort and other anti-submarine duties gathered in United Kingdom ports. On April 28 the first such operations began when Canadian corvettes

Woodstock and *Regina* began to escort small convoys to and from ports on the Thames Estuary. On the last day of April, nine Canadian destroyers and eleven corvettes arrived at Moelfre Bay in North Wales and set to work to establish a 90,000-square-kilometre submarine exclusion zone covering the western entrance to the Channel.

The role played by the Royal Canadian Navy in the landings themselves is often overlooked, but that role was by no means a minor one. The RCN's contribution included not only the pre-invasion Channel sweeps by the Canadian Tribals and the anti-U-boat patrol duties of the corvettes, but also the vital work performed by the RCN's minesweepers, including the 31st Minesweeping Flotilla, in helping to clear mines from the waters off the beaches. Oddly enough, the Canadian Bangor Class minesweepers were assigned the responsibility of clearing mines off the US Utah assault beach. The sweepers moved very close inshore but were not detected in the darkness. As they finished their job and steamed northward, Lieutenant J.C. Marston, captain of HMCS *Blairmore*, recalled, "The dark of the night began to give way to twilight [and] one could begin to appreciate the immensity of the operation. As light increased more and more dark shapes began to make distinctive forms, and what had appeared to be just a few ships in close proximity now became a whole panorama of sea power as far as the eye [could see] to seaward."[8] The Canadian infantry landing ships (LSIs) *Prince Henry* and *Prince David* were among those ships. They had ferried men from the United Kingdom to the Normandy coast while five flotillas of RCN landing craft of various sorts prepared to bring infantry, tanks, trucks, self-propelled artillery, and other equipment directly to the beaches.

* * * *

The C-47s (Dakotas) that passed Murray Peden's B-17 as he and his crew returned to the United Kingdom in the early morning hours of June 6 carried elements of three airborne divisions—the US 82nd and 101st and the British 6th—destined to be the first of the Allied invaders to land on French soil. The two US airborne divisions were to land to the south and west of the beach designated Utah, which was on the southeast corner of the Cotentin Peninsula. They were supposed to secure the key inland routes leading to the beaches, to stop the Germans from reinforcing their coastal defences as the US infantry stormed ashore. The British 6th Airborne, which contained the 1st Canadian Parachute Battalion, was to be airdropped or glider-landed to the east of the Orne River, south of the easternmost British beach (Sword), in order to secure the river crossings and stop German troops and armour from mounting a flanking attack against Sword Beach.

Late on June 5, 1944, thirty-six Dakotas carrying the main body of 1st Canadian Parachute Battalion took off from the southern United Kingdom and headed for the coast of France. The Canadians' planes were a small part of a huge fleet of transport aircraft carrying thousands of other paratroopers or towing British and American gliders; as the aircraft crossed the French coast, German anti-aircraft fire opened up. Some of the aircraft were shot out of the sky almost immediately. Others were damaged but not destroyed; they flew on as best they could as the jumpers tried to get out of their planes. And others flew on, untouched, but weaving and jinking to avoid the ground fire. Nineteen-year-old paratrooper Bill Lovatt later remembered, "As we approached the D[rop] Z[one] the aircraft took violent evasive moves and as I approached the door I was flung back violently to the opposite side of the aircraft in a tangle of arms and legs." Private Anthony Skalicky's plane was hit, and one of the engines burst into flame. The paratroopers "just ran out the door," he remembered. "I couldn't get out of the plane fast enough."[9] Instead of landing at their designated drop zone, the Canadian paratroopers were scattered over a wide area between the Orne and Dives Rivers. Some never made it to the ground alive. Others were caught in trees or landed in bogs. Their first challenge was to find one another. Their next step was to organize to fulfill their assigned objectives: to capture the Merville Battery, located just a few kilometres from Gold Beach and situated to enable firing into the flanks of the British landings; to destroy the bridge over the Dives at Robehomme; and to destroy a small bridge at Varaville, near their drop zone. After these jobs were done, the Canadians were to take and hold an important crossroads at Le Mesnil-Patry, a few kilometres to the east of Pegasus Bridge, which was to be captured by British glider troops. Many of the paratroopers who survived the landing were hopelessly lost. A mere one-third of the battalion was eventually able to assemble and attack their objectives, and more than 70 percent of their heavy equipment was lost. Had it not been for the superb physical fitness of the men, they could not have accomplished their missions, but by noon the next day, they had—at a cost of 116 casualties out of the 541 who had jumped into Normandy the night before.[10]

The great bulk of the Canadian seaborne troops were to assault Juno Beach, which stretched from St-Aubin-sur-Mer on the east to halfway between La Rivière and Courseulles-sur-Mer on the west. To the right of Juno Beach lay Gold Beach, to be assaulted by the 50th British Infantry Division, and to its left was Sword Beach, the objective of the 3rd British Infantry Division. The three beaches were to be under the command of the 1st British Corps, then attached to the 2nd British Army; once a successful lodgement had taken place, the Canadians were to revert to the command of 2nd Canadian Corps under Lieutenant-General

Guy Simonds. Montgomery did not intend to bring Crerar and his First Canadian Army headquarters to Normandy for some time yet.

Much controversy would erupt in the years after the war as to exactly what Field Marshal Montgomery had planned for D-Day and the days following. He was to claim after the battle that he had intended to fight a defensive battle on the British-Canadian front in order to draw the bulk of the German troops and especially armour to his front, and then loose the Americans on his left—at Omaha Beach, to the west of Gold Beach; and at Utah Beach, at the foot of the Cotentin Peninsula— to break through the German defences and make a wide sweep toward both the Brittany ports to the west and the River Seine and Paris to the east and south. The historical record shows otherwise. Montgomery clearly intended to seize Caen on the first day and then drive rapidly beyond it to take the high ground to the south (the Verrières and Bourguébus Ridges). Caen was the chief administrative centre of Normandy, the main rail, road, and canal junction behind the beaches, and the key to any further inland advance on the British and Canadian flank. The quicker this could be done the better, since the land south of Caen was ideal for airfields to be used by the forwardmost units of the tactical air forces. The role assigned to the Canadians after they had secured their bridgehead was to drive eastward and capture the important ports of Le Havre and Rouen. This latter operation was dubbed Axehead.

The British and Canadians were assigned the easternmost beaches, and the Americans the two on the west, because of where those armies had been based in the United Kingdom (i.e., the British and Canadians in the southeast, the Americans in the south and west) and because it was thought that the US troops might be resupplied by ships arriving directly from the United States. That created a major strategic imbroglio for the Allies in the coming weeks. The Americans were by far the stronger of the three Allies in both men and equipment and, because of that, had the best chance of fighting a successful battle to break out of the bridgehead. But inland from them was the bocage country—hundreds of square kilometres of small fields and pastures bordered by earthen embankments with thick hedgerows growing on the top. Each field afforded the Germans excellent defensive positions, and when the Americans did push inland, they had to literally fight a small battle for each one. It was slow and it was very costly. Inland from Juno and Sword Beaches, on the other hand, lay mostly rolling country, which tempted commanders to launch mass armoured attacks. Such attacks generally proved disastrous, since well-positioned and camouflaged German anti-tank guns could easily destroy tanks from long distances. What may have appeared to some commanders as good tank country was, therefore, usually fatal. Montgomery could not afford to risk heavy casualties in a breakout battle, so he chose to be much more cautious than an American commander facing the same terrain might have been.

The German defenders had stepped up their preparations for D-Day since the start of the year when Field Marshal Erwin Rommel had been designated Inspector of Fortifications for the western front (he was also in command of Army Group B). Field Marshal Gerd von Rundstedt was in overall charge of German forces in France. The two men disagreed as to the best way of meeting an Allied invasion, and their disagreement was reflected in the way the Germans deployed their troops. Rommel wanted to stop the Allies on the beaches, then smash them with powerful armoured thrusts from panzer units located only a short distance away. Von Rundstedt took the more traditional German approach to defence: he wanted to keep the German armour farther back to be used in a powerful counterattack once the Allies got ashore. Most of the German commanders (but not Rommel) also fell for the

Allied ruse that Calais was to be the invasion point, not Normandy. Thus the Fifteenth Army (with its panzer divisions) was to be held in reserve near Calais until Hitler himself agreed to release it, or its tanks, to be used elsewhere. This left a number of static infantry divisions manning the coastal defences with a handful of powerful armoured divisions stationed from 10 to 20 kilometres south of the beaches. On the Sword-Juno-Gold front, the Germans placed the 716th Infantry Division; the armoured backbone was initially to be provided by the 21st Panzer Division located just north of Caen.

* * * *

As dawn broke along the beach, the British, Canadian, and American infantry climbed down into their landing craft and waited. Ashore, the paratroopers of the 6th British Airborne had seized the bridge across the Orne River south of Ouistreham in the early hours of D-Day and had been beating back German counterattacks ever since. The American paratroopers had an even more difficult time of it. Widely scattered in their drops, they suffered heavy casualties and were delayed by the need to reorganize and consolidate before moving to their objectives; they achieved most of them, due to German confusion and the bravery and innovation of officers and NCOs leading mixed units of both airborne divisions.

At approximately 0715, the heavy guns aboard the cruisers and battleships opened up on the beach defences. The fire plans had been carefully prepared. The largest-calibre naval guns were used to bombard the massive concrete gun emplacements along and behind the beaches; the lesser guns of the destroyers were aimed directly at the smaller bunkers and gun emplacements along the beach fronts. Rocket-equipped landing craft and self-propelled artillery (105mm "Priests") on other landing craft drenched the beaches with fire designed not so much to destroy German defences as to force the defenders to keep their heads down as the landing craft headed in to shore. Much of the heavy gunfire was wasted because the large German bunkers were designed to provide flanking fire onto the beaches and were not open on the sea side. The rockets were completely unguided and the crews of the self-propelled 105mm Priests had great difficulty hitting specific targets from landing craft pitching and rolling in the heavy sea.

On the British and Canadian beaches, the infantry were supposed to be supported by a variety of specially designed armoured fighting vehicles, such as flail tanks to clear paths through minefields, fascine-carrying tanks to fill in gulleys and anti-tank ditches, and the Duplex Drive (DD) tanks. The Americans, for the most part, eschewed these "funnies," as they were called by the British and Canadian troops, though they did use a small number of DD tanks. They had faith that their infantry could successfully assault the beaches without direct support from armour. By then, however, there was plenty of evidence available to them from numerous assault landings carried out by US Marines in the South Pacific that unprotected infantry could be subject to very heavy casualties in a well-opposed landing.

On Gold, Juno, and Sword Beaches, it was planned to have the DD tanks come ashore alongside and even before the infantry to give them cover fire. The rough sea almost completely upset that scheme. Several DD tanks sank like stones, taking crew members with them; others were brought directly to the beaches in their LCTs (tank landing craft). In some sectors the tanks went ashore ahead of the infantry as planned, but in most cases they arrived well after the infantry, leaving the riflemen to charge the beach defences without heavy covering fire. Because the pre-invasion bombings and the bombardment had had only a limited effect on the beach fortifications, some of the Canadian assault battalions ran into heavy defensive fire immediately upon reaching the beaches. It was largely a matter of luck as to whether a man lived or died in the rush across the sand and in the attacks on the fortifications the Germans had built above the high-tide line. On the 7th Brigade's Mike Beach, C Company of the Canadian Scottish landed on the right flank, on a stretch of relatively open sand, to find that their objective had already been destroyed by naval gunfire. They pushed inland with few casualties. Not more than a few hundred metres to their left the two assault companies of the Royal Winnipeg Rifles came under heavy fire even before touching down; B Company suffered a great many casualties as it attacked four German strongpoints without any covering fire. Only one officer and twenty-five men managed to get off the beach unscathed. On the leftmost sector of the beach, the Regina Rifles A Company had been assigned to clear a strongpoint in the northwest corner of the village of Courseulles-sur-Mer. They received a nasty surprise as they neared their objective:

> The bombardment had not cracked the huge casemate . . . [the] fortress had reinforced concrete walls four feet thick and housed an 88mm gun as well as machine-guns. In addition there were concrete trenches outside the fort liberally sprinkled with small arms posts. It was grim going but eventually they executed a left flanking attack and with the support of tanks succeeded in breaking through the defences.[11]

On the 8th Brigade's Nan Beach, the Queen's Own A Company was put ashore right in front of a new German defensive position not indicated on the maps. They took heavy casualties from mortars and machine guns. On the left of the beach, the farthest left platoon of the North Shore Regiment had practically a walkover and "went into the village in nothing flat," but the platoon to its right ran into intense small-arms fire and

Our Finest Hour

sought refuge behind a seawall. Lieutenant G.V. Moran knew that he and his men could not stay there: "In order to get the men moving . . . I stood in the open and shouted at the top of my voice and, making vigorous motions with my arms, urged the sections around the wall forward."[12] A German sniper easily spotted Moran and aimed for the centre of his back. If shot there, Moran would have been killed, but the instant the German pulled the trigger, Moran began to turn around and was hit in the left arm instead. By midday, the assaulting companies were past the initial line of beach defences and into the towns or fields beyond, as the reserve companies came ashore.

Behind them, traffic off the beaches had slowed to a crawl. As the assault troops rooted out German resistance inland, the beaches began to fill, as reserve battalions, engineers, beach movement troops, and others landed faster than the lead elements could move off the beaches. The Priests of the 14th Field Regiment, Royal Canadian Artillery, stood with engines running for what must have seemed like hours: "Immediately a hazard loomed—the congestion of vehicles on the beach with only one narrow exit in the low sea-wall for the traffic now piling up on the sand. The wait for our turn to leave the beach seemed endless as our anxiety increased, for we had been repeatedly warned that the beach itself was the most critical area of danger."[13] Later in the day, the 9th Brigade headquarters landed, as did Major-General Keller and his divisional headquarters. Keller was incensed by the traffic jams on the beaches and ordered his subordinates and staff to get things moving.

The forwardmost company of the Queen's Own Rifles advanced as far as the small hamlet of Anisy before setting up their defences for the night. It was only then, when the mad rush to get off the beach and push inland as far as possible had expended itself, that Charlie Martin and his comrades had time to think about the awful reality of war:

It was on this evening that a moment came when some reality sank in about all the things that had happened during the day. It hurt. We had reached only the edges of Bernières-sur-Mer when we learned that half of our original company—those I had joined up with in June of 1940—had been killed or wounded. And we'd taken still more casualties as we'd gone on to Anguerny. The tears came. I went behind a wall. So many had been lost.[14]

That was true for the other battalions as well. Although the casualties were not nearly as high as the most pessimistic of the predictions (the worst of which had forecast that there would be about 1,980 casualties), they were high enough; more than 600 men were wounded, and 335 killed.

* * * *

From the lowest ranks of the beach defence regiments to the high command, the Germans reacted to the landing with confusion, disorganization, and despair. Rommel was in Germany celebrating his wife's birthday and rushed to get back to the beaches. Hitler was sleeping, and his chief of staff refused to wake him, thinking that Normandy was only a feint to cover up the real landing, which would take place at the Pas de Calais. The closest armour to the Allied beachheads was 21st Panzer Division, which received orders to attack toward the beaches hours after the British and Canadians were safely ashore. The division advanced against the right wing of the 3rd British Division at Sword Beach but were strongly resisted by British anti-tank guns and infantry. The panzers then turned northwest and accidently found the weak boundary between the British and Canadians, but as they advanced, resistance grew stiffer and more tanks were destroyed. They almost reached the beach between the British and Canadians before withdrawing in confusion on orders from their corps commander, who feared for the safety of the division with both flanks exposed to the British and Canadians.

The Canadian brigades continued to push inland toward the village of Carpiquet, just west of Caen on the south side of the Caen–Bayeux highway, which was their first day's objective. The 9th Brigade, on the Canadian left, was within striking distance of Carpiquet when orders reached the divisional commanders from Lieutenant-General Miles Dempsey, General Office Commanding Second British Army (which included 3rd Canadian Infantry Division), to halt in place for nightfall. The fronts of Dempsey's three divisions did not form a continuous line inland from the beaches; the Canadians, for example, were much farther inland than either the British 3rd Division to their left or the British 50th Division to their right, and he feared more counterattacks by German armour.[15] Dempsey was right to have done so, because the best-armed and heaviest German division in Normandy, 12th SS Panzer Division, was moving into position to counterattack the Canadians just on the other side of the Caen–Bayeux highway.

The Canadians finally met the German armour the morning of D+1, when spearheads of the 12th SS Panzer counterattacked the North Novas and the 27th Canadian Armoured Regiment at Authie. That town lay just to the north of the Caen–Bayeux road. If Authie had been taken and held as planned, the Canadians would have been in a good position to advance on Carpiquet, just to the west of Caen, as the first part of a manoeuvre to outflank Caen and encircle it. Caen was the key to virtually everything around it, and as long as the Germans held it, the British and Canadian forces would move neither eastwards nor to the south.

The Germans were determined to defend Caen at all costs, and the Caen–Bayeux road and the rail line that paralleled it just to the south were as good a place as any to drive back the Canadian spearheads. Thus they quickly moved two more armoured divisions into the Caen sector, in addition to 21st Panzer, which had been there before D-Day. The 12th SS marched all night and was the first of the two to arrive. It deployed before dawn on June 7 (the other, Panzer Lehr, followed in short order). A heavy division of almost 20,000 men, the 12th SS was known as the "Hitlerjugend" since most of its recruits were young and fanatical Nazis from the Hitler Youth organization. Most officers and NCOs were veterans of the brutal war on the eastern front. Although not yet battle tested, they had been thoroughly trained and imbued with the racist culture of Nazi ideology. The division was stiffened by more armour, artillery, and anti-tank guns than were assigned to normal Wehrmacht or even SS divisions.

The first 12th SS attack was coordinated by the commander of the 25th SS Panzergrenadier Regiment, SS Obersturmbannführer Kurt Meyer —a battle-hardened and committed Nazi. Meyer stationed himself in the Abbaye Ardenne, an abandoned Gothic ruin in the fields to the northwest of Caen. From atop one of the towers, he could see almost all the way to the beaches and track the progress of the oncoming Canadian armour: "Did I see right? An enemy tank pushed through the orchards of St. Contest. Suddenly it stops. The commander opens the hatch and scours the countryside before him. Is the fellow blind? Has he not noticed that he stands barely 200 yards from the grenadiers of my 2nd Battalion, and that the barrels of their anti-tank guns are pointed at him?"[16]

Meyer suddenly realized that the Canadians were heading to Authie and that their eastern flank was totally unprotected. That was where he would strike. As the 9th Canadian Infantry Brigade rolled toward the Caen–Bayeux road, the Germans attacked their left flank. There was a short, sharp tank battle before the Germans swept past the lead Canadian tanks and into Authie. Due to communications foul-ups and the failure of 14th Field Regiment, Royal Canadian Artillery, to position itself to support the North Novas, the North Novas could not hold, even with the support of the 27th Canadian Armoured Regiment. They were driven farther back to Buron, taking heavy casualties. The Germans moved on to Buron and again overcame Canadian resistance. The North Novas then withdrew to Villons-les-Buissons where they dug in; they suffered 245 killed, wounded, or missing in one day, but Meyer's SS had paid a heavy price for their success, losing fifteen tanks and 300 men.[17]

The 12th SS hit the 7th Canadian Infantry Brigade the next day. Strongly supported by armour and artillery, the 26th SS Panzergrenadier Regiment attacked the Royal Winnipeg Rifles in Putot-en-Bessin, about 8 kilometres west of Authie and on the south side of the Caen–Bayeux road. The three forward companies of the Winnipegs were encircled by the SS tanks and infantry and took heavy casualties before managing to withdraw. The 7th Brigade commander, Brigadier Harry Foster, then ordered a counterattack by the Canadian Scottish, which went in at nightfall and drove the SS back with the support of five Canadian field regiments. Putot was recovered and held. Then the SS came at the Regina Rifles at Norrey-en-Bessin. A desperate night-long tank/infantry battle swirled around the Reginas' battalion headquarters before the Germans were driven back with heavy casualties, leaving several destroyed tanks, including Mark V Panthers, in the smoking ruins of the town.

As the survivors of the Royal Winnipeg Rifles withdrew from Putot-en-Bessin, they were forced to leave a number of men behind, some of whom were wounded. The SS took them to the Abbaye Ardenne. After being punched and beaten, eighteen were systematically murdered in a little courtyard of the abbey (two more were shot some ten days later).

Their bodies were hastily buried there and not discovered for some time after. Meyer, who took command of the 12th SS Panzer Division on June 14, was charged with war crimes after the war, tried by a military court, found guilty, and sentenced to death. His sentence was then commuted to life in prison, which he was supposed to serve in Canada. He was brought to Dorchester Penitentiary in New Brunswick but sent back to Germany in September 1954. He was subsequently released. The Winnipegs were not the only Canadian prisoners murdered in cold blood by 12th SS troopers. In fact, more than 100 met their deaths this way over the span of several days after June 7.

From their positions near Carpiquet, the SS tried again and again to dislodge the Canadians in three villages—Norrey-en-Bessin, Le Mesnil-Patry, and Bretteville-l'Orgueilleuse—which dominated the Caen–Bayeux highway to the west of Caen. These positions had to be taken in order for 12th SS to establish a start line for a general attack northward toward the beachhead. One major attack went in against Bretteville after nightfall on June 8. The German tanks had virtually no artillery support, and very few infantry accompanied them. With the sky lit by magnesium flares that blinded the German drivers, the Canadians took a heavy toll with artillery and anti-tank fire. When the German tanks drove into the town, they were swarmed by Canadian infantry, which destroyed all but two; these actually penetrated to the centre of the town, virtually in front of the battalion headquarters of the Regina Rifles, before one was destroyed and the other raced away. The next day just after noon, the SS tried again with another ragged attack, this time aimed at Norrey. The young Nazis tried to make up with fanaticism what they lacked in artillery and sufficient infantry, and the Canadians held again, destroying large numbers of German tanks and killing dozens of troopers. The last major German attack on the 7th Brigade positions was made on June 9.

This time the tanks—Panther Mark Vs, much superior to the Canadians' Shermans—outran the German infantry and lost seven Panthers in a matter of minutes. Once again, Canadian anti-tank guns, tanks, and artillery helped the infantry hold off the SS attack.[18]

The Canadians battled the 12th SS again on June 11, when the 6th Canadian Armoured Regiment (1st Hussars) and the Queen's Own attempted to advance from Norrey-en-Bessin through Le Mesnil-Patry toward Cheux, thereby beginning to outflank Carpiquet to the west. As they approached Le Mesnil, the Germans poured heavy mortar and machine-gun fire down on the infantry who were riding aboard the Shermans. Then they opened up with 88mm anti-tank guns. The tanks slewed and swerved to avoid being hit. The infantry jumped off and headed for cover as the Shermans drove on to try to deal with the German fire. Some penetrated into the town. "We were just sitting ducks with that kind of exposure," Charlie Martin would later write, "and we could move just as fast on foot."[19] In the town, the 1st Hussars were slaughtered by German tanks and anti-tank guns. Only two of the Shermans that had entered the town survived; fifty-nine men were killed and twenty-one wounded. The Queen's Own lost fifty-five killed and forty-four wounded. The attack was a total failure. The men were learning the hard way just how vulnerable the Shermans were to German anti-tank fire. The men nicknamed them Ronsons (as in Ronson Lighters) because they "brewed up" (i.e., caught on fire) so easily when hit by an 88mm armour piercing shell.

The defeat at Le Mesnil-Patry shows how difficult it was for the Allies or the Germans to mount effective attacks in the open country around Caen. Indeed, by June 11 the 3rd Canadian Infantry Division had advanced about as far as it was going to get for many weeks, as the Germans poured every armoured fighting vehicle, every gun, and every infantryman they could scrape together to hold the British and the Canadians in front of Caen while the Americans tried doggedly to fight their way through the bocage to the west. Yet the Canadians had done well to get ashore as fast as they did, penetrate as far as they did, and hold off the determined attacks of what was touted by the Germans as an elite division of fanatical seventeen- and eighteen-year-old Hitler Youth led by experienced officers and NCOs. As historian Marc Milner put it, "The men who saw them off were the utterly inexperienced and rather ordinary citizen soldiers of the 3rd Canadian Division."[20]

After the failure at Le Mesnil-Patry, the 3rd Canadian Infantry Division was effectively withdrawn for the better part of the next three weeks while the British and Americans bore the brunt of the fighting. The failure to take Caen produced a long and deadly stalemate as the Germans strengthened their defences in an effort to hold the Allies to a relatively small and shallow bridgehead. Although the US forces were able to drive westward across the Cotentin Peninsula, then north to take Cherbourg, that port itself had been almost completely destroyed by the Nazis—and was therefore unuseable—while the Allies could not break through to the south. Thus a deadly war of attrition followed the quick success of Overlord itself. In the six days between the D-Day landings and nightfall of June 11, 1,017 Canadian soldiers were killed in action and 1,814 were wounded on or near the Normandy beaches. As bad as they were, however, the mounting casualties were only a sombre sign of the terrible price that would have to be paid before the battle for Normandy would be won.

CHAPTER 15

THE ORDEAL OF
NORMANDY

Dieppe, France: September 3, 1944. This fifth anniversary of Britain's declaration of war against Germany was to be a solemn one for the men of the 2nd Canadian Infantry Division; a little over two years after assaulting Dieppe, the division had returned to the place of its greatest single-day loss of the war. Two days earlier the division's lead elements had entered Dieppe from the south after a long and almost uneventful drive from Rouen, the cathedral city on the north bank of the Seine. They had encountered no Germans; the port town had been taken without a shot being fired.

On the morning of September 3 the survivors of the Dieppe attack attended religious services at the Canadian war cemetery on the southern outskirts of the town. The people of Dieppe had built and maintained the cemetery during the many long months of German occupation since the Canadian raid. In that cemetery lay more than 700 of the Canadians killed on August 23, 1942, as well as other Allied servicemen killed in the raid or shot down in the vicinity of Dieppe in the months afterwards.

In the afternoon, the citizens of Dieppe officially welcomed their liberators as the entire division paraded through the main part of the town, led by the massed pipe bands of its Highland regiments. First came the armoured cars of the 8th Reconnaissance Regiment, followed in order by the division's three infantry brigades. Army Commander H.D.G. Crerar took the salute; standing beside him was Divisional Commander Charles Foulkes and the mayor of Dieppe. Crerar had been ordered to a staff conference with Montgomery and Lieutenant-General Miles Dempsey, Commander of Second British Army, that day, but he had chosen to attend the ceremony in Dieppe instead. Montgomery was angry with him, but Crerar stood his ground. It was his duty as national commander to be with the 2nd Division that day, and that was that, whether Montgomery understood or not. This was just the latest dust-up between him and Montgomery. Ross Ellis, battle adjutant of the Calgary Highlanders of 5th Brigade, was there, and at the end of the day he wrote his wife Marjorie, "This is quite a day in history, 5 years of war . . . Today also brought back memories of another Sunday 5 years ago (when Britain declared war on Germany) and I find that I can remember several points quite clearly . . . Day by day doesn't count anymore because so often there is no distinction between days."[1] For Ellis, as for so many other Canadian soldiers, one day of war was pretty much like another.

The road to Dieppe had been long and bloody for the 2nd Canadian Infantry Division. It had landed in France at the beginning of July and had first been blooded on July 18 in Operation Atlantic—the final stage of the capture of Caen. Within a week of its first day in battle, one of its battalions—the Black Watch (Royal Highland Regiment) of Canada of the 5th Canadian Infantry Brigade—had walked up Verrières Ridge and, within only a matter of hours, had suffered the worst single-day defeat inflicted on a Canadian battalion in the Second World War. By

Our Finest Hour

the time the battle for Normandy ended, the 2nd Division had changed almost beyond recognition from what it had been when it first landed in France. But then, so had the other two Canadian divisions of the 2nd Canadian Corps and the many other units that fell under corps command. From D-Day until the crossing of the Seine in late August, 18,444 Canadians had become casualties in Normandy, and 5,021 of them were dead. The story of the long and costly battle of attrition in Normandy is often ignored when the history of the successful D-Day landings is related, but Normandy was one of the bloodiest campaigns in the history of modern war.

* * * *

After the initial success of the D-Day landings and the establishment of a contiguous Allied lodgement in the days immediately afterward, the Battle of Normandy quickly degenerated into a costly stalemate. The failure of a thrust to the southwest of Caen by the British 7th Armoured Division on June 12 had left the front lines about 6 kilometres to the north of Caen, except on the eastern side of the Orne River and the Caen Canal, where the British 51st (Highland) Division had taken over the ground won by the airborne on D-Day. On that flank, the front looped to the south, almost flanking the industrial suburb of Colombelles, immediately east of Caen.

The 7th Armoured Division's failure on June 12 was dramatic. In an advance west of Caen, the British thought they had discovered a hole in the German defences and rushed the 7th Armoured into it. That famed and battle-hardened division headed rapidly toward the strategic hilltop town of Villers-Bocage, about 16 kilometres southwest of Caen. But instead of pushing through as far and as fast as possible, the column stopped and rested at Villers-Bocage, watched by SS Hauptsturmführer Michael Wittman, leader of a group of five Tiger tanks. Singlehandedly, Wittman attacked and badly shot up armoured cars, trucks, and tanks. The SS then attempted to take the town itself but were held off by the British, who decided, nevertheless, to withdraw the next day. The pullback of the 7th Armoured marked the end of the Allied scramble to push south and ushered in almost a month of stalemate north of Caen.

Because of Allied air superiority, the Germans had great difficulty moving reinforcements up by day, but they could and did move by night, as Wittman's Tiger tanks had done. In the weeks following the invasion, three more panzer divisions were moved to the Caen front, in addition to the two sent there just after D-Day and 21st Panzer Division that was in place near Caen when the landings took place. The German armour stiffened German resistance but was unable to overcome the very effective Allied artillery and anti-tank guns, as the experience of 12th SS in attacking the Canadians along the Caen–Bayeux road just after D-Day had shown. On the other hand, German tenacity and effective anti-tank weapons and tactics neutralized Allied air superiority. By mid-June the Germans had lost any hope they may have had of throwing the Allies into the Channel, but they were able to keep the Allies bottled up in the bridgehead, delaying the further buildup of Allied military formations because, quite simply, there was no room to put them.

The weeks-long stalemate and the tenacious defence mounted by the Germans both then and for the rest of the Normandy campaign has been the source of great controversy among British, American, and Canadian historians, who tend to fall into two camps. Some believe that the Germans were better fighters and more effective tacticians who were eventually simply overwhelmed by the tide of Allied equipment and Allied air superiority. Others deny German superiority, pointing out that some German units were well trained and highly motivated—the SS divisions, to be sure—but that other German formations were poorly trained and equipped, and were made up of conscripts from conquered nations, mostly in the east, whose main motivation was to find a safe way to surrender to the Allies. This debate over "combat power" forms the context for a similar, though less technical, debate among Canadian military historians about how well prepared the Canadian Army was to meet the Germans in Normandy; how well they performed, from the lowliest private to the highest divisional and corps commanders; and how much their accomplishments contributed to the eventual Allied victory in Normandy.

Unexpressed in much of the Canadian writing is knowledge harking back to the First World War. By the spring of 1917 the Canadian Corps in France had become a very effective fighting formation; on August 8, 1918, together with the Australian Corps, it spearheaded the key Battle of Amiens, which broke the back of German resistance, re-established manoeuvre warfare, and led to Allied victory 100 days later. The Germans called August 8, 1918, "the black day of the German army." During the battle for Normandy, many Canadians hoped that the Canadian Army might play the same role and, at some point, score a resounding victory over the German defenders. In fact, Lieutenant-General Guy Simonds's Operation Totalize, launched on August 8, 1944, is sometimes compared to August 8, 1918, in what it was intended to do—finally smash the German defences south of Caen—but fell short of (more on this later).[2]

There is, of course, a simple explanation for the inability of the Canadian Army in 1944 to replicate its success of twenty-six years previously: the Canadian Corps of August 8, 1918, had endured three and a half years of war, learned valuable lessons in how to fight and win, and was commanded by a man—Arthur Currie—who had had front-line battle experience over that whole forty-four months. The Canadian Army in France on August 8, 1944, was still virtually green, with only two months of battle behind it and a corps commander with some five months of experience since taking over 1st Canadian Infantry Division just before the Sicily invasion.

This is not to say that the Germans did not have significant advantages in holding back the Allied buildup in Normandy. Their most important advantage is that they were on the strategic defensive; it is much more difficult to attack successfully than it is to defend successfully. The Allies were not in Normandy just to hold on. They were there to attack and to keep on attacking until the Germans were destroyed or driven from the battlefield. The Germans could win just by holding out. To some degree, German equipment was better than that of the Allies. The bulk of the German tanks in Normandy were the older Mark IVs, a match for the Sherman medium tank, but the Sherman was no match for the newer and much heavier- and better-gunned Panthers and Tigers or the superb flat-trajectory, high-power, long-range 88mm anti-tank gun. Allied Shermans mounted 75mm low-velocity guns designed to kill infantry, not tanks, but they were able to destroy Tigers and Panthers from the flank or back when they gained a chance. Much of the fighting around Caen and south of it took place in flat country, interrupted by copses, ravines, and narrow water courses. There was lots of dead ground to mask German anti-tank guns. The Germans took full advantage of the stone-walled villages, narrow roads, thick hedgerows, tall wheat, and other terrain features when laying out their defences. In response to the German buildup, Montgomery altered his original intentions at the end of June and decided to fight an essentially defensive battle on the Caen front in such a way (with, for example, limited offensives) as to convince the Germans that his object was to break out near Caen and strike for Paris. This, he believed, would lead them to place the bulk of their armour opposite him, giving the Americans a chance to break out. The trouble with that strategy was that the Americans first had to fight their way through the bocage, a difficult and costly operation.

Virtually all of the units of the 3rd Canadian Infantry Division spent the last half of June in reserve. That hiatus ended on July 4 when Major-General Keller's troops opened an attack on the town of Carpiquet and the airport that lay just to the south of the town. The offensive was to be the first stage of a major British effort to take Caen: Operation Charnwood. The 8th Brigade, with the Royal Winnipeg Rifles under command, had already suffered heavy casualties on D-Day (as had the Winnipegs) but was given the assignment anyway. It was supported by the 10th Canadian Armoured Regiment (Fort Garry Horse) and the "funnies," or AVRE (Assault Vehicles, Royal Engineers), of the 79th British Armoured Division.

With support from the artillery, Royal Air Force Typhoons, and the guns of the battleship HMS *Rodney*, the Canadians swept in from the west to meet the formidable firepower of the well-dug-in SS defenders. As so often happened, the massive barrages left the bulk of the defenders still alive and the core of the defence unshaken. From low concrete bunkers surrounding the control buildings and hangars, the SS made the airfield into a killing zone with interlocking fields of machine-gun fire backed by mortars and artillery. Major J.E. Anderson of the North Shore Regiment, which sustained more casualties on that day than any other of the war, later reflected on the nature of the battle: "I am sure that at some time during the attack every man felt he could not go on. Men were being killed or wounded on all sides and the advance seemed pointless as well as hopeless."[3] The Canadians took the town but could not secure the southern part of the airfield, even after a second attempt mounted by two battalions. The attack was only a partial success bought at very high cost. The reason? Too little direct fire support and too few tanks. A hesitant effort produced disappointing results. Charlie Martin and the Queen's Own were there: "It was terrible. We had to dig in along the runway and in part of an old hangar building. The enemy were watching every move from a slightly higher level. At best it's difficult crossing open ground, but the terrain surrounding an airport is about as level as can be found anywhere."[4]

Keller's two superior officers, army commander Miles Dempsey and corps commander Sir John Crocker, blamed him for failing to control the battle and not recognizing when to throw additional resources into it. They thought him unfit for divisional command. Canadian military historian John English essentially agreed with them when he wrote, "The decision to send the [reinforcements] over 2 kilometres of open ground without any intimate direct fire support was questionable. The decision to hurl them in again with the minimum tank support they should have had in the first place could also be categorized as too little, too late."[5] The 8th Brigade itself concluded that the battle ought to have been fought in one sweeping movement, simultaneously, on a broad front, so as to cancel the ability of the Germans to create interlocking fields of fire.[6]

For the next five days, the 8th Brigade remained in its exposed salient in Carpiquet village and the northern portion of the airfield until the Germans were driven out of Caen by the Charnwood attack. That offensive began with a massive bombing of the northern fringe of Caen in the early morning hours of July 8. Then the entire 1st British Corps, assisted by the 3rd Canadian Division, moved into the city. The 9th Canadian

Infantry Brigade captured Buron and Authie, to the northwest of Caen; the 7th Brigade captured the small hamlets of Cussy and Ardenne; while the 8th completed its capture of Carpiquet as the Germans pulled back.

Caen, or what was left of it after the heavy bombing and fighting, was secured by the night of July 9; 1,194 Canadians had become casualties in taking the city, 334 of them fatal. But the suburbs of Colombelles, east of Caen, and Vaucelles, across the Caen canal to the south of it, remained in German hands as did the key Verrières and Bourguébus Ridges that lay about 6 kilometres to the south of Vaucelles. Those were to be Montgomery's next objectives. The Orne had to be crossed on the western side of Vaucelles, and Colombelles had to be secured; that would leave the Germans outflanked and force their withdrawal farther south. Once that happened, the Canadians and British could continue their push toward Falaise, southwest of Caen, preferably along Route Nationale 158, which ran straight as an arrow from Caen to Falaise. In the meantime, General Omar Bradley, commander of the First US Army to the west, would continue to prepare for a major breakout offensive.

The country to the south of Caen was ideal for defence. From the stone-walled Norman villages atop Bourguébus and Verrières Ridges, the Germans could see many kilometres to the north; it would be virtually impossible to surprise them in daylight, and yet mounting a well-coordinated night attack is one of the most difficult things to do in war. The old Norman villages provided excellent protection for German troops and armour; the tall grain and the many clumps of trees could hide troops and even armour when it was properly camouflaged. Demolished, the towns provided excellent cover, as in the case of the hamlet of Tilly-la-Campagne, situated near the Caen–Falaise highway. There the Germans built bunkers in the basements of the houses, then blew up the houses atop the bunkers. The rubble gave excellent protection to the defenders. Backed by German armour, they threw back repeated British and Canadian attacks in July and August, exacting a heavy toll.

On July 11 Lieutenant-General Guy Simonds's 2nd Canadian Corps took over operational command of the 3rd Canadian Infantry Division from the British and also assumed command of the 2nd Canadian Infantry Division, which had started to arrive in France from the United Kingdom on July 6, as well as the independent 2nd Canadian Armoured Brigade. The 4th Canadian Armoured Division was to be held in the United Kingdom until near the end of the month, primarily because there was simply no room for it in the increasingly crowded Allied bridgehead. Although Harry Crerar and much of the staff of First Canadian Army HQ had arrived in France before the end of June, he was not due to activate his command until the end of July. At that point the 1st British Corps, under command of Lieutenant-General John Crocker, was to pass under his control along with the 2nd Canadian Corps. Still later, on August 5, the 1st Polish Armoured Division would also be placed under Simonds's (and Crerar's) command. First Canadian Army's eventual configuration until 1st Canadian Corps rejoined it from Italy in the spring of 1945 would thus basically consist of two corps, one British and one Canadian, with the Canadian corps being made up of four divisions, three Canadian and one Polish. On July 23 Crerar's First Canadian Army assumed operational command of Simonds's 2nd Canadian Corps and Crocker's 1st British Corps. His relationship with Crocker got off to a bad start when Crocker questioned the utility of an operation Crerar ordered him to carry out; the matter was settled within a day or so but appears to have confirmed Montgomery in his view that Crerar and his Canadian Army were simply not as competent at war as the British were. He observed, "Harry Crerar has started off his career as an Army Comd by thoroughly upsetting everyone . . . I fear he thinks he is a great soldier and he was determined to show it the very moment he took over command at 1200 hrs on 23 July. He made his first mistake at 1205 hrs; and his second after lunch."[7]

Simonds's first campaign as General Officer Commanding (GOC) 2nd Corps was Operation Atlantic, the Canadian end of a joint Canadian-British effort to secure Vaucelles and Colombelles, to draw the Germans to the eastern end of the Allied lodgement and away from the Americans, and, if possible, to punch an armoured fist through the German defences, which the infantry could then exploit. Simonds is a controversial figure in Canadian military history. He graduated from Royal Military College in 1925, winning the Sword of Honour for best all-round cadet, before joining the Royal Canadian Horse Artillery. He attended British Army Staff College at Camberley in the United Kingdom for two years and graduated with distinction. In the late 1930s he wrote several notable articles for *Canadian Defence Quarterly* specifically on the role of the division in the attack. In the early stages of the war, he served in a number of staff and planning positions and was sent to North Africa to observe the fighting there. That's when he was first noticed by Montgomery, who quickly came to believe that Simonds had great potential as a senior commander. Indeed, when Major-General Salmon was killed in an air crash on his way to take command of 1st Canadian Infantry Division prior to the Sicily landings, Simonds was his obvious successor. Simonds was highly intelligent, somewhat ascetic (like his mentor, Montgomery), and hard on his subordinates when his often elaborate plans failed the test of combat. He thought and wrote about war and combat systematically, and his military planning reflected the theories he had developed by studying and observing war. By the time he led 2nd Canadian Corps in action, he had acquired a comprehensive view of how the Germans should be fought, based on his reading of military history, his observations in the desert, and his experience as a divisional commander. As a gunner he had great faith in the winning power of artillery; as a commander he believed that guns were the key to defeating the Germans' main tactical premise, which was that every attack must be met with an immediate counterattack, even if the men and resources to do so had to be scraped together on the spot.[8] Was he the best Canadian field commander of the war? He certainly was the best and most systematic Canadian thinker when it came to planning, at both the tactical and operational levels, but his style of leadership never inspired his subordinates as did that of Bert Hoffmeister, for example.

The British part of Operation Atlantic was known as Goodwood and was aimed at securing the high ground to the east and south of Caen, particularly Bourguébus Ridge. Simonds planned Atlantic as a two-pronged assault: Keller's 3rd Division would lead, cross the Orne in the vicinity of Colombelles, then move south to secure the country to the west of Route Nationale 158. It would stay in contact with the British 8th Corps, attacking to its left. Major-General Charles Foulkes's 2nd Division would follow with an attack southeastward from Caen across the Orne into the western outskirts of Vaucelles and secure the territory between the Orne and Route Nationale 158.

The attack began early on July 18. On the left, the British ran into the 1st SS Panzer Division (Leibstandarte Adolf Hitler) with its Panther tanks and anti-tank guns deployed well forward. Without adequate infantry protection or sufficient artillery support, the British armour was vulnerable; the British 11th Armoured Division quickly lost 126 tanks and was forced to halt its attack well short of its objective. The 7th Armoured Division tried without success to capture the Verrières and Bourguébus Ridges against a strong German defence with many tanks and anti-tank guns. To the British right, the 3rd Canadian Division's troops, aided by artillery and following a massive bombing attack against the German positions, pushed across the Orne River into Colombelles, and to the south and east of the steelworks there. Despite great disorder in the attack, the Queen's Own Rifles was able to capture Giberville, while the rest of the 8th Brigade worked its way south. By nightfall 3rd Division's troops were in Cormelles, just to the east of the main highway, and had secured the eastern part of Vaucelles.

On the Canadian right, engineers trying to bridge the Orne came under heavy mortar fire and were unable to bridge the river on the 18th. But next day the 5th Brigade's Black Watch made a successful assault crossing of the Orne, followed by further advances to St-André-sur-Orne on the right and to the northern edge of Verrières Ridge on the left. Then Simonds sent the 6th Brigade, with the Essex Scottish under command, into the centre to take Verrières Ridge. Backed by artillery and air support, their assault began at 1500. It went well at first, but then a torrential rain swept the battlefield, putting an end to the work of the Typhoons and making it difficult for the artillery observers to see the battle develop. The Germans took advantage of the rain to launch a heavy counterattack; their tank fire and machine guns quickly killed and wounded scores of Canadian infantrymen and destroyed the few Canadian tanks that had ventured forward. In danger of being encircled and losing men by the minute, the Canadian troops in the centre broke; they threw away their weapons and ran back, chased by the advancing Germans. Two companies of the Fusiliers Mont-Royal were cut off and virtually wiped out. The German attacks resumed at dawn, and the Canadians lost more men before a counterattack by the Black Watch helped to stabilize the situation. The Essex Scottish lost more than 300 men killed and wounded in the fighting. Operation Atlantic was a failure; the rookie 2nd Division suffered 1,149 casualties, and Simonds blamed Foulkes for the failure. He concluded that Foulkes was not competent to run a division and was determined to fire him if he could. But Foulkes was a favourite of Harry Crerar, and that counted more than Simonds's disapproval.

The failure of Goodwood/Atlantic put great pressure on Montgomery to try again, especially since Bradley was finally ready to launch his major effort (Operation Cobra) to break out from the Normandy bridgehead after penetrating through heavy bocage country and reaching St-Lô in the west. This time Monty's main thrust would be made on his right; Simonds's Canadians, with the British Guards Armoured and 7th Armoured Divisions under command, would mount Operation Spring at dawn on July 25 with heavy artillery support and tactical air power. The goal was to use the two Canadian infantry divisions to break through the German defences on Verrières Ridge, then to send the two armoured divisions through the hole to exploit as far south as possible, and certainly as far as the high ground around Bretteville-sur-Laize and Cintheaux, where the Germans were already preparing a second line of defence. Although Simonds was to claim after the war that Operation Spring was intended only as a "holding action" to draw German armour to his front while the Americans broke out to his right, there is no indication of that in the pre-attack orders circulated to his divisional commanders.

Simonds planned Operation Spring to be fought in four phases; the first and most important was to begin at 0330 on the morning of July 25 and be completed by 0530, with the first light of dawn. Within those two hours, troops of the two Canadian infantry divisions were to secure May-sur-Orne, at the bottom of the western slope of Verrières Ridge, Verrières village, on the crest of the ridge, and Tilly-la-Campagne, about 1.5 kilometres east of Verrières village, across the Route Nationale

158. Once secured, the ground between these villages would give the armoured divisions a good assembly area from which to launch their attacks southward. They would be led by 7th Armoured, followed by Guards Armoured, and then both they and the 3rd Canadian Infantry Division would leapfrog toward Falaise. The initial night attacks would be aided by artificial moonlight—searchlights played against the clouds. Simonds planned the attack this way to avoid the mass slaughter of armour that had occurred in the Goodwood attack. He reasoned that once the ridge had been secured by the infantry, the armour would be able to manoeuvre as necessary.

In the pre-dawn darkness of July 25, the North Nova Scotia Highlanders moved off as planned on the 3rd Division front, supported by tanks of the Fort Garry Horse. One company went straight at Tilly from the start line, two others moved around to outflank it from the south and east. At 0545 they reported that they had reached their objective and had taken it. But dawn broke to reveal that they had captured only half of Tilly; the Germans had the other half and were beginning to move back in strength, supported by armour. Most of the Canadian tanks were destroyed; the North Novas in and around Tilly were cut off. After nightfall, the remnant made it back to their start lines.

In the centre, the Royal Hamilton Light Infantry stormed up the gentle forward slope of Verrières Ridge and took Verrières village. They held it despite intense German fire, but the Royal Regiment of Canada, due to use the village as a starting point for an attack on Rocquancourt, about 3 kilometres farther south, could move almost no farther. The capture of Verrières village was the only success, partial as it was, that Spring was to produce.

July 25 was one of the blackest days of Canadian arms; that morning, on the far right flank of Operation Spring, the attack of 5th Brigade went wrong from the beginning. The start line was not secured on time. The forwardmost companies of the Calgary Highlanders reached the vicinity of May-sur-Orne after a confused and somewhat disorganized night approach, but were quickly driven out by German armour and self-propelled guns. As the Germans counterattacked, the Highlanders were first driven back to a locality known as "the factory" (actually a set of mine buildings) about halfway between their original start line and May-sur-Orne. Later they were again driven back, this time to the vicinity of their start line. The Calgaries were a green battalion. In their first action on July 19–20 they had secured and held Point 67 as part of Operation Atlantic, but that was the sum total of their battle experience prior to Operation Spring. Yet Simonds's battle plan called for them to advance at night over ground they had never seen, with the rifle companies taking their objectives according to a strict timetable in order to secure the flank for the main thrust; this was to be made at dawn by the Black Watch, on the Highlander left, to capture the village of Fontenay-le-Marmion. To make matters worse, the radio sets that were supposed to allow the battalion commander to coordinate the movement of his companies in the dark failed to operate, leaving runners as the only means of communication. This was a recipe for disaster.

The Black Watch advance should have started at 0530, after May-sur-Orne was supposed to have been secured by the Highlanders, but neither the Black Watch Commanding Officer nor Brigadier Bill Megill, OC of the 5th Brigade, actually knew where the Highlanders were and, most importantly, whether they had secured May-sur-Orne. The Black Watch were themselves delayed by having to fight their way to their own start line; in that fighting, the OC and the senior company commander were killed. The delay meant that a new artillery plan was needed. At 0930 acting battalion Officer Commanding Major F.P. Griffin, not knowing for certain where the Calgary Highlanders were, advanced up the slope. He and his men were caught in a maelstrom of German tank, anti-tank, mortar, machine-gun, and sniper fire. It came from the northern crest of the ridge and from tanks disguised as hay stacks. It also came from their flanks; from the high ground west of the Orne and from May-sur-Orne. Griffin and a handful of survivors reached the crest of the ridge where he, and most of them, were killed. On that one morning, the Black Watch lost 123 men who were killed in action or died of their wounds, 101 wounded, and 83 taken prisoner, of whom 21 were wounded. It was the worst single day of losses suffered by any Canadian infantry battalion in the war.

In Simonds's mind, the overall plan for Spring had been sound but subordinate units—2nd Division, 5th Brigade, and the attacking infantry battalions—had dropped the ball. It was "errors of judgment in minor tactics" that had produced the debacle, he subsequently declared; he was more ready than ever to fire Foulkes. But Simonds's analysis was as much self-seeking rationalization as it was cool judgment of events. For Simonds's concept to work would have required virtually split-second timing, by troops and commanders who were still very green, in an uncoordinated series of night attacks across a front of some 8 to 10 kilometres, over largely unknown and unreconnoitred ground. It was too much to ask, too much to expect, even of brave men. Simonds had also underestimated the German strength on the ridge as badly as he had overestimated the abilities of his subordinate units.[9]

Although Spring was a failure, it did serve one valuable purpose: it continued to persuade the Germans that the main Allied push would come on Montgomery's front, even at the very moment when Bradley's First US Army was launching Cobra. In the words of US military historian Russell Weigley, "Through the critical first hours of Cobra the Canadians [with Operation Spring] reinforced Field Marshal Günther von Kluge's fatal conviction that the Anglo-Americans remained principally interested in rolling across the Falaise plain, and that it was the American attack farther west that was diversionary."[10] Weigley points out that on July 25 von Kluge went to the Canadian front, not the American one, to direct the German defence.

Bradley's Operation Cobra had been twice stalled due to bad weather; it went ahead on the morning of July 25, opening with the by now standard massive heavy-bomber attack, which (also all-too common) killed many front-line US troops. At first the offensive stumbled, but then US VII Corps commander J. Lawton "Lightning Joe" Collins realized that his troops had slogged their way right through the main German line of resistance and had broken into open country. He drove his corps forward like a man possessed; his division commanders were ordered to keep moving no matter what, to bypass and isolate German strongpoints if necessary, and to push ahead at all costs. Collins's flanks were protected by US fighter bombers, but the Germans had almost no reserves in their rear on the American front; in the next few days VII Corps spearheaded First US Army's drive to the south and opened the door for Patton's Third Army, just activated, to go through the door and then swing westward into Brittany, as the original Overlord plan had called for. At that point Brittany was no longer of immediate value to the Allies, but the "fog of uncertainty," as Clausewitz called the chaos of battle, hid the real picture of the battlefield.

The American breakthrough to the west put the Germans on the Caen front in danger of encirclement. They should have withdrawn at least to the Seine, if not across it, which would have meant a loss of territory but the preservation of what was left of their fighting power. In anticipation of that withdrawal, Montgomery ordered Dempsey's Second British

Army to attack southwestwards, on the American flank. Dempsey thus sent his 8th and 30th Corps southward on July 30. Dempsey's attack—Operation Bluecoat—accomplished little, due mostly to the thick bocage through which his army had to fight. The net result of Montgomery's plan was to thin out the forces available to him south of Caen to attack down the road from Caen to Falaise—a logical next move to push the Germans back toward Paris and one that Crerar anticipated as early as July 29. In the meantime, and in response to Montgomery's orders to continue to hold the Germans on his front, Crerar called for a renewed effort to take Tilly-la-Campagne. The Calgary Highlanders tried unsuccessfully to capture it on August 1, while units of the newly arrived 4th Canadian Armoured Division, under Major-General George Kitching, tried again on August 2 and 5, also without success.

Instead of ordering a general withdrawal in response to Bradley's breakthrough, Hitler told his commanders to mount a major counterattack (Operation Lüttich) westward toward Mortain in an attempt to cut off the southward-thrusting US spearheads. In preparation for that counterattack, the Germans began moving the bulk of their armour westward. On August 6 the Germans attacked the American left flank, using virtually every German armoured unit north of the Seine. It was a disaster. Warned of the impending attack by Ultra, the Americans fought it to a stop. Hitler had gambled all and, in losing, placed the great bulk of his armour into an even more untenable position than it had been before, since it was now much farther away from the safety of the Seine.

While the Germans were preparing to assault the Americans at Mortain, Simonds was planning a major attack southwards from the Caen area toward Falaise. At this point, neither of the three Allied high commanders, Eisenhower, Bradley, or Montgomery, realized the precarious position the Germans had placed themselves in and were still focused on the Brittany ports to the east. Thus the Canadian attack, dubbed Operation Totalize, was not conceived as a means to trap the Germans in a pocket, because no one on the Allied side quite realized that a potential pocket was forming. Monty's real aim, as late as August 4, was to trap the German armour retreating from the front of Dempsey's British Second Army. Montgomery had no choice but to give the Canadians this important task, because Crerar's 2nd Canadian Corps was on the far left of Montgomery's flank and clearly in the best position to attack toward Falaise without delay. As matters unfolded in the next ninety-six hours, the Canadians would need to do a great deal more than that, but they would have to do it essentially alone, because Dempsey's forces, just coming out of Operation Blue Coat, were in no position to help them.

The eventual shape of Simonds's plan was strongly influenced by what he had seen on the battlefield so far and by his belief that whatever his troops did, they would face a German counterattack from a second German defensive line he believed was being prepared farther south. To enable his tanks to get forward quickly without exposing them to undue danger, he planned Totalize as a night attack. In order to surprise the German defenders, he eschewed the usual preliminary artillery bombardment and arranged for a saturation bombing of not only the area immediately in front of his attacking forces but also five fortified villages, which he believed the Germans would use to launch their counterattack. After the bombing, in the pre-dawn hours of August 8, the British 51st (Highland) Division, accompanied by the British 33rd Armoured Brigade on the left, and the 2nd Canadian Infantry Division, with the 2nd Canadian Armoured Brigade on the right, were to advance down both sides of the Caen–Falaise road. They would be kept going in the right direction by light beams, radio beacons, and tracer fired parallel to their advance. They would be aided by artificial moonlight (searchlights shone on low clouds). The infantry would be carried in armoured personnel carriers (APCs)—surplus Priest 105 self-propelled guns with the guns removed and reinforced by steel plate welded on both sides. The APC was Simonds's own invention; the new vehicles, prepared in Canadian Army repair shops, were dubbed kangaroos. They were designed to move the infantry along with the tanks, protecting them from rifle and machine-gun fire. When the initial phase of the assault was completed, there was to be an eight-hour hiatus to consolidate, prepare for a German counterattack (Simonds believed that 12th SS would lead the counterattack, but they were, in fact, in the process of withdrawing westward), and to bring up artillery. Then another heavy bombing, this time by the Americans was to take place, hopefully destroying Germans setting up in defensive positions south of the new Canadian front line. Then the attack was to resume with the 4th Canadian Armoured Division on the right flank of the Canadian thrust and the 1st Polish Armoured Division on the left. Ahead lay the German infantry, considerably weakened by the westward movement of the panzers but with, Simonds believed, enough armour, anti-tank weapons, and SS infantry to make things very difficult.

In the last twenty-four hours before Totalize began, Bradley and Montgomery began to realize that the German attack at Mortain had drawn the bulk of the German armour and anti-tank guns westward, including some who had been in position to oppose Simonds's attack. This therefore presented an opportunity for a major envelopment—if Totalize could put the First Canadian Army into the vicinity of Falaise without delay, and if the Americans could reverse the flow of their breakout into Brittany, drive eastwards instead, and then north in the Falaise area. A large pocket of the bulk of the German army and SS in Normandy would thus be created and might be closed somewhere near

Falaise. As Terry Copp put it, "Operation Totalize was . . . transformed from an attack designed to assist the Second British Army into the wing of a vast pincer movement, but no new resources were allocated to carry out this much more ambitious task."[11]

The attack began as planned the night of August 7–8 with the infantry jumping off at 2330. There was some confusion among the advancing armoured units, due to the massive amounts of dust thrown up by the columns of APCs and tanks and by the resistance of the Germans in some localities. But for the most part the great weight of men and tanks, moving like a river of steel in the dark after the heavy pounding from the air, finally succeeded in smashing through the main German defences that had held for so many weeks. Then, as planned, the great mass of men and vehicles halted to regroup and to bring up the field artillery.

There has been considerable debate among Canadian military historians about the wisdom of following the Phase I and Phase II plan of Totalize to the letter. By the morning of August 8, some have reasoned,[12] the main German line of resistance on the Caen–Falaise road had been cracked and Simonds had but to cancel the pause and order his troops to keep rolling forwards, perhaps as Collins had done on the American front after the initial stages of Cobra. There are several factors to explain why Simonds didn't. First, neither Simonds nor anyone else was quite sure what the Germans held farther south on the road to Falaise. There were strong indications that most of 12th SS Panzer had pulled west to Mortain, but the German division that took over, 89th Infantry, was no slouch. The 1st Polish and 4th Canadian Armoured Divisions had to get in place to continue the attack. There was also the matter of having ordered up a second heavy bombing, also by the US Eighth Air Force, which would have been very difficult to cancel. But another major factor, and one that may have far outweighed the others, was that as good as he was at planning, Simonds was heavily influenced by the staff training and experience of the British Army and its style of command. Britain was severely short of manpower and always inclined to use firepower (artillery or heavy bombers) instead of men; plans were artillery-centric; generals laid out their objectives, relied on their staffs to plan the best way to achieve those objectives, and whether they were actually at their desks when the battle started (as SS General Kurt Meyer, commanding 12th SS Panzer, once claimed) or asleep—which was often the situation with Montgomery—they were rarely up front, feeling the battle and preparing to seize an unforeseen opportunity if it came along. For them, leaving flanks unprotected, leaving the artillery umbrella too far back, ordering troops to ignore the phases of an operation and just "push on," was just not on.

During the hiatus between Totalize I and II, local German resistance tried to grind away at the southernmost Canadian positions. Kurt Meyer ordered some of his armour and anti-tank guns to return to shore up 89th Infantry Division resistance. The Germans still held three key French villages across the front or on its flanks. The daylight bombing attack, designed to punch through the second German line of defence, was much less successful than the first phase had been. Essentially a repeat of the first phase, it got off to a very bad start when the preparatory bombing by the US Eighth Air Force also hit the 3rd Canadian and 1st Polish divisions, killing and wounding a great many men. Among the wounded was Canadian divisional commander R.F.L. Keller. Making matters worse, the few tanks but many 88mm anti-tank guns that Meyer had positioned in front of the Canadians rushed back and forth across the front of the attack, fought for every metre of ground, and destroyed large numbers of advancing tanks. Instead of flowing around the German resistance points and pushing on, as Simonds had wished them to do, the Canadian and Polish armoured divisions wasted time and momentum by trying to deal with every strongpoint. The growing losses included much of Worthington Force, consisting of the armour of the British Columbia Regiment and the infantry of the Algonquin Regiment, which, in the pre-dawn hours of August 9, somehow managed to swing to the eastward of the main Canadian thrust and plant themselves on the wrong hill. They were quickly surrounded by the Germans and lost 247 men killed, wounded, or captured, along with forty-seven armoured vehicles and half tracks.[13] The Canadian advances ground to a halt by nightfall. Although the 1st Polish and 4th Canadian Armoured divisions tried to get forward the next day, they could make no further progress. Totalize was over. The combined assaults had moved the Canadian lines about 12 kilometres to the south, but they were still nowhere near Falaise or even the high ground to its north.

Simonds was not pleased by the performance of Kitching's division or of the Poles. In his memoirs Kitching chalked up his division's failure to high casualties among senior officers, poor radio communications, and general inexperience in a very green division: "I do not think these factors were appreciated sufficiently by General Simonds whose vision was focussed on the horizon and whose thoughts were often a day or two ahead of us," he later wrote.[14] He did not know it, but he was a marked man in Simonds's eyes. Rod Keller was also through as a divisional commander. He had wanted Simonds to relieve him for days; now his wounds from the American bombing made that a foregone conclusion. He was relieved on August 8, to be replaced ten days later by Major-General D.C. "Dan" Spry, who was to command the 3rd Division until late March 1945.

Totalize had opened a large salient in German lines, but the situation on the morning of August 10 was completely fluid all across the Normandy front; the bulk of the German armour was still in the Mortain area, as the Germans tried to decide whether or not to withdraw. Now Eisenhower, too, realized the opportunity the Germans had handed him. With the Canadians closing in on Falaise, and the British after Bluecoat on the Canadian right flank, and with the Americans sweeping northeastward toward Alençon and Argentan beyond it, the Germans who had moved to the Mortain area were in the bag. If Crerar's army could join Patton somewhere near Falaise, or to the east of it, the Germans would be cut off. Thus instead of trying a "long" envelopment, to encircle the Germans along the line of the Seine, the Allies (Patton dissenting) decided on a "short" envelopment in the Falaise area.

The American XV Corps had reached Le Mans and was swinging north toward Argentan. The Americans may well have been able to drive most of the way to the Canadian sector—they had more men and armour, and had seen less grinding combat—but Montgomery overestimated Crerar's ability to push south with great speed and underestimated the American ability to drive northward. Monty ought to have sent an additional armoured division or two from Second British Army to bolster the Canadian thrust, but he did not. He insisted, instead, that the Canadians meet the Americans at the pre-established boundary between 12th Army Group (American) and 21st Army Group (British and Canadian), just south of Argentan. Since Montgomery, in overall command of both army groups, made no move to shift that boundary to the north, the Americans had no choice but to pull up and wait for Crerar to meet them. In any case, the American drive into Argentan stalled when Leclerc's 2nd French Armoured Division—attached to the XV Corps—disobeyed orders to drive directly into the town and took a more circuitous route instead. By the time they approached Argentan, the Germans had greatly strengthened their troops there.

On August 11 Montgomery ordered Crerar to capture Falaise as quickly as possible. If that key road junction were in Allied hands, it would be very difficult for the Germans to withdraw their armour to the east. On that very day, German commander Field Marshal Günther von Kluge decided to risk Hitler's wrath and do just that. Once again, Crerar handed the job to Simonds; once again, Simonds designed a large set-piece attack much along the lines of Totalize. This time the offensive was code-named Tractable, but unlike Totalize, it would be launched in daylight, its attacking elements and its flanks hidden from the enemy by smoke laid down by artillery. Before Simonds could actually launch the attack, Montgomery changed his mind and gave the job of capturing Falaise to the Second British Army (he would later change his orders yet again) and directed Crerar to take the high ground north and east of Falaise, then drive southeast to Trun, a key road junction about 18 kilometres east of Falaise. The left flank of the attack was to be made by Kitching's 4th Armoured, the right by Spry's 3rd Infantry, with the 2nd Armoured Brigade under command. H-Hour was set for August 14; the Germans learned of the attack the day before when a Canadian officer lost his way and drove into enemy lines. He was killed and his driver taken prisoner; in the jeep was a copy of Simonds's orders.

★ ★ ★ ★

Tractable began on time with another strike of heavy bombers, this time from Bomber Command. Again, some of the bombs fell short, and efforts by both the advancing troops and army observation aircraft to stop the bombing by the use of yellow or red flares—exactly the wrong colour as far as the bomb aimers knew—made the situation even worse. Then smoke shells were fired by the artillery to hide the advancing men and armour. The Germans could not see much because of the smoke and the dust thrown up by the vehicles, but, warned of the attack, they had sited their artillery and anti-tank guns on the expected line of approach. They fired furiously into the smoke and dust, hitting many tanks and causing many casualties, including Brigadier Leslie Booth, the commander of the 4th Armoured Brigade, who was killed. Many of the Canadian tanks bunched up at the few crossing points over the Laison River, which ran across the line of advance, though the infantry got forward as planned. Much territory was captured, but the attackers ended the day short of the objective, a hill immediately to the north of Falaise, known as Point 159. Despite their paucity in both men and armour, the Germans put up fierce resistance that the Canadians could not easily overcome. Little progress was made the next day; it was not until August 16 that Point 159 was taken. That same day troops of the 2nd Canadian Division finally entered Falaise.

That did not close the gap, which was still about 18 kilometres wide, with the Germans pouring through it to the east. Simonds then ordered the Poles and Kitching's division to attack southeast to Trun to cut the Germans off; the next day orders were changed again, and the Poles were directed to Chambois, about 6 kilometres east of Trun, to meet the Americans who were about to attack to the north. As the Germans desperately tried to keep the gap open, the Canadians and the Poles struggled just as desperately to close it. The Canadians reached Trun early on the 18th, but the Poles, under heavy attack, could not reach all the way to Chambois until the next day. That same day, first contact was made with advancing US troops from the south.

As thousands of Germans streamed eastward through the narrowing pocket, others attacked the Poles and Canadians in order to keep the escape route open. Now Allied fighter bombers began to exact a fearful toll of men, equipment, and horses (much of the German equipment was still horse-drawn). Even battle-hardened veterans would find the carnage incredible. On the 19th, in the midst of the intense ground fighting and the air attacks, a unit of the 4th Canadian Armoured Division under Major D.V. Currie fought its way into St-Lambert-sur-Dives and held for the next three days as the Germans tried to break out. In those three days, they captured about 2,000 Germans and killed many others. Not far to the east, but totally cut off from the Canadians, the Poles held Chambois and Point 262, a strategic hill that commanded what was left of the German escape route. They were attacked violently and continuously by German forces on the 20th, but managed to hold while destroying much German equipment and taking many prisoners; on August 21 they were so low on ammunition that they had to be resupplied by airdrop.

Late on the afternoon of August 21, the Canadians finally struggled through to the Poles on Point 262 and in Chambois. The Falaise gap was closed, and the battle for Normandy was effectively over. The Germans lost about 300,000 men in total; the Canadians alone took more than 13,000 prisoners in the closing phases of the Falaise battle. Many thousands more Germans were slaughtered by Allied fighter bombers as they pushed toward the ever-narrowing gap; their heaviest casualties came in the last three days of the fight. The fate of two of the SS's once-powerful divisions was typical. Meyer's 12th SS had been a division of more than 20,000 men with 150 tanks on D-Day; by August 25 it had been reduced to fewer than 300 men, ten tanks, and no artillery. The 1st SS Panzer was left with no tanks, no artillery, and only a handful of men.

Despite the heavy losses, many thousands of Germans did manage to escape as the Poles and Canadians struggled to close the gap in the week from the beginning of Tractable (August 14) until the gap was closed on August 21. Among those who got away were a large number of divisional, corps, and army staff officers, who would later form the basis upon which destroyed and new German army units would be rebuilt. Precious days had been lost as the bedraggled German defenders had succeeded time after time in delaying the advances of the numerically powerful Canadian and Polish armour, backed by an overwhelming preponderance of artillery and air support. The 4th Canadian Armoured Brigade—the armoured component of Kitching's division—was especially to blame for having been ponderous and indecisive in its operations. Kitching would later chalk that up to the death of Brigadier Booth in the first hours of Tractable, and on his division's inexperience in battle, but there is evidence to suggest that Booth himself was responsible before his death.

Simonds was not happy about the performance of his two leading armoured divisions in Tractable or in the closing of the gap. He had no authority to remove the Polish commander, Major-General S. Maczek, but Kitching was another matter. Simonds relieved him on August 21, and replaced him with Brigadier Harry Foster, who was still in Italy. Within a matter of days, then, two out of the three Canadian divisional commanders in France were gone. It was one measure of how difficult an ordeal Normandy had been.

In the end, the failure to close the gap more quickly and score a truly decisive victory in the west must be shared around. Bradley and Eisenhower must take part of the blame for allowing large numbers of American troops to advance into Brittany after the Cobra breakout as though nothing had changed. Montgomery gave the Canadians too large a job to do without adequately backing them up (he would do that again in the opening phase of the Battle of the Scheldt Estuary). Leclerc's 2nd French Armoured Division's failure to move quickly into Argentan when ordered gave the Germans a chance to block the American move north. Simonds's failure to exploit the initial success of Totalize gave Kurt Meyer a chance to reorganize his defences and thwart the second phase of Totalize, thereby delaying the closure even further. The tactical shortcomings of the rookie 4th Canadian and 1st Polish Armoured Divisions gave the Germans further chances to escape.

* * * *

With the Falaise gap closed, Montgomery directed Crerar's troops to advance from the Trun-Chambois area to Elbeuf, where they were to cross the River Seine near Rouen. The Second British army was to advance to the right of the Canadians. Units of the 2nd and 3rd Canadian Divisions began to move on August 20, even before the gap was fully closed. They made good progress, only occasionally meeting German rearguards or being attacked from the air at night. What remained of the German army in Normandy made quick tracks to the Seine, where other German rearguards, including a handful of SS panzer troops, fought as long as possible to hold up the Allied advance until their comrades could get across the river. The Germans took a heavy toll of units of the 2nd Canadian Infantry Division advancing through the Forêt de la Londe, just south of the Seine, in the last days of August. The tragedy was that the division should not have fought in the forest in the first place. By the time that Foulkes issued the orders to clear it, the two other Canadian divisions had bypassed it and were crossing the river at Elbeuf.

By August 30 the 2nd Canadian Corps was across the Seine and pushing toward the Channel coast. The 2nd Division was directed to Dieppe, the other troops to the important Channel ports of Boulogne and Calais, around which large numbers of V-1 sites were to be found.

For a time it was feared that the Germans would put up a ferocious struggle for Dieppe, but they did not. Early on the morning of September 1, the lead elements of the 2nd Canadian Infantry Division crossed the height of land to the south of the port and cautiously began the long descent to the town itself. As the citizens cheered the Canadians on, the division's long journey back to Dieppe finally ended.

CHAPTER 16

THE SCHELDT

Albert Canal near Antwerp: 0130, September 22, 1944. Sergeant Clarence Kenneth Crockett and nine men of C Company, the Calgary Highlanders, of the 5th Canadian Infantry Brigade, left their forward positions on the south bank of the canal and crept stealthily toward the damaged lock gate that awaited them in the drizzly gloom. A veteran of many battles, Crockett had been selected by his company commander to lead a small patrol over the lock gate and seize a bridgehead on the north bank of the canal. All the men of his platoon had volunteered to go, but Crockett could take only nine with him. He chose two Bren gunners and seven others armed with Sten guns. He wanted as much automatic fire as he could get. Each man carried two or three bandoliers of ammunition over his shoulders. One took a PIAT (Projector, Infantry, Anti-Tank), another a two-inch mortar, and a third carried a small Mark 38 radio set. For better footing, they doffed their combat boots and put on sneakers. That was because the lock gate was damaged halfway across, and they would have to make the last part of the crossing over a water pipe 15 centimetres in diameter, with just a bent catwalk rail to hold on to.

In the fall of 1944 the canal ran through open farm country about 3 kilometres north of the Antwerp suburb of Wommelgem. It was about 30 metres wide and connected the port of Antwerp to Liège, about 130 kilometres to the east. The north side of the canal was lined by fields, brush, and patches of woods and was regularly patrolled by its German defenders. If the Germans were going to be rooted out of the northern suburbs of Antwerp, the Canadians would have to take and hold a bridgehead over the canal from which to begin the clearing operations. The Black Watch, also of the 5th Brigade, had attempted to cross the canal at roughly the same spot the night before, but had been discovered and beaten back.

Crockett inched his way over the south part of the lock gate, walking carefully on an undamaged catwalk until he reached a small island in the middle of the canal. When he saw it was all clear, he returned to the south bank to beckon his men forward. They moved silently over the catwalk, then waited on the island while Crockett made his way carefully over the water pipe to the north side of the canal. The night was damp, and the pipe was slippery; Crockett slung his Sten gun on his back so that he could better grasp the partly demolished handrail. When he reached the north side of the canal, he found a barbed-wire barrier blocking his way, so he returned to the island to bring the rest of the patrol forward with him. In complete silence, they crept along until they reached the north bank; then Crockett and Corporal R.A. Harold, crouching behind him, carefully inched the barbed-wire barrier out of the way.

Suddenly a flare popped and a voice called out in German. The men on the pipe froze in position as machine guns opened up in the dark. One man was hit immediately; the others rushed on to the north side of the canal, automatic weapons blazing away at the machine-gun flashes. Crockett cut down one German soldier with his Sten, then poured several magazines into a machine-gun position, silencing it. He and one of his men destroyed two more German machine guns with the PIAT. The mortar man quickly went into action, killing yet another German gun crew.

As Crockett's men battled for their lives on the north bank of the canal, the rest of his company began to pour over the lock gate from the south bank. Then A and D Companies of the Highlanders followed. The Germans brought up reinforcements, and German mortar fire began to blanket the Canadian perimeter. For the next several hours the fight raged back and forth, first one side holding the upper hand, then the other. It was not until early afternoon, as the drizzle stopped and the sun began to push through the clouds, that the Highlanders were able to secure the area. Then a unit of engineers came up to construct a bridge across the canal. By nightfall, most of the 5th Brigade were across and the job of clearing the entire area began in earnest. The Highlanders paid a heavy price for this first permanent Canadian foothold across the canal: fifteen killed and thirty-four wounded; Crockett was awarded the Distinguished Conduct Medal for his incredible act of bravery. For the Calgary Highlanders and the 5th Brigade, the Battle of the Scheldt Estuary had commenced in memorable fashion.

* * * *

The struggle of the First Canadian Army to clear the banks of the Scheldt Estuary dominated Canadian war news in September and October of 1944. Even as that battle raged, however, other Canadian soldiers, airmen, and sailors were fighting the forces of the Axis over thousands of kilometres of land, sea, and sky and on almost every war front in western Europe and the Mediterranean. In the Mediterranean theatre, for example, the 1st Canadian Corps in Italy spent the first two weeks of September deeply engaged in a struggle to break the Pisa–Rimini line. At the same time, Canadians of the Royal Air Force and the Royal Canadian Air Force in Bomber Command increasingly took advantage of the growing weakness of the German day-fighter forces (and the strength of the Allied day-fighter escorts) to fly daylight raids into Germany itself. The German day fighters had been decimated beginning in early 1944 when the United States Army Air Force's new long-range Mustang fighters began to escort American bombers deep into Germany and range ahead of the bomber formations to destroy German fighters on the ground. The thinness of German day-fighter defences allowed more and more Bomber Command missions to be launched in daylight. Such missions included an area attack against Emden on September 6, 1944, and raids against synthetic oil installations at Dortmund and other locations in Germany on September 12, as well as against the key communications centre of Osnabrück on the 13th. On the night of September 15–16 the bombers returned to Kiel for the only night raid of the month. No. 6 Group lost only six aircraft in all of September; the crews of three bombers were saved after ditching in the North Sea. Most of its twenty-three missions that month were against tactical targets or synthetic oil plants.

The constant bombings destroyed aircraft factories, tank production lines, U-boat pens, and synthetic oil facilities, but perhaps more important, they cut huge holes in the German transportation system. Attacks on bridges, railway yards, canals, and marshalling yards began to dissect the German economy. In the area of aircraft production, for example, decentralization had helped keep aircraft construction going in much smaller factories, but with the rail system under constant attack, it grew harder for the aircraft parts to be brought together in a systematic way to construct new planes. As one economic historian of Nazi Germany put it, "The way in which the bombers achieved that effect [bringing production to a halt] was by severing the rail links and the waterways between the Ruhr and the rest of Germany . . . On 11 November Speer reported to Hitler that the Ruhr was effectively sealed off from the rest of the Reich. The shortfall in hard coal deliveries from the Ruhr between August 1944 and January 1945 was a massive 36.5 million tons, at least six weeks of normal consumption."[1]

* * * *

As the First Canadian Army moved up the Channel coast in the first two weeks of September, a growing shortage of infantry reinforcements stymied efforts to keep the front-line rifle companies up to war-establishment strength. The problem was not an overall shortage of reinforcements in the army as a whole, just too few spare trained infantrymen available. A projected shortfall of some 20,000 men was expected to occur by the spring of 1945, and talk about the need for conscription to solve this problem began to be heard again from opposition benches, Tory newspapers, and even within the officer corps—the latter, of course, without attribution. How and why had this happened?

The key reason was that the Canadian Army had too few infantry and too many of all other types of military occupations. When new recruits entered the army, most were taken up by the artillery, the engineers, the pay corps, the military police, and so on. Only a relatively small number were sent to become infantrymen. What's more, the army had tended since the start of the war to pick what it considered the best men—intelligent, ambitious, well-educated—for everything but the infantry. Thus the Canadian Army had too few fighting troops for its size. As one example, the weakness of the Luftwaffe left many thousands of Canadian soldiers in anti-aircraft units doing very little in the way of combat in the summer and fall of 1944, while their counterparts in the infantry could barely carry out their assigned tasks. A second important reason was that the army had utilized British combat-loss projections based on the fighting in the North African desert to forecast how many casualties (the army called this "wastage") it would need to replace once the fighting in Italy and northwest Europe began in earnest. Those figures were far too low for the intense ground combat in Italy and Normandy, which produced far more infantry casualties than the fighting in the desert had.

After the war, the former commander of 1st Canadian Corps, E.L.M. Burns, produced a study of manpower in the Canadian Army, which told the tale rather succinctly. By the fall of 1944, Burns found, the Canadian Army had expanded to almost half a million men and women, with a quarter million serving in northwest Europe, Italy, or the United Kingdom. About 100,000 of these people worked at jobs in supply depots, hospitals, offices, communications centres, and in other non-combat situations, or were waiting in reinforcement units for assignment to active units. Some 158,000 served in the field formations—the five divisions and two independent armoured brigades of the First Canadian Army. But few people in a Canadian division actually fought; most did something else. What all this boiled down to was that the actual front-line fighting strength of an infantry division consisted of the riflemen, Bren gunners, mortarmen, and anti-tank gunners in the four rifle companies and the one support company of each infantry battalion—about 5,400 men in a division of more than 17,000. These, and the close support troops such as combat engineers and signallers, suffered the highest casualties—killed, wounded, captured, or psychologically afflicted—and this was the root of the growing crisis: Canada had enough soldiers but not enough fighting soldiers, and the ones it did have were being "used up" more quickly than anyone had forecast.

One solution to the shortage of combat soldiers, especially infantry, was to remuster men from non-infantry units, especially the artillery, into the infantry. There was great potential in remustering, but it was a slow process to retrain men for the infantry. In the meantime, the army worried, its infantry battalions would fall far below strength and be rendered ineffective before any appreciable number of reinforcements could be trained. Thus the army's top commanders put pressure on the government, through Minister of National Defence J.L. Ralston, to conscript those trained infantrymen serving in Canada who had been drafted under the National Resources Mobilization Act (NRMA) of 1940. Often referred to disparagingly as zombies, these men had been conscripted for home defence and under the laws of Canada could not be sent to an active theatre of war overseas. Many NRMA men volunteered for active (i.e., overseas) service during the war, but by the fall of 1944 a hard core had emerged in Canada of men who appeared dead set against going active. Eventually, after a serious crisis in the Canadian Cabinet in November 1944, 16,000 of these men were ordered sent to the fighting fronts. About 2,400 actually reached front-line units before the war ended; in virtually all cases, they were welcomed by the veterans and integrated without difficulty into the line rifle companies.

* * * *

On September 4, 1944, the 11th British Armoured Division of the 30th British Corps entered the port of Antwerp. Located on the Scheldt Estuary, the massive port (the second-largest in northwest Europe) was protected from the rising and falling of the North Sea tide by two sets of massive locks. The Germans had neglected to destroy those locks until almost the last minute before they pulled out of the dock area; when they did try, they were prevented from doing so by the Belgian resistance. Thus the port of Antwerp—with its almost 50 kilometres of docks, quays, and warehouses, its hydraulic and electric fixed and floating cranes, its grain elevators, its hundreds of kilometres of railway track, and its capacity to handle well in excess of 10,000 tons of cargo per day—was taken virtually intact.

That was vitally important because, by the late summer of 1944, the Allied armies were facing a severe supply problem. Most of the food, ammunition, gasoline, and other necessities of war were still being unloaded over the original Normandy invasion beaches and trucked forward hundreds of kilometres. The Allies possessed no major ports near the front lines. The US armies, on the Allied right flank and farther from the coast than the British and Canadians, were especially hard pressed; shell rationing was imposed on American artillery regiments by late August. The problem was growing so severe that Eisenhower declared he would not permit an offensive into Germany until it was resolved.

The capture of Antwerp promised relief from the supply problem, but not until both banks of the Scheldt Estuary were taken from the Germans. When the British rolled into Antwerp at the start of September, they could have done that easily. The Germans were still in retreat and in disarray. All that would have been needed was for the commander of 30 Corps, Sir Brian Horrocks, to order his units forward some 30 kilometres up the right bank of the Scheldt to seize the narrow neck of land where the South Beveland peninsula connects to the mainland, thus isolating any German defenders on South Beveland or the island of Walcheren. He did not; Montgomery had more important matters on his mind at that stage of the campaign—a lightning thrust to capture a bridge over the Rhine as preparation for a campaign to capture the Ruhr.

In the days and weeks that followed the British entry into Antwerp, the Germans (under express orders from Hitler to hold the Scheldt) reinforced their men, prepared to defend every metre of the Estuary, and planted thousands of mines in the waterway. Needless to say, these mines could not be swept, nor could ships pass to Antwerp, as long as German guns dominated the Estuary. The reinvigorated German presence in the Scheldt area was only one sign of a general stiffening of German resistance all across the Allied front in early September. In what the Germans referred to as the "miracle in the west," new divisions and *Kampfgruppen* were scraped together, rearmed with new weapons, and dispatched to the front. Most of these units were built out of the remnants of units that had been badly mauled in Normandy but had nonetheless managed to squeeze through the narrowing Falaise gap in late August, taking the bulk of their divisional and corps headquarters and staff with them. By mid-September the Germans were actually able to match the Allies almost man for man in Holland and Belgium, although they were still vastly outnumbered in artillery, tanks and, of course, aircraft.

Montgomery was fully aware of the new German buildup, but he was preoccupied with planning his thrust to the Rhine: Operation Market Garden. Put together with Eisenhower's blessing, Market Garden was to consist of a combined airborne/ground assault to drive a narrow salient deep into German lines and seize the river and canal crossings leading to the German border. The ultimate objective of the attack was the bridge across the Neder (Lower) Rhine at Arnhem, in Holland. Both Montgomery and Eisenhower believed that a victory at Arnhem would allow the Allies immediate entry to the Ruhr and bring a quick victory. If that happened, access to a major port might not be so crucial. But it did not happen. The ten-day campaign utilizing the First Allied Airborne Army of two US and one British Airborne divisions, and a Polish paratroop brigade was a spectacular failure and ended ten days after it started with the remnants of the 1st British Airborne Division being evacuated across the Neder Rhine near Arnhem. Losses were in the thousands. In the meantime, the campaign to capture the Scheldt was not cancelled, but ground on under Crerar without additional resources while part of his army also continued trying to liberate the Channel ports.

* * * *

Hitler had ordered his commanders to hold these ports at all costs, and the garrison commanders did their best to oblige. Extensive fortifications were prepared; artillery, mortars, and machine guns were sited; and patrols were pushed out to find and harass the Canadians. To make matters worse, it seemed to rain constantly throughout the first weeks of September. Large stretches of the coastal plain lie below sea level near Dunkirk and Ostend, as do parts of the landward side of Calais. With the rains, this ground was sodden and muddy. Wherever they could, the Germans blew open canal locks and dykes to flood low-lying polders and force the Canadians, men and vehicles, to stick to the roads—where they were easy targets for German shells or mortars. The Canadians might have had an easier time of it had they been able to concentrate on each port at a time, but they could not—they were spread thin over some 320 kilometres of coast. It was, therefore, decided to mask off Dunkirk, but to capture Boulogne and Calais as quickly as possible, and thereafter to concentrate on the Scheldt. Boulogne contained a 10,000-man garrison behind strong fortifications backed by plenty of artillery. Much of the defence faced seaward, however, while the defending troops were not first class and morale was low. The initial Canadian ground assault on September 17 was preceded by a massive bombardment from the air with 690 Bomber Command aircraft taking part; the impact of this bombing was questionable. When the ground attack began, the Canadians were immediately met by strong defensive fire. It took five days and thousands of shells and aerial sorties by fighter bombers before the outer defences could be overcome. Boulogne finally fell on September 22; the Canadians took some 9,500 German prisoners, but the harbour facilities had been systematically destroyed and were not useable until mid-October.

Calais and Cap Gris Nez came next. On September 25 the usual bombing and heavy artillery barrage signalled the start of a Canadian infantry and armoured offensive. On the evening of September 28 the German garrison commander met Canadian divisional commander Dan Spry to ask that Calais be declared on open city. Spry refused, but allowed twenty-four hours for the evacuation of the town's civilians. The following day the guns momentarily fell silent around Calais, but the fighting continued at Cap Gris Nez to the west as the 9th Canadian Infantry Brigade assaulted and captured the massive guns that the Germans had been using to bombard Dover and other points along the English coast since the summer of 1940. At noon on September 30, the ceasefire at Calais ended and the Canadians resumed the assault, but the Germans had lost their taste for the fight. Resistance ceased the next day, and more than 7,000 Germans were taken prisoner.

The taking of Dieppe, Boulogne, and Calais did virtually nothing to ease the Allied supply problem. The ports were too small (and in the case of Boulogne too damaged) to make any difference. Antwerp was still the prize, but a prize unusable until the seaward approaches to it were cleared. Throughout the first weeks of September, Montgomery was preoccupied with Market Garden, but on September 15, two days before Market Garden was to begin, he ordered Crerar to hurry on to the Scheldt Estuary. He was asking the impossible; there were simply not enough troops in the small First Canadian Army to mask off Dunkirk, capture Boulogne and Calais (and Cap Gris Nez), and make any real headway in clearing the Germans from the banks of the Scheldt, all at the same time.

British troops were trucked into the Dunkirk area in mid-September to relieve the 2nd Canadian Infantry Division (which was sent to Antwerp to begin the initial stage of the attack on the Scheldt), but the Canadians received no other reinforcements. Put simply, Montgomery underestimated both German strength and the need to take the Scheldt quickly. But then, he and Eisenhower were banking on Market Garden to shorten the war. In addition, Montgomery was placing burdens on Crerar's army that no small army could possibly carry. As if to emphasize his total disregard for the realistic when it came to the Canadians, he also ordered Crerar on September 27 to protect the left flank of the Second British Army (Crerar was to do this with his 1st British Corps), which was about to begin an offensive toward the Ruhr from the newly captured Nijmegen salient. Thus when the 2nd Canadian Infantry Division began to clear the area north of the Albert Canal on September 22—led by the Calgary Highlanders and the rest of the 5th Brigade when Sergeant Crockett won his Distinguished Conduct Medal—that activity was really only preliminary to a major attack that still lay in the future. In effect, the 2nd Canadian Division was trying to establish the base from which an offensive aimed at capturing South Beveland might later be launched when sufficient forces would become available.

The very day that Montgomery ordered Crerar to cover Dempsey's left flank (September 27), Crerar took ill and flew to the United Kingdom to be admitted to hospital. The burden for planning and commanding the Scheldt battle now fell on Simonds, who became acting army commander in Crerar's absence (Foulkes took over temporarily from Simonds at 2nd Canadian Corps Headquarters). Simonds decided that the Scheldt offensive should be conducted in three stages. First, the area between the south bank of the Scheldt and the Leopold Canal and the Canal de Dérivation de la Lys—called the Breskens pocket—would be cleared. This would be done primarily by the 3rd Canadian Infantry Division, aided by elements of the 52nd British (Lowland) Division and the 4th Canadian Armoured Divisions. Then, the neck of South Beveland would be cut and the rest of South Beveland taken primarily by the 2nd Canadian Infantry Division. Finally, the island of Walcheren, which dominated the entrance to the estuary, would be assaulted from South Beveland over the Walcheren causeway and by seaborne landings (by British troops) at Westkapelle and Flushing. The last part of the plan depended on flooding Walcheren—most of which lay below sea level—to deny the German garrison movement and confine them to the small areas of the island that lay above sea level. It was a controversial proposal, but eventually it was approved by Eisenhower and Churchill, and the Dutch government-in-exile. The Walcheren dykes were destroyed from the air beginning on October 3, when 243 heavy bombers dropped over 1,200 tons of high explosives on the dykes. Other attacks followed on subsequent days; by the third week of October, most of the island lay under water.

★ ★ ★ ★

In the last week of September, the 2nd Canadian Infantry Division pushed the Germans back on the north side of the Albert Canal, cleared the area between it and the Turnhout Canal, and forced a crossing over the Turnhout Canal as well. Then, on October 2, it began the long-awaited push toward the point where the isthmus of South Beveland joins the mainland. The 4th Brigade struck north from Antwerp, while the 6th Brigade attacked westward from the Turnhout Canal. Their objective was to push the Germans back from Antwerp and clear the ground for a 5th Brigade attack toward Hoogerheide and Woensdrecht, two small towns barely 3 kilometres apart that dominated the road and rail links from the mainland through South Beveland to Walcheren.

W. Denis Whitaker, then Commanding Officer of the Royal Hamilton Light Infantry, 4th Canadian Infantry Brigade, later described the opening moments of the attack:

> At H-Hour, a deafening barrage went up and C Company began its advance. To our horror, we observed that one of our own field guns was firing short, right into the path of my advancing men. I had a terrible decision to make—and it had to be made instantly. If I aborted the operation at this point many lives would be lost, more than if I risked some of the troops being hit by fragments from our own shellfire. I had little choice but to carry on.[2]

Whitaker's terrible gamble paid off; the opening stages of the attack were successful and the two brigades spent the next few days advancing steadily to the northwest, the 6th Brigade protecting the flank of the 4th Brigade.

On October 6 the offensive to crush German resistance in the Breskens pocket began. The attack started with a flame-throwing assault by twenty-seven Wasps—Bren carriers equipped with flame-throwers—on the north bank of the Leopold Canal followed by an assault crossing of the canal by two battalions of the 7th Canadian Infantry Brigade. The flame-throwers momentarily stunned the German defenders, but they quickly recovered and counterattacked. The two Canadian battalions managed to hold on to their bridgeheads, but could not link them up, even with the assistance of a third battalion that crossed soon after. The German troops in the Breskens area were very good and were determined to follow Hitler's orders to the last man.

To the east, in the battle for South Beveland, the Calgary Highlanders began to lead the 5th Brigade advance toward Hoogerheide and Woensdrecht on October 7. By nightfall they had pushed into Hoogerheide against stiffening German resistance. The following day they and the other battalions of the 5th Brigade—the Black Watch and the Maisonneuves—began to advance cautiously toward Woensdrecht, just a few kilometres to the west. But the Germans were ready to push back with *Kampfgruppe Chill*, a force of some 2,000 men, many of them paratroopers, backed by tanks, self-propelled artillery (SPs), and assault guns. Battle was joined in the afternoon when the Germans slammed into the Canadian positions; it raged all night and into the next day. The Black Watch intelligence officer observed, "The [German] troops we are now meeting are the cream of the crop . . . fine physical specimens, keen to fight and with excellent morale."[3] At one point an entire Highlander company went missing for several hours; it was cut off, and with its radios malfunctioning, battalion headquarters had no idea of its status. After dark a 68-ton German "Ferdinand" SP packing an 88mm gun penetrated to the very centre of the Black Watch positions before it was destroyed.

The 5th Brigade held; the German attack was spent by dawn on October 10. Now preparations began for the seizure of Woensdrecht and the final push to the East Scheldt, just beyond it, to cut off the supply lines and line of retreat for the German defenders on South Beveland. In the meantime, in the Breskens area, the 9th Canadian Infantry Brigade climbed into amphibious Buffalo vehicles at Terneuzen just after midnight on October 9 and began a 7-kilometre journey westward to land behind the German lines at just after 0200. As dawn broke the surprised German defenders reorganized themselves and began counterattacking. Nonetheless, the 9th Brigade was soon reinforced by the 8th Brigade, and the Germans began to give ground.

The Canadians were making progress, but it was slow progress. The cold, wet rains of autumn turned the battlefield into a quagmire—at least that part of it not already flooded by the Germans, who resisted strongly. In the Breskens pocket, the fighting seemed unending, the men had little respite, the water was everywhere, and death came quickly and sometimes unexpectedly. Donald Pearce was serving with the North Nova Scotia Highlanders of the 9th Brigade on October 10, leading a small convoy of Bren carriers of the anti-tank platoon to B Company:

> Tense ride down an open one mile stretch of country road, every moment expecting a big explosion to occur underneath us . . . We have to make a sharp turn up a little lane that heads to Baker Company, so I stop just beyond the intersection to ask for covering fire before turning into the exposed laneway. The second carrier pulls up just a few yards back of ours and with a noise like the bursting of a ship's boiler simply blows up—men, equipment everything. . . . My gun crew and I were appalled . . . I was sick all day.[4]

As the 8th and 9th Brigades pushed westward, the 10th Infantry Brigade of the 4th Canadian Armoured Division joined the battle, pushing west along the north side of the Leopold Canal. On October 14 the three brigades linked up; five days later they joined the lead elements of the 52nd (Lowland) Division, which had pushed across the Leopold

Canal from the south, using the bridgehead originally established by the 7th Brigade. By now the original Breskens pocket had been reduced by about half, but the Germans fought on, their guns at Breskens still dominating the water passage between Breskens and Flushing, on Walcheren. The Royal Air Force's No. 84 Group sent Typhoon fighter bombers to bomb, strafe, and rocket German troops, artillery, and fortified positions whenever the foul weather allowed flying operations. On twelve of the twenty-seven days of Operation Switchback, the planes were grounded, but when they did fly, they greatly impeded German movement by day and limited the effectiveness of the German artillery.[5] The town of Breskens fell on October 22, but the Germans still refused to quit. The Canadians pushed on to the west, bypassing a large flooded area north of the Bruges-Sluis Canal, and closed in on the remnant of the German defenders, near Zeebrugge. Charlie Martin and the men of the Queen's Own were given the dubious honour of assaulting the last German stronghold. As usual, the attack was preceded by an artillery bombardment:

We were on both sides of the road, spaced, running fast and making ourselves as difficult targets as possible. The moment we hit the gate our artillery stopped—perfect timing . . . now we had to cover open ground to get close enough to drop in our grenades or smoke bombs . . . so we're all running at top speed . . . the miracle we prayed for happened. Out from all the slits in the strongpoint came the white flags. They had surrendered. The battle for Breskens was won.[6]

★ ★ ★ ★

As the 10th Brigade neared its intended junction with the 8th and 9th Brigades southeast of Breskens on October 13, the fight for Woensdrecht was beginning to reach a bloody climax some 40 kilometres to the northeast. At 0645 that morning, C Company of the Black Watch passed through positions of the Royal Regiment of Canada some 3 kilometres west of Woensdrecht, to begin an advance toward the railway embankment carrying the main line from Bergen op Zoom to Walcheren. The plan was to shoot two companies onto the position with the aid of tank, mortar, and artillery fire; the aim of the advance was to cut the rail line leading to South Beveland.

The attack ran into difficulty almost from the start. C Company began to take heavy casualties from small-arms fire not long after leaving its jumping-off point. B Company, assigned to pass through C Company, was heavily mortared at its start line. Under cover of smoke, these two companies were eventually able to advance to the embankment, but were then pinned down, taking more casualties. Both company commanders were wounded. Later, under cover of artillery fire and air strikes, and accompanied by Wasp flame-throwers, the other two Black Watch rifle companies tried to complete the battalion's assigned task. But the artillery spotters found it difficult to pinpoint targets in the almost featureless landscape, while the fighter bombers could not attack the far side of the curving railway embankment without gravely endangering the Canadian troops. By nightfall, the offensive was called off. It was a complete failure; fifty-six Black Watch were killed or died of their wounds, sixty-two were wounded, and twenty-seven were taken prisoner. It was the second, and second worst, disaster to befall the regiment since the start of the campaign. Most of the Black Watch dead lay exposed and unburied along the railway embankment until October 24 when the Calgary Highlanders finally took and held this small piece of contested and bloody ground.

The Black Watch attack was a disaster for many reasons, including the failure of the infantry to use their artillery cover properly. But some of the blame must also be laid at higher levels. Put simply, the advance was another case of too few men asked to do too difficult a job against a well-dug-in enemy especially skilled at defence. Even though Simonds had only about half of his army to work with, and certainly no reinforcements from Montgomery at the start of the Scheldt campaign, his plan had called for two widely separated campaigns at the same time, one in the Breskens area and one at the eastern end of South Beveland. Had he masked off the Breskens pocket with, say, the 3rd Canadian Infantry Division and assigned the 4th Canadian Armoured Division to the South Beveland attack in a two-divisional operation, the fight for Woensdrecht might have been completed much quicker and with fewer casualties.

Ultimately, however, the fault lay at Montgomery's door. He had given the First Canadian Army too much to do, and it could not accomplish everything he was asking of it in short order. With the failure of Market Garden it became obvious that the Allies would need to mount a coordinated offensive into Germany and, thus, that they would need the Antwerp port facilities as quickly as possible. But Montgomery continued to have his eye on the Ruhr. As October dragged on, Eisenhower put increasing pressure on Montgomery to make the Scheldt battle his first priority. Amid reports that the Canadians were short of ammunition and making slow progress, Eisenhower wrote Montgomery that "of all of our operations on our entire front from Switzerland to the Channel, I consider Antwerp of first importance and I believe that the operations to clear up the entrance require your personal attention."[7]

Monty was forced to give in. He closed his Ruhr offensive down, ordered Dempsey's army to cover the Canadians' right flank and help them take Bergen op Zoom, and gave Simonds two additional divisions, one British and one American, to work with. As C.P. Stacey noted, "As soon as the new orders took effect, the situation north of Antwerp was transformed."[8] Montgomery was not a man to concede that he ever made a mistake, but he did admit to making one when it came to the Scheldt battle. In his memoirs he wrote, "Here I must admit a bad mistake on my part—I underestimated the difficulties of opening up the approaches to Antwerp so that we could get the free use of that port. I reckoned that the Canadian Army could do it while we were going for the Ruhr. I was wrong."[9] He never clarified whether his mistake was in overestimating the ability of First Canadian Army to do the job, or underestimating the scope of the job he called on them to do.

On the morning of October 16, the Royal Hamilton Light Infantry finally took Woensdrecht; in the days that followed, the 5th Brigade cut the road and rail links between the mainland and Walcheren, while the rest of the 2nd Division turned westward along the South Beveland peninsula. Led by the 4th Brigade, the advance began October 23 as the division's other two brigades completed the task of securing the area north of Woensdrecht. They were aided by units of the 4th Canadian Armoured Division, which joined the fight the following day. Then they, too, headed westward.

Despite heavy traffic, German shelling, and German demolition of the bridges over the Beveland Canal, the division made steady progress. On October 26 the 52nd (Lowland) Division crossed the Scheldt from Terneuzen and began landing on the southeast coast of South Beveland. Then it, too, began to advance toward the western end of the peninsula. On the 29th they linked with the Canadians. By the 31st, all resistance had ceased on South Beveland; the island of Walcheren lay ahead.

Simonds's plan called for a three-pronged attack on Walcheren. On November 1 the British 4th Special Service Brigade was to land near

Westkapelle, on the western tip of Walcheren, while the British No. 4 Commando, accompanied by a brigade of the 52nd (Lowland) Division, were to storm Flushing from Breskens. The land attack from South Beveland over the long and narrow Walcheren Causeway was to get underway as soon as possible. The 5th Canadian Infantry Brigade was given the task.

The western end of the causeway was well fortified by the Germans; their mortars and artillery were sited on every metre of it. The salt marshes on both sides of the causeway did not have enough water to float assault boats, but were too muddy to support men and vehicles. The only way to get to Walcheren was by crossing the almost totally exposed causeway. The Black Watch were the first to try. At about 1040 on October 31, they sent three companies forward; German shells rained down, forcing the men to hit the ground. Some were lucky enough to be near brick-lined slit trenches that the Germans had built for their own use. Most lay exposed, with little prospect for movement. They remained on the causeway until dark, then pulled back.

The Calgary Highlanders went next. After a heavy barrage on the German positions atop the dykes to the north and south of the western end of the causeway, the Highlanders moved out just after midnight. German mortar, machine-gun, and shellfire blanketed the causeway. Some men got as far as a large tank trap on the south slope of the causeway, about two-thirds of the way across, others took refuge in slit trenches and shell holes. Company Commander Frank "Nobby" Clarke set up his headquarters in a large crater that the Germans had blasted out of the middle of the causeway, and quickly concluded that he could not hold. By 0300, the Highlanders had pulled back, taking some Black Watch wounded with them. Three hours later, the Highlanders moved back onto the causeway under cover of a new and more extensive fire plan. This time they made it all the way across and began to fan out on the eastern end of Walcheren. By midday it began to look as if they might succeed, but the Germans counterattacked with flame-throwers, threatening to cut off at least one Highlander company. Late in the day, the Highlanders pulled back, their rifle companies reduced to about twenty men each.

That same day, to the west, the landing at Flushing was a complete success, and although the troops coming ashore at Westkapelle met stiff resistance at first, they were able to fan out to the north and south before the day ended. It was clear that the German hold on Walcheren was loosening fast, but the 5th Brigade was still under orders to assault over the causeway. Thus the Maisonneuves sent two companies onto the causeway after midnight on the night of November 1–2. They never came closer than 200 metres from Walcheren and had to be rescued by the Scottish troops of the 52nd (Lowland) Division.

Major-General Charles Foulkes, still in temporary command of 2nd Canadian Corps, insisted on another go across the causeway and turned to Major-General Edmund Hakewell-Smith, General Officer Commanding (GOC) the 52nd (Lowland) Division. Hakewell-Smith refused to make a direct assault and ordered his men to find another way. This they did when scouts discovered a place where troops could, in fact, walk across the mud flats. They outflanked the Germans at the end of the causeway, hastening the surrender of the last defenders on Walcheren on November 8. It then took almost three weeks to clear the mines from the Scheldt. The first cargoes did not arrive until November 28; ironically, a Canadian merchantman led that first convoy.

As the Battle of the Scheldt Estuary ended, the men of the First Canadian Army retired eastward to the vicinity of Nijmegen. Taking over from the US 82nd Airborne Division, which had captured the town and its dominant highway bridge during Market Garden, the men encamped in the forests to the southeast of Nijmegen (against the German border), in the town itself, and in nearby towns and villages to the west. Much of the land near Nijmegen was dotted with the wreckage of American gliders, relics of Market Garden. For the next few months, the war would largely be fought elsewhere on the western front; the Canadians were only too happy to be left out. As they dug their slit trenches, sited their mortars and machine guns, and watched the falling snow cover the war-scarred countryside, they awaited the sixth Christmas of the war.

CHAPTER 17

VICTORY

Late August, 1945: Nippon Kokan shipyards, Kawasaki, Japan. The slave labour prisoners at Camp B had known for at least a week that Japan had announced its surrender; the Canadians among them had been prisoners since that bleak December day in 1941 when the Commonwealth forces on Hong Kong Island had surrendered to Japan. They had survived the unspeakable horrors of the post-surrender atrocities the Japanese had meted out. They had lived through almost four years of captivity in Hong Kong and Japan in unspeakable conditions of filth, starvation, brutality, and constant physical exhaustion. They had endured months of air raids from US carrier–borne aircraft and the massive fire raids of the great silver American B-29 bombers. Now they waited to be rescued and to go home.

One of the men was William Allister. An army signaller, Allister had been born in Montreal and had grown up in Manitoba. In the fall of 1941 he had been attending a signals course in Nova Scotia, with little prospect of going overseas for a least a year, when the chance arose to volunteer for a secret mission to an unknown destination. He grabbed it and, within weeks, was aboard the SS *Awatea* bound for Hong Kong. Allister became a prisoner of war on Christmas Day 1941; it had been the beginning of his life as a slave to the Japanese Empire—an ordeal that changed him forever.

The news of the Japanese surrender brought the promise of release, but days went by with no sign of the Americans. Most of the thousands of American, British, Canadian, and other Allied prisoners in Japan were in desperate straits; even a few days' early release could mean the difference between life and death. Then fighter planes began to appear in the sky, circling, searching for POW camps. Usually they were too far away to signal. Each day the aircraft seemed to come nearer but not near enough. The men grew frustrated: "We felt like castaways on a desert island trying to signal ships," Allister later remembered.

Then one day, about August 21, it happened. A fighter plane circled closer and spotted the camp. The pilot flew straight at the jubilant men, then swooped low, coming in just over the telephone wires. As he flew past he dipped his wing in salute. It was a moment Allister would remember all his life: "I was shrieking, waving, laughing, howling insane gibberish, freaking, weeping uncontrollably—the tears spurting up like an irrepressible orgasmic release. My dam had burst at last and out it all came, as though all the anguish of the planet had found me, and out of my bowels all the murders, tortures, all the Jews burning in Belsen, all the hellish years, had gathered in a million voices bursting all bounds."[1]

Allister and his comrades-in-arms were among the first Canadian soldiers taken prisoner in the Second World War; they were the last to be liberated.

* * * *

As 1944 ended, one of the coldest winters on record gripped northern Europe. Along the western front from Holland to southern France stood seven Allied armies—one Canadian, one British, four American, and one French—close to ninety divisions. Opposing them were the supposedly defeated remnants of the Wehrmacht, who had suddenly come to life to put up a skilled and tenacious defence against the British at Arnhem, the Canadians at the Scheldt, and the Americans and French advancing toward the Saar.

In the other theatres of war, Allied victory had become certain, though months of hard fighting and heavy casualties obviously remained. In Italy, the American and British forces had broken through the Gothic Line, but stalled south of Bologna as winter closed in in the high passes of the Apennines and along the Adriatic coastal plain. On the eastern front, three Soviet army groups with fifteen armies stood poised for the last great Soviet offensive of the war. By then the Soviets had regained all of the Soviet Union and most of Poland, stood on the very borders of East Prussia, and were preparing to take Warsaw. In the southwest Pacific, the United States had regained most of the Philippines and prepared to invade Luzon, the principal island and site of Manila, the Philippine capital. In the central Pacific, US Marines prepared to invade Iwo Jima, which was close enough to Japan to be used as an air base for long-range fighters to attack Japan directly.

As the Allied commanders on the western front bickered about what to do next, the Canadian Army gathered in and around Nijmegen. The Canadian mission was simple: to hold the Nijmegen salient and the small piece of Allied-held territory north of the Maas River, across the Nijmegen bridge, known as "the island." Montgomery was planning a major offensive, to start in early January, aimed at clearing the Germans from the Rhineland as a first step to crossing the Rhine.

He planned to use the Nijmegen salient as the jumping-off point for the initial attack.

The three months that the Canadians spent in the vicinity of Nijmegen was the longest period of time after D-Day that the Canadians in northwest Europe mounted no major operations. That does not mean there was no action. North of the Maas, the Germans did their best to push the Canadians out of "the island." The flood gates of the Neder (Lower) Rhine were opened and the flood waters rose in the polderland between that river and the Maas. The Canadians north of the Maas were confined to an ever-smaller slice of dry land and were under constant German harassment.

Southeast of Nijmegen, near the towns of Berg-en-Dal and Groesbeek, the Canadian and German positions faced each other along the Dutch-German border. The German positions were the outposts of the much vaunted Siegfried Line, with its concrete fortifications, pillboxes, dragon's teeth, and other obstacles, that lay just a few kilometres out of sight in the forest to the east. Both sides patrolled aggressively to probe positions, take prisoners, and gather intelligence. Artillery barrages regularly made life difficult, if not deadly. The men dug deep slit trenches, covered them with whatever was handy—often portions of the gliders that still dotted the landscape—and tried to keep warm. On Christmas and New Year's Eve they serenaded one another with both music and mortar fire before returning to the grim business of survival in a hostile environment.

As much as they may have grumbled about the snow and the cold and need for constant vigilance, especially at night, the Canadians had nothing to complain about compared to their American allies farther south in the Ardennes Forest. There, on December 16, the Germans loosed two panzer armies through General Courtney Hodges's First

US Army. The Germans called the attack Autumn Fog; the Americans dubbed it the Battle of the Bulge. New armour from German tank factories had been channelled to reinvigorated units smashed in the Normandy fighting or to new units recently formed. Gasoline and diesel, in ever shorter supply in the Reich, had been hoarded for months to fuel the attack. It was all part of Hitler's last great gamble; if his troops could cut deep into Allied territory and retake Brussels and Antwerp, the Allied cause in the west would suffer a serious setback. Then Hitler could turn the bulk of his troops eastward to meet the Russians. The German plan called for the Fifth and Sixth Panzer Armies to drive west and north and then to form the anvil for Army Group H, which would attack westward across the Maas to encircle and then destroy the 21st Army Group. Allied air superiority was neutralized by the bad weather; for days Hitler's tanks moved underneath a cover of thick clouds.

Stunned, the Americans managed to rush the 101st Airborne Division to the key Belgian road junction town of Bastogne; there they were besieged but refused to surrender. Other American troops fought tenaciously at St-Vith, another important crossroads, until they were forced to pull back. The Germans drove to within 30 kilometres of Namur on the Meuse River but could get no farther. Their lines of supply and communication were hopelessly snarled. Even if they had reached the Meuse, however, they would have encountered a stiffened defence organized by Montgomery, who had been asked by Eisenhower to take the Ninth US Army under command for the duration of the emergency because Bradley's 12th US Army Group Headquarters was on the other side of the Bulge from it. Monty placed US and British troops at strategic locations to hold the shoulder of the Bulge and alerted Crerar's Canadians to a possible attack on the Nijmegen salient by the German First Parachute Army.

That attack never came. The US Army suffered thousands of casualties—dead, wounded, and missing—but fought back stubbornly after the initial panic. Patton's Third Army, which had been poised to launch an attack against the Saar, swung north in one of the most difficult manoeuvres called for in war and broke through to Bastogne just after Christmas. Then, when the weather cleared, Allied fighter bombers took a frightful toll of German troops and tanks. Hitler had gambled his last significant reserve and had lost. The Germans would still put up a determined defence of their borders, but the panzers that would have added so much punch to that defence lay wrecked on the roads and among the trees of the Ardennes Forest.

* * * *

As the Allied armies drove to the very borders of Germany in the late fall of 1944, Bomber Command's assault on Germany had intensified. Sir Arthur Harris's bombers had been tied in to the Normandy operations since the spring; when Normandy had been won, he regained control over his aircraft. For a time in late summer the RAF and RCAF "heavies" had concentrated on V-1 sites, but for the most part, these aircraft were ineffective against such targets, which were better attacked by medium bombers and fighter bombers. Harris's heavies attacked oil and other strategic targets, especially transportation nodes, though Bomber Command also continued its area attacks against German cities whenever the opportunity arose. The winter of 1944–45 proved especially bad over northern Europe, and much of the bombing conducted both by Bomber Command and the US Eighth Air Force was, in effect, blind bombing or area bombing using radar to identify ground targets through cloud.

By now the night bomber war had swung in favour of the Royal

Air Force, though night fighters continued to pose a significant danger to the bomber crews whenever interceptions did take place. As Allied armies advanced toward Germany's borders, Oboe stations were set up on the Continent, greatly improving the crews' ability to pinpoint their positions. The aircraft also carried improved H2S, which allowed them to locate their targets with much greater accuracy at night or when bombing through clouds in daylight. The acute German shortage of aviation gasoline played havoc with the Luftwaffe's efforts to field an effective night-fighter force. The German propeller day-fighter force had long since been driven from the skies. The new Me-262 jets, much faster than Spitfires or Mustangs, were almost invincible when attacking bombers in daylight, but large numbers of these new jets were either destroyed on the ground or shot down when landing or taking off. A few were even destroyed in air-to-air combat.

Through the fall and into the winter, the bomber force attacked target after target, wreaking havoc at a shrinking cost. In fact, of the more than 300,000 tons of bombs dropped in area raids on Germany throughout the war, the greatest part by far was used after July 1, 1944. In just one week in October, for example, the RCAF's No. 6 Group took part in four area bombing attacks against Duisburg (twice), Wilhelmshaven, and Stuttgart. A total of 677 aircraft sortied in these raids; only eight failed to return. The pace of the attacks picked up in November and December, with No. 6 Group routinely dispatching 150 or more bombers to a single target each night for the loss of just one or two aircraft.[2]

The previous summer the Air Ministry had examined, then shelved, Operation Thunderclap—a series of "overwhelming raids" designed to destroy German morale and end the war. The original plan was for an attack—on Berlin alone—so powerful that it might inflict some 220,000 casualties, of whom some 50 percent would be killed. The plan envisaged "that such an attack resulting in so many deaths, the great majority of which will be key personnel, cannot help but have a shattering effect on political and civilian morale all over Germany."[3] Thunderclap was shelved for five months but revived in January 1945 as a means of helping a new Red Army offensive on the eastern front. Thunderclap itself was never carried out. Instead, planning shifted to the use of both British and American bombers to hit targets behind the German-Soviet front to cause confusion and panic; to aid the Red Army; and to hit major transportation targets, thus choking off the Germans' ability to reinforce their troops to meet the Russian advances. Three key cities were added to the target list: Chemnitz, Leipzig, and Dresden. As one historian of the Dresden raid put it, "The Saxon cities were closer to the front [than Berlin] and in order to really damage the Germans' ability to move large amounts of men and *materiél* between fronts [east and west], their rail networks (as well as Berlin's) would have to be attacked."[4] Thus an attack on Dresden was ordered on January 27, 1945, just days before Stalin, Churchill, Roosevelt, and their military advisors met at Yalta to plan the final stages of the offensive against Germany. At Yalta the Russians sought the establishment of a bomb line beyond which British and American flyers would not go—to protect the Red Army from possible air attack by its Allies—but it is unclear whether or not they specifically asked for air attacks on eastern German cities, specifically Dresden. As Taylor points out, however, the question of whether the Russians asked for an air attack on Dresden or not "is merely a technical one . . . since the attack had already been ordered."[5] Dresden had been bombed before but had never been subject to a sustained attack. And although it contained important war plants, particularly involved in the production of radars, precision optical equipment for bombsights, etc., its inhabitants had come to believe that its nineteenth-century architectural splendour—it was often referred to as Florence on the Elbe—gave it a special status and that it would never be heavily attacked. But to those who accepted both the logic and necessity of area bombing, there was no reason why Dresden should be spared when other German cities had not been. As Carter and Dunmore concluded in their history of No. 6 Group, "At this stage of the conflict, the Allies were in no mood to show mercy to the perpetrators of such horrors as Auschwitz, Belsen, and Dachau. The pressure had to be maintained . . . The Allies had already suffered far too many casualties in the invasion of Europe. The bloodletting had to be brought to a halt as rapidly as possible."[6]

On the night of February 13–14, 1945, Bomber Command sent close to 800 Lancasters and nine Mosquitos to Dresden. They started bombing at 2215; within forty-five minutes the heart of the city was engulfed in a firestorm. The blaze could be seen by approaching bombers at least 200 kilometres away. Bomber Command later estimated that 85 percent of the built-up area of Dresden was destroyed. Recent estimates have placed the number of dead at some 25,000 people.[7] Since the city was filled with refugees, an accurate death count was not possible. Goebbels's propaganda ministry wasted no time spinning the casualty number to over 100,000 killed, while playing up the architectural legacy of the city and ignoring its great strategic value not only as a transportation centre but also as a location of extensive war production. Nazi lies about both the number of dead and the nature of the target persist to this day.[8] Many No. 6 Group squadrons were still flying Halifaxes of various types, so only sixty-seven RCAF Lancasters took part in the raid; none were lost.

In one of the greatest acts of hypocrisy of the entire war, Churchill now sought to distance himself from the Dresden bombing in particular and the area bombing campaign in general. It was time to re-examine the policy, he wrote in late March 1945, when the Allied armies were already deep into Germany and victory was both certain and only weeks away. His reversal was shameless and had no impact on the course of the war, but it helped create a postwar climate of disapproval both of Harris and of the area bombing campaign that was manifest in a number of ways: from the failure to honour Harris as other Allied military leaders were to the refusal to issue a special medal to Bomber Command aircrew. Echoes of this hypocrisy reverberate to this day as the drums against the area bombing campaign continue to be beaten by men and women who experienced nothing of the horror of the Second World War and who ignore the context within which the bombing campaign took place.[9]

The bombing continued until late April, even as the Russians closed in on Berlin. As city after city was occupied by the Allies, target after target was removed from the Bomber Command list. By the end of the fighting, thousands of square kilometres of Germany's most important cities lay ruined, hundreds of thousands of city dwellers had been killed, and many more had been injured or rendered homeless. The debate about the strategic effectiveness of the bomber war will continue for a long time, but there was one indisputable result of that bombing campaign: when the German people dug themselves out of the ruins of their cities, they knew beyond doubt that they had suffered a terrible and costly defeat and had paid a heavy price for the war they had begun and waged. As the *Globe and Mail* put it in March 1945, "The real victory of Allied air power [was] a thing of the mind—a lesson so terrible as never to be forgotten . . . The German People will not need the presence of Allied armies to persuade them that they lost this war. The storm which is engulfing them from the air . . . is convincing them that they have suffered the most terrible defeat ever inflicted on a people in all history."[10] That was as good a guarantee as any that Germany would not repeat the mistake a third time in the twentieth century.

Our Finest Hour

★ ★ ★ ★

In the early hours of April 16, 1945, the RCN Bangor Class minesweeper *Esquimalt* departed Halifax on a routine anti-submarine sweep on the approaches to Halifax harbour. The ship was to meet up with HMCS *Sarnia* just before noon. It was calm and clear. *Esquimalt* was not using its SW2C radar, which was, in any case, obsolete. The ship's asdic beam swept the waters close ahead, but *Esquimalt* was neither zigzagging nor streaming its CAT gear. At 0635, near the Sambro light ship, an acoustic torpedo tore into the minesweeper. It had been fired by U-190, which had been lying at ambush ready to attack ships coming into or leaving Halifax harbour. *Esquimalt* went down in less than four minutes with no chance to issue a distress call. The survivors clung to four Carley floats in the bone-chilling water for some seven hours before being spotted by *Sarnia*. Many died of exposure; the final death toll was forty-four. *Esquimalt* was the last Royal Canadian Navy vessel to be lost in the war; its sinking was all too typical of the last phases of the Allied campaign against the U-boats.

From the late summer of 1944 until the end of the war, Dönitz sent his U-boats into the shallow waters of the English Channel and the approaches to the major East Coast ports of North America such as Halifax. His reasoning was simple: Allied anti-submarine capability had developed to the point where a renewal of the wolf-pack tactics of 1940–43 were unthinkable; thus his submarines would have to hunt alone. Sending lone submarines to search the vast areas of the mid-ocean for convoys was a waste of precious resources; it was too easy for a lone boat to miss a convoy. But the experiences of his submariners in the Gulf of St. Lawrence in 1942 had demonstrated two things: tricky currents and thermal layers made it easy for U-boats to hide in coastal waters, and it was also easy for them to find targets at particular choke points, especially approaches to harbours.

The Canadians had had a difficult enough time hunting U-boats in their own coastal waters in 1942; they and their Allies had an even tougher time in late 1944 and 1945 because the U-boats were much better equipped than they had been two years earlier. The snorkel was virtually undetectable from the air and could be picked up from the sea only by the very newest radars and only when a submarine hunter was in close proximity to the snorkeling U-boat. The newest snorkel heads also contained the latest in radar-detection equipment while the submarines carried the still-dangerous Gnat acoustic torpedo. It is, therefore, understandable though ironic that of the fifteen RCN ships sunk by submarines during the war, three were destroyed in Canadian coastal waters in the last six months of the conflict: *Shawinigan* in the Cabot Strait on November 25, 1944; *Clayoquot* near Halifax on December 24, 1944; and *Esquimalt*.

The new tactics and equipment enabled the U-boats to approach close to the East Coast ports of both Canada and the United States, as they had done in 1942. Even the much-vaunted United States Navy's hunter-killer groups had a difficult time finding and sinking the invaders. But because of the overwhelming presence of Allied air cover and ocean-going escorts, there was nothing like the slaughter that had taken place more than two years before. Snorkeling U-boats still had to stay submerged to avoid detection from the air. This restricted their speed and ability to get into attack position. When they placed themselves on known routes into and out of major ports they could sink merchantmen in relatively large numbers, as U-1232 had done in early January 1945, when it had destroyed five ships near Halifax in only a matter of hours. But the days of wide-open roving of the convoy lanes, on the surface or submerged, were over. Even the best equipped U-boats could not sink ships they could not detect or reach.

In the final months of the war, Dönitz dreamt about a great new submarine offensive using the new faster, longer-range submersibles still on the drawing boards or being built in German shipyards. Reports appeared in some North American newspapers that the Germans would use these U-boats to launch V-2 rockets at East Coast cities. But dreams of sub-launched missiles remained dreams (or nightmares); the advanced U-boats Dönitz needed to renew his mid-ocean campaign against Allied shipping were destroyed, still in their dry docks, by Allied bombers.

The Royal Canadian Navy lost twenty-four ships and 1,800 sailors to all causes in the Second World War; more than a thousand other Canadians were killed at sea aboard Canadian-registry merchant ships. But four of every five U-boat crew members who left European ports on war patrol never returned, and the RCN could take some satisfaction from that; it and the Royal Canadian Air Force had sunk, or participated in the sinking of, fifty-two Axis submarines in the course of the war. More to the point, its vessels had escorted millions of tons of vital Allied shipping from North America to the United Kingdom and back. Without that shipping, the Allied invasion of Europe would have been impossible. That was quite an achievement for a navy that had all but disappeared in the early 1930s.

* * * *

In the pre-dawn darkness of February 8, 1945, the rifle companies of the Calgary Highlanders took up their forward positions in the dense but leafless woods on the road to the German border town of Wyler. They and the Régiment de Maisonneuve had been chosen to lead the 2nd Canadian Infantry Division in the great attack about to begin. That attack, code-named Veritable, was to be the first stage in Montgomery's campaign to clear the Rhineland. Its object was to secure the ground between the Dutch-German border and the Hochwald, a forest reserve that guarded the approaches to the crossroads town of Xanten. Xanten was the key to the Rhine crossings at Wesel. After the Hochwald had been reached, the attacking forces were to halt for regrouping and redeployment. The artillery would be brought forward in classic set-piece fashion. Then stage two of the offensive—code-named Blockbuster—would begin.

To the south, along the Roer River, the US Ninth Army, usually under the command of Lieutenant-General W.H. Simpson, had been placed under Montgomery's command for this operation; it was to attack northward (Operation Grenade) to meet the British and Canadian forces opposite Wesel. Montgomery had put the entire 30 Corps and several other British divisions under command of First Canadian Army to ensure that Crerar had the strength needed to break through the German frontier defences. For a time Crerar's headquarters would control thirteen divisions, of which only three were Canadian, while the total manpower strength of the forces under his command would reach almost half a million. Montgomery believed that the Germans would never suspect that his major offensive would begin on the Canadian front, and he was right. It is no mean task for an army headquarters to take responsibility for planning, coordinating, and supplying a major attack such as Blockbuster. Crerar's team could never have attempted such a huge undertaking six months earlier. But Canadian infantrymen, engineers, gunners, and tankers had learned how to fight the Germans in towns and villages, fields and forests; their superiors had also learned how to carry out successful operations at the army, corps, and divisional levels.

Our Finest Hour

The attack began at 0500 on February 8 with a massive artillery barrage. The field, medium, heavy, and super-heavy guns of seven British and Canadian divisions and five Army Groups Royal Artillery were joined by the deadly projectiles of the 1st Canadian Rocket Battery and virtually every anti-aircraft gun, tank gun, medium machine gun, and 4.2-inch mortar along the front. The initial barrage lasted for 160 minutes, then ceased abruptly for 10 minutes as spotters and listeners pinpointed answering German artillery. Those guns were then targeted when the firing resumed. Five hours after the initial barrage, a moving barrage led the first waves of British and Canadian troops toward their assigned objectives. One Calgary Highlander was awed by the spectacle: "I never saw anything like that in my life," William Powell would remember. "The ground just rocked . . . that was the first time I saw those multiple rockets fired. There was a farm and a grove of trees near Wyler . . . that place just disintegrated, all in one smack."[11] Behind the front, heavy bombers attacked and virtually destroyed the road-junction towns of Kleve, Goch, and Emmerich. The fighter bombers and medium bombers of the RAF's 2nd Tactical Air Force and the US Ninth Air Force provided close air support whenever the weather permitted.

Canadian divisions played a small but vital role in Veritable. On the northern, or left, flank the 3rd Division, aptly nicknamed the Water Rats because of the polder fighting they had done during the Scheldt campaign, advanced in amphibious vehicles across flooded fields to take possession (if one could take possession of flooded land) of the area between the Waal River and the Nijmegen-Kleve-Kalkar road, which was one of the main axes of attack. The task of the 2nd Division (especially the 5th Brigade) was to secure the left flank of the 15th (Scottish) Division by taking the fortified towns of Wyler and Den Heuvel. The Calgary Highlanders and the Maisonneuve did that in one day, though the Highlanders suffered heavy casualties when one of their assault companies ran into a well-prepared killing zone sown with mines and covered by German mortars and machine guns. Only quick thinking by battalion Officer Commanding Lieutenant-Colonel Ross Ellis saved the situation when he crawled forward under fire to do his own reconnaissance, then ordered a new fire plan to shoot his reserve company on to its objective and to the rescue of those men who were pinned down.

The 2nd Division got into the fight once again, several days later, when it was called upon to clear a thick forest reserve known as the Moyland Wood, about 8 kilometres southeast of Kleve, but for the most part this first stage of the offensive was borne by the British troops of 30 Corps, who slogged their way forward over muddy and congested roads, through bombed-out or shelled-out villages and, worst of all, through the thick wood of the Reichswald.

Like many of the forests that dotted the Rhineland, the Reichswald was actually a forest reserve. Hiking and bicycle paths ran through it, as did a number of narrow dirt roads. In the forest itself, thick stands of both evergreen and deciduous trees made movement difficult, as did the snow, mud, and wet leaves and pine needles on the forest floor. The Germans had planted mines and booby traps everywhere and had constructed low bunkers to protect their machine-gun and sniper emplacements. Using the paths and narrow roads in the forest was suicide; pushing through the thick brush was almost impossible. Tree bursts from 88s sent deadly shards of wood and shell fragments crashing on the advancing infantry. It was slow going against a determined enemy, but by nightfall of the first day, the Siegfried Line (which ran through the western part of the forest) had been breached and the defending German 84th Division smashed.

At first the Veritable offensive went well. The Germans had not expected the main 21st Army Group attack to come from the Canadian sector. That and a lavish use of air power and artillery gave the British and Canadians a good jumpoff. Within forty-eight hours 30 Corps had captured "virtually all its objectives for Phase One of 'Veritable.'"[12] But no battle ever runs smoothly, and major problems began to beset Montgomery's armies on the third day of the attack. The northward thrust of Simpson's Ninth US Army from the Rur River had to be postponed when the Germans blew up the Rur dams, flooding the river and inundating the land over which the attack was to be launched. For the most part, the German defenders who faced the British and Canadians were not as skilled at war as the well-trained Wehrmacht and SS troops who had fought in Normandy, but the Germans were now defending the very soil of their country and battled with great determination.

On the northern flank of the attack, the rising flood waters made the area between Kleve and the Rhine into a shallow lake; movement was all but impossible. Donald Pearce of the North Nova Scotia Highlanders was one of the Canadians who fought there. He kept a diary of his time on that sodden battlefield:

February 15
Took up new positions on the flooded dykes and farms bordering the Rhine opposite Emmerich. Our duties purely defensive—maintaining constant contact with neighbouring companies and, at night, patrolling the dykes, most of which were submerged . . . we managed our night patrols in row boats, splashing from one flooded farm to another, docking at windows, or at high points along the dykes . . . this was one of the ugliest assignments we have ever been handed—cold, wet, cut off from the rest of the brigade by acres of standing water.[13]

In the centre of the front an early thaw turned the dirt roads into morasses forcing the British armour to use only the few paved roads in the region. To add to their troubles, the destruction of Kleve and Goch by bombing made movement through those towns very difficult. Whereas the British and Canadians had made good progress on the first two days, it took six days more to move an additional 15 kilometres. Veritable was running out of steam well short of its initial objective, the Hochwald.

On the night of February 19–20, the Royal Hamilton Light Infantry and the Essex Scottish of the 4th Brigade were hit hard in their positions on the Goch-Kalkar road by a German battle group scrounged from elements of the 116th Panzer Division. It took almost twenty-four hours of continuous fighting before the German counterattack was thwarted, but the cost was very high. The brigade, and the Queen's Own Cameron Highlanders from the 6th Brigade, suffered some 400 casualties in that twenty-four-hour period. The Essex Scottish alone lost 204 killed, wounded, and missing.

* * * *

On February 23 the US Ninth Army finally launched its long-delayed attack, code-named Grenade. But the Germans continued to maintain a strong presence west of the Rhine, especially in the Hochwald and the area to the east and south of Xanten. To effect a junction with Simpson's forces, Crerar's army would have to move much farther to the southeast than was originally planned. That advance, code-named Blockbuster, as mentioned, was set to start on February 26. This time the 2nd Canadian Corps would play the major role, and the 30th British Corps would guard the right flank of the Canadians.

The Canadian attack plan was simple in conception. The 2nd and

3rd Canadian Infantry Divisions were to take possession of the Hochwald and the smaller Tüschenwald and Balbergerwald that lay south of it and were separated from it by a cleared area about 2 kilometres wide. The rail line from Goch to Wesel ran through that gap. Once in possession of the forest north and south of the gap, the 4th Canadian Armoured Division was to sweep through the gap, south of Xanten and then toward Wesel. Then the two infantry divisions would follow, with the 2nd directed to take Xanten itself. The British 43rd Division would cover the Canadian left flank between the Rhine and the Kalkar-Xanten road.

The Hochwald is on a plateau that slopes up from west to east. Like the Reichswald, it is thickly forested and was easily defended. In front of the Hochwald was the Schlieffen Position, a belt of strong defences backed up by nine German infantry divisions. It stretched from Rees, on the south bank of the Rhine, to Geldern. The line would have to be assaulted by infantry in a dawn attack, because the land to the west of the forest was gently rolling and mostly open farm country; infantry or armour trying to cross that area by daylight would be cut down by machine-gun, mortar, and anti-tank fire from the woods. Just prior to the main attack, a diversionary assault would be launched at a height of land to the west of the forest and south of Kalkar. Simonds hoped this attack would draw the main German strength to the north.

Blockbuster began on schedule, and for a time the diversion worked, but German resistance soon stiffened; the fighting on the edges of the Hochwald and in the forest itself was especially vicious and costly. Crack German paratroopers defended the gap; other German soldiers contested every metre of the forest itself. Although troops of the 2nd and 3rd Divisions pushed through the Schlieffen Position on the first morning of the attack (February 26) to reach the edge of the Hochwald, the forest itself was not cleared for another six days.

To the south, the US Ninth Army continued its attack to the north, threatening the German defenders west of the river with encirclement. On March 3 troops of 30 Corps effected a junction with the Americans south of Üdem. Henceforth, the Germans began to concentrate on getting over the Rhine with as many men and as much equipment as possible. As the German paratroopers prepared to defend Xanten to the last man, their comrades-in-arms started to pull back to the highway and rail bridges at Wesel, and over them to the east bank of the river.

On March 7 came the electrifying news that the First US Army had captured a railway bridge across the Rhine at Remagen, between Bonn and Koblenz, and were pushing straight across the river. The next day the 5th Brigade of the 2nd Canadian Infantry Division began the battle for Xanten, while other troops from the division moved past it to the Alter Rhine, an oxbow lake some 3 kilometres south of the Rhine River.

By March 9 the battle for the Rhineland was almost over. Three British divisions—the 3rd, the Guards Armoured, and the 53rd—were sweeping toward Wesel from Geldern in the west while the Americans closed in from the south. As his troops neared the river, Simonds gave some thought to seizing one or both of the bridges there, despite being warned not to do so by Montgomery. But at 0700 on the morning of March 10, with the bulk of their surviving forces withdrawn to the east bank of the Rhine, the Germans blew up the bridges. By 2200 that night, all resistance west of the river had ceased; now, only the Rhine stood between the Canadians and Germany itself.

Though the Americans in the Remagen bridgehead were driving as many troops and as much equipment across the Rhine as they could, Montgomery characteristically made extensive and careful preparations for a massive assault crossing of the great river in his sector. That operation, code-named Plunder, began at 2100 on March 23. The crossing took place on a wide front between Wesel and Rees. Though the Canadians had played such a key role in clearing the ground for the crossing, Montgomery reserved the bulk of the operation for the British Second Army; only the 9th Canadian Infantry Brigade took part on the extreme left of the bridgehead, though 1st Canadian Parachute Battalion formed part of the British airborne forces that assaulted across the Rhine in the first hours of the attack. The 3rd Canadian Infantry Division crossed the Rhine five days later over a pontoon bridge at Rees, and the 2nd Division followed soon after.

* * * *

The crossing of the Rhine by Montgomery's 21st Army Group was one of the last acts of the war. Victory was now finally in sight. On the eastern front, the Soviet armies, two million strong with more than 40,000 artillery pieces, over 6,000 tanks, and with some 500 ground assault aircraft, stood on the Oder River 65 kilometres from Berlin. In the west, four American armies were across the Rhine; two were driving east into Austria and Czechoslovakia, and two others began to encircle the Ruhr. On the northern flank, Dempsey's Second British Army prepared to assault northeast toward Bremen, Hamburg, and Kiel—Montgomery was especially anxious to beat the Russians to Denmark. Canada's Cinderella army was to be denied the chance to help cut out the heart of the Nazi enemy. Instead, Crerar's forces—united at last with the arrival from Italy of the 1st Corps—were given the less glamorous but no less important task of liberating Holland.

Simonds's 2nd Canadian Corps was initially directed north and east from its Rhine bridgehead to push the Germans out of eastern Holland, secure the Dutch coast along the north sea, and then move into northern Germany on the left flank of the British Second Army. Foulkes's 1st Canadian Corps, which had formally come under Crerar's command on March 15, was to clear the "island" north of the Waal, capture Arnhem, then drive to the Ijsselmeer (once known as the Zuider Zee). Following those operations, it was to swing westward to clear northwestern Holland, including the major cities of Amsterdam, Rotterdam, the Hague, and Utrecht.

The 2nd Corps drive began April 1 with the 2nd Division moving up the central axis of advance to Groningen; the 3rd Division, to the left of the 2nd Division, directed toward Leeuwarden; and the 4th Canadian and 1st Polish Armoured divisions, on the corps' right flank, advancing northeast toward the Dutch-German border. In the words of one Canadian Army report, the objective was to drive the Germans "into the [POW] cage, into the grave, or into the North Sea."[14] The corps swept north, delayed primarily by blown bridges, flooded polders, and mined roads. A German self-propelled artillery (SP) might occasionally lob some shells toward the advancing Canadians before scuttling away or being destroyed. In some of the more important road-junction towns, scattered units of German army or SS tried to delay the advance, but could not. Brigadiers would assign a battalion to clear them out, while the rest of the brigade would sweep around the centre of resistance and continue on the move. The Canadians made little effort to protect their divisional flanks, but then the Germans were hardly in a position to threaten them. On the night of April 7–8, French paratroopers were dropped forward of the advancing corps to seize bridges and other important positions and help clear the way for the Canadians. The Canadian spearheads met up with the paratroopers three days later.

Within two weeks after beginning the advance, the 3rd and 2nd Divisions were in reach of the North Sea. Then, on April 13, the battle for Groningen was joined. A one-time port city dating back to the thirteenth century, Groningen was home to some 100,000 people and was the capital of Groningen province. It was defended by a mixed force of German troops, including naval personnel, and members of the Dutch Nazi party (NSB) and Dutch SS. This last group was made up of Dutchmen who had joined the SS after Holland had been occupied by the Germans. Many had fought on the eastern front. Knowing they would be killed either in battle or at the hands of their compatriots once Holland was liberated, they mounted a fanatical resistance. The fight was long and bloody, and much of the historic town centre was destroyed. The Canadians were handicapped by Simonds's order not to use artillery unless absolutely necessary so as to preserve civilian lives. On April 16, however, the German garrison commander surrendered and resistance died out. Thereafter, the 2nd and 3rd Divisions were trucked rapidly over the Dutch-German border to begin operations aimed at clearing the area between the Küsten Canal and the North Sea, taking the important port of Wilhelmshaven.

The 1st Canadian Corps went into action on April 2 with the 5th Canadian Armoured and the British 49th (West Riding) Divisions under Foulkes's command (the 1st Canadian Infantry Division began operations under Simonds, then switched back to Foulkes). There was some hope that the Germans might withdraw from western Holland because they were now in great danger of being entirely cut off from Germany, but they did not. Accordingly, Foulkes launched his forces at Arnhem from across the Ijssel River. The Germans fought for each house in the already battered town, but by April 14 Arnhem—or what was left of it—was in Canadian hands. As one visiting Canadian officer later wrote, "This city is one of the most saddening sights I have seen in this war, for though the destruction is very far from total every building is smashed in some degree . . . the greater part of it . . . entirely empty of civilians, and the doors of many houses . . . standing open."[15]

On April 11 the 1st Canadian Infantry Division joined the battle by attacking westward across the Ijssel toward Apeldoorn. Then Foulkes sent the 5th Canadian Armoured Division dashing northward toward the Ijsselmeer; it reached Harderwijk, on the edge of the Ijsselmeer, on April 18. Foulkes's corps now stood on a north-south line from the Ijsselmeer to the Neder Rhine, poised for a major assault westward toward Utrecht.

The Germans had about 120,000 troops in western Holland, still a formidable opposition for Foulkes's two division corps. Those Germans were isolated and could have no further impact on the outcome of the war, so there was a good argument to be made to leave them in place. The most important problem facing the Allies in this sector, however, was not a military one: the civilian population of western Holland was slowly starving to death. It was far more important to get food supplies to them than it was to defeat the Germans there. Under Eisenhower's threat to deal harshly with the Nazi occupation authorities and the Dutch puppet government of Arthur Seyss-Inquart if they did not agree to allow food supplies to be sent into their administrative area, an agreement was worked out. The Canadian offensive would be halted and, in turn, the Germans would allow food convoys in to feed the civilian population, and take no further repressive measures against them. On April 22 Montgomery ordered Crerar to cease operations in western Holland; six days later a full truce went into effect. On April 29 Allied aircraft began dropping tons of food supplies into the beleaguered area, and truck convoys rolled in shortly after.

On April 25 Soviet and American troops met at Torgau on the Elbe; Germany had been cut in half. In the north, the Second British Army penetrated to the centre of Bremen, while Crerar's forces prepared to attack Wilhelmshaven. In southern Germany, US forces had swept through to the Czech border. In Berlin, the Soviet army was taking the German capital block by block in some of the bitterest and bloodiest fighting of the war. In Italy, German troops prepared to surrender. SS Chief Heinrich Himmler betrayed Hitler by offering to surrender the German armies on the western front, an offer refused. Hitler prepared for his marriage and for his suicide.

By May 4 Simonds's corps was within 15 kilometres of Wilhelmshaven preparing to enter the city. Just after noon, Crerar received a telephone call from 21st Army Group Headquarters with the news that the Germans were meeting with Montgomery to discuss the surrender of all their forces on the 21st Army Group front. Crerar called Simonds and told him to hold his troops until further word came. That evening the news broke that the Germans on the northern front would definitely surrender the next day. On the evening of May 5, German generals Blaskowitz and Straube formally surrendered the troops under their command to Foulkes and Simonds respectively. The formal surrender of Germany was received by Eisenhower at his headquarters at Reims on May 7, and May 8 was declared "VE-Day." For the Canadians in Europe, the war was over. In the days between the launching of Veritable and the end of the war, they had lost 5,515 officers and men killed, wounded, and missing. The fighting had continued almost to the last; Canadian units were still taking significant casualties right up to the truce.

The war did not end on May 8, 1945. In the Pacific theatre, the Japanese fought on; their army exacted a terrible toll of US Marines on Okinawa, while their kamikaze pilots accounted for the loss of many good ships and good sailors. Canada had played little part in the Pacific war, but prepared to field naval, air, and ground forces that would participate in the looming invasion of Japan. That invasion never took place; Japan surrendered after losing two entire cities—Hiroshima and Nagasaki—to atomic bombs. Those bombs killed tens of thousands of Japanese, but spared tens of thousands of Allied soldiers' lives, including those of the many Canadians who would have been killed in the final battle for Japan.

In the end, they went home—to wives, husbands, lovers, children (some they had never seen), and families. Most rebuilt their lives; all participated in some way in Canada's postwar economic growth and in its maturity and development as a modern nation. Although many chose to join veterans' organizations and some continued to participate in the militia, most wanted nothing more than to put the war behind them. Over the years, however, the memories often flooded back—of men trapped in the engine room of a sinking destroyer, of bombers exploding like fireworks in the dark night skies, of close friends lying with bodies shattered in sodden polderland, or in the hot, dusty wheat fields of Normandy. Just as war begins and ends inside each individual human being, so too does the process of healing. Victory is a concept celebrated by nations, but to warriors from time immemorial to now, it really means only one thing: a chance to go home, the promise of a normal existence, and a good possibility of surviving the next twenty-four hours. As a beleaguered Europe celebrated its liberation from Nazi tyranny, the Canadians turned to home and peace.

AFTERWORD

There were only four Allied nations to field a force of at least one army in western Europe in the fight to destroy Nazi barbarism: the United States, Britain, France, and Canada. That was a distinction Canada earned at a high price—12,579 officers and men killed in action in the Canadian Army and 35,373 wounded, missing, or taken prisoner. Those losses are in addition to the casualty totals for the Royal Canadian Air Force, the Royal Canadian Navy, the Canadian Merchant Marine, and those Canadians serving in other, mostly British, formations. The total for the nation was 42,042 killed in action and 54,414 wounded out of about 1,100,000 Canadians who served in all theatres, including Canada. For a nation of barely more than 12,000,000 people, it was a marvellous achievement. For a country that had begun the war six years earlier with fewer than 10,000 Permanent Force soldiers, sailors, and airmen, it was a miracle.

The Canadian war was as sweeping as it was varied. Canada's fleet of escort vessels, from the lowly corvettes to the thoroughbred Tribal Class destroyers, patrolled from the warm waters of the Caribbean to the freezing ocean on the run to North Russia. Canadian airmen flew transport and supply missions over the jungles of Burma, fighters with the Desert Air Force, and bombing missions in the dark night air over Germany. Canadian soldiers fought and died from Hong Kong to northern Germany. Canadian dead can be found at Commonwealth War Graves

Commission cemeteries from the Japanese home islands to the United Kingdom.

The Canadian war did not begin well. In the time-honoured way of virtually all Canadian governments past and present, those who governed Canada between 1919 and 1939 were not thinking of war, or even military preparation, but of partisan political advantage. As in the First World War, therefore, Canada's soldiers, sailors, and airmen went to war undertrained, poorly equipped, and, for the most part, badly led. They had no choice but to learn on the job. They did learn, but the initial price—Hong Kong, Dieppe, Verrières Ridge, the disastrous convoy battles of late 1942, the heavy losses suffered by No. 6 Group (RCAF) in the first eight months of 1943—was very high.

It is sometimes observed that Canada was rather fortunate in its total casualties in the Second World War as compared to the First World War. In that war there were 60,661 fatal casualties or 9.28 percent of all those who served. In the Second World War, only 3.86 percent of the total who served were killed or died on active service. But the figure is misleading. Although aircrew casualties were much higher than anticipated in the Second World War, especially among bomber crew, nothing destroys lives quicker and in larger numbers than sustained ground combat. In the First World War, the Canadians fought in virtually every major battle on the Western Front from April 1915 on—three years and seven months. In the Second World War, sustained Canadian ground action did not begin until the invasion of Sicily in July 1943 and even then, the bulk of the Canadian ground forces were not committed to action until the summer of 1944 in Normandy. Thus they went in harm's way for a much shorter time. The simple fact is that in several major battles in which Canadians participated in the Second World War, casualty rates were the equal of, and sometimes even higher than, some of the more famous battles of the First World War. Normandy was as ferocious and as costly a battle of attrition as any First World War battle on the Western Front.

There will always be controversy about the quality of the military leaders to whom the nation entrusted its young men and women. It ought not to be surprising that the quality of that leadership was at best uneven on the ground, at sea, and in the air, for at least the first half of the war. With few exceptions, Canada's military leaders were too old, too stuck in old ways, and too simple in their understanding of the demands of modern war to provide the leadership necessary to not only survive but win. Then, however, they either learned how to make modern war or were forced out of their leadership positions. As that happened—as the brutal but inexorable battlefield process of the "survival of the fittest" took hold—the quality of Canada's military leadership improved dramatically. When that happened, and when Canada's forces began to receive the very best in equipment and learned how to fight by doing it and surviving, Canadian performance on the ground, at sea, and in the air improved as well. By the end of the war it was second to none.

The war changed Canada and Canadians in ways that could only be guessed at in 1939. Canadian industry, Canadian science, and Canadian technology made huge leaps in design, production, and sophistication of product. Canadian society was changed by new collective bargaining legislation, mothers' allowances, veterans' benefits, and other government schemes to ensure a fairer distribution of the nation's wealth and a rapid expansion of the Canadian middle class after the war. Canada's people became more aware of the world around them, came to question traditional moral and social values, came to see themselves more as a distinct North American society than they had before the war; they became more inclined to look south, to the United States rather than

Britain, for both social and intellectual leadership, for the new consumer products of postwar society, and for leadership in world affairs.

Although the government of William Lyon Mackenzie King began to come to grips very quickly with the economic, industrial, and consumer issues posed by a major war, Mackenzie King himself eschewed any role in participating in higher strategic decisions in the war, even those directly involving Canadian fighting forces. In mid-war the government began to push for Canadian representation in some of the key joint US-British boards that regulated food production and distribution, munitions production, refugee relief, and other war-related activities; it met with only mixed success, and its determination to have some say over at least the deployment of Canadian forces was weak, hesitant, and ultimately unsuccessful. Much of the time Ottawa's knowledge of Allied war planning was at best imprecise because the British and the Americans closely controlled Canadian access to high Allied strategic decisions. In making policy decisions about what to deploy and where, therefore, Ottawa often acted without full knowledge of the larger picture. That was as true of Hong Kong as it was of the campaign in Italy.

War is a terrible evil. Among all the many species that share this good earth, homo sapiens is the only one that willfully organizes wars for abstract purposes, or for purposeless conquest. War has been part of human history and human civilization from time immemorial and, barring some fundamental change in human nature, it will form part of human activity far into the future. But although war in the abstract is both terrible and evil, human beings have, from time to time, rightly chosen to fight wars rather than allow themselves to be enslaved. That is as it should be. All human beings are destined to die, but slavery is the deserved destiny of no one. As long as evil men and women plot to enslave and murder other men and women, and use the force of arms to achieve their tyrannical goals, there will be a need to take up arms to preserve the basic human right to be free. The Talmud declares, "He who saves one life saves the whole world." Between 1939 and 1945, Canada's soldiers, sailors, and airmen willingly went into harm's way to fight the Axis until it was shattered. In doing so, they helped save the world many times over.

ENDNOTES

Introduction

1. Gordon C. Case, "The Lessons of Munich: Mackenzie King's Campaign to Prepare Canada for War," *Canadian Military Journal*, Winter 2004/5, 73–82.

2. Paul Dickson, *A Thoroughly Canadian General: A Biography of General H.D.G. Crerar* (Toronto: University of Toronto Press, 2007), 100–117.

3. Britton Wade MacDonald, "The Policy of Neglect: The Canadian Militia in the Interwar Years, 1919-1939" (PhD dissertation, Temple University, 2009).

4. John A. English, *The Canadian Army and the Normandy Campaign* (New York: Praeger, 1991), 47.

5. Stephen Harris, *Canadian Brass* (Toronto: University of Toronto Press, 1988), 210–211.

6. David Moule, "The Burns-Simonds Debate Revisited: *The Canadian Defence Quarterly* and the Principles of Mechanized Warfare in the 1930s," *Canadian Military History*, Winter 2013, 17–23; Jamie Hammond, "The Pen Before the Sword: Thinking About 'Mechanization' Between the Wars," *Canadian Military Journal*, Summer 2000, 93–102.

7. David Zimmerman, *The Great Naval Battle of Ottawa* (Toronto: University of Toronto Press, 1989), 10.

8. Marc Milner, *Canada's Navy: The First Century* (Toronto: University of Toronto Press, 1999), 69–75.

9. W.A.B. Douglas, *The Creation of a National Air Force* (Toronto: University of Toronto Press, 1986), 34; William J. McAndrew, "Canadian Defence Planning

Between the Wars: The Royal Canadian Air Force Comes of Age," *Canadian Military History*, Winter 2013, 57–70.

Chapter 1

1. Farley Mowat, *The Regiment* (Toronto: McClelland and Stewart, 1973), 30–31.

2. Quoted in J.L. Granatstein, *The Generals* (Toronto: Stoddart, 1993), 21.

3. Marc Milner, "The Battle of the Atlantic," in *Decisive Campaigns of the Second World War*, ed. John Gooch (London: Routledge, 1990), 45.

4. W.A.B. Douglas, *The Creation of a National Air Force* (Toronto: University of Toronto Press, 1986), 343.

5. Matthew Chapman, "BCATP Revisited: The Evolution of Flight Training in Canada," *Canadian Air Force Journal*, Spring 2011, 35–44.

6. Dave McIntosh, *High Blue Battle* (Toronto: Stoddart, 1990), 38.

Chapter 3

1. C.M. Maltby, "Operations in Hong Kong from 8th to 25th December, 1941," January 1948 (The Maltby Report).

2. Oliver Lindsay, *The Lasting Honour: The Fall of Hong Kong, 1941* (London: Hamish Hamilton, 1978), 96.

3. For a summary of recent discussions on these questions, see Galen Roger Perras, "Defeat Still Cries Aloud for Explanation: Explaining C Force's Dispatch to Hong Kong," *Canadian Military Journal*, Autumn 2011, 37–47.

4. Terry Copp, "The Defence of Hong Kong; December 1941," *Canadian Military History*, Autumn 2001, 5–19; Christopher M. Bell, "'Our Most Exposed Outpost': Hong Kong and British Far Eastern Strategy, 1921–1941," *Journal of Military History*, January 1996, 61–88.

5. Franco David Macri, "C Force to Hong Kong; The Price of Collective Security in China, 1941," *Journal of Military History*, January 2013, 141–171.

6. Paul Dickson, *A Thoroughly Canadian General: A Biography of General H.D.G. Crerar* (Toronto: University of Toronto Press, 2007), 163–173.

7. Copp, "The Defence of Hong Kong."

Chapter 4

1. Denis Whitaker and Shelagh Whitaker, *Dieppe: Tragedy to Triumph* (Toronto: McGraw-Hill Ryerson, 1993), 252.

2. Library and Archives Canada, Historical Section, Army Headquarters, Reports Nos. 89, 98, and 108, "Concerning Operation Jubilee, the Raid on Dieppe," August 19, 1942.

3. Ibid.

4. John English, *The Canadian Army and the Normandy Campaign* (New York: Praeger, 1991), 132.

5. Ibid., 107

6. Nigel Hamilton, *Monty: The Making of a General, 1887-1942* (Toronto: McGraw-Hill, 1981), 546–47.

7. *National Post*, August 19, 2013.

8. Dickson, 199.

9. Ibid., 203.

10. This is the conclusion of Brian Loring Villa in *Unauthorized Action: Mountbatten and the Dieppe Raid* (Toronto: Oxford University Press, 1990).

11. John Nelson Rickard, *The Politics of Command: Lieutenant-General A.G.L. McNaughton and the Canadian Army, 1939–1943* (Toronto: University of Toronto Press, 2010), 63.

12. Hugh G. Henry, "The Calgary Tanks at Dieppe," *Canadian Military History*, vol. 4, p. 99.

13. J. L. Granatstein, *Canada's Army: Waging War and Keeping the Peace* (Toronto: University of Toronto Press, 2002) 208–209.

14. John Mellor, *Forgotten Heroes: The Canadians at Dieppe* (Toronto: Methuen, 1975), 74.

15. C.P. Stacey, *Six Years of War: The Army in Canada, Britain and the Pacific* (Ottawa: The Queen's Printer, 1966), 332.

16. Whitaker, 290.

Chapter 5

1. Randall T. Wakelam, *The Science of Bombing: Operational Research in RAF Bomber Command* (Toronto: University of Toronto Press, 2009), 94.

2. Brereton Greenhous et al., *The Crucible of War, 1939-1945, The Official History of the Royal Canadian Air Force,* Volume III (Toronto: University of Toronto Press, 1994), 44–47.

3. George Beurling and Leslie Roberts, *Malta Spitfire: The Buzz Beurling Story* (Toronto: Penguin Books, 2002).

4. There are literally dozens of works on this subject. Some of the best include *Why The Allies Won* by Richard Overy (New York and London: W.W. Norton & Company, 1995), *Rhetoric and Reality in Air Warfare* by Tami Davis Biddle (Princeton: Princeton University Press, 2002), *Air Power* by Stephen Budiansky (New York: Penguin Books, 2004), *The Bomber War* by Robin Neillands (New York: Overlook Press, 2001), *Lancaster* by Leo McKinstry (London: John Murray, 2009), and *The Wages of Destruction* by Adam Tooze (London: Allen Lane, 2006).

5. McKinstry, *Lancaster.*

6. Ibid.

7. Wakelam and Ehlers Jr.

8. Randall Hansen, *Fire and Fury: The Allied Bombing of Germany, 1942–1945* (Toronto: Anchor Canada, 2008).

9. Williamson Murray, *Luftwaffe* (Baltimore: Nautical & Aviation Publishing, 1985).

Chapter 6

1. Milner, 100–101.

2. Alan Easton, *50 North* (Toronto: Ryerson Press, 1963), 99.

3. Lamb, *The Corvette Navy,* 92.

4. Sarty, location 2036.

5. Milner, 109.

6. Sarty, location 3643.

7. Easton, 139.

8. Milner, 113.

9. Roger Sarty and Jürgen Rohwer, "Intelligence and the Air Forces in the Battle of the Atlantic 1943-1945," *International Commission of Military History*, Helsinki, 1991.

Chapter 7

1. David J. Bercuson, *True Patriot: The Life of Brooke Claxton, 1898-1960* (Toronto: University of Toronto Press, 1990), 111–126.

2. Robert Bothwell and William Kilbourn, *C.D. Howe: A Biography* (Toronto: McCleland and Stewart, 1979) is still the best single source on Howe's role in the war, especially pages 120–179.

3. One of the best histories of the Canadian home front is Jeff Keshen, *Saints, Sinners and Soldiers: Canada's Second World War* (Vancouver: University of British Columbia Press, 2004). See especially Chapter 3, 71–93.

4. J.L. Granatstein, *Canada's War: The Politics of the Mackenzie King Government, 1939–1945* (Toronto: Oxford University Press, 1975), 159–200 still presents the best summary of how the government paid for the war.

5. James Pritchard, *A Bridge of Ships: Canadian Shipbuilding during the Second World War* (Montreal and Kingston: McGill-Queen's University Press, 2011).

6. Daniel Byers, "Mobilizing Canada: The National Resources Mobilization Act, the Department of National Defence, and Compulsory Military Training in Canada, 1940-1945," *Journal of the CHA*, Vol. 7, 175–203.

7. C.P. Stacey, *Arms, Men and Governments: The War Policies of Canada* (Ottawa: Minister of National Defence, 1970), 397–484.

8. Ruth Roach Pierson, *"They're Still Women After All": The Second World War and Canadian Womanhood* (Toronto: McClelland and Stewart, 1986) is still the standard work on the subject of Canadian women in the Second World War.

9. Diane G. Forestell, "The Necessity of Sacrifice for the Nation at War: Women's Labour Force Participation, 1939-1946," *Histoire Sociale—Social History*, November 1989, 333–348.

10. Ruth Pierson, "Woman's Emancipation and the Recruitment of Women into the Canadian Labour Force in World War II," *Historical Papers*, 1976, 141–173.

11. For National Selective Service see Michael D. Stevenson, *Canada's Greatest Wartime Muddle: National Selective Service and the Mobilization of Human Resources during World War II* (Montreal & Kingston: McGill-Queen's University Press, 2001).

12. Keshen, Chapter 5, "(Im)moral Matters," 121–144.

13. See Sarah Kathleen Sewell, "Making the Necessary Sacrifice: The Military's Impact on a City at War, Calgary, 1939–1945" (unpublished master's thesis, University of Calgary, 2013).

14. As one example, see Eswyn Lyster, *Most Excellent Citizens: Canada's War Brides of World War II* (Victoria: Trafford Publishing, 2009).

15. See, for example, Timothy Balzer, "'In Case the Raid is Unsuccessful…' Selling Dieppe to Canadians," *The Canadian Historical Review*, September 2006, 409–430.

16. Wendy Cuthbertson, *Labour Goes to War: The CIO and the Construction of a New Social Order, 1939–1945* (Vancouver: University of British Columbia Press, 2012).

17. Ken Adachi, *The Enemy That Never Was: A History of the Japanese Canadians* (Toronto: McClelland and Stewart, 1991) was one of the first works to tackle this important subject. A more recent study is Aya Fujiwara, "Japanese-Canadian Internally Displaced Persons: Labour Relations and Ethno-Religious Identity in Southern Alberta, 1942–1953," *Labour/Le Travail*, Spring 2012, 63–89.

Chapter 8

1. Stacey, *Arms, Men and Governments*, 182.

2. *Mackenzie King Diary*, entries for July 19 and July 23, 1943.

3. Winston S. Churchill, *The Second World War: Closing the Ring* (Boston: Houghton

Mifflin, 1951), 66-67. C.P. Stacey mistakenly attributed this quote to the preceding volume of Churchill's memoirs, *The Hinge of Fate.*

4. Andrew Roberts, *Masters and Commanders: The Military Geniuses Who Led the West to Victory in WWII* (London: Penguin Books, 2008), 273.

5. Adrian W. Preston, "Canada and the Higher Direction of the Second World War 1939-1945," *Royal United Institute Journal,* published online September 25, 2009. See especially p. 33. See also John Alan English, "Not an Equilateral Triangle: Canada's Strategic Relationship with the United States and Britain, 1939-1945," in J.C. McKercher and Lawrence Aronsen (eds), *The North Atlantic Triangle in a Changing World: Anglo-Canadian Relations, 1902-1956* (Toronto: University of Toronto Press, 1996), 147-183.

6. Preston, 33.

7. Paul Dickson and Michael Roi, *Canadian Civil-Military Relations, 1939-1941: A Case Study in Strategic Dialogue* (Ottawa: Defence R&D Canada, 2011), 25ff.,

8. Ibid., 27.

9. Ibid., 31.

10. Quoted in Stacey, *Arms, Men and Governments,* 159.

11. Quoted in English, "Not an Equilateral Triangle," 164.

12. See David Bercuson and Holger Herwig, *One Christmas in Washington: The Secret Meeting Between Roosevelt and Churchill That Changed the World* (New York: Overlook Press, 2005).

13. See the often overlooked but very important Maurice A. Pope, *Soldiers and Politicians: The Memoirs of Lt.-Gen. Maurice A. Pope, C.B., M.C.* (Toronto: University of Toronto Press, 1962), especially 182–208.

14. Stacey, *Arms, Men and Governments,* 163.

15. Quoted in J.L. Granatstein, *Canada's War: The Politics of the Mackenzie King Government, 1939–1945* (Toronto: Oxford University Press, 1975), 30.

16. The William Lyon Mackenzie King quote is from Abe Roof, "The Empire at Sunset: Production, Finance, and British Grand Strategy 1941–42" (unpublished PhD dissertation, University of Calgary, 2014), 72–73.

17. See Daniel Byers, "Mobilizing Canada: The National Resources Mobilization Act, the Department of National Defence, and Compulsory Military Service in Canada, 1940–1945," *Journal of the Canadian Historical Association*, Vol. 7, Number 1, 1996, 175–203.

18. These discussions and much more on these developments can be found in Granatstein, *Canada's War*, 210ff.

19. Ibid., 211.

20. E.L.M. Burns, *Manpower in the Canadian Army: 1939–1945* (Toronto: Clarke Irwin, 1956) is still the most authoritative study.

21. Christine Leppard, "Fighting as a Colony: 1st Canadian Corps in Italy, 1943–1945" (unpublished PhD dissertation, University of Calgary, 2013), 23

22. Ibid, 7

23. Quotes in Ibid., 49.

24. *King Diary*, June 6, 1944.

25. For a comparison of the way Borden and Mackenzie King led Canada in the two wars, see Tim Cook, *Warlords: Borden, Mackenzie King, and Canada's World Wars* (Toronto: Allen Lane, 2012).

Chapter 9

1. Randall T. Wakelam, *The Science of Bombing: Operational Research in RAF Bomber Command* (Toronto: University of Toronto Press, 2009), 98.

2. Brereton Greenhous et al., *The Crucible of War, 1939–1945* (Toronto: University of Toronto Press, 1994), 764.

3. See McKinstry.

4. Quoted in Ibid., location 4756.

5. See Wakelam, especially 98–100.

6. See Robert S. Ehlers Jr, *Targeting the Third Reich: Air Intelligence and the Allied Bombing Campaigns* (Lawrence: University Press of Kansas, 2009).

7. David Bercuson, "Errant Aircrew: A Case for 'Grey' Insubordination in No. 6 Group

(Royal Canadian Air Force), Bomber Command in 1943," in Howard G. Coombs
(ed.), *The Insubordinate and the Noncompliant: Case Studies of Canadian Mutiny and
Disobedience, 1920 to Present* (Toronto: Dundurn Press, 2008), 125–140.

8.   Allan D. English, *The Cream of the Crop: Canadian Aircrew, 1939-1945* (Montreal
     and Kingston: McGill-Queen's University Press, 1996), 128.

9.   Quoted in L. Nuttal "Canadianization and the No. 6 Bomber Group, RCAF,"
     (unpublished PhD dissertation, University of Calgary, 1990), 265.

10. Quoted in S. Dunmore and W. Carter, *Reap the Whirlwind: The Untold Story of 6
     Group* (Toronto: McClelland and Stewart, 1991), 129.

11. Quoted in John Terraine, *The Right of the Line: The Royal Air Force in the European
     War* (London: Hodder and Stoughton, 1985), 548.

12. Quoted in Max Hastings, *Bomber Command* (London: Pan Books, 1981), 147.

13. Randall Hansen, *Fire and Fury: The Allied Bombing of Germany, 1942–1945*
     (Toronto: Anchor Canada, 2008).

14. Adam Tooze, *The Wages of Destruction* (London: Allen Lane, 2006), 648.

15. Hansen, 271.

16. Martin Middlebrook, *The Peenemünde Raid* (London: Allen Lane, 1982), 125.

17. McKinstry, location 7689.

18. Gordon W. Webb, "Nuremburg—A Night to Remember" in *Airforce Magazine*,
     March 1982, 12.

19. Ibid.

Chapter 10

1.   Richard Goette, "The RCAF and the Creation of an RCN Air Arm: A Study of
     the Command and Control of Maritime Air Assets," *Canadian Military History*,
     Volume 13, Number 3, 5–13.

2.   Dan van der Vat, *The Atlantic Campaign* (New York: Harper and Row, 1988), 315.

3.   All these issues are dealt with in great detail in W.A.B. Douglas et al., *No Higher
     Purpose: The Official History of the Royal Canadian Navy in the Second World War*,

1939–1943, Volume II, Part 1 (St. Catharines: Vanwell Publishing, 2002). See especially 579–594.

4.   Ibid., 593–594.

5.   Milner, *The RCN*, 122.

6.   Peter Cremer, *U-boat Commander* (Annapolis: Naval Institute Press, 1984), 147.

7.   Milner, *The RCN*, 125.

8.   Quoted in Tony German, *The Sea Is at Our Gates* (Toronto: McClelland and Stewart, 1990), 148.

9.   Richard Oliver Mayne, "Bypassing the Chain of Command: The Political Origins of the RCN's Equipment Crisis of 1943," *Canadian Military History*, Summer 2000, 7–22. See also "A Political Execution: Expediency and the Firing of Vice Admiral Percy W. Nelles, 1943–44," in *The American Review of Canadian Studies* (Winter 1999), 557–592, by the same author.

Chapter 11

1.   Quoted in W.J. McAndrew, "Fire or Movement? Canadian Tactical Doctrine, Sicily—1943," in *Military Affairs*, July 1987, 143.

2.   Strome Galloway, *A Regiment at War: The Story of the Royal Canadian Regiment, 1939–1945* (Privately printed, 1979), 81.

3.   Quoted in Grant N. Barry, "Beyond Consensus: 1st Canadian Infantry Division at Agira, Sicily, 24-29 July 1943," in *Canadian Military History*, Spring 2010, 44.

4.   See, for example, Lee Windsor, "The Eyes of All Fixed on Sicily": Canada's Unexpected Victory, 1943," in *Canadian Military History*, Summer 2013, 4–34. The special issue marking the 70th anniversary of the Sicilian campaign contains several other articles on the campaign as does the issue of *Canadian Military History* published in the summer of 2003. Biographies of Generals McNaughton, Crerar, and Hoffmeister have added much to our knowledge of Sicily as have regimental histories of many of the battalions and regiments that fought there. Mark Zuehlke's *Operation Husky: The*

Canadian Invasion of Sicily, July 10–August 7, 1943 (Toronto: Douglas & McIntyre, 2008) is the latest full history of the Canadian campaign there.

5. See, for example, J.L. Granatstein, *Canada's Army: Waging War and Keeping the Peace*, 213.

6. Alex Danchev and Daniel Todman (eds), *War Diaries: 1939–1945: Field Marshal Lord Alan Brooke* (London: Weidenfeld & Nicolson, 2001), 329.

7. *King Diary*, February 5, 1943.

8. Ibid., March 17, 1943.

9. John Nelson Rickard, *The Politics of Command: Lieutenant-General A.G.L. McNaughton and the Canadian Army, 1939–1943* (Toronto: University of Toronto Press, 2010), 74–77.

10. *King Diary*, April 24, 1943.

11. Farley Mowat, *And No Birds Sang* (Toronto: Seal Books, 1980), 52.

12. Peter Stursberg, *The Sound of War* (Toronto: University of Toronto Press, 1993), 100.

13. Carlo D'Este, *World War II in the Mediterranean* (Chapel Hill: University of North Carolina Press, 1990) 63.

14. Quoted in W. McAndrew, "Fire or Movement? Canadian Tactical Doctrine, Sicily—1943," *Military Affairs*, Summer 1987, 140–145. This is an excellent short piece that explains much about Simonds and Canadian tactical doctrine generally.

15. Barry, "Beyond Consensus," 41–43.

16. Strome Galloway, *A Regiment at War*, 85.

Chapter 12

1. Charles Comfort, *Artist at War* (Toronto: Ryerson, 1956),104–105.

2. G.C. Case, "Trial by Fire: Major-General Chris Vokes at the Battles of the Moro River and Ortona, December 1943," in *Canadian Military History*, Summer 2007, 13–28.

3. Quoted in Mark Zuehlke, *Ortona: Canada's Epic World War II Battle* (Toronto: Stoddart, 1999), 289

4. One notable exception is Rick Atkinson, *The Day of Battle: The War in Sicily and Italy, 1943 -1944* (New York: Henry Holt and Company, 2007).

5. Ian Gooderson, "Assimilating Urban Battle Experience—the Canadians at Ortona," *Canadian Military Journal*, Winter 2007-2008, 64–73.

6. Comfort, 21.

7. Lee A. Windsor, "'Boforce'" 1st Canadian Infantry Division Operations in Support of the Salerno Bridgehead, Italy, 1943," *Canadian Military History*, Volume IV, No. 2, 1995, 51–60.

8. Quoted in Case, 15.

9. Chris Vokes, *Vokes: My Story* (Ottawa: Gallery Books, 1985), 123.

10. Farley Mowat, *And No Birds Sang*, 154.

11. Atkinson, Kindle Edition, 298, Location 5993.

12. Christine Leppard, "Fighting as a Colony? 1st Canadian Corps in Italy, 1943–1945," (unpublished PhD dissertation, University of Calgary), 2013.

13. See Dickson, 218–225; Rickard, 187–207.

14. *Mackenzie King Diary*, August 31, 1943.

15. Ibid., August 10, 1943

16. Rickard, 150–167.

17. Stacey, *Arms, Men and Governments*, 246–247.

18. Brereton Greenhous, "Would it not have been better to bypass Ortona completely...? A Canadian Christmas, 1943," *Canadian Defence Quarterly*, April, 1989, 55.

19. Ibid.

20. Case, 24.

21. Ibid., 19.

22. Farley Mowat, 154.

23. Strome Galloway, *A Regiment at War*, 109.

24. Quoted in Shaun R.G. Brown, "'The Rock of Accomplishment': The Loyal Edmonton Regiment at Ortona," *Canadian Military History*, Vol. 2, No. 2, 16.

25. The most recent analysis of Canadian street fighting in Ortona is by Ian Gooderson. The now-standard narrative of the battle is Mark Zuehlkes, *Ortona*.

26. Comfort, *Artist at War*, 109.

Chapter 13

1. William McAndrew, "Fifth Canadian Armoured Division: Introduction to Battle," in *Canadian Military History*, Volume 2, No. 2, 45.

2. The best source remains Terry Copp and Bill McAndrew, *Battle Exhaustion: Soldiers and Psychiatrists in the Canadian Army, 1939-1945* (Montreal: McGill-Queen's University Press, 1990).

3. Quoted in Carlo D'Este, *Fatal Decision: Anzio and the battle for Rome* (New York: HarperCollins, 1991), 347

4. Uvic Archives, Roy Collection, interview with Cameron Ware.

5. William J. McAndrew, "Fifth Canadian Armoured Division: Introduction to Battle," *Canadian Military History*, Vol. 2, No. 2, 1993, 62.

6. J.P. Johnston, "E.L.M. Burns—A Crisis of Command," in *Canadian Military Journal*, Spring 2006, 53.

7. Ibid.

8. Leppard, 218.

9. Ibid., 218-219.

10. Quoted in Douglas E. Delaney, *The Soldier's General: Bert Hoffmeister at War* (Vancouver: University of British Columbia Press, 2005), 180-181.

11. Ibid., 179-191.

12. D'Este, *World War II in the Mediterranean*, 185.

13. William J. McAndrew, "Eighth Army at the Gothic Line: The Dog Fight," *Journal of the Royal United Service Institute*, June 1986, 62.

14. Mowat, *The Regiment*, 227.

15. Johnston, 54.

16. Brian Horrocks, *Corps Commander* (London: Sidgwick and Jackson, 1977), xiii.

Chapter 14

1. Charles Cromwell Martin (with Roy Whitsed), *Battle Diary: From D-Day and Normandy to the Zuider Zee and VE* (Toronto: Dundurn Press, 1994), 1–6.

2. "The Technique of the Assault: The Canadian Army on D-Day; after action reports by commanders," *Canadian Military History*, Summer 2005, Comments by Major-General R.F.L. Keller, 58.

3. Ibid.

4. Ibid., 60

5. Murray Peden, *A Thousand Shall Fall* (Stittsville, ON: Canada's Wings, 1979), 383.

6. Paul Johnston, "Tactical Air Power Controversies in Normandy: A Question of Doctrine," *Canadian Military History*, Spring 2000, 59–71.

7. Robert Vogel, "Tactical Air Power in Normandy: Some Thoughts on the Interdiction Plan," *Canadian Military History*, Vol. 3, No. 1, 1994, 37–47.

8. Quoted in Michael Whitby, "'There Must Be No Holes in Our Sweeping: the 31st Canadian Minesweeping Flotilla on D-Day," *Canadian Military History*, Vol. 3, No. 1, 1994.

9. Bernd Horn and Michel Wyczynski, "A Most Irrevocable Step: Canadian Paratroopers on D-Day; The First 24 Hours, 5-6 June, 1944," *Canadian Military History*, Summer 2004, 15–16.

10. Ibid., 28.

11. Quote is from the regimental war diary, cited in Reginald H. Roy, *1944: The Canadians in Normandy* (Toronto: Macmillan of Canada, 1984), 13.

12. Terry Copp and Robert Vogel, *Maple Leaf Route: Caen* (Alma, ON: Maple Leaf Route, 1983), 42.

13. Quoted in Wesley M. Alkenbrack, "First Deployment of the 14th Field Regiment, RCA: D-Day—Bernières-sur-Mer—6 June 1944," *Canadian Military History*, Autumn 2007, 65.

14. Martin, *Battle Diary*, 14.

15. Terry Copp, *Fields of Fire: The Canadians in Normandy* (Toronto: University of Toronto Press, 2003), 55–56.

16. Craig W.H. Luther, *Blood and Honor* (San Jose: R.J. Bender Publishing, 1987), 133.

17. Ibid., 65–67.

18. This account of the battles between 7th Canadian Infantry Brigade and 12th SS Panzer Division is based on Copp, *Fields of Fire*, 67–76; Marc Milner, "The Guns of Bretteville: 13th Field Regiment, RCA, and the Defence of Bretteville-l'Orgueilleuse, 7–10 June, 1944," *Canadian Military History*, Autumn 2007, 5–24; Oliver Haller, "The Defeat of the 12th SS: 7-10 June, 1944," *Canadian Military History*, Vol. 3, No. 1, 1994, 9–25.

19. Martin, *Battle Diary*, 10.

20. Marc Milner, "Reflections on Caen, Bocage and the Gap: A Naval Historian's Critique of the Normandy Campaign," *Canadian Military History*, Spring 1998, 13.

Chapter 15

1. Quoted in D.J. Bercuson, *Battalion of Heroes: The Calgary Highlanders in World War Two* (Calgary: Calgary Highlanders Regimental Funds Foundation, 1994), 124.

2. Given the importance of the Normandy campaign in the Allied victory, it is not surprising that there is a long list of Canadian books and articles and sections of books and articles about the Canadian Army's performance in Normandy. Some of the best and more recent of these include Copp, *Fields of Fire*, Brian A. Reid, *No Holding Back: Operation Totalize; Normandy, August 1944* (Toronto: Robin Brass Studio, 2005); Roman Johann Jarymowycz, *Tank Tactics from Normandy to Lorraine* (London: Lynne Rienner Publishers, 2001); Russell A. Hart, *Clash of Arms: How the Allies Won in Normandy* (London: Lynne Rienner Publishers, 2001); Marc Milner, *D-Day to Carpiquet: The North Shore Regiment and the Liberation of Europe* (Fredericton: Goose Lane Editions, 2007); Angelo N. Caravaggio, "Commanding the Green Centre Line in Normandy: A Case Study of Division Command in the Second World War," (unpublished PhD dissertation, Wilfrid Laurier University, 2009), Jody Perrun, "Best Laid Plans: Guy Simonds and Operation Totalize, 7–10 August, 1944," *The Journal of Military History*, January 2003, 137-173.

3. Quoted in Terry Copp and Robert Vogel, *Maple Leaf Route: Caen* (Alma, Ontario: Maple Leaf Route, 1983), 98.

4. Martin, *Battle Diary*, 37.

5. John English, *The Canadian Army and the Normandy Campaign* (New York: Praeger, 1991), 217.

6. Copp, *Fields of Fire*, 101.

7. Dickson, 288.

8. On Simonds, see Terry Copp, *Guy Simonds and the Art of Command* (Kingston: Canadian Defence Academy Press, 2007).

9. A good summary of the issues involved in planning and executing the attack can be found in Terry Copp, "Operation 'Spring': An Historian's View," *Canadian Military History*, Winter/Spring 2003, 63–70.

10. Russell F. Weigley, *Eisenhower's Lieutenants*, Vol. 1 (Bloomington: Indiana University Press, 1981), 241.

11. Copp, *Fields of Fire*, 194

12. Including myself in an earlier version of this book. For more recent and more accurate literature on this subject see Copp, *Fields of Fire*, 187–252; Brian A Reid, *No Holding Back: Operation Totalize; Normandy, August 1944*, 220–249, 333–394; Jody Perrun, "Guy Simonds and Operation Totalize, 7–10 August, 1944" in *The Journal of Military History*, January 2003, 137–173.

13. Mike Bechtold, "Lost in Normandy: The Odyssey of Worthington Force, 9 August, 1944," in *Canadian Military History*, Spring 2010, 5–24.

14. George Kitching, *Mud and Green Fields* (Langley, BC: Battleline Books, 1985), 219.

Chapter 16

1. Tooze, 650–651.

2. W. Denis Whitaker and Shelagh Whitaker, *Tug of War* (Toronto: Stoddart, 1984), 154.

3. Bercuson, *Battalion of Heroes*, 169–170.

4. Donald Pearce, *Journal of a War* (Toronto: Macmillan of Canada, 1965), 76.

5. Mike Bechtold, "Air Support in the Breskins Pocket: The Case of First Canadian Army and 84 Group Royal Air Force," *Canadian Military History*, Vol. 3, No. 2, 53–62.

6. Martin, 97.

7. Quoted in Terry Copp, *Cinderella Army: The Canadians in Northwest Europe; 1944-1945* (Toronto: University of Toronto Press, 2006), 139.

8. Stacey, *The Victory Campaign*, 390.

9. B.L. Montgomery, *The Memoirs of Field Marshal Montgomery* (London: Collins, 1958), 297.

Chapter 17

1. William Allister, *Where Life and Death Hold Hands* (Toronto: Stoddart, 1989), 218.

2. Robin Neillands, *The Bomber War: The Allied Air Offensive Against Nazi Germany* (Woodstock: The Overlook Press, 2001), 323-350; Sebastian Cox, Head of Air Historical Branch (RAF) to the author, October 4, 2011.

3. Quoted in Frederick Taylor, *Dresden: Tuesday, February 13, 1945* (New York: HarperCollins, 2004), 181.

4. Ibid., 183.

5. Ibid., 191.

6. Dunmore and Carter, 344.

7. McKinstry, *Lancaster*, 463.

8. Ibid., 462–475. Taylor also deals extensively with the historiography of Dresden.

9. Possibly the best recent example of such scholarship is Randall Hansen, *Fire and Fury: The Allied Bombing of Germany, 1942-1945* (Toronto: Anchor Books, 2008).

10. *Globe and Mail*, 23 March, 1945.

11. Bercuson, *Battalion of Heroes*, 202.

12. Stacey, *The Victory Campaign*.

13. Donald Pearce, *Journal of a War: North-West Europe, 1944-1945* (Toronto: Macmillan of Canada, 1965), 140.

14. Stacey, *The Canadian Army: 1939-1945* (Ottawa: The King's Printer, 1948), 265.

15. Stacey, *The Victory Campaign*, 474.

BIBLIOGRAPHY OF SOURCES CITED

Books

Adachi, Ken. *The Enemy That Never Was: A History of the Japanese Canadians*. Toronto: McClelland and Stewart, 1991.

Allister, William. *Where Life and Death Hold Hands*. Toronto: Stoddart, 1989.

Atkinson, Rick. *The Day of Battle: The War in Sicily and Italy, 1943–1944*. New York: Henry Holt and Company, 2007.

Avery, Donald H. *The Science of War: Canadian Scientists and Allied Military Technology during the Second World War*. Toronto: University of Toronto Press, 1998.

Bercuson, David J. *True Patriot: The Life of Brooke Claxton, 1898–1960*. Toronto: University of Toronto Press, 1990.

Bercuson, David J. *Battalion of Heroes: The Calgary Highlanders in World War Two*. Calgary: Calgary Highlanders Regimental Funds Foundation, 1994.

Bercuson, David J. and Holger Herwig. *One Christmas in Washington: The Secret Meeting Between Roosevelt and Churchill That Changed the World*. New York: Overlook Press, 2005.

Berger, Monty, and Brian Jeffrey Street. *Invasions Without Tears*. Toronto: University of Toronto Press, 1994.

Beurling, George, and Leslie Roberts. *Malta Spitfire: The Buzz Beurling Story*. Toronto: Penguin Books, 2002.

Biddle, Tami David. *Rhetoric and Reality in Air Warfare*. Princeton: Princeton University Press, 2002.

Bothwell, Robert, and William Kilbourn. *C.D. Howe: A Biography*. Toronto: McClelland and Stewart, 1979.

Budiansky, Stephen. *Air Power.* New York: Penguin Books, 2004.

Burns, E.L.M. *Manpower in the Canadian Army, 1939–1945.* Toronto: Clarke Irwin, 1956.

Churchill, Winston S. *The Second World War: Closing the Ring.* Boston: Houghton Mifflin, 1951.

Comfort, Charles. *Artist at War.* Toronto: Ryerson, 1956.

Cook, Tim. *Warlords: Borden, Mackenzie King, and Canada's World Wars.* Toronto: Allen Lane, 2012.

Copp, Terry. *Fields of Fire: The Canadians in Normandy.* Toronto: University of Toronto Press, 2003.

Copp, Terry. *Cinderella Army: The Canadians in Northwest Europe, 1944–1945.* Toronto: University of Toronto Press, 2006.

Copp, Terry. *Guy Simonds and the Art of Command.* Kingston: Canadian Defence Academy Press, 2007.

Copp, Terry and Robert Vogel. *Maple Leaf Route: Caen.* Alma, ON: Maple Leaf Route, 1983.

Copp, Terry, and Bill McAndrew. *Battle Exhaustion: Soldiers and Psychiatrists in the Canadian Army, 1939–1945.* Montreal: McGill-Queen's University Press, 1990.

Cuthbertson, Wendy. *Labour Goes to War: The CIO and the Construction of a New Social Order, 1939–1945.* Vancouver: University of British Columbia Press, 2012.

Danchev, Alex, and Daniel Todman, eds. *War Diaries: 1939–1945: Field Marshal Lord Alan Brooke.* London: Weidenfeld & Nicolson, 2001.

Delaney, Douglas E. *The Soldier's General: Bert Hoffmeister at War.* Vancouver: University of British Columbia Press, 2005.

D'Este, Carlo. *World War II in the Mediterranean.* Chapel Hill, NC: Algonquin Books, 1990.

D'Este, Carlo. *Fatal Decision: Anzio and the Battle for Rome.* New York: HarperCollins, 1991.

Dickson, Paul. *A Thoroughly Canadian General: A Biography of General H.D.G. Crerar.* Toronto: University of Toronto Press, 2007.

Dickson, Paul, and Michael Roi. *Canadian Civil-Military Relations, 1939–1941: A Case Study in Strategic Dialogue.* Ottawa: Defence R&D Canada, 2011.

Douglas, W.A.B. *The Creation of a National Air Force.* Toronto: University of Toronto Press, 1986.

Douglas, W.A.B., Roger Sarty, and Michael Whitby. *No Higher Purpose: The Official History of the Royal Canadian Navy in the Second World War, 1939–1943*, Volume II, Part 1. St. Catharines: Vanwell Publishing, 2002.

Dunmore, S., and W. Carter. *Reap the Whirlwind: The Untold Story of 6 Group.* Toronto: McClelland and Stewart, 1991.

Easton, Alan. *50 North.* Toronto: Ryerson, 1963.

Ehlers Jr., Robert. *Targeting the Third Reich: Air Intelligence and the Allied Bombing Campaigns.* Lawrence, KS: University Press of Kansas, 2009.

English, Allan D. *The Cream of the Crop: Canadian Aircrew, 1939–1945.* Montreal and Kingston: McGill-Queen's University Press, 1996.

English, John A. *The Canadian Army and the Normandy Campaign.* New York: Praeger, 1991.

Evans, Gary. *John Grierson and the National Film Board: The Politics of Wartime Propaganda.* Toronto: University of Toronto Press, 1984.

Frankland, A. Noble, and Charles Kingsley Webster. *The Strategic Air Offensive Against Germany.* 4 volumes. London: Her Majesty's Stationery Office, 1961.

Galloway, Strome. *A Regiment at War: The Story of the Royal Canadian Regiment, 1939–1945.* Privately printed, 1979.

German, Tony. *The Sea Is at Our Gates.* Toronto: McClelland and Stewart, 1990.

Graham, Dominick. *The Price of Command.* Toronto: Stoddart, 1993.

Granatstein, J.L. *The Generals: The Canadian Army's Senior Commanders in the Second World War.* Toronto: Stoddart, 1993.

Granatstein, J.L. *Canada's Army: Waging War and Keeping the Peace.* Toronto: University of Toronto Press, 2002.

Greenhous, Brereton, Steven Harris, William Johnston, and William Rawling. *The Crucible* of War, 1939–1945: The Official History of the Royal Canadian Air Force, Volume III. Toronto: University of Toronto Press, 1994.

Hamilton, Nigel. *Monty: The Making of a General, 1887–1942*. Toronto: Fleet Books, 1982.

Hansen, Randall. *Fire and Fury: The Allied Bombing of Germany, 1942–1945*. Toronto: Anchor Canada, 2008.

Harris, Stephen. *Canadian Brass: The Making of a Professional Army, 1860–1939*. Toronto: University of Toronto Press, 1988.

Hart, Russell A. *Clash of Arms: How the Allies Won in Normandy*. London: Lynne Rienner Publishers, 2001.

Harvey, J. Douglas. *Boys, Bombs and Brussel Sprouts*. Toronto: McClelland and Stewart, 1981.

Hastings, Max. *Bomber Command*. London: Pan Books, 1981.

Horrocks, Brian. *Corps Commander*. London: Sidgwick & Jackson Ltd., 1977.

Jarymowycz, Roman Johann. *Tank Tactics from Normandy to Lorraine*. London: Lynne Rienner Publishers, 2001.

Keshen, Jeff. *Saints, Sinners and Soldiers: Canada's Second World War*. Vancouver: University of British Columbia Press, 2004.

Kitching, George. *Mud and Green Fields: The Memoirs of Major-General George Kitching*. Langley, BC.: Vanwell Publishing, 1985.

Lamb, James. *The Corvette Navy: True Stories from Canada's Atlantic War*. Toronto: Signet, 1977.

Lindsay, Oliver. *The Lasting Honour: The Fall of Hong Kong, 1941*. London: Hamish Hamilton, 1978.

Luther, Craig W.H. *Blood and Honor: The 12th SS Panzer Division*. San Jose, CA: R.J. Bender Publishing, 1987.

Lyster, Eswyn. *Most Excellent Citizens: Canada's War Brides of World War II*. Victoria, BC: Trafford Publishing, 2009.

Martin, Charles Cromwell (with Roy Whitsed). *Battle Diary: From D-Day and Normandy to the Zuider Zee and VE*. Toronto: Dundurn Press, 1994.

McIntosh, Dave, ed. *High Blue Battle: The War Diary of No. 1 (401) Fighter Squadron.* Toronto: Stoddart, 1990.

McKinstry, Leo. *Lancaster: The Second World War's Greatest Bomber.* London: John Murray, 2009.

Mellor, John. *Forgotten Heroes: The Canadians at Dieppe.* Toronto: Methuen, 1975.

Middlebrook, Martin. *The Peenemünde Raid.* London: Allen Lane, 1982.

Milner, Marc. *North Atlantic Run: The Royal Canadian Navy and the Battle for the Convoys.* Toronto: University of Toronto Press, 1985.

Milner, Marc. *Canada's Navy: The First Century.* Toronto: University of Toronto Press, 1999.

Milner, Marc. *D-Day to Carpiquet: The North Shore Regiment and the Liberation of Europe.* Fredericton, NB: Goose Lane Editions, 2007.

Montgomery, B.L. *The Memoirs of Field Marshal Montgomery.* London: Collins, 1958.

Mowat, Farley. *The Regiment.* Toronto: McClelland and Stewart, 1973.

Mowat, Farley. *And No Birds Sang.* Toronto: Seal Books, 1980.

Murray, Williamson. *Luftwaffe.* Baltimore: Nautical & Aviation Publishing, 1985.

Neillands, Robin. *The Bomber War: The Allied Air Offensive against Nazi Germany.* New York: Overlook Press, 2001.

Overy, Richard. *Why The Allies Won.* New York and London: W.W. Norton & Company, 1995.

Pearce, Donald. *Journal of a War: North-West Europe, 1944–1945.* Toronto: Macmillan of Canada, 1965.

Peden, Murray. *A Thousand Shall Fall.* Stittsville, ON: Canada's Wings, 1979.

Pierson, Ruth Roach. *"They're Still Women After All": The Second World War and Canadian Womanhood.* Toronto: McClelland and Stewart, 1986.

Pope, Maurice A. *Soldiers and Politicians: The Memoirs of Lt.-Gen. Maurice A. Pope, C.B., M.C.* Toronto: University of Toronto Press, 1962.

Pritchard, James. *A Bridge of Ships: Canadian Shipbuilding during the Second World War.* Montreal & Kingston: McGill-Queen's University Press, 2011.

Reid, Brian A. *No Holding Back: Operation Totalize: Normandy, August 1944.* Toronto: Robin Brass Studio, 2005.

Rickard, John Nelson. *The Politics of Command: Lieutenant-General A.G.L. McNaughton and the Canadian Army, 1939–1943.* Toronto: University of Toronto Press, 2010.

Roberts, Andrew. *Masters and Commanders; The Military Geniuses Who Led the West to Victory in WWII.* London: Penguin Books, 2008.

Roy, Reg. *1944: The Canadians in Normandy.* Toronto: Macmillan of Canada, 1984.

Sarty, Roger. *War in the St. Lawrence: The Forgotten U-Boat Battles on Canada's Shores.* Toronto: Allen Lane, 2012.

Stacey, C.P. *The Canadian Army: 1939–1945.* Ottawa: The King's Printer, 1948.

Stacey, C.P. *The Victory Campaign.* Ottawa: The Queen's Printer, 1960.

Stacey, C.P. *Six Years of War: The Army in Canada, Britain and the Pacific.* Ottawa: The Queen's Printer, 1966.

Stacey, C.P. *Arms, Men and Governments: The War Policies of Canada.* Ottawa: Minister of National Defence, 1970.

Stevens, G.R. *Princess Patricia's Canadian Light Infantry: 1919–1957.* Vol. III. Griesbach, AB: Historical Committee of the Regiment, 1959.

Stevenson, Michael D. *Canada's Greatest Wartime Muddle: National Selective Service and the Mobilization of Human Resources during World War II.* Montreal & Kingston: McGill-Queen's University Press, 2001.

Stursburg, Peter. *The Sound of War.* Toronto: University of Toronto Press, 1993.

Taylor, Frederick. *Dresden: Tuesday, February 13, 1945.* New York: HarperCollins, 2004.

Terraine, John. *The Right of the Line: The Royal Air Force in the European War.* London: Hodder and Stoughton, 1985.

Thompson, Walter. *Lancaster to Berlin.* Toronto: Totem, 1987.

Tooze, Adam. *The Wages of Destruction.* London: Allen Lane, 2006.

van der Vat, Dan. *The Atlantic Campaign.* New York: Harper and Row, 1988.

Villa, Brian Loring. *Unauthorized Action: Mountbatten and the Dieppe Raid.* Toronto: Oxford University Press, 1990.

Vokes, Chris. *Vokes: My Story.* Ottawa: Gallery Books, 1985.

Wakelam, Randall T. *The Science of Bombing: Operational Research in RAF Bomber Command.* Toronto: University of Toronto Press, 2009.

Weigley, Russell F. *Eisenhower's Lieutenants.* Vol. 1. Bloomington: Indiana University Press, 1981.

Whitaker, W. Denis, and Shelagh Whitaker. *Tug of War.* Toronto: Stoddart, 1984.

Zimmerman, David. *The Great Naval Battle of Ottawa.* Toronto: University of Toronto Press, 1989.

Zuehlke, Mark. *Ortona: Canada's Epic World War II Battle..* Toronto: Stoddart, 1999.

Zuehlke, Mark. *Operation Husky: The Canadian Invasion of Sicily, July 10–August 7, 1943.* Toronto: Douglas & McIntyre, 2008.

Chapters in Books

Bercuson, David. "Errant Aircrew: A Case for 'Grey' Insubordination in No. 6 Group (Royal Canadian Air Force), Bomber Command in 1943." In *The Insubordinate and the Noncompliant: Case Studies of Canadian Mutiny and Disobedience, 1920 to Present,* edited by Howard G. Coombs. Toronto: Dundurn Press, 2008.

English, John Alan. "Not an Equilateral Triangle: Canada's Strategic Relationship with the United States and Britain, 1939–1945." In *The North Atlantic Triangle in a Changing World: Anglo-Canadian Relations, 1902–1956,* edited by J.C. McKercher and Lawrence Aronsen. Toronto: University of Toronto Press, 1996.

Milner, Marc. "The Battle of the Atlantic." In *Decisive Campaigns of the Second World War,* edited by John Gooch. London: Frank Cass, 1990.

Articles

Alkenbrack, Wesley M. "First Deployment of the 14th Field Regiment, RCA; D-Day—Bernières-sur-Mer—6 June 1944." *Canadian Military History* 16, no. 4 (Autumn 2007): pp. 65–72.

Balzer, Timothy. "'In Case the Raid Is Unsuccessful...' Selling Dieppe to Canadians." *The Canadian Historical Review* 87, no. 3 (September 2006): pp. 409–430.

Barry, Grant N. "Beyond Consensus: 1st Canadian Infantry Division at Agira, Sicily, 24–29 July 1943." *Canadian Military History* 19, no. 2 (Spring 2010).

Bechtold, Mike. "Air Support in the Breskens Pocket: The Case of First Canadian Army and 84 Group Royal Air Force." *Canadian Military History* 3, no. 2 (Autumn 1994): pp. 53–62.

Bechtold, Mike. "Lost in Normandy: The Odyssey of Worthington Force, 9 August, 1944." *Canadian Military History* 19, no. 2 (Spring 2010): pp. 5–24.

Bell, Christopher M. "'Our Most Exposed Outpost': Hong Kong and British Far Eastern Strategy, 1921–1941." *Journal of Military History* 60, no. 1 (January 1996): pp. 61–88.

Brown, Shaun R.G. "'The Rock of Accomplishment': The Loyal Edmonton Regiment at Ortona." *Canadian Military History* 2, no. 2 (Autumn 1993): pp. 10–23.

Byers, Daniel. "Mobilizing Canada: The National Resources Mobilization Act, the Department of National Defence, and Compulsory Military Service in Canada, 1940–1945." *Journal of the Canadian Historical Association* 7, no. 1 (1996): pp. 175–203.

Canadian Military Commanders. "The Technique of the Assault: The Canadian Army on D-Day: After-Action Reports by Commanders." *Canadian Military History* 14, no. 3 (Summer 2005): pp. 57–70. Comments by Major-General R.F.L. Keller.

Case, Gordon C. "The Lessons of Munich: Mackenzie King's Campaign to Prepare Canada for War." *Canadian Military Journal* 5, no. 4 (Winter 2004/5): pp. 73–82.

Case, G.C. "Trial by Fire: Major-General Chris Vokes at the Battles of the Moro River and Ortona, December 1943." *Canadian Military History* 16, no. 3 (Summer 2007): pp. 13–28.

Chapman, Matthew. "BCATP Revisited: The Evolution of Flight Training in Canada." *The Canadian Air Force Journal* 4, no. 2 (Spring 2011): pp. 35–44.

Copp, Terry. "The Defence of Hong Kong: December 1941." *Canadian Military History* 10, no. 4 (Autumn 2001): pp. 5–19.

Copp, Terry. "Operation 'Spring': An Historian's View." *Canadian Military History* 12, no. 2 (Winter/Spring 2003): pp. 63–70.

Evans, Christopher. "The Fighter-Bomber in the Normandy Campaign: The Role of 83 Group." *Canadian Military History* 8, no. 1 (Winter 1999): pp. 21–36.

Forestell, Diane G. "The Necessity of Sacrifice for the Nation at War: Women's Labour Force Participation, 1939–1946." *Histoire Sociale-Social History*, November 1989: pp. 333–348.

Fujiwara, Aya. "Japanese-Canadian Internally Displaced Persons: Labour Relations and Ethno-Religious Identity in Southern Alberta, 1942–1953." *Labour/Le Travail*, Spring 2012, pp. 63–89.

Goette, Richard. "The RCAF and the Creation of an RCN Air Arm: A Study of the Command and Control of Maritime Air Assets." *Canadian Military History* 13, no. 3 (Summer 2004): pp. 5–13.

Gooderson, Ian. "Assimilating Urban Battle Experience—the Canadians at Ortona." *Canadian Military Journal* 8, no. 4 (Winter 2007-2008): pp. 64–73.

Greenhous, Brereton. "Would it not have been better to bypass Ortona completely...? A Canadian Christmas, 1943." *Canadian Defence Quarterly* 18, no. 5 (April 1989): p. 55.

Haller, Oliver. "The Defeat of the 12th SS: 7–10 June, 1944." *Canadian Military History* 3, no. 1 (Spring 1994): pp. 9–25.

Hammond, Jamie. "The Pen Before the Sword: Thinking About 'Mechanization' between the Wars." *Canadian Military Journal* 1, no. 2 (Summer 2000): pp. 93–102.

Henry, Hugh G. "The Calgary Tanks at Dieppe." *Canadian Military History* 4, no. 1 (Spring 1995): pp. 61–74.

Horn, Bernd and Michel Wyczynski. "A Most Irrevocable Step: Canadian Paratroopers on D-Day: The first 24 hours, 5–6 June, 1944." *Canadian Military History* 13, no. 2 (Summer 2004): pp. 15–16.

Johnston, J.P. "E.L.M. Burns—A Crisis of Command." *Canadian Military Journal* 7, no. 1 (Spring 2006).

Johnston, Paul "Tactical Air Power Controversies in Normandy: A Question of Doctrine." *Canadian Military History* 9, no. 2 (Spring 2000): pp. 59–71.

Leigh-Mallory, Trafford. "Air Operations at Dieppe." *Canadian Military History* 12, no. 4 (Autumn 2003): pp. 55–70.

Macri, Franco David. "C Force to Hong Kong: The Price of Collective Security in China, 1941." *Journal of Military History* 77, no. 1 (January 2013): pp. 141–171.

Mayne, Richard Oliver. "A Political Execution: Expediency and the Firing of Vice Admiral Percy W. Nelles, 1943–44." *The American Review of Canadian Studies* 29, no. 4 (Winter 1999): pp 557–592.

Mayne, Richard Oliver. "Bypassing the Chain of Command: The Political Origins of the RCN's Equipment Crisis of 1943." *Canadian Military History* 9, no. 3 (Summer 2000): pp. 7-22.

McAndrew, W. J. "Eighth Army at the Gothic Line: The Dog Fight." *Journal of the Royal United Service Institute* 131, no. 2 (June 1986): pp. 55–62.

McAndrew, W. J. "Fire or Movement? Canadian Tactical Doctrine, Sicily—1943." *Military Affairs* 51, no. 3 (July 1987): pp. 140–145.

McAndrew, W. J. "Fifth Canadian Armoured Division: Introduction to Battle." *Canadian Military History* 2, no. 2 (Autumn 1993): pp. 43–56.

McAndrew, W. J. "Canadian Defence Planning Between the Wars: The Royal Canadian Air Force Comes of Age." *Canadian Military History* 22, no. 1 (Winter 2013): pp. 57–70.

Milner, Marc. "Reflections on Caen, Bocage and the Gap: A Naval Historian's Critique of the Normandy Campaign." *Canadian Military History* 7, no. 2 (Spring 1998): pp. 7–18.

Milner, Marc. "The Guns of Bretteville: 13th Field Regiment, RCA, and the Defence of Bretteville-l'Orgueilleuse, 7–10 June, 1944." *Canadian Military History* 16, no. 4 (Autumn 2007): pp. 5–24.

Moule, David. "The Burns-Simonds Debate Revisited: *The Canadian Defence Quarterly* and the Principles of Mechanized Warfare in the 1930s." *Canadian Military History* 22, no. 1 (Winter 2013): pp. 17–23.

Perras, Roger. "Defeat Still Cries Aloud for Explanation: Explaining C Force's Dispatch to Hong Kong." *Canadian Military Journal* 11, no. 4 (Autumn 2011): pp. 37–47.

Perrun, Jody. "Best Laid Plans; Guy Simonds and Operation Totalize, 7–10 August, 1944." *The Journal of Military History* 67, no. 1 (January 2003): pp. 137–173.

Pierson, Ruth. "Woman's Emancipation and the Recruitment of Women into the Canadian Labour Force in World War II." *Historical Papers*, 1976, pp. 141–173.

Preston, Adrian W. "Canada and the Higher Direction of the Second World

War 1939–1945," *Royal United Institute Journal* 110, no. 637 (1965). Published online September 25, 2009, especially p.33. http://www.tandfonline.com/doi/abs/10.1080/03071847609421223#.VCHfG2OxrF8

Sarty, Roger, and Jürgen Rohwer. "Intelligence and the Air Forces in the Battle of the Atlantic, 1943–1945." *International Commission of Military History.* Helsinki, 1991.

Vogel, Robert. "Tactical Air Power in Normandy: Some Thoughts on the Interdiction Plan." *Canadian Military History* 3, no. 1 (Spring 1994): pp. 37–47.

Wallace, Jack. "Shermans in Sicily: The Diary of a Young Soldier, Summer 1943." *Canadian Military History* 7, no. 4 (Autumn 1998).

Whitby, Michael. "Masters of the Channel Night: The Tenth Destroyer Flotilla's Victory off Île De Batz, 9 June, 1944." *Canadian Military History* 2, no. 1 (Spring 1993): pp. 5–22.

Windsor, Lee A. "'Boforce'" 1st Canadian Infantry Division Operations in Support of the Salerno Bridgehead, Italy, 1943." *Canadian Military History* 4, no. 2 (1995): pp. 51–60.

Windsor, Lee A. "The Eyes of All Fixed on Sicily": Canada's Unexpected Victory, 1943." *Canadian Military History* 22, no. 4 (Summer 2013): pp. 4–34.

Newspapers and Magazines

National Post, August 19, 2013.

Globe and Mail, March 23, 1945.

Webb, Gordon W. "Nuremburg—A Night to Remember." *Airforce Magazine*, March 1982, p. 12.

Archival Sources

British National Archives, Cab/66/40/18, War Cabinet, Relations with Canada, 14 August, 1943.

National Library and Archives Canada. King, William Lyon Mackenzie. *The Mackenzie King Diaries, 1932–1949* [microform]. Toronto: University of Toronto Press, 1980.

See also Library and Archives Canada. The Diaries of William Lyon Mackenzie King. Mackenzie King Diary, entries for July 19 and July 23, 1943. http://www.bac-lac.gc.ca/eng/discover/politics-government/prime-ministers/william-lyon-mackenzie-king/Pages/diaries-william-lyon-mackenzie-king.aspx

Doctoral Dissertations and Masters Theses

Caravaggio, Angelo N. "Commanding the Green Centre Line in Normandy: A Case Study of Division Command in the Second World War" (PhD dissertation, Wilfrid Laurier University, 2009).

Leppard, Christine. "Fighting as a Colony: 1st Canadian Corps in Italy, 1943–1945" (PhD dissertation, University of Calgary, 2013).

MacDonald, Britton Wade. "The Policy of Neglect: The Canadian Militia in the Interwar Years, 1919–1939" (PhD dissertation, Temple University, 2009).

Nuttal, L. "Canadianization and the No. 6 Bomber Group, RCAF" (PhD dissertation, University of Calgary, 1990).

Roof, Abraham. "The Empire at Sunset: Production, Finance, and British Grand Strategy 1941–42" (PhD dissertation, University of Calgary, 2014).

Sewell, Sarah Kathleen. "Making the Necessary Sacrifice: The Military's Impact on a City at War, Calgary, 1939–1945" (MA thesis, University of Calgary, 2013).

Young, W.R. "Making the Truth Graphic: The Canadian Government's Home Front Information Structure and Programmes During World War II" (PhD dissertation, University of British Columbia, 1978).

Oral References

Sebastian Cox (Head of Air Historical Branch [RAF]) in discussion with the author, October 4, 2011.

University of Victoria Archives, Reg Roy Collection, interview with Cameron Ware.

PHOTO CREDITS

1. Dept. of National Defence/ Library and Archives Canada/PA-114820

2. Library and Archives Canada/C-017291

3. Dept. of National Defence/Library and Archives Canada/PA-115875

4. Dept. of National Defence/Library and Archives Canada/PA-037456

5. Canada. Dept. of National Defence/Library and Archives Canada/PA-105306

6. Dept. of National Defence/ Library and Archives Canada/PA-112877

7. Kenneth Maclean/Dept. of National Defence/Library and Archives Canada/PA-150156

8. Dept. of National Defence/Library and Archives Canada/PA-104199

9. Ronny Jaques/National Film Board of Canada/Library and Archives Canada/PA-116178

10. Dept. of National Defence/Library and Archives Canada /PA-151743

11. National Film Board of Canada. Photothèque/Library and Archives Canada/e000760403

12. Library and Archives Canada, Acc. No. 1983-30-805

13. Library and Archives Canada/The Gazette (Montreal) fonds/PA-108300

14. Library and Archives Canada, archival reference number R2057-78, e008406108

15. National Film Board of Canada. Photothèque/Library and Archives Canada/C-031186

16. Library and Archives Canada/e011079727

17. Dept. of National Defence/Library and Archives Canada/PA-119399

18. National Film Board of Canada. Phototheque/Library and Archives Canada/C-026922

19. Dept. of National Defence/Library and Archives Canada/PA-116273

20. Harold G. Aikman/ Dept. of National Defence/Library and Archives Canada/PA-151501

21. Dept. of National Defence/Library and Archives Canada/PA-176977

22. Dept. of National Defence/Library and Archives Canada/PA-163415

23. NFB/Library and Archives Canada/C-008853

24. Dept. of National Defence/Library and Archives Canada/PA-114029

25. Dept. of National Defence/Library and Archives Canada/PA-144723

26. Dept. of National Defence/Library and Archives Canada/PA-130337

27. Library and Archives Canada/C-004796

28. Lieut. Terry F. Rowe/Dept. of National Defence/Library and Archives Canada/PA-141662

29. C.E. Nye/Dept. of National Defence/Library and Archives Canada/PA-134177

30. Frank L. Dubervill/Dept. of National Defence/Library and Archives Canada/PA-132652

31. Lieut. Frank L. Dubervill/Dept. of National Defence/Library and Archives Canada/
    PA-136280

32. Frank L. Dubervill/Dept. of National Defence/Library and Archives Canada/PA-131541

33. Frank L. Dubervill/Dept. of National Defence/Library and Archives Canada/PA-163919

34. Frank Dubervill/Dept. of National Defence/Library and Archives Canada/PA-132887

35. Ken Bell/ Dept. of National Defence/Library and Archives Canada/PA-169273

36. Dept. of National Defence/Library and Archives Canada/PA-115543

37. Ken Bell/Dept. of National Defence/Library and Archives Canada/PA-138268

38. Ken Bell/Dept. of National Defence/Library and Archives Canada/PA-168703

39. Dept. of National Defence/Library and Archives Canada/PA-154826

40. Dept. of National Defence/Library and Archives Canada/PA-145613

41. Dept. of National Defence/Library and Archives Canada/PA-144537

42. Lieut. Donald I. Grant/Dept. of National Defence/Library and Archives Canada/
    PA-111565

43. Dept. of National Defence/Library and Archives Canada/PA-107907

44. Ken Bell/Dept. of National Defence/Library and Archives Canada/PA-177798

45. Library and Archives Canada/C-32420

46. Daniel Guravich/Dept. of National Defence/Library and Archives Canada/PA-167198

47. Lieut. Dan Guravich/Dept. of National Defence/Library and Archives Canada/
    PA-134486

48. Capt. Alexander M. Stirton/Dept. of National Defence/Library and Archives Canada/
    PA-113696

49. Barney J. Gloster/Dept. of National Defence/Library and Archives Canada/PA-132443

50. J.H. Smith/Dept. of National Defence/Library and Archives Canada/PA-138052

51. Ken Bell/Dept. of National Defence/Library and Archives Canada/PA-114965

52. K. Bell/Library and Archives Canada/Dept. of National Defence/PA-137473

53. PO Jack Hawes/Dept. of National Defence/Library and Archives Canada/PA-145986

INDEX

McAndrew, William, 336
McCreery, Richard, 338
McEwen, Clifford "Black Mike" Mackay, 241–42
McFarland, Stephen L., 237
McKinstry, Leo, 241
McNaughton, A.G.L. "Andy," 10–11, 12, 40, 41, 317
    commands First Canadian Army, 11, 27–28, 88, 213, 270
    and Dieppe Raid, 93, 95, 96, 97, 105
    and Exercise Spartan, 106, 304
    insists that Canadians stay together, 91, 271, 273, 274, 300–301, 303, 304, 306
    as minister of national defence, 212
    and Sicily, 283
Megill, Bill, 385
Meighen, Arthur, 207–208, 209
Melfa River, 319–20, 332, 339
Menard, Joe, 86–87
Mencken, H.L., 323
Mennonites, 177–78
Menzies, Robert, 194
Merritt, Cecil, 102
Merville Battery, 356
Messerschmitt Bf-109s (Me-109s), 17–18, 47
Messerschmitt Me-110s, 18, 217, 243
Messerschmitt Me-262s, 430
Messina, 282, 288, 289
Metauro River, 335
Meuse River, 428
Meyer, Kurt, 365, 367, 392, 399
Michell, Steve, 99
Middlebrook, Martin, 238
Middle Wallop, 47
Mid-Ocean Escort Force (MOEF), 139–40, 143, 147, 244, 251, 255
Mid-Ocean Meeting Point, 151
Midway, Battle of, 316
Mike Beach, 361
Miquelon, 50
Milner, Marc, 31, 148, 256, 369
Minotaur Class light cruisers, 265
Modica, 279–80
MOEF. See Mid-Ocean Escort Force
SS Monowai, 341
Monte La Difensa, 328
Montgomery, Bernard L. "Monty," 11, 392
    and Battle of the Bulge, 428
    and Battle of Normandy, 375–76, 383, 387–89, 390, 394, 395, 398, 399
    and Battle of the Rhineland, 426–27, 437, 443, 444
    and Battle of the Scheldt Estuary, 408–409, 412, 419–20
    and Canadian Army, 26, 90, 322, 334, 357, 371, 412, 419, 420
    and D-Day, 357, 358

and Dieppe Raid, 91, 92–93, 95, 96
and German surrender, 448
and Holland, 447
and Italy, 294, 298, 300, 309
and Operation Market Garden, 409–410, 411–12
and Sicily, 274, 280, 281, 283, 285, 288, 289
HCMS Moosejaw, 60, 62, 63
Moran, G.V., 362
HMCS Morden, 244
Moro River, 210
Mortain, 388, 390, 391, 394
Mosquito fighter bombers, 218, 228, 229, 241, 346, 351, 432
Mountbatten, Louis, 91–92, 95, 96
Mowat, Farley, 21, 41, 278, 299–300, 310–11
Moyland Wood, 439
SS Muneric, 60
Munich crisis, 6, 7, 18
Munitions and Supply, Department of, 162, 165–66, 189, 191
Munro, Ross, 175
Murchie, J.C., 192
Murray, Leonard W., 54, 253–54
Murray, Williamson, 130
Mussolini, Benito, 287
Mustang fighters, 348, 349, 404

NAAFI (Navy, Army, Air Force Institute), 325
Nagasaki, 449
Nagumo, Chuichi, 82
Namur, 428
Nan Beach, 361
Naples, 296, 300
Narvik, 40
National Defence, Department of, 167
National Defence for Air, Department of, 189–90
National Defence Headquarters (NDHQ), 28, 74, 188
National Defence for Naval Services, Department of, 189–90
National Labor Relations Act (The Wagner Act), 176
National Research Council, 15
National Resources Mobilization Act (NRMA), 42, 83, 167, 190, 206–207, 209–12, 407
National Selective Service, 170
National War Service Regulations, 177
National War Services, Department of, 166–67, 190
Navy, Army, and Air Force Institute (NAAFI), 325
Nazi–Soviet Pact, 23
NDHQ (National Defence Headquarters), 28, 74, 188
Neatby, H. Blair, 7
NEF. See Newfoundland Escort Force
Neilands, Robin, 237

destroyers, 13, 29, 34–35, 45–46, 49, 53, 54, 64, 66–68, 137, 150, 197, 244, 251, 255, 264–66
and E-boats, 353
escort groups, 244–45, 249–50, 251: C1, 249, 250; C3, 251; C5, 255
frigates, 138–39, 252, 255
during interwar period, 8, 13, 14–15
minesweepers, 29, 35, 133, 143, 434; 31st Mine-sweeping Flotilla, 354
motor launches, 136, 143
obsolete equipment and weaponry, 55, 59, 63, 137–38, 139, 150, 151, 158, 251, 260–62
Operational Intelligence Centre, 252
and Pacific theatre, 83–84
and Royal Navy (RN), 14–15, 30–31, 34–35, 45, 54–55, 84, 142, 158, 244, 352
and shipping system in western Atlantic, 142
size of, 14, 29, 186
tactics, 150
and training, 14–15, 36, 55, 58, 63, 64, 151, 249–50
and U-boats/submarines, 15, 34, 36, 45, 46, 58, 60–64, 68, 150, 152–53, 157–58, 244–45, 250, 252, 254, 260–61, 266, 352
and United States Navy (USN), 66, 141, 252, 253
Royal Canadian Regiment (RCR), 24, 267–69, 275, 286, 288, 299, 311, 313
Royal Flying Corps, 8, 16
Royal Hamilton Light Infantry (RHLI), 85, 100, 104, 384, 414, 420, 441
Royal Highland Regiment. See Black Watch
Royal Marines, 103
Royal Military College (RMC), 9, 27
Royal Naval Air Service, 8
Royal Navy (RN), 197
    and Battle of the Atlantic, 51–52, 150–51, 237, 244–46, 251
    and bulk cargoes to UK, 145
    and Canadian shipbuilders, 166
    and Coastal Command (RAF), 65
    casualties/ships lost, 52, 53, 246, 247, 266
    codes, 34, 44, 57, 149
    and convoy escort, 30, 33, 34, 52, 57, 58, 60, 64, 137, 150–51, 247
    corvettes, 56, 137, 251, 261
    and D-Day, 344, 359–60
    destroyers, 15, 16, 29, 52, 197
    and Dieppe, 97, 104
    escort carriers (CVEs), 247
    escort groups, 244–45
    and interwar period, 15
    and Royal Canadian Navy (RCN), 54–55, 158, 249, 251
    10th Destroyer Flotilla, 352
    and U-boats/submarines, 45, 56–58, 60, 150–51, 251, 254

See also Western Approaches Command
Royal Regiment of Canada, 43, 99, 103, 384, 418
Royal Rifles of Canada, 71, 74–75, 76, 77, 78, 80
Royal 22e Regiment (the Van Doos), 24, 275, 297–99, 312, 330
Royal Winnipeg Rifles, 361, 366–67, 376
Ruhr, 118, 119, 232, 405, 409, 412, 419
    Battle of the, 232–33, 237, 239
Rur River, 440
Russia, 451. See also Red Army; Soviet Union

HMCS Sackville, 139, 152–53, 244
HMCS Saguenay, 13, 30, 45, 49
Sai Wan War Cemetery, 84
St-André-sur-Orne, 382
St-Aubin-sur-Mer, 1
St-Aubin-sur-Scie, 94
HMCS St. Clair, 46
HMCS St. Croix, 46, 49, 50–51, 152, 157, 244, 245–46, 250, 263
HMCS St. Francis, 244
St. John's, 54, 140, 142
St-Lambert-sur-Dives, 397
HMCS St. Laurent, 16, 30, 45, 49
St. Lawrence, Battle of the, 134–36, 143–48
St-Nazaire, 92
St-Pierre and Miquelon, 50
St-Vith, 428
Salerno, Bay of, 294, 296, 297, 298
Salmon, H.L.N., 276, 380
San Fortunato Ridge, 337–38
San Leonardo, 310, 311
San Martino, 337
San Nicola, 317
San Tommaso, 317
HMCS Sarnia, 434
Sarty, Roger, 143, 148, 154
Saskatoon Light Infantry, 315
KMS Scharnhorst, 51
Scheldt Estuary, Battle of the, 398, 401–403, 407–408, 410–22
Schlieffen Position, 442
Schräge Musik cannon, 218
Schweinfurt, 227
Schwerte, 115
Scie, River, 101, 102
    Seaforth Highlanders of Canada, 286–87, 291, 310, 313, 314–15, 323
Second British Army. See British Second Army
Seine, Bay of the, 344
Senio River, 338
Seyss-Inquart, Arthur, 447
Sham Shui Po, 76
HMCS Shawinigan, 435